THE POETICS OF GREEK TRAGEDY

The Poetics of Greek Tragedy

Malcolm Heath

Stanford University Press
Stanford, California
1987

Stanford University Press
Stanford, California
© 1987 by Malcolm Heath
Originating publishers: Gerald Duckworth & Co. Ltd.
First published in the U.S.A. by
Stanford University Press, 1987
ISBN 0-8047-1398-7
LC 86-63248

Printed in Great Britain

Contents

Preface

This book is a slightly revised version of the latter parts of a doctoral thesis submitted to Oxford University in the summer of 1983. The manuscript was closed in substance in April 1984; since then I have added a few references to more recent work, but I have not attempted any systematic revision.

The first part of the thesis contained methodological prolegomena to the exercise undertaken here. It was my original intention to publish the two parts simultaneously; this has not proved possible, but I still hope that the theoretical material will be forthcoming in some form in due course.

A number of friends and colleagues have improved the book by their comments on earlier versions. Those who are conscious of having done so will, I hope, forgive me if I make express acknowledgement only of my more pressing debts: to my supervisor, Hugh Lloyd-Jones; to my examiners, John Gould and Myles Burnyeat; and – above all – to my friend and former tutor, the late Tom Stinton.

If I were able adequately to express my gratitude to Gerard and Bernadette O'Reilly, I would so so.

Hertford College, Oxford   M.H.
January 1987

Introduction

When a Greek tragedian competed at a dramatic festival, the work which he displayed was unique, composed as no one else among his contemporaries would have composed it; moreover, it was displayed to an audience that must itself have been diverse in the tastes and the beliefs, the settled dispositions and the transient moods, which they had brought with them to the theatre. This aspect of tragedy, its particularity and uniqueness, must not be neglected by an interpreter who wants to understand the individual plays; but it is not the only aspect to consider. The various texts which we label 'Greek tragedies' are related to one another by more than a name; and their familiar resemblance is clearly not coincidental. Greek tragedy is a *genre*. The poets and their audiences, for all their diversity, shared certain assumptions about and expectations of serious drama, which guided both the composition of the plays and their reception: which, in short, made possible communication in the tragic theatre.

If this is true, then a modern reader who wants to find his way into the individual plays must attempt to reconstruct the presuppositions and expectations which made tragedy possible in its native context; that is to say, he is committed first of all to the discipline which I shall call *poetics*. This discipline will be a preliminary to his reading of the plays no less important than his learning of their language: indeed, in the strictest sense, it is part of learning their language, for no sense can be given to the notion of the Greek language simply as such, in abstraction from the various specific registers which, so far from being mere modifications of a neutral substrate, themselves collectively make up the language. The purpose of this book, then, is to lay the foundations for such a poetics of Greek tragedy.[1] I must emphasise 'foundations', and not only for the obvious reason that an exhaustive and detailed treatment of the subject is impossible in so brief a compass. Technical studies of the 'grammar' of tragedy have proliferated in recent years, to good effect.[2] But genre is essentially a semantic concept: that is, a genre or register is a set of possible meanings, and only secondarily the

---

[1] When I write 'tragedy' from here on, I will mean *Greek* tragedy unless I state otherwise. On theoretical grounds I am sceptical of broader generic categories, believing that poetics can only be profitable as a historical enquiry into the workings of a particular system of conventions in a given historical and cultural context.

[2] The term is Fraenkel's (1950: 305), and has been taken up by (e.g.) Taplin (1977), Bain (1977, 1981), Halloran (1985), Mastronarde (1979); see also Jens 1971 and its satellite dissertations.

resources for the realisation of those meanings.[3] Therefore, although poetics must indeed pay careful attention to matters of form and technique, this is not its most fundamental task; any study of such resources – of tragic 'syntax', so to speak – will be pointless, unless we can clarify the meanings which those resources were used to realise: and this in turn will need reference to the typical range of meaning definitive of the genre. It is with this more fundamental question, therefore, with the general shape or structure of tragedy's *meaning-potential*, that I am chiefly concerned.

The internal evidence for this enquiry is the extant tragic corpus: thirty-two plays, more or less complete, though all to some degree lacunose and interpolated, written by up to five poets, with one probable exception in the last three quarters of the fifth century;[4] in addition, there are several thousand fragments, mostly very small, somewhat more widely distributed by authorship and date, but most heavily concentrated in the same range. The external evidence is mainly to be found in fourth-century philosophical texts (Plato, Aristotle), supplemented by some anecdotal evidence, incidental references in other authors, and later criticism and scholarship (including that preserved in the scholia); sources strictly contemporary with the main body of extant tragedy are disappointingly meagre, and the use of our most substantial contemporary witness (Aristophanes) is complicated by the fact that his evidence takes the form of parody and comic fantasy. We can to some extent supplement these *testimonia* by seeing tragedy in the light of other aspects of contemporary culture, and in particular of the broader literary tradition within which tragedy flourished.

This motley collection of evidence poses formidable problems of method. First, with respect to the internal evidence, there is the threat of circularity inherent in the use of interpretations of tragedy as evidence in the interpretation of tragedy. This circle is inescapable, but not (I believe) vicious; it is, in fact, a variant of the hermeneutic circle. The point cannot be pursued here; I remark only that, because the orienting discipline of poetics depends on interpretations, the study of tragic meaning, although more fundamental in principle, will in practice have to advance in the closest cooperation with the study of tragic technique. Secondly, there is the need for a critical element in our approach to the external sources: we must always reckon with the possibility that the author's attitude to tragedy is eccentric, or (since introspection is notoriously fallible) that he is misreporting his own attitudes, or (since most of our sources are not strictly contemporary) that his attitudes are anachronistic. Since our critical testing of these sources will inevitably involve matching them against the plays themselves, to see whether their suggestions fit the textual data, the external sources are thus

[3] The terminology here, and occasionally elsewhere, draws on systemic linguistics, which I have found to provide an extremely useful framework for poetics. Halliday 1978 is fundamental; see also de Joia & Stenton 1980, Gregory & Carroll 1978.

[4] I accept the late dating of A.*Su.* (see Garvie 1969, Taplin 1977: 194-8; below, 4.23, 4.42); I reserve judgment on the authenticity of *PV* (see Griffith 1977, Taplin 1977: 460-9; below ch.3 n.33) – the question will not bear on my argument; *Rhesus* must, I suppose, be fourth-century (see Fraenkel 1965), despite appearances.

drawn into the same circular system of interpretation.[5] Problems of this kind cannot be eradicated: evidence in historical enquiry can, in the nature of things, never be rigorously conclusive. But when we are dealing with the evidence of witnesses who are contemporary or near contemporaries, there is at least a presumption of general reliability; certainly, they are more likely to prove reliable guides than the untutored intuition of a modern reader – which is, in practice, the only alternative, and a patently treacherous one.

The charge of anachronism is frequently levelled against those sources which are not contemporary with the plays when they seem to deny or neglect the preoccupations of modern tragic criticism; it is, as I have said, always a possibility to be reckoned with. But although we have some evidence for changes of taste and technique between the fifth and fourth centuries, we cannot know until we have proved it that these changes affected the basic principles of the poetics of tragedy. So we would do well not to set the fourth-century evidence lightly aside; we will need in each case to show by careful argument just where and why its claims are untenable. And we must insist again that even a fourth-century writer is *a priori* more likely to be a reliable guide to tragedy than the unreconstructed prejudices of the modern reader. Moreover, if (as I shall argue in the following chapters) a broad consensus can be established across the whole range of external sources – if writers of the fifth and fourth centuries agree, and if this agreement coheres with the whole Greek literary tradition – then attempts to set aside the evidence of later writers, even in points where there is no earlier corroboration, will even more take on an air of special pleading.

The problem of anachronism is posed most acutely by the scholia: why should we look for evidence of fifth-century aesthetics in a tradition of commentary with its roots in Hellenistic scholarship? The reputation of the tragic scholia does not stand very high; I was pleasantly surprised, therefore, to discover that the, admittedly scanty, remains of literary critical commentary in the tragic scholia display what I take to be a good general grasp of the basic principles of tragic aesthetics, and that it was instructive to observe the kinds of question they found it appropriate to ask. (With their answers in particular cases, I naturally find myself more often in disagreement; but it is from the underlying presuppositions that we have most to learn, and these can be recovered even when they appear to have been misapplied.) My surprise was perhaps unreasonable. The tragic scholia do, after all, fall within a tradition of literary activity broadly continuous with the fifth century, in a culture generally conservative of its traditions; significantly, the scholiasts are more evidently at sea in those cases (for example, Old Comedy and epinician lyric) in which there had been a sharp discontinuity in the tradition.[6] Those who remain sceptical may prefer to treat my references to the scholia as an argument for their usefulness, rather than as corroborative evidence for my discussion of tragedy; my argument

---

[5] Or rather, *further* in; for it would be naive to deny that even our initial reading of the 'external' sources is prejudiced by our familiarity with the genre.

[6] I do not find the defence of the Pindaric scholia in Wilson 1980 persuasive (see now Lefkowitz 1985).

does not depend at any point on a sympathetic predisposition towards the scholia.

I shall supplement my references to the tragic scholia with references to those on Homer, since comparable literary attitudes are to be found there. This similarity might raise the suspicion that one or other set of notes is insensitive to genre, and therefore useless for our present purpose. But the Homeric scholia explicitly regard their author as, at least in one aspect of what they see as a complex literary character, a tragedian;[7] this implies that they drew on their understanding of tragedy in interpreting Homer, so that the similarity of attitudes is natural and, for our present purposes, fruitful. We may note in this one slight token of the continuity of literary traditions of which I have spoken, since the notion of Homer as tragedian is already taken for granted by fourth-century authors; there is no reason to doubt that it went back to the fifth century.[8]

---

[7] For the complexity of Homer's art see Σ *Il*.2.478-9 ABT; for Homer as tragedian, 1.1 A, 3.306 B, 10.349-50 T; cf. 6.58-9 BT. In particular, as *prôtos heuretês* of tragedy and its devices: 1.332 ABT (*kôpha prosôpa*), 2.156 BT (*mêkhanê*), 5.446 T (child characters), 21.34 BT (*peripeteia*). Cf. Richardson 1980: 270-1 & n.15; this article and Griffin 1976 urge the value of the scholia for our understanding of Homer – in my judgment, persuasively.

[8] Pl.*Ion* 536a, *Tht*.152e, *Rep*.595c, 602b, 606e-7a, *Laws* 598d; Ar.*Poet*.1448a25ff., 48b34ff., 49b9ff.; Isocr.2.48.

1. First Principles

1.1 Pleasure and pathos

1.11 The tradition

In the Introduction, I suggested that the broader literary tradition within which tragedy flourished could provide one supplementary source of external evidence for the poetics of tragedy; and I drew attention to the connections which were traced in the ancient world between tragedy and epic. I propose to begin this enquiry, therefore, by considering the image of poetry in early hexameter verse, taking Hesiod first for the sole reason that the proem to his *Theogony* makes in a conveniently explicit way a number of points about poetry and its effects that have to be inferred more obliquely from Homer's narrative presentation of the bards and their role in heroic society. (In what follows, I use the name 'Homer' as a Greek might, for convenience; I am not trying to beg the Homeric question.)[1]

Consider first the range of epithets which Hesiod applies to the divine patrons of poetry: the voice of the Muses is beautiful (*perikallês* 10; *kalê* 68), sweet (*hêdeia* 39-40) and lovely (*eratê* 65; *epêratos* 67); so, too, is their dancing (7-8, 70); they live near the Graces and Desire (64); when they sing they give Zeus pleasure (36-7, 51) and fill his palaces with joyful laughter (40-2). So their names, derived from words for delight, beauty and love, are apt: Euterpe, Terpsichore, Erato, Calliope (77-8). Their gifts, too, are fitting: they pour a sweet liquid (*glukerê eersê*) on the tongue of their favourite, so that his words are like honey (*meilikha* 84) and his voice sweet (*glukerê* 97); the song they taught Hesiod was beautiful (*kalê* 22) and awakens desire (*himeroessa* 104). In sum: Hesiod's hymn to the Muses is an unrestrained celebration of the pleasures of poetry and song; indeed, the only other sphere of human experience which Hesiod describes in comparable terms is that of erotic pleasure (*Th.*201-6; cf. *h.Hom.*4.484).

In the light of this evidence, it is astonishing that scholars can discuss Hesiod and his view of poetry with scarcely a mention of aesthetic pleasure.[2] What Hesiod does say with complete clarity has too often been overshadowed by insubstantial speculations precariously founded on the Muses' enigmatic address to the poet (26-8). 'We know,' they assure him, 'how to utter many plausible falsehoods, and we know (if we wish) how to speak the truth.' It is not easy to believe that before Hesiod no one had suspected that, for example, such narratives as Odysseus' at the court of

---

[1] For what follows, cf. Lanata 1963, Maehler 1963, Fränkel 1975: 6-25.
[2] Cf. (e.g.) Maehler 1963: 35-48.

5

Alcinous were perhaps not wholly truthful; nor is it obvious that in making this point Hesiod's Muses are promising to adhere more faithfully to the truth in his own poems than elsewhere.[3] It is rash, therefore, to see in these lines a great step forward in poetic theory or the formulation of a *Wahrheitsanspruch*. In them, the Muses appear to do no more than declare, in a teasing ironical manner, how it is that they are accustomed to behave: poetry contains some truth, and some fiction which (doubtless just because poetry is sweet and lovely and captivating) will carry its audience away to at least a temporary willingness to believe.

If we cannot have faith in the truthfulness of Hesiod's Muses, is there then no more to their gift than a superficial and deceptive loveliness? There is more: for these Muses provide men (whose life is harsh, as Hesiod explains in *Works and Days*) with a respite: they are forgetfulness of ills and release from cares (55); when a bard sings, he takes away a man's grief and helps him to forget his troubles (98-103): and he does so precisely because of the sweetness and beauty of song (97, 104). This is the heart of the Hesiodic view of poetry.

If we turn now to the *Odyssey* (the military circumstances of the *Iliad* preclude the portrayal of poetry in its normal social context)[4] we find this view of poetry realised in a representation of human life. We may note first of all that the range of epithets is similar: song is sweet (*hêdeia* 8.64), lovely (*himeroessa* 18.304, cf. 17.519), full of charm (*khariessa* 24.197-8); 'delight' (*terpein* and its cognates) is frequent (1.347, 369, 421-2, 8.46, 91, 368, 429, 17.385, 606, 18.305-6), and the bard Phemius is given the significant patronymic Terpiades (22.330). In the life of this society, the bard is an entertainer, who performs at feasts: Odysseus observes that it is a fine thing (*kalon*) to listen to a bard, indeed that there is nothing more charming (*khariesteron*) when people are enjoying themselves at a feast (9.1-11).[5] Odysseus makes this observation in reply to Alcinous' complaint that his own bard is failing to give pleasure to all his guests (*ou kharizomenos* 8.538): Demodocus had, in fact, moved Odysseus to tears by a story that touched on his own personal sorrows; something similar had happened on two previous occasions (1.325-71, 8.43-107). Now, it is observable that the repertoire of the Homeric bards is tragic in tendency: the story of Ares and Aphrodite is in a lighter vein (8.266-366), but elsewhere we are offered the inauspicious homecomings of the Greeks from Troy (1.326-7) and the Trojan War itself (8.72-82, echoing *Il*.1.1ff.; see also *h.Hom.* 3.191-3). Pleasure is required, and

---

[3] A poet who takes such evident delight in the dynastic rivalries and crimes of the gods, in Gigantomachies, and in all the things that were later to serve as stock examples of wicked poetic falsehood, is not (one might have thought) the most obvious candidate for the role of religious thinker, incipient philosopher and purifier of poetry from untruth. Hesiod's poetic practice makes it clear, at any rate, where his main interests lay. Commentators have been perplexed by the apparent imbalance in his treatment of the Pandora episode in *WD* (e.g. West 1978a: 155); he has simply chosen to elaborate most fully that part of the story which offers greatest scope for his artistry, the part that is potentially most pleasing. (For a fuller discussion see Heath 1985.)

[4] The only occasion on which we find someone performing in *Il*. is at 9.186-7, where it is the amateur Achilles amusing himself while out of the fighting.

[5] We see, then, that Thalia is also an aptly named Muse: see West 1966: 177-8, 410 (on *Th*.65, 917).

tragic tales can give pleasure; but not one's own tragedy: the charm is expelled when one's own tragedy is told, since (as Hesiod said) song is supposed to be forgetfulness of one's ills and a refuge from care.

Characteristic of the successful bardic performance in the *Odyssey* is the silent, rapt attention which it wins from its audience: so, for example, in 1.325-6. In 11.333-5 (= 13.1-3) imagery of enchantment is used to describe this effect (*kêlêthmôi eskhonto*): to be sure, these two passages are the concluding formulae for the two stages of Odysseus' story-telling, but the force of his narrative is clearly equivalent to that of the professional bards; Alcinous explicitly pays this compliment to his guest's narrative skills (11.368). Eumaeus, too, speaks of Odysseus' stories as enchantments (*ethelge*), and compares them to the lovely words (*epe' himeroenta*) of a professional bard's performance (17.513-21). And Penelope speaks of songs as magic charms (*brotôn thelktêria* 1.337).[6]

The same themes can be traced in other early hexameter poetry. In the *Hymn to Apollo* (already cited for its emphasis on tragic themes) a choir's singing is said to bewitch its audience (*thelgousi* 160-1); their song is beautiful (*kalê* 164); and the highest praise for a bard is that he gives the most pleasure (*hêdistos, terpesthe malista* 169-70). When Hermes strikes up on the lyre in the *Hymn to Hermes*, Apollo's anger is assuaged: he laughs for joy (*gelasse ... gêthêsas* 420-1) and is filled with sweet longing (*glukus himeros* 422); firm friends, they go off delighting in the music of the lyre (*terpomenoi phormingi* 506). Other early poetry could be used to illustrate these themes; but little or nothing would be added to the impression we have already gained. We can sum up thus: in the earliest recoverable stages of the Greek literary tradition, the attitude to poetry and song is markedly hedonistic; poetry is a pleasant bewitchment, and the poet's task is to enthrall and charm his audience.

Against this traditional background, the preoccupations of Gorgias in his *Helen* (DK 82 B 11.8-14) are readily intelligible. He is interested in the power of words, a power so great that Helen, if she was overcome by it, cannot be held responsible for her misdeeds. Speech, Gorgias observes, can assuage fear and take away grief (the Hesiodic motif again); it can move us to joy and to pity. Poetry is cited in illustration of this power of words: it produces in us fearful shuddering (*phrikê periphobos*), tearful pity (*eleos poludakrus*), and a yearning after grief (*pothos philopenthês*); it makes us respond within ourselves to the good and bad fortune of others. Gorgias speaks here of poetry in general (*tên poiêsin hapasan*): but he can hardly be thinking of comedy, and there must be a tacit limitation to the 'serious' forms, tragedy and epic. His account of the emotional effects of poetry is, as we shall see, amply confirmed by other discussions of both these genres. Two points may be made in passing: first, that Gorgias takes as another illustration of the power of words magical incantations; in the light of the enchantment imagery which we noted in the poets, this juxtaposition of magic and poetry will not appear fortuitous. Secondly, although Gorgias does not explicitly mention rhetoric in

---

[6] There was an interpretation of *Od*.4 in antiquity that linked Helen's drug and her story: Plut.*Mor.*614bc, Macrobius *Sat.*7.1.18-19.

this passage, we can hardly doubt that it is close to his thoughts. If so, this connection also has its roots in the tradition: compare *Il*.1.247-9 with the passages cited earlier on poetry; in the proem to the *Theogony*, Hesiod exploits this connection to bring poets and kings together in a *captatio benevolentiae*. We may note that Nestor is sweetly spoken (*hêduepês*: *Il*.1.247), as are the Muses (*Th*.965-6 = 1021-2; Hes. *fr*.1.1; *h.Hom*.32.1-2) and their poets (*h.Hom*.21.4-5; Pi.*N*.7.21 of Homer himself).[7]

In this light some lines of Plato's attack on poetry may seem less odd. In the dialogue named after Gorgias (501e-2d), Plato argues that poetry and related arts are in essence no different from the titillating skills of the pastry-cook, which aim to provide pleasure rather than to make a sound contribution to man's physical or moral well-being. Even tragedy, solemn and serious though it may seem, falls under this condemnation. The question is posed whether it would be willing to use material that was beneficial although less pleasant; the conclusion, not surprisingly, is that tragedy aims above all at pleasure or enjoyment (*hêdonê*), at pleasing the spectators (*to kharizesthai tois theatais*). Tragedy therefore, can be written off as a species of rhetoric (*dêmêgoria, rhêtorikê*) – a now familiar connection, but transformed by Plato's contempt for rhetoric (502c12-d3). So tragedy can be dismissed as morally worthless, a mere knack of pandering to low-grade tastes (*kolakikê* 502d7). This judgment is repeated in the *Laws*, where the tragedian is refused license to practise rhetoric (*dêmêgorein*) before a morally vulnerable audience – children, women, the general mob (817ad). In *Phaedrus* we are told that rhetoric is a means of swaying the mind by words (*psukhagôgia tis dia logôn* 261a); so too in poetry, a god, using poets and performers as intermediaries, drags the human mind about at will (*Ion* 535a9-6a2). This brings us back to Gorgias' account of the effects of poetry, for the context in *Ion* makes it clear that poetic *psukhagôgia* is a matter of emotional stimulus; a successful performance in Ion's view is a particularly emotive one, one which produces the greatest *ekplêxis* (we shall have more to say on this term in 1.12), leaving the audience in tears (535be). We may note that actors are mentioned along with rhapsodes as performers (536a1), confirming that what is said here about epic recitations is equally applicable to tragedy (*Laws* 800cd provides evidence for the emotivity of non-dramatic lyric as well).

Much the same is to be found in the more systematic critique of poetry in *Republic*. Even the best of us, we are told, are carried away by enjoyment when we hear a pathetic rhesis or a lyric lament in a tragic performance or in epic recitation; we surrender to the experience, allowing ourselves to be led in sympathy with the sufferers; and we admire most the poets who affect us most powerfully in this way (605cd). Moreover, the restraints which in normal circumstances keep our emotional reactions in check are, in this special context, relaxed; we admire and pity the sufferers with their exaggerated expressions of grief; and we take pleasure in this, never realising that we are in this way allowing our own emotional stability to be undermined and giving rein to the worst part of our personality (606ab).

---

[7] For Hesiod's *captatio* cf. West 1966: 44; for the whole connection see further de Romilly 1975.

These two passages contain many echoes of material we have already examined: the *psukhagôgia* of rhetoric in *Phaedrus* and *Ion*, the response to others' sufferings emphasised by Gorgias. The paradox of our taking pleasure in painful emotions like grief (in *Philebus*, too, Plato observes that at tragic performances the audience takes pleasure in its tears: 48a) recalls especially Gorgias' *pothos philopenthês*.[8] Plato even uses the imagery of enchantment in his summing-up: *sunismen ge hêmin kêloumenois hup' autês* (606c).

Poetic enjoyment is discussed also in the *Laws*. The majority opinion, Plato says, is that pleasure given is the sole criterion of poetic excellence (655cd). This view is not rejected outright: but we have seen that the kind of pleasure which the majority finds in poetry is that of emotional excitement; as the author of the (probably spurious) *Minos* says, tragedy is the kind of poetry which gives most pleasure to the masses (*dêmoterpestaton*) and has the most powerful emotional effect (*psukhagôgikôtaton*) – more precisely, it gives the most pleasure *because* it is the most emotive. This kind of pleasure Plato regards as morally harmful. The hedonistic principle is conceded, therefore, only with a qualification that utterly transforms it: it is the pleasure of the best educated and morally soundest (that is, of those who will not be beguiled by corrupting emotionalism) which is to provide the criterion by which poetry is judged (658e-9c, cf.700ab).

Plato is a hostile witness, and it might be thought that his account of the emotional effect of tragedy is tendentiously exaggerated; his agreement with Gorgias counts against this supposition, however, and other scraps of fourth-century evidence uphold their joint testimony. Isocrates, who elsewhere links poetic pleasure and *psukhagôgia* (2.49), and explains that metre and rhythm in poetry give it a charm (*kharis*) which lends itself to *psukhagôgia* (9.10), complains that the very people who shed tears over the disasters concocted by poets are unmoved by the genuine sufferings (*alêthina pathê polla kai deina*) resulting from the war (4.168). Aeschines invites a jury to recall the tears shed over tragedies and the sufferings in them of heroes (*epi tais tragôidiais kai tois hêrôikois pathesi* 3.153). Xenophon mentions an actor who prided himself on his ability to move an audience to tears (*Symp.*3.11). In this connection, we may recall the reaction to Phrynichus' *Sack of Miletus* as recorded by Herodotus (6.21.1-2): the poet was fined and the play banned, not simply because the audience was moved to tears (this, as we have seen, was required of a tragedian), but because the tears were shed over misfortunes that touched the audience too closely, reminding them of their own troubles (*hôs anamnêsanti oikêia kaka*); Phrynichus' mistake was that of the bard in *Od.*8.499ff., and in the similar passages mentioned earlier; he had forgotten the Hesiodic function of poetry.[9]

A characteristic phrase in Aristotle's discussion of tragedy (and of epic, for in this respect he declines to distinguish the two genres: *Poet.*1462b12-15) is 'the appropriate kind of pleasure' (*oikeia hêdonê*: 53a36, 53b10-11, 59a21,

---

[8] Cf. D.L.2.90, citing Aristippus and his school: 'We listen to those who imitate lamentation with pleasure (*hêdeôs*): but to those whose grief is genuine, without.'
[9] On Phrynichus see Marx 1928, and below 2.33. I should mention here also the comic exploitation of the traditional theme of forgetfulness by the fourth-century poet Timocles (fr.6).

62b13-14): the appropriate kind being in this case that which accompanies the emotions of fear and pity. To afford this pleasure is, on Aristotle's view, the function (*ergon*: 50a30-1, 52b29-30, 62b12-13) of tragedy, its purpose or end (*telos*: 60b24-5, 62b14-15). This is not contradicted by his statement that it is plot that is the *telos* of tragedy (50a22-3). Aristotle says elsewhere that the duty of the tragedian is to provide the pleasure which accompanies fear and pity, and to do so by means of 'imitation' (*mimêsis*: 53b10-13): the plot is the *mimêsis* (a *mimêsis praxeôs*: 51a31, 52a13), and so it is there in order to provide the *oikeia hêdonê* of tragedy; it is itself a *telos* only in relation to the other constituent elements of a play: character, thought, diction, song and 'spectacle' are there to facilitate the representation of an action in the plot, with a view to the pleasurable emotions which that representation will excite.

In this definition of the purpose of tragedy we can now recognise a further manifestation of the entirely traditional assumption that poetry exists to give pleasure, and specifically the pleasure of emotional response, to its audiences. To be sure, Aristotle is aware that the gratification of the audience's taste can corrupt the tragic art (1455a33-6); but this does not lead him to abandon the principle; indeed, he styles Euripides 'most tragic' of tragedians precisely because his plots are of the kind most conducive to fear and pity, and hence to tragedy's proper pleasure (52b29). Aristotle's account of the facts, therefore, agrees with Plato's, but his moral judgment of them is utterly different; in fact, his example of the influence of the audience's bad taste is, in complete opposition to Plato's view, the *deflection* of the poet from the pursuit of tragic emotion.

Finally, the scholia, in which literary critical comment is concerned above all with the relationship between poet and audience; as in the whole tradition surveyed above, the play is regarded as a rhetorical medium, through which the poet seeks to evoke a certain response from his audience, and it is this response which the scholia consider with most interest in their comments. The picture is a simple one: the poet tries to secure the sympathetic attention of his audience, in order to gratify them by the play to which they then attend (cf.1.2). Like Aristotle, they are aware that a poet may compromise his art by the inappropriate indulgence of his audience's taste (unlike Aristotle, they worry most about this when the pursuit of tragic emotion leads the poet to violate one of the constraints which the nature of tragedy imposes: cf.1.3); but the gratification of the audience by legitimate means is nevertheless central to their view of tragedy. For the scholia, as for the earlier sources, this gratification is primarily that which accompanies emotional excitement; indeed, they regard emotion, *pathos*, as the defining quality of the genre.[10]

---

[10] *Pathos* refers in Aristotle to the tragic events (cf. Aeschines, 3.153); in the scholia the term ranges over the events, their inherent emotive quality, and the emotional response which they do or should evoke from the audience. References in the scholia: (a) *kinêsis*: S.*Aj*.1168, *El*.86, 271, *OT* 141, cf.264; E.*Ph*.1606; *Il*.1.3 AT, 1.446 BT, 21.34 BT, 22.201 A, 24.776 BT. (b) *psukhagôgia*: S.*Aj*.864 (of an actor); *Il*.3.306 B. (c) *ekplêxis*: A. *Vita* 7, *Ag*.hyp.; S.*Aj*.346, 815. (d) *pathos*: S.*Aj*.66, 1123 (cf. *Il*.6.499 BT), 1409, *El*.1137; E.*Hec*.689, *Ph*.4, *Tro*.36, 1129; intensification of *pathos*: S.*Aj*.57, 66, 421, *El*.1098, *OT* 175, *OC* 1687; E.*Hec*.421; *Il*.2.698ff. B, 12.154-5 T, 18.18 A, 18.324-5 A, 22.201 A; *pathêtikon* etc.: S.*OT* 34, *OC* 845, 1333, 1725; E.*Ph*.618, *Med*.1; *peripathes* etc.: S.*Aj*.312, 346, 434, 566, 570, 596, 633, 791, 819, 1266, 1305, *El*.95, 209, 269, 312, 451, 755,

1.12 The tragic emotions

Our survey of the tradition has disclosed a view of tragedy which one might – discounting the derogatory connotations which both words have acquired in modern usage – term 'emotive hedonism'; according to this view, the tragedian aims primarily to evoke an emotional response from his audience, while the audience for their part value his work because of the pleasure that accompanies such emotional excitation under the controlled conditions of a theatrical fiction. Our next task is to attempt a closer definition of the characteristically tragic emotions. For this, it will be convenient to begin with Aristotle's standard formula, 'fear and pity';[11] and the most obvious place to turn for an elucidation of this formula is to the more detailed analysis of these emotions in the *Rhetoric*. But we should not rely uncritically on the definitions which Aristotle gives there. First, Aristotle is taking over a traditional motif in his theory of tragedy; this is clear if one recalls the similar formulations in Gorgias and Plato (*Phdr.*269cd, *Ion* 536bc); so Aristotle's own usage elsewhere is not necessarily of special relevance to the interpretation of the terms in this context. Secondly, the context of the discussion in *Rhetoric* is in any case rather different; what it may seem relevant to say about an emotion when describing the orator's tasks need not carry over directly into the rather different circumstances of dramatic composition. Finally, one has to bear in mind the possibility that the definitions in *Rhetoric* have succumbed to the dangers of scholastic oversimplification, rigidity and even distortion that always beset formulations of this kind. The chapters of the *Rhetoric* are still of the greatest importance: but they must be treated with caution; and I will argue that they are in fact misleading in a number of respects. I also believe that the summary formula 'fear and pity', though suggestive and conveniently concise, is too narrow to be adequate in the last analysis.

(i) *Fear*: In the *Poetics*, the noun is *phobos*, the adjective *phoberon* or *deinon* (1456b3: cf. *Rhet.*1386a22, Pl.*Ion* 535c, *Rep.*387b8-9); the verb is *phrittein* (1453b5; cf. *Rep.*387c and Gorgias' *phrikê periphobos*): the use of this strong verb emphasises that we are dealing with emotions sufficiently intense and basic to evoke physical symptoms (cf. Pl.*Ion* 535c). The definition in the *Rhetoric* (1382a21-2, with the subsequent discussion) yields the following points:

(a) fear is a painful emotional disturbance (*lupê tis ê tarakhê*);
(b) it is occasioned by the expectation of an impending harm, such as to cause destruction or pain;[12]
(c) it is conditional upon uncertainty (83a5-7);
(d) it is egocentric (82b25-6).

846, 1123, *OT* 251 (cf. 137, 141, 236), 1071, *Ant.*82; E.*Or.*241, *Ph.*hyp., *Tro.*189, 343, *Hi.*566; *Il.*6.411-12 T, 12.154-5 T, 15.610-14 BT (for the link made with pleasure here cf. 17.197 T). (e) *pathos* as distinctively tragic: S.*Aj.*66, 1123, 1409, cf. *OT* 93; E.*Hec.*698, *Tro.*1129, *Hi.*566. The contrast with comedy in E.*Or.*1691 (cf. hyp. and *Alc.*hyp.) is stock, and misleading: cf. 1.12vi.

[11] See Schadewaldt 1955; on pity see also Burkert 1955.
[12] Cf. Pl. *Laches* 198b8-9: *deos* is defined as *prosdokia mellontos kakou*.

Of these points, (c) is surely too narrow: this is perhaps an instance of the rhetorical concerns of the treatise influencing the account. If the purpose of inspiring fear is to recommend a course of action to a deliberative body, it is certainly relevant that fear may make people deliberate; but fear does not always have this effect (it may paralyse us), and the emotional response to expected harm that does not seem avoidable is at least cognate with fear, and is surely relevant to tragedy. Point (d), too, is not straightforwardly applicable in the theatre: the examples given by Plato in *Ion* 535b (Odysseus poised to engage the suitors, Achilles setting out to do battle with Hector)[13] suggest situations of tense excitement, and perhaps fear for the characters involved in the action of the poem: and this, certainly, rather than fear for its own safety, is what we would expect of an epic or tragic audience. There is a partial correction in *Rhet.*1386a18-20, where it is admitted that we feel about those very close to us as we do about ourselves; but this is not very helpful, for Aristotle is saying that for these people we feel fear but *not* pity, which he treats as an other-regarding emotion incompatible with self-regarding fear. We hardly want fear and pity to be mutually exclusive responses to tragedy, and can again set down the narrowness of Aristotle's definitions to the rhetorical concerns which have influenced the account: in a speech, one uses fear to recommend a course of action by showing that one's audience, or some others for whom they are already concerned, are in danger; pity, by contrast, is used to sway those who are not already committed to be concerned for the welfare of some others. When Aristotle says in the *Poetics* that fear is about someone like ourselves (*peri ton homoion* 1453a4-6), he shows clearly that fear in tragedy is fear for a character; it is a sympathetic emotion, like pity.[14]

However, it is doubtful also whether point (b) is apt for tragedy, in which fear is perhaps more characteristically a reactive than an anticipatory emotion. Plato's words in *Rep.* 387bc point to that species of fear which is a shuddering recoil from the gruesome, horrid or awe-inspiring (he uses *phrittein* and *phrikê* for the response, *deina te kai phobera* for the objects: Cocytus, Styx, ghosts). Aristotle himself speaks of a response of *phrikê* and pity when one is simply told what happens in a tragedy, which suggests reactive fear; and clearly, it would make no sense to treat the emotion evoked by fearful spectacle as an anticipatory fear (*Poet.*1453b1-8). The kind of reactive fear here in question, and its natural objects, can easily be illustrated from the tragic corpus: the bellowing of a supernatural bull is *phrikôdes* (E.*Hi.*1216); the sight of Prometheus and of Io in their sufferings evokes a *phrikê* (*PV* 540, 695); so does mention of the Thyestean banquet (A.*Ag.*1242-3) and the sight

[13] Plato does not say explicitly that these are examples of *phobera* and *deina*: but he is working with the fear-pity pair (535c5-8), and goes on to give examples of *eleina* explicitly, so that the inference is natural.

[14] It has sometimes been held that tragic fear is fear for onself occasioned by the display of human insecurity on stage – which is a display *a fortiori* of the insecurity of the audience, men less great than the heroic sufferers. Since the Greek concept of pity included (as we shall see) a perception of one's own analogous vulnerability, this is presumably an element in sympathetic fear as well: but this is not what the Greeks had in mind when they spoke of tragic fear; it is at most a corollary of its being sympathetic.

of the blinded Oedipus (S.*OT* 1306). The sight of Philoctetes, wild and unkempt, excites fear, but presumably not because he poses a threat (S.*Ph*.225-7: *oknôi deisantes*); so too the sight of Orestes (E.*Or*.385ff.: *deinon*), while the mere mention of matricide is sufficiently horrible to excite the same kind of recoil from a barbarian king (E.*IT* 1174). The nocturnal apparition in Aristophanes' Euripidean monody was, we may recall, a *phrikôdê deinan opsin* (Ar.*Frogs* 1385).

In sum: 'fear' in the formula 'fear and pity' must be understood to cover a wide range of related emotional responses. It includes the species of fear described rather too narrowly in *Rhet*.1382a21ff.: the emotional disturbance felt when someone for whom our emotions are closely engaged is threatened by impending harm; also, presumably, our response to tension, suspense and excitement in narrative is to be included. But no less important is the instinctive shuddering recoil from what is made horrific by tabu, superstition, numinous awe, physical grisliness or unpleasantness.[15]

(ii) *Pity*: In the *Poetics* the noun is *eleos*, the adjective *eleeinon*; we may add *oiktron* and *oiktos* (cf.*Poet*.1453b14, *Rhet*.1417a12; Pl.*Phdr*.268cd, A.*Ag*. hyp. and scholia on S.*El*.271, E.*Ph*.1606, *Il*.1.13-34 BT, 3.305 BT, 3.306 B); we may note again the recurrent mention of physical symptoms (Gorgias' *eleos poludakrus*, and the other references to weeping mentioned in 1.11). The definition in the *Rhetoric* (1385b13-15, with the subsequent discussion) yields the following points:

(a) pity is a painful emotion (*lupê tis*);
(b) it is felt at apparent destructive or painful harm;
(c) the harm must be suffered by someone not sufficiently close to make it count as harm to oneself, although with this proviso pity is otherwise intensified if the sufferer is known to one or is in a similar status or condition as onself;
(d) the harm must be such as might be suffered by oneself or by a friend;
(e) the harm must be undeserved.

Points (c) and (d) indicate the balance that must be kept between suffering that is so close to home as to be one's own (as was the case in Phrynichus' *Sack of Miletus* discussed in 1.11), and that which is so remote as to be meaningless or incomprehensible. Pity must not collapse into a species of egocentric emotion, like the species of fear discussed in the *Rhetoric*, but must (like the rather wider fear of *Poet*.1453a4-6) be *peri ton homoion*. There is a certain difficulty here: another important requirement of tragedy was that its characters be elevated, removed from ordinary people in status and condition

---

[15] This last kind of fear is perhaps more characteristic of tragedy than of epic: hence the contrast of atmosphere that has been observed between Homer and Aeschylus ('haunted, oppressive': Dodds 1951: 40). But a historical explanation (of the kind that Dodds offers), as well as being implausible on other grounds (Lloyd-Jones 1971: 70-8), is unnecessary if the difference can be explained on generic grounds (see further Parker 1983: 14-16). This difference of generic tone would qualify the association of epic and tragedy: see further Ar.*Poet*.1460a11-18, 61b26ff.

(1.3); if, as Aristotle says elsewhere, the characters of serious poetry are to be 'better than us', how can they be 'like us', as his accounts of the sympathetic emotions require? Like in some respects, but not others? Which respects, and how like? And as for the nature of the harm, how many Athenians felt themselves likely to sleep with their mothers, or in danger of pursuit by Furies? Is not the whole point of such tragic ordeals the extremity which makes them untypical and astounding? The answer to these problems lies, perhaps, in the notions of deception (*apatê*) and vividness (*enargeia*) so important to Greek thinking about literary art; it is part of the dramatist's job to make the remote and improbable seem so vivid and credible (we may recall Hesiod's *pseudea ... etumoisin homoia*) that the experiences and emotions of the characters can be grasped imaginitively by the audience despite their remoteness and unfamiliarity. But this element of dramatic deception means that very little weight can be placed on points (c) and (d) in our discussion of pity in tragedy.

Point (e) is also, in my view, open to question; but it touches on a more complex problem, to which I will return in 2.5; I therefore set it to one side for the present.

In general, one could say that 'pity' is one's instinctive response to another's grief, suffering or misfortune (we pity Oedipus before he finds out the truth, and not only because he is going to find out; it is therefore objective wretchedness that we pity, as well as and independently of subjective suffering); this instinct prompts us, when it is possible to do so, to alleviate the suffering or to refrain from inflicting suffering (so that 'Have pity!' is often equivalent to 'Spare me!'), and the cluster of words round 'pity' tends to cover the action as well as, and sometimes rather than, the feeling;[16] when there is no possibility of such action, as is necessarily the case in the theatre, the instinct seeks expression by prompting one to give rein to and freely to express one's grief: hence the audience's tears.

Euripides provides an illustration in his *Suppliants* (286ff.). Theseus at first rejects the suppliants' plea, for sound moral and political reasons. He has no obligations to Adrastus and the others (for example, as *philos*); and their misfortune is the direct consequence of their own folly and misconduct. On these grounds, Theseus can deny that they have a claim to his aid as of right; and so he does no wrong when a prudent concern for the well-being and goodwill of his people constrains him to reject the plea. Even so, the defence of the suppliants, as punishment of injustice and impiety, would carry glory: the more so, indeed, in that he is not obliged to act thus.[17] Refusal, on the other hand, could be turned to his dishonour by enemies who would misrepresent his wise caution as cowardice. The pathos of the suppliants' laments in the face of his rejection of their plea moves his mother to tears (286-8); but Theseus, too, has been touched (*kame gar diêlthe ti* 288), so that he is now open to his mother's appeal, which lays stress on these points; he

---

[16] Dover 1974: 195ff.

[17] The act is supererogatory; Dover misses this point when he sets out a simple dilemma: 'If his later feeling is right, his earlier feeling was wrong' (1974: 16).

finally takes pity on the suppliants in the full and active sense.[18]

(iii) *Sympathy:* We have seen that both fear, in one of its relevant species, and pity are sympathetic emotions; and sympathetic responses are clearly central to tragedy: as Gorgias observed, poetry makes the soul undergo a response of its own to others' good and bad fortune (*ep' allotriôn te pragmatôn kai sômatôn eutukhiais kai duspragiais idion ti pathêma dia tôn logôn epathen hê psukhê* B11.9; cf. Pl.*Rep.*605d *hepometha sumpaskhontes*, 606b; Ar.*Rhet.*1386b13 *sunakhthesthai kai eleein, Pol.*1340a12 *eti de akroômenoi tôn mimêseôn gignontai pantes sumpatheis*). It would be conventional to speak here of 'identification'; but I would prefer to discourage the casual use of this term, which is surely misleading in its implication that the audience imaginitively acts out the roles of characters in the play. The audience's position is more accurately thought of as that of an observer – but of an observer whose emotional responses are readily drawn out by the condition and emotions of the dramatic characters; 'involvement' or 'engagement' would be less misleading terms for this attitude.[19] The point is not that the audience is made to undergo in imagination the experiences and emotions of the tragic characters, but that it is made to *respond* to those experiences and emotions: a distinction which does not, however, imply that the audience's response is in any sense muted or restrained; on the contrary, it is precisely on the readiness and intensity of the tragic audience's emotional response that I wish to insist. I shall argue in subsequent chapters that this prompt and intense responsiveness has important consequences for our approach to the interpretation of the plays.

(iv) *Ekplêxis:* We met this term in 1.11. It and its cognates are used of any emotional reaction, and especially of those which are particularly intense: for example, of love (E.*Med.*8, 639, *Hi.*38), joy (S.*Tr.*629, A.*Ch.*233, Pl.*Prot.*355a), but most characteristically of fear and terror (A.*Per.*606, E.*Tro.*183, Th.6.36.2; in Ar.*Rhet.*1385b32 *hoi ekpeplêgmenoi* is equated with *hoi sphodra phoboumenoi*). In Pl.*Ion* 535b2 it refers to the emotional effect which is essential to the success of a recitation, and the following explanation seems to refer to both fear and pity. In Aristotle, the term appears several times: *Poet.*1454a4, when someone acts in ignorance and then learns what he has done, the *anagnôrisis* is *ekplêktikon*; cf. 55a17, 52a2ff. (noting that *ekplêxis* is defined as *huperbolê thaumasiotêtos* in *Topics* 126b14); 60b25, the *telos* of poetry

---

[18] 'If this were a Just War, it would be inspired by high motives; in fact, the straight appeal of Adrastus fails, and the motivation appears as a tangle of national pride, personal egoism and maternal compulsion' (Fitton 1961: 435). One might say, less tendentiously: a complex of patriotism, personal honour and filial piety – to say nothing of humane pity; none of these motives is discreditable in Greek eyes. Fitton's description of Theseus as 'more a cautious politician than a national hero' is also strange: a national hero who is also a king cannot help being a politician (the derogatory implications which Fitton imports are gratuitous: and Theseus' attitudes are, for a democratic audience, exemplary: cf. 2.33), and *ought* to be cautious – that is, wise and prudent – as Adrastus disastrously was not. Fitton's article is an exemplary failure of interpretative method; we shall have occasion to refer to it again.

[19] Cf. Vickers 1973: 58; on 'identification' see Harding 1962.

is *ekplêxis*, and so an impossibility or other *prima facie* artistic flaw is justified if it makes the passage *ekplêktikôteron*. The same *telos* is ascribed to poetry by 'Longinus' (15.2); and Plutarch associates *ekplêxis* with the pleasure (*hêdonê*, *kharis*) at which most poets, he says, aim (*Mor*.16a-17e, 25d; cf. Plb. 2.56.7-12). Demetrius links *ekplêxis* and *phrikê* (*Style* 100-1). In the scholia, note the hypothesis to Agamemnon, in which Cassandra's scene is admired for having *ekplêxis* and *oiktos hikanos*, as well as the comments on S.*Aj*.346, 815.

It will be observed from these examples that the term does not necessarily imply sensationalism or crudity of technique; it does, however, have this implication in *Frogs* 962 (in Euripides' criticism of Aeschylus), and perhaps in the Aeschylean *Life*, where however *teratôdê* may do more to convey this meaning (cf. Ar. *Poet*.53b9).[20]

(v) *Other tragic emotions*: Aristotle writes in his definition of tragedy of fear and pity, and of 'emotions of that kind' (*ta toiauta pathêmata* 1449b27): does this imply that he recognises a wider range of emotions appropriate to tragedy, for which 'fear and pity' is merely a convenient brachylogy? If so, what other emotions would be in question? Grief would be an obvious example: so Gorgias' *pothos philopenthês*, S.*OT* 1225, or the scholion on S.*El*.86. Since Aristotle defines emotions in terms of pleasure and distress (*hois hepetai hêdonê ê lupê EN* 1105b23, cf. *Rhet*.1378a19-22), it would be plausible to treat the distressing or 'painful' emotions in general as the specifically tragic emotions: both fear and pity are defined in *Rhetoric*, as we have seen, as *lupê tis*. If so, then the next obvious candidates would be anger and hatred, emotions which involve distress (*estô de orgê orexis meta lupês timôrias Rhet*.1378a30), and which Aristotle frequently mentions in one breath with fear and pity.[21] Arguably, the antipathetic emotions are inevitably engaged when a tragic plot has an adversarial structure (cf.3.13); and I will argue in Chapter 5 that they carry the main emotional charge (and therefore, the main reward) of the latter scenes of *Ajax*. We should add that, although (as Aristotle rightly observes in *Rhet*.1378b1-10) there is a pleasurable element in anger (in the anticipation of revenge), it is not primarily for this reason that anger is pleasurable for the tragic audience; rather, it is the distressing and painful emotional disturbance itself which, as with fear and

[20] Cf. Taplin 1977: 46-7.

[21] Cf. Janko 1984: 160-1; note (e.g.) *EN* 1105b25, 33-4; *Rhet*. 1354a17, 1378a21, 1419b25-6; *Poet*. 1456b1 – this is the only passage which mentions anger as a tragic effect, but the reference is to the effects of rhetoric *ad intra*, so that it should not be pressed in this connection. (There is, of course, a good deal of anger and hatred *in* tragedy, but that is not the question: we are here concerned with the emotional effect *on an audience* of plays which contain, among other things, representations of the emotions of the *dramatis personae*. One of the faults in Stanford's disappointing book on tragedy and the emotions [1983] is that he is only intermittently aware of this distinction: e.g. on p.47 he expects an audience to 'identify' *either* with a character *or* with the Chorus – and so he cannot do justice to a passage like S.*Aj*.693-718 [see pp. 47, 116], where the audience must find the Chorus' joy, which they know to be groundless, painful: cf. 5.32. I welcome, nevertheless, the principle of Stanford's protest against the neglect of tragic emotion in modern scholarship.)

pity, can be enjoyed, once it has been detached from our extradramatic concerns – the Hesiodic motif once more.

(vi) *Happy endings*: Joy is obviously not one of the painful emotions which would, on this account, be proper to tragedy: and Aristotle does indeed argue that plays with a happy ending are second-rate, since they provide the *oikeia hêdonê* of comedy rather than that of tragedy; happy endings, he claims, are preferred only in deference to the weakness of the audience (*Poet.*1453a23-9: Aristotle himself seems to succumb to that weakness in 54a4-9). This argument was influential: a scholiast on E.*Or.*1691 tries to formulate a criticism of the play based on the assumption that the happy ending is more characteristic of and appropriate to comedy or satyric drama than tragedy (so too the hypotheses to this play and to *Alc.*); the attempt breaks down, however, because he is compelled to admit that the phenomenon to which he takes exception is really rather common in tragedy. A tragedy, then, 'may end happily (though only after troubling vicissitudes)'.[22] Because of the necessary vicissitudes, fear and pity and the painful emotions remain central to and definitive of tragedy; but we must recognise that the lighter emotions are also to be found in the tragedian's repertoire. The evaluative question is, of course, separate; some doubt may be cast on Aristotle's disparagement of eucatastrophic plays when one recalls that the *Oresteia* ends with great joy in reconciliation. I propose to turn to this trilogy in the next subsection, hoping to illustrate some of the themes discussed in the preceding pages through a brief survey of the emotional demands which it makes on its audience.

1.13 Aeschylus: Oresteia

(i) *Agamemnon*: The trilogy begins with a prayer: a look-out, posted by Clytaemnestra to keep watch for the beacon that will signal the capture of Troy, gives voice to his longing for release from that burdensome duty, for *apallagê ponôn* (1). It is not solely the physical discomfort of his post that troubles him: when he mentions his mistress's purpose his language is guarded and paradoxical, its implications strange and perhaps disturbing; the speaker, at any rate, is disturbed, for his thoughts at once take a more sombre turn as he recalls and deplores the troubles which beset the house of Atreus. So when, in the manner of ring-composition, his prayer for *apallagê ponôn* recurs (20) its significance has been broadened and deepened; it refers now, not to the troubles of one lowly individual, but to those of the whole royal house. To this deepening gloom Aeschylus juxtaposes an exuberant outburst of joy. As if in answer to the look-out's prayer, the beacon appears; from his excited celebration one would guess that all is now well. Not so: his exultation abruptly ebbs, leaving once more only veiled hints of disorder rooted deeply in the house. The appearance of the beacon has not brought release from care, as the look-out had supposed; despondency reasserts itself, and the prologue ends in obscure disquiet.

[22] Dale 1967: ix.

An audience responsive to the emotional currents of the tragic stage will readily catch the moods of this prologue; and the pattern of emotions which it displays is potent: a movement from gloom and apprehension to joy is checked by the onset of deeper gloom. As we shall see, this pattern pervades the trilogy.

The long parados takes us back ten years to the departure of the expedition to Troy. In the anapaests, the emphasis is on the rightfulness of the vengeance which the Greek army is to exact as agents of the justice of Zeus (*Dikê*), and on the inevitability of retribution for transgressors. But the extended lyric narrative which follows gives an account of the events which marred the army's dispatch, and so draws out the darker side of the affair: first, there is the ambivalence of the omen which assured the Greeks of victory; then, working out the adverse aspect of that omen, the manifestation of Artemis' anger, with its shocking sequel.

There are too many complex problems in the interpretation of this ode for my treatment to be other than superficial and dogmatic. The eagles' appearance on the right hand is propitious, and their feasting on the prey portends victory; but the killing of the young hare is hateful to Artemis in one of her divine capacities, and it can therefore be inferred that the victory of the Atreidae which it portends is also somehow hateful to her. Why this is so we are not told, and speculation is idle; Aeschylus has not told us why Artemis is angry, because it is the consequence of her resentment, and not its cause, that is significant in his narrative. The consequence is that Artemis will obstruct the departure of the fleet until Agamemnon has sacrificed his daughter. To do this would be a terrible thing, as Agamemnon sees; but it appears to him also that there is no other course of action not equally fraught with disaster: and so he yields to the necessity which his hopeless dilemma appears to impose on him.[23] From that moment – the moment of his fateful decision, when he yielded to perceived necessity – Agamemnon lost the scruples which had given him pause as he weighed up the alternatives, so that he now devoted himself to the sacrifice ruthlessly; for when a man is in the grip of *atê* (and what else could explain a man's taking such a decision at all?) he will become reckless:

βροτοὺς θρασύνει γὰρ αἰσχρόμητις
τάλαινα παρακοπὰ πρωτοπήμων·

For mortals are emboldened by the evil counsel
of cruel derangement, beginner of woe.   (222-3)

---

[23] 'Appears': the device of direct quotation means that Aeschylus has, strictly speaking, not endorsed Agamemnon's analysis; does this mean that there was in fact no necessity, i.e. that there may have been a course of action that was not *bareia kêr* (for this use of *anankê* to describe an unwelcome choice forced by the disastrous consequences of the only alternatives, cf. A.*Su*.440, 478)? The question is idle since, as we shall see, Agamemnon was swayed by *atê*. One should not inquire too closely either *why* the alternative was, or seemed to Agamemnon, intolerable: Aeschylus wishes to convey the impression of a dilemma, but a dramatist is not obliged to fill in the circumstantial background to his impressions where an audience would not normally have the time or inclination to look (cf.3.3).

Dawe argues that the transmitted order of these stanzas makes the onset of *atê* follow the taking of the fatal decision, uniquely; he suggests that the transposition of 160-91 to follow 217 would heal this fault.[24] It is not clear to me that the transmitted order does require the tardy onset of *atê*, or that the transposition which Dawe proposes would solve the problem if it did. But I do find the transposition attractive on other grounds (indeed, it is primarily on other grounds that Dawe urges it). The allegedly misplaced stanzas speak of the supremacy of Zeus and the moral order which he upholds; the explanatory role of these lines, as well as their ominous implications, are plainer if they are brought into closer relation with the onset of *atê*. Furthermore, it is easier to give sense to *mantin outina psegôn* and *empaiois tukhaisi sumpneôn* (186-7) if these expressions refer, not to the inconclusive prophecy of 126-55, but to the disaster of the contrary winds and the unquestionably distressing prophecy of 198ff.; and the syntax of 184-91 is easier if it leads into 218. So let us tentatively accept the transposition; then the digressive stanzas on the supremacy of Zeus, abruptly and inexplicably placed after 159, acquire a clear structural role. Aeschylus brings his emotive account of the events at Aulis to two successive climaxes: first, Agamemnon's decision; then there is a pause, followed by a resumption of the narrative, which leads up to the second climax, the sacrifice itself. Rhetorically, this seems much more effective.

The narrative, then, has two stages. In the first, we see Agamemnon put into an intolerable dilemma, and are moved to pity him as he works through an agonising analysis of his situation; but the decision he takes is shocking, one of those monstrous things from which we recoil in instinctive horror. In the second stage this horror is present as a constant undertone, but the focus shifts as Aeschylus recounts the sacrifice itself in a narrative of great pathos; the abrupt aposiopesis with which the Chorus turns at the last moment from the death-blow reflects the repugnance of the killing; and so the ode closes on a note of apprehension: Agamemnon has done a terrible thing, and what does the stern theology of retribution implied by the stanzas on the sovereignty of Zeus hold for him? If infatuation is *prôtopêmôn*, beginner of woe, what woe lies in wait for him?

The parodos explores a little way into the background of the plot; we will be taken deeper into this at a later stage. But what we have been told already confirms the despondent mood of the prologue: if the king has slaughtered the daughter that adorned his house (*domôn agalma* 208), we can begin to see what is wrong with the house. And Calchas has warned that this sacrifice will awaken conflict with no fear of the husband (*ou deisênora*), that child-avenging wrath (*mnamôn mênis teknopoinos*) haunts the house (150-5). The entry of Clytaemnestra gives palpable form to these obscure worries. Her presence is chilling: she rapidly establishes a personal ascendancy over the Chorus, which she treats with condescension; her manner, and the ironical emphasis she lays on the weakness of her sex, recall the discordant paradox of the prologue; worst of all is her evident dissimulation and the covert threat of

[24] Dawe 1966, taken up in 1967.

346-7 (we can hardly miss the sinister undertones of this, after the Chorus has told us of Iphigeneia's death and the child-avenging wrath that haunts the house without respect of the husband). The news of the fall of Troy should have been good: but as in the prologue, good news is turned sour; and if the Chorus goes on to celebrate the victory of Dike over the Trojan malefactors, a painful irony insinuates itself into the celebration: for if we ask again what Dike holds for Agamemnon, the preceding scene has given us clear indication. Aeschylus is evoking his painful expectation of impending destructive harm (cf.1.12i).

The emotional development of the first stasimon reflects the painful ambiguity that is becoming apparent in the principle of Dike, and so reproduces the basic emotional pattern of a movement to joy checked by renewed fear. The celebration of victory slides into a lament over those fallen in the war; and from there we pass into apprehension for the future: what of the people's resentment of their losses in such a cause? what of the anger of the dead? the anger of Zeus? The position of the sacker of cities is a precarious one. But then, who knows if the rumour is true? One cannot trust a woman's judgment. There is a notorious inconcinnity here with the opening of the ode; but we should not look for a psychological explanation of the Chorus' inconsistency. Rather, we should note the song's linear continuity: if we had passed directly from celebration to doubt, then indeed the clash of moods might jar; as it is, the route is an indirect one, and each new mood seems to arise without strain from what has gone immediately before – what transition is smoother than that from uncertainty about the future to uncertainty about the present? So there is no point at which the ode as it unfolds for the audience gives rise to a sense of dislocation. It is only to the synoptic view of the critic that the overall coherence of the ode becomes problematic; and for that viewpoint, the song was not designed.

Aeschylus picks up his Chorus, therefore, in a celebratory mood appropriate to the news which they had received in the preceding act, and by gentle stages he undermines their celebration, bringing them round first to share the audience's apprehensiveness, and then to the state of uncertainty necessary for their role as audience *ad intra* of the Herald's report. In this scene there is a poignant tension between the obtuse cheerfulness of the Herald and the countertheme of fear which the Chorus maintains in their dialogue with him. He blithely misses the point of their hints that all is not well at home (550ff.), and launches again into a triumphant rhesis; his mood now infects even the Chorus (583-6). At once Clytaemnestra returns, and brings a chill to the proceedings.[25] She again lays a disquieting, ironical emphasis on her sex; she is offensively patronising; she is brazenly hypocritical. Her appearance is brief, but sufficient to effect a new change of mood; the latter part of the scene is devoted to the loss of Menelaus – bad news, as the Herald says, polluting the celebration (636ff.). The basic pattern asserts itself again: the use of Clytaemnestra, the sinister figure who

[25] I assume that she has been off-stage since 354: see Taplin 1977: 288-90, 294-300. If she has been present from the beginning of the act, my point will stand (for 'returns' read 're-engages in the dialogue'), although the visual realisation will be less effective.

embodies the threat to Agamemnon, as pivot, and of the recital of Menalaus' loss (otherwise scarcely relevant) to give substance to the change of mood, is masterly.

After the news of this disaster the second stasimon must begin already in a sombre mood; when the Chorus reflects on the fall of Troy, it is now no longer in triumph, but to remark on the damage wrought by Helen. Once again, we can see how the intervention of Dike coincides with the turning-point into tragedy: the playful lion-cub, when it turns savage, becomes a priest of Ate; and the marriage which that fable reflects, although beginning in exquisitely tender poetry (737-42), ends bitterly with the Fury bringing tears to brides (*numphoklautos Erinus*). Here the harsh contrast in diction, imagery and thought drives home the repetition of the pattern of thwarted joy.

At last Agamemnon arrives. The homecoming of a victorious king should, and in other circumstances would, be an occasion for joy and celebration. But the cumulative pattern of disappointment, and the shadows cast by the Chorus' reflections on Dike, rule out any unambiguous sense of triumph; moreover, we are aware of the threat posed to Agamemnon by Clytaemnestra. So the king enters, unwittingly, under a cloud; and we are made to watch this compromised triumph slide gradually, painfully to a disaster that is the more pitiful for the victim's helpless ignorance of his true situation.

After the Chorus' enthusiastic greeting, Agamemnon delivers a long and dignified speech (although even here there are traces of his triumph's souring, as he calls to mind the loss of his loyal comrade Odysseus: 841ff.). Characteristically, it is the entry of Clytaemnestra that changes the tone: she welcomes him with prolonged and unctuous hypocrisy, and then begins her 'temptation' of him; her speech ends with another covertly threatening allusion to Dike. In reply, Agamemnon flatly refuses her invitation to trample underfoot the expensive weavings, and the dry wit with which he puts her down at the beginning of his speech suggests a dominance that should delight us: has this odious woman at last met her match? As the dialogue proceeds and Agamemnon's defences crumble, we realise that she has not; she wins her point. It is made clear that for Agamemnon to make this concession is dangerous; it is the kind of action that invites divine anger. Nevertheless, that he does so is in no sense the *cause* of his death: that has been settled long ago, by ancestral crimes and by his own wrongdoing at Aulis. Strict causality, however, has no necessary connection with dramatic effect. The point is, first, that Agamemnon must be vanquished on some point in full view of the audience, so that when he leaves the stage he is seen to be under Clytaemnestra's power – fatally; then, that the issue on which he is vanquished should be a symbolically weighty one, with fearful implications for Agamemnon's safety: this is secured by the religious qualms which prompt his irresolute resistance. Beyond that, the ill-defined complexity of the ominous symbol, suggestive as it is of the dangers of wealth, of the house destroying itself, of an entry along a path of blood, accentuates and deepens these overtones and implications; to force too precise or limited a meaning on the scene would diminish its force: what is essential is the action's indefinite suggestiveness of evil.[26] To this, the confused fear of the third stasimon is an appropriate response.

The scene of Agamemnon's homecoming, then, ends with his surrender, and his entry into the palace takes place in ominously suggestive circumstances. Once more, would-be triumph has been poisoned, and issues in fear and pity as we watch the victor going to his death. But if as we watch that fatal exit we expect a swift *dénouement*, we are cheated, for another long and important scene intervenes. Cassandra, who had arrived in the king's retinue and maintained an inconspicuous silence, was brought to our attention towards the end of the scene (950); she remained on stage during the subsequent stasimon, thus becoming a more striking enigma; now Clytaemnestra returns to take her inside: but the long, immobile silence is sustained, and inflicts on Clytaemnestra her first rebuff. When Cassandra does at last break her silence after the queen's retreat, it is in a lyric outburst the violence of which is in stark and shocking contrast to her previous silence: *ekplêxis* is brilliantly achieved; and to the sheer shock of the outburst is added a *phrikê* of horror as she vividly portrays her vision of the murdered children of Thyestes – and of the impending murder of the king; then her thoughts move on to her own part in the coming events, and the emotional demand on the audience expands to embrace pity for her. The same range of emotion is recapitulated in the iambic speeches: observe how the repeated exclamations (1214, 1256) keep the emotional pitch intense, as she ranges over the haunting of the house by the Erinyes, the Thyestean banquet (observe 1242-4 for the appropriate reaction to this), the impending murder, and her own fate – and here the speech rises to a majestic climax with the prophecy of vengeance (1279-85), before closing on a quieter, more pathetic note. The horrific vision is renewed as she recoils twice from the doors of the palace; and when she steels herself at last to enter, the pathos is suddenly deepened by being set against a universal backdrop of human insecurity (1327ff.; cf.3.11).

This scene, then, is emotionally rich and turbulent; it is, as the hypothesis observes, remarkable for its emotional intensity and pathos (*touto to meros tou dramatos thaumazetai hôs ekplêxin ekhon kai oikton hikanon*). It has also extended our understanding of the background of the tragedy. The crime of Atreus is brought into the open; and we see that it is the Erinys infesting the house of Atreus that is bringing Agamemnon to his death. In this disclosure, we come upon another and still darker aspect of the working of Dike, and a more striking evidence of the threat that it poses to human security. It seems likely that 374-5 contained a reference to the visitation of paternal sins on the children;[27] and the fourth strophe of the second stasimon made it clear how corruption sinks deep into the fabric of whole families (763-71). Cassandra's prophecies now confirm these hints, and show how the process is at work in

[26] A good discussion in Taplin 1977: 308-16, 1978: 78-83.

[27] The text is controversial: but since this was a standard defence of the doctrine (impugned in the preceding lines) that the gods concern themselves with human wrongdoing, it is likely to have occurred here.

the family of Atreus, with the present generation suffering the consequences of ancestral crime. The implications of this doctrine are summed up in the brief anapaestic interlude before Agamemnon's death-cries, an epitome of the theological apparatus which brings about the death: if Agamemnon, victor returning (to all appearances) with the favour of the gods (1337) is doomed by ancestral crime – who is safe? Every man must hold himself at risk of retribution both unpredictable and inexorable.

The interlude is brief: Agamemnon's death, so long held back, follows swiftly; then there is a pause, in which the Chorus' indecision is used to delay and build up tension towards a disclosure. Clytaemnestra's sudden appearance abruptly interposes a commanding figure. At first, as she describes and glories in her deed with bloodthirsty relish, she is an object unequivocally of shock, of loathing, of hatred – emotions which the Chorus articulate on behalf of the audience; but as the kommos progresses, this simple reaction is complicated. The two parties begin their confrontation holding bitterly opposed views of the responsibility for and justification of the killing, but they gradually advance towards a shared understanding founded on the recognition of two points: that Agamemnon's death was ultimately the outworking of the family curse; and that it was proximately the merited consequence of his killing of Iphigeneia. Clytaemnestra's crime is therefore on one level absorbed into a broader pattern of the operation of Dike; on another, it is seen as in some degree justifiable: right clashes with right and judgment is contestable (*dusmakha d' esti krinai* 1561). This latter point must qualify our inclination to see the threat of vengeance that now hangs over Clytaemnestra as the punishment of a mere criminal and an unmixed good; and so we are now free to consider it in the light of the former point, and to see that it is also another stage in the history of the Atreid house, another step towards utter destruction, and so to be feared and deplored. It is towards this end that the Chorus looks bleakly at the end of the exchange:

τίς ἂν γονὰν ἀραῖον ἐκβάλοι δόμων;
κεκόλληται γένος πρὸς ἄται.

Who could expel the brood of curses from the house?
The family is fastened to destruction.   (1565-6)

Clytaemnestra seizes on this and expresses the hope that some way might now be found to placate the Erinys and rescue the house from final disaster. This hope should not be dismissed as worthless or hypocritical; we have seen how the precarious equilibrium which the debate attains shows Clytaemnestra in a new light: her defence is persuasively urged; and there is genuine pathos both in her maternal grief and in her awareness of the potency of the curse. Nevertheless, the compromise she suggests is theologically unworkable: the divinely ordained justice which, through her agency, destroyed Agamemnon for his crimes must apply with equal rigour to the crimes of his killers also; for Dike is the rule of Zeus, and while Zeus remains sovereign it is immutable and inexorable:

μίμνει δὲ μίμνοντος ἐν θρόνωι Διὸς
παθεῖν τὸν ἔρξαντα· θέσμιον γάρ.

It abides while Zeus abides upon his throne:
to him who does shall it be done; for so it is ordained.   (1563-4)

Her hope is futile, the Chorus' despair to all appearances justified.

The kommos, therefore, has brought us to a point where our anticipation of vengeance for the death of Agamemnon must be ambivalent: we must see it as indeed merited and morally necessary, but also as impending doom for the house of Atreus. This ambivalence will be present as an undertone throughout *Choephori*, together with our horror of matricide; but it is an undertone: for most of the play Aeschylus desires that the dominant mood be far closer to the simpler adversarial relation with which the kommos began. Sympathies must be realigned, therefore, before the end of *Agamemnon*, and it is the entry of Aegisthus that destroys the balance of the kommos: he is an odious man, whose violence exhibits clearly the futility of the hope that has been expressed and the inescapability of further bloodshed. It is appropriate, therefore, that he should begin with a recital of the power of the curse and of Dike: the very things which have made the prolongation of the struggle and his own eventual downfall inevitable.

(ii) *Choephori*: The second play of the trilogy is built of three contrasting sections. The first part is long and static; more than half the play has passed before any active steps are taken towards implementing the plan of revenge. When the plan is taken in hand, however, the play is transformed into a drama of intrigue, rapid and exciting in its movement; but this development is itself diverted into a third, more sombre and reflective stage. As we have learnt to expect, the joy of success is swiftly soured.

What the earlier scenes lack in activity they make up in emotion and atmosphere. The prologue is unfortunately too fragmentary for us to be able to trace its mood in detail; but it is clear that the two prayers to Hermes (1ff., 124ff.) are meant to balance each other: Aeschylus introduces the two children of Agamemnon separately, and displays their longing for redress. The pair must then be brought together: the recognition scene takes the form of a prolonged, anxious uncertainty for Electra as she discovers the signs of Orestes' presence, released into joy after a tense and wary encounter with him.[28] The last words of her speech of welcome are taken up by Orestes and

---

[28] There is evidently some disruption in the text of 201-30, but the theory of interpolation is not attractive. I would not myself wish to rest a defence of the footprints on Wilamowitz's observation that the prints provide a more certain indication of Orestes' presence (so Lloyd-Jones 1961: 176-7): for although that would of course be true, the inference is not drawn by the characters – Electra is not reassured, but is plunged into further uncertainty by her discovery; so this was not the use that Aeschylus was making of the sign. Rather, the second sign is designed to prolong Electra's period of anxiety, achieving a more pathetic effect. As for details: it is argued that 212 should follow directly from 204; if it did, the way in which Orestes takes up Electra's words would indeed be effective; but it does not, and 212-13 are sufficiently plausible as an opening to stand independently of what preceded. More weighty is the observation that to

turned into another majestic prayer; finally, in a horrifying passage, Orestes reviews the pressures and sanctions which compel him to act.

The opening scenes, therefore, are forward-looking and dwell on the justice and necessity of the vengeance; thus they build up a pressure towards the murders – a pressure which is held in check for more than two hundred lines by the 'conjuration'. It should not be supposed that this scene is designed to reinforce Orestes' determination. He has taken his decision long ago, and shows no signs of faltering; the end of his speech at 305 is strong and confident in tone. Moreover, the chief reason why he might falter is through a horror of matricide; but that would be ruinous here, for Aeschylus has with some care refrained from emphasising this darker and more horrific aspect of the vengeance. This is being held in reserve for the climactic confrontation between Orestes and his mother, and for the abrupt reversal of mood with which the play ends; if the idea were brought into prominence at this early stage, the impact of those scenes would be impaired, and it would inhibit the expectation of and desire for the vengeance that Aeschylus is building up as the dominant mood in his audience throughout the early scenes of the play. The conjuration is, therefore, what it purports to be: an attempt to enlist the dead man's aid by stirring up his slumbering wrath. An invocation of the dead moves in those underworld regions which, as Plato knew (*Rep.*387bc: cf.1.12i), evoke a horrified shudder; this effect is enhanced here by the dark emotions which pervade the passage, the bitterness and hatred of living and dead. It is this emotional effect, the horrified *phrikê* which it should evoke from the audience, that is the tragic motivation of the passage.

After the long invocation of the dead, the more detailed account of Clytaemnestra's dream (523ff.: taking up 32ff.) serves as a sign of the wakefulness of the wrath that has been evoked (cf.41-2), and as an omen of success; thus it serves also as a transition to the play's second stage, in which the plot is put in motion and vengeance achieved. Orestes' outline of his plan is carefully contrived to deprive the audience of any accurate expectations, so that the unfolding of the plot loses none of its tension and excitement (554ff.: note also that the killing of Clytaemnestra is not mentioned; as I have observed, Aeschylus wishes to play down the darker aspects of the vengeance at this stage). The execution of the plan begins immediately after an ode which prepares for the vengeance by placing the murder of Agamemnon at the climax of a catalogue of female crimes,[29] and which looks towards the work of Dike and the Erinys. The same theology is at work here as in *Agamemnon* (cf.48, 61ff., 312-14, etc.); but a different aspect is displayed, so that the theology now makes a new demand on our emotions. In the earlier play, we were invited to perceive and respond to the working of Dike as a

---

close with a prayer would be more regular; but 204 *is* a close: 205 introduces a surprising new observation (cf. 166). If any change is necessary, Hermann's lacuna after 208 is sufficient. In the later passage, I would favour a lacuna after 228 (retaining the order of M); this gap makes confident treatment of 229-30 impossible.

[29] Accepting Preuss's transposition; '*a* is bad, and so is *b*, and worst of all is *c*: but Clytaemnestra is even worse than that' is obviously required; '*a* is bad, and so is *b*, and so is Clytaemnestra: but none of them compare with *c*' is nonsense in this context.

threat; now we are made to look forward to and celebrate its work, because our sympathies have been aligned with the avengers, rather than with the victim. Nevertheless, a shock is in store for us.

As we have already mentioned, the scenes of conspiracy differ from the slow opening in pace and tone;[30] the brief door-knocking scene prefaced to the (as always) commanding appearance of Clytaemnestra[31] has a hint of colloquialism about it; both this act and the one which follows (after only a short anapaestic interlude) are brief; and the Nurse's appearance in the latter again has the suggestion of a more vulgar tone than is usual in tragedy. These two incidents show the weaving of the net: Clytaemnestra is deceived, the avengers gain entry to the palace, Aegisthus is lured without protection. At this point, with all the preparations in hand, a pause: the Chorus prays for success, and looks forward with optimism to the end of the series of murders that has troubled the house (806).

Aegisthus arrives, and very soon goes inside to his death: his death-cries are only briefly delayed by anapaests; then there is a new flurry of action – the servant's panic and the reappearance of Clytaemnestra – that comes to a sudden halt in the confrontation of mother and son. Now at last Aeschylus begins to bring home to us the horror of matricide (896-8, its import emphasised by Orestes' hesitation and the momentous words of the 'silent' character Pylades). But as Clytaemnestra is led off to the slaughter, the Chorus are still celebrating the work of Dike, beginning from the paradigm which the history of Troy affords (935-8: cf. *Ag*.357ff. etc.); and they end by celebrating the resurrection of the house, the end to its troubles for which they had earlier looked. That naive optimism, which Aeschylus has fostered by his suppression of the darker side of the vengeance in the earlier parts of the play, is to be shattered in the play's last scene. Orestes foresees his ordeal, and publicly displays the evidence for his plea of justification: then he lapses into madness with the onset of the Erinyes, as yet unseen. So when the play ends with a meditation on the sufferings of the Atreid house, the mood of the Chorus has undergone a profound change; the future now appears obscure and menacing.

We can see, then, how the structure of this play fits into the basic pattern established at the beginning of *Agamemnon*. In the first two parts of this play Aeschylus has given us an atmospheric set-piece and an exciting and lively intrigue. In them, we move from the initial gloom of the dead king's dispossessed children towards triumph and liberation; the vengeance is the act which is looked forward to as the healing of the situation: and that is what it ought to be; but it is in the event flawed, matricidal, sinful; and so the ordeal of the house is again prolonged, and the incipient movement into joy is abruptly checked in the closing scenes. Dike had seemed, in the course of this play, less threatening and intolerable than it did in *Agamemnon*; the reversal of mood with which the play ends once again calls that appearance of benignity into question.

---

[30] An excellent appreciation in Taplin 1977: 346-8, 351-3.

[31] The grief of 691ff. is of course sincere: we saw how the closing scenes of *Ag.* drew a more complex picture of her character, and allowed her genuine pathos.

(iii) *Eumenides*: We have observed in the earlier plays of the trilogy how Aeschylus strives for the effect of *ekplêxis*, for surprise or shock with the onset of violent emotion. The opening scenes of *Eumenides* pursue the same end through devices of stage technique that have been well described by Taplin:[32] the contrast between the dignity of the opening speech and the terrified scramble of the Pythia's return, followed by a fearsome description of the Furies designed to set our imagination to work; the ghost; the weird noises of the unseen monsters, feeding our images; at last the eruption from the scene of the Furies themselves – so costumed, we must assume, that the images of horror that have been evoked are not bathetically cheated. Horror, then, and fear are the dominant emotions of the scene.

The Chorus is horrific because it embodies the workings of Dike; this, as we have seen, has a dark and threatening aspect in the earlier plays: the reversal at the end of *Choephori* in particular has heavily underscored this aspect, and the victim in this play is once again the focus of the audience's sympathy, not an antagonist. Nor is the audience alone in its recoil from the horror of the Furies; Apollo treats the Chorus with a contempt and loathing which his dramatic role requires (for he is one of the conflicting parties), but which also articulates the revulsion felt by the audience. But a more favourable estimate of the Furies is also offered: their own estimate of themselves. This begins to come across in the stasimon at 307ff.: they are upholders of justice (*euthudikaioi* 312); though Zeus may affect to despise them (365-6) their role is an essentially honourable one (389-96). It is fitting that this statement of their *timê*, their honour and office, is followed by the entry of Athene, for she restrains natural repugnance and treats the Furies with courtesy and respect (as they treat her, though not their antagonist Apollo). The second stasimon, the prelude to the trial itself, serves to emphasise its importance by showing how much hangs on the issue; thereby it serves also to explicate Athene's words at 470ff. In this song, the Furies develop their case more fully. The inexorable harshness of Dike which the Erinyes represent is not arbitrary, but is a vital bastion of the moral and natural order; if the restraint of terror were removed men would bitterly regret its loss in the moral chaos that would ensue; that terror, therefore, is salutary, though cruel, since it alone makes possible a free life without anarchy. This doctrine Athene herself explicitly endorses in her speech instituting the new court (513-37, cf.696-706).[33]

The theological consensus thus reached does not mitigate the harshness of this order of things; if life bounded by terror is preferable in theory to moral anarchy, it (and the agents of Dike who enforce it) remain in practice grimly unattractive. Moreover, the crucial issue, the fate of Orestes, remains to be

---

[32] Taplin 1977: 362ff.

[33] The doctrine is, of course, received wisdom: cf. Solon fr.6 W. As for Athene's speech of institution, Taplin is surely right to conclude (1977: 395-401) that the early part of this act has suffered damage; and this must raise the possibility that the speech has been displaced. The oddity of the later placing of the institution; the apparent clash with 674-5; the interruption of the series of couplets (678 is difficult in any case): all these conspire to make the theory of displacement hard to dismiss; but one sympathises with Taplin's hesitancy.

settled: hence the trial. To many interpreters the course and outcome of the trial have been a stumbling-block; they have found in it only slippery rhetoric and mythological quibbles leading to a decision based arbitrarily on private predilection. In fact, the trial is fought on issues that are clearly indicated, and its outcome is (in my judgment) both rational and dramatically satisfying. The Erinyes invoke their simple maxim: he did it, therefore he must pay the fixed penalty. Then why was the rule not applied also to Clytaemnestra when she committed murder? Because the husband is not a blood-relation of the wife. And the son is a blood-relation of the mother? Orestes is made to raise this curious question in 606, though he makes nothing of it; its function is to emphasise at the climax of the Erinyes' cross-examination the issue that will be crucial. Of course the son is a blood-relation of his mother, say the Erinyes; not, Apollo replies, in the strictest sense: the death of a woman is in any case less important than that of a man, and of such a man (625ff.); but the mother is also of less significance specifically as a parent, since she is entirely passive in procreation (657ff.). Granted that premise, there can be no doubt that the avenging of the father must take precedence over the claims of the mother; the oracle's command is vindicated, and Orestes must be acquitted. And the crucial premise must be granted; Athene is to hand as incontrovertible proof of the relative insignificance of the mother as parent.[34]

Orestes, then, is acquitted; but the theological vision of the Erinyes is limited: they are unimpressed by the case for the defence, and can only interpret the acquittal that has deprived them of their prey as *atimia*, an attempt to strip them both of their office and of their honour. Athene tries to placate them; but the heedless verbal repetitions of their complaint (778-92 = 808-22; 837-47 = 870-80) give a terrifying impression of implacable fury. Yet, as Athene explains, their anger is misguided. That the judgment was evenly balanced testifies to the seriousness with which they have been taken (795-6); and the decisive consideration, that which swayed Athene's vote (735ff.), was the superior claim of the father: that does not abolish the rights of the mother or lightly set them aside, since it is only in the unique circumstances of Orestes' moral dilemma that such a plea could stand; in general, therefore, the penalty for matricide must be exacted. So the verdict does not involve *atimia*: that is, it neither shows contempt for the Furies, nor deprives them of their office.

The Furies are not easily persuaded that they have not been dishonoured, and the crisis which their resentment precipitates is crucial to the structure of the whole trilogy. We saw at the end of *Choephori* that Dike had again acquired a predominantly threatening aspect; this has been accentuated in *Eumenides* by the horrific character and appearance of its agents, and above all by the terrible fate that awaited Orestes. His acquittal represents a

---

[34] It may be relevant that the premise was granted by some Greek thinkers (cf. Aristotle's remarks at *de gen. anim.*763b30); but it is more important that the premise is secured *within the play* by mythological data that are beyond question. The relative devaluation of the female also provides a corrective to Clytaemnestra's subversion of male and female roles: it therefore comes as a welcome restoration of normality.

liberation from this fear and a movement towards joy; but, in accordance with the basic pattern of emotions that we have traced through *Agamemnon* and *Choephori*, this movement is checked: the Erinyes in their fury threaten to devastate Attica in retaliation for the contempt shown them by the Athenian judges. Athene's attempt to placate them leads to a high-point of tension that is maintained through a dozen lines of wavering dialogue before the Furies at last give way and turn their curses into blessings. But now, the renewed fear which checks the movement to joy is itself checked, and turned back into a more powerful movement to joy that is this time not defeated. The Furies' change of mind breaks, not only the tension of this crisis, but also the pattern that has haunted the trilogy since its opening lines: hence its great force. Athene interposes commentary between the stanzas of benediction, but this is not a dialogue; the impression is rather of a monologue attended by an observer, for the blessings sweep past her comments heedless – echoing and inverting the effect of the Chorus' earlier heedless anger. From this device arises the momentum which contributes so much to the buoyant and uplifting effect of this magnificent hymn of joy.

It is widely supposed that the institution of the Areopagus in this play represents the transition to a new order of justice: due process of law has superseded the vicious *lex talionis* that the Erinyes had embodied; and the Erinyes themselves are, by their reconciliation, incorporated in the new order, with the result that their role and character is in some measure changed.[35] This interpretation, if accepted, would cohere well with the account I have given of the emotional pattern of the trilogy; the pattern of thwarted joy is broken, it would be pointed out, precisely when Dike – which has so often plunged joy into despair – is transformed. Nevertheless, this is a misunderstanding of the play.

The decisive objection to such an interpretation is this: that it needs to place its emphases at points quite different from those which Aeschylus has chosen to emphasise; for what Aeschylus has emphasised is the *continuity* between the Erinyes – the unreformed Erinyes – and the court of the Areopagus. This continuity is impressively brought out in the echo of the Chorus' self-justification in Athene's speech of institution: the court is seen here as nothing but the civic analogy of the Erinyes at the cosmic level, an extension of the same principles of justice. Nor is there any indication later in the play that the Erinyes surrender or alter their former role when they accept new cultic honours at Athens. On the contrary, Athene's denial of their *atimia* presupposes that their former office is upheld, and this is clearly implied by the commentary which she offers on their benedictions: they still destroy the sinner and the sinner's descendants (930-7), and in the fear which they inspire there is gain for this city – an echo of the principle of salutary terror on which the Erinyes had previously rested their self-defence, and which Athene had taken up in founding the new court. In all of this, therefore, continuity.

---

[35] The most recent version of this theory is also the most cogent: Macleod 1983: 20-40 Contrast Lloyd-Jones 1971: 92-5.

It is perhaps just because the court is seen as no more than an extension of the Erinyes that its institution fails to resolve the problem in hand; when the judges vote on Orestes' fate, they are deadlocked, and only the casting vote of Athene resolves the issue.[36] The deadlock which the human jurors reach is expressive of the nature of the problem: it is a conflict of right with right, a consequence of the dilemma which Orestes faced when he had to make a choice between two courses of action each of which was criminal and pollutant. This conflict of rights is a conflict within the existing moral order: for that reason, the only way the problem could be resolved is through a clarification of the mind of Zeus; and this Apollo and Athene provide in determining the order of precedence between the ordinances of Zeus that have here come into conflict. This brings out the crucial point: that the principle to which the Erinyes adhered in their persecution of Orestes was indeed an ordinance of Zeus, which is not set aside or abolished even though subordinated to another divine law; it is for this reason that their defeat in the trial involved no *atimia*. But for this very reason also there could not be (in terms of Aeschylean theology there could not be) any surrender or alteration in their office; for they are the agents of Dike, which is upheld by Zeus himself, and:

μίμνει δὲ μίμνοντος ἐν θρόνωι Διὸς
παθεῖν τὸν ἔρξαντα· θέσμιον γάρ.

It abides while Zeus abides upon his throne:
to him who does shall it be done; for so it is ordained   (*Ag.*1563-4)

The old order is identified with the sovereignty of Zeus; it is therefore fixed and immutable (cf. *Ag.*160-183).

At the fundamental level, therefore, nothing has or could have changed of a general nature; but why should we expect it to be otherwise? The decisive changes have occurred at the level of particulars: Orestes has been acquitted, a particular chain of suffering and death has been broken, Athens has been saved from the Erinyes' curse. For a tragic audience, sympathetically involved in the fortunes of the characters of the drama, these are matters of no small importance; certainly, they are of more concrete and more urgent importance than the generalities to which the reading of the play I have criticised would distract our attention. This, however, is to touch on issues that will concern us in subsequent chapters (cf.3.11); at this point I wish only to emphasise that an interpretation of the *Oresteia* must, as the tradition we have surveyed in 1.11-2 would lead us to expect, be above all an interpretation of its emotional and emotive economy.

The trilogy has given us fear and pity in abundance; its climax resolved these emotions into celebration. This climax is not, as some have supposed, a loosely attached addition: on the contrary, it is precisely the *apallagê ponôn* to which the trilogy has been looking from the very beginning; and it is a fitting

[36] If the vote of Athene is not casting, but brings about the deadlock, the human jury does even less well; but that I regard as the less likely view.

and satisfying conclusion to the recurrent emotional pattern that has dominated the trilogy. This makes it hard to accept that eucatastrophe is, as Aristotle would have it, a compromise of the tragic art.

1.14 A note on method

In the last subsection I tried to give a concise account of the emotional demands of the *Oresteia*. Inevitably, this will be regarded by some as a hopelessly 'subjective' undertaking; as A.M. Bowie puts it, 'one cannot prove that pathos "exists" by any objective criterion'.[37] Now, one could plausibly argue that appropriateness of response is a more objective matter than this comment implies: if someone finds it irresistibly amusing when a child is maimed in a road accident, then he is either failing to notice something of importance about the incident, or he is morally defective; similarly, it might be argued, if someone is insensitive to the joyful climax of *Eumenides*, then he has either failed to see it clearly, or his aesthetic sensitivity is sadly curtailed. But quite apart from this line of argument, objection to the 'subjectivity' of what I have tried to do would miss the point.

The charge might hold against someone who asked the purely descriptive question: what effect *does* this text have? For such a question might plausibly be answered introspectively; one might, so to say, observe the moistening of one's eyes, and mark down a passage as 'pathetic'. But I am not asking that question, nor even at present the critical question: what effect *ought* this text to have? Rather, I am asking the *interpretative* question: what effect was this text *meant* to have? My subjective response may indeed have a heuristic role in answering this question; if my eyes moisten, it is worth asking whether they were meant to do so. But an initial response must then be tested by a more objective analysis, which (in my experience) will often curb or correct it; were this not so, the whole enterprise of poetics, which is designed precisely to restrain our use of anachronistic responses as evidence in interpretation, would be pointless. So my question is essentially a historical one; and a hypothesis about what an author was trying to achieve is as objective, as open to rational discussion and disconfirmation, as any other historical claim. Admittedly, we are dealing always with conjectures and hypotheses; but that is true of any historical, indeed of any empirical, enquiry, and the objection is trivialised if 'proves' is taken in so strong a sense . as to exclude this. I do not believe, therefore, that my critical method is viciously subjective in principle; to be sure, particular applications may be open to objection for relying excessively on purely subjective impressions: that is a different question.

This approach commits me to the 'intentional', as well as to a variant of the 'affective', fallacy; and to some this will seem no less grave an objection. I shall explain why I think otherwise elsewhere; here I will merely point out that classical scholars who remain sceptical with respect to authorial intention are on treacherous ground. Will they abandon textual criticism, for

[37] *CR* 31 (1981) 158, reviewing Griffin 1980.

example? For we cannot decide what an author probably wrote until we have decided what he probably meant; and this will mean also: what effect he meant to achieve – which must include no less the *emotional* effects he meant to achieve.

1.2 Ancillary pleasures

I argued in 1.1 that Greek audiences valued tragedy primarily because of the pleasure afforded by the emotional stimulus that it was designed to, and did, provide. But clearly, the tragic emotions were not the only source of aesthetic reward for the audience, and we should now remind ourselves briefly of some subsidiary sources of value in tragedy. Aristotle himself, although somewhat strict about the kinds of enjoyment appropriate to tragedy (*Poet.*1453a35-6, 53b10-11, 62b13), recognises other legitimate sources of pleasure: the visual presentation, for example (*opsis*: 1450b16, 62a16; for Aristotle's reserved attitude to this aspect of tragedy, see 4.3), or the musical setting of its lyrics (*hê melopoiia megiston tôn hêdusmatôn* 1450b15, 62a16; cf. *Pol.* 1339b20, 40b16 and, for *hêdusma*, *Rhet.* 1406a18-19); indeed music and the rhythmical qualities of poetry are such important sources of pleasure in Aristotle's eyes that he felt obliged to build them into his very definition of tragedy: it is a *mimêsis* in 'language made pleasurable' (*hêdusmenôi logôi* 1449b25), which he glosses as 'language having rhythm and harmony or song' (*ton ekhonta rhuthmon kai harmonian kai melos* (1449b29). With this one may compare Isocrates: he congratulates the inventors of tragedy for enhancing the pleasures of *muthos* by adding to it a visual dimension (2.48-9), and he numbers among the ornamentations (*kosmoi*) available to poets, but not to writers in prose, a diction that is out of the ordinary (compare ch.22 of the *Poetics*), and metre and rhythm: these latter, he says, have such charm (*kharis*) that poets can please their audiences by these means alone, even if their poetry is deficient in what Aristotle would call *lexis* and *dianoia* (*an kai têi lexei kai tois enthumêmasin ekhêi kakôs, homôs autais tais eurhuthmiais kai tais summetriais psukhagôgousi tous akouontas* 9.8-11; cf. 4.46-7). The scholiasts, who are very much aware of the dramatist's need to hold the attention of the audience by stimulating their interest and enhancing and varying the reward which that attention yields, often comment on the value of poetic embellishment, of visual effect, of suspense and anticipation, and of a varied dramatic texture, to this end.[38]

[38] Securing attention and gratification: (a) *prosokhên ergazesthai*: S.*Aj*.9: cf. *Aj*.326, *El*.2, 22, *OT* 8; *Il*.7.479 BT, 15.610-4 BT; also *PV* 88. (b) *therapeuein ton theatên*: S.*Aj*.762; cf. *OC* 457, 712; E.*Tro*.209. (c) *kharizesthai tôi theatêi*: A.*Eu*.11; S.*Aj*.14, *El*.707, *OC* hyp.I, 92, 457; cf. also E.*Tro*.31 (*pros kharin*), S.*Aj*.202, 861, *El*.731 (*pros* or *eis eunoian*). (d) *terpein ton akroatên*: S.*OT* 928; cf. *Aj*.1221 (*euphrainein*). (e) *nearopoiêsein tous akouontas*: A.*PV* 631. Various kinds of ancillary pleasure: poetic embellishment, such as lyric (S.*Aj*.693); visual interest (S.*Aj*.14; cf. Demetrius *Eloc*.195); suspense and anticipation (S.*Aj*.9, 326, *El*.2, 22); varied dramatic texture (A.*PV* 631, *Eu*.94; S.*Aj*.295, 719, *El*.328, cf. 632; E.*Ph*. hyp. – *poluprosôpon* is used as a term of praise; in Homer, e.g., *Il*.21.34 BT: for further reference to *poikilia* – to which I shall return in 3.2 – see Richardson 1980: 266 & n.4); appeal to patriotic sentiment (see Chapter 2 n.49, and 2.33).

These aspects of tragedy I shall call 'ancillary pleasures'. By this, I do not mean to imply that they will always have been used directly or indirectly to enhance the primary emotive force of a passage. Often this is the case: for if an emotional stimulus is presented by means of a vehicle that is attractive and rewarding in other ways as well, then an audience is likely to be more attentive and more readily responsive than they might otherwise have been. But the devices by which the dramatist may thus seek to render his audience attentive and responsive have this effect just because they are interesting and pleasant in their own right, and it is often clear that they have been cultivated either primarily or even purely for the sake of their intrinsic aesthetic reward; they are therefore in some degree independent of the primary pleasure of tragedy. But it would not have been thought proper for these autonomous pleasures to become the chief interest and reward of a tragedy: this would have been untragic, since they are, in Aristotelian terms, pleasures derived from the means of tragic representation, not from its *telos* or true end; one should seek in tragedy, not just any pleasure, but its proper pleasure, the *oikeia hêdonê*. The tragedian may, indeed must, use these elements of the dramatic medium to attract and hold the attention of his audience, to enhance and diversify their pleasure; and so they may be allowed a degree of autonomy. But they remain in the last analysis less important to tragedy than the emotive pleasure that is central to Greek accounts of the genre; hence, and in this sense, they may be spoken of as 'ancillary' pleasures.

1.3 Tragic restraints

I have discussed the primary (1.1) and ancillary (1.2) pleasures of tragedy, and argued that the tragedian's task was thought to be the gratification of the audience by these means. But there is in our sources also a recognition that the pursuit of this gratification could lead the tragic poet into a compromise of his art. Aristotle, as we have observed, saw the risk of a deflection from the pursuit of tragic emotion in this light (*Poet.*1455a33-6, cf.1.11); but it is also recognised that some means of achieving the tragic emotions are illegitimate, or at least questionable. That is to say: the nature of tragedy imposes some restraints on the pursuit of its primary, and *a fortiori* of its ancillary, pleasures.

The most important of these restraints is that which I have called 'tragic dignity'; Aristophanes provides a convenient starting-point for a discussion of this concept. In the agon of *Frogs* Aeschylus is shown as priding himself on his portrayal of noble and heroic characters, and on his use of elevated language and splendid costume to match their semi-divine stature (1040-1, 1058-61). Euripides, on the other hand, fills his plays with ragged beggars and women no better than prostitutes (842, 846, 850, 1043-4); 'democratically' he allows to all his characters, even to women and slaves, the right of free speech (for the inferiority of women and slaves, cf. Ar. *Poet.*1454a19-22); he fills his plays with homely, commonplace things, *oikeia pragmata* (959: brilliantly taken up in the parody of Euripidean monody at

1331-64); if he does bring on noble figures, he demeans them by putting them in rags (1058-61: a stock joke, amusingly exploited at *Ach.*393ff.). The common theme of these criticisms is the elevation proper to tragedy and its absence in the work of Euripides; but this theme has two sides. In the case of the *oikeia pragmata* the implication is that the subjects are too trivial to sustain the emotional demands of a tragedy: it is absurd to get worked up about a stolen cock. But in the case of the rags, the point is quite the reverse; Euripides' motive in demeaning kings and heroes is precisely to accentuate the pathos of their position: *hin' eleinoi tois anthrôpois phainoint' einai* (1063-4: note the recurrence of *eleeinos* and *athlios* in the passage from *Ach.*, and see the scholion on *Ach.*384). Here we see with peculiar clarity a clash between the primary pleasure of tragedy, emotional stimulus, and the most important of the tragic restraints, dignity. We should add at once that Aristophanes does not conduct either the defence of Aeschylus or the attack on Euripides with a straight face and judicious honesty: the presentation of both sides is meant to be funny, and is therefore delightfully caricatured. The jokes are of course unfair to Euripides; but that Aristophanes thought that *these* were the jokes to make is enough to show something about the common perception of tragedy in fifth-century Athens: and that is what we are interested in.

Plato makes ironical use of this view of tragedy as an essentially serious and dignified form in his polemics against poetry. In *Gorgias* he speaks of *hê semnê hautê kai thaumastê, hê tês tragôidias poiêsis* ('that dignified and admirable poetic genre, tragedy': 502b1), only to deflate it with the conclusion that it is mere *kolakeia*, on a par with fancy cookery, since it aims only to gratify, not to edify. The same note of scepticism is found in *Laws*: having dismissed comedy (*hosa ... peri gelôta estin paignia*) he turns to the tragedians, the 'so-called serious poets' (*tôn de spoudaiôn, hôs phasi, tôn peri tragôidian poiêtôn* 817a1-3), and ushers them out of his city with mock respect. In the *Republic* he concludes that artistic imitation, of which 'tragedy' (he is subsuming epic) is the supreme example, is 'mere play, not really serious' (*paidian tina kai ou spoudên* 602b6-10), because of its ignorance of the transcendent objects of its imitation; and in 606ab the exaggerated emotionalism of tragic characters is found to be inconsistent with true moral seriousness: tragic dignity, in Plato's view, is a contradiction in terms.

Aristotle defines tragedy as the imitation of a serious action (*spoudaia praxis* 1449b24); the point is expressed elsewhere in a slightly different form: tragedy is the imitation of serious agents (*mimêsis spoudaiôn* 1448a27, 49b10; this links tragedy with epic in opposition to comedy, which shares with tragedy the medium but not the object of imitation: cf. 1448a11-18, 25-8, 48b34-49a2, 49a31-2, 49b9-12). 'Serious' agents are glossed as men 'better than we are' (48a1-5 etc.: in the context of epic and tragedy the phrase recalls Homer's heroes, superior to men 'as they are today'): men of high status and fortune (*tôn en megalêi doxêi ontôn kai eutukhiai* 52a10), endowed with the excellences which one would require of a man – men, precisely, to be taken seriously.[39]

[39] Lucas 1968: 63.

Aristotle's analysis passed into the critical tradition. His pupil Theophrastus defined tragedy is the reversal of *heroic* fortune (*hêrôikês tukhês peristasis*: Aeschines spoke of *hêrôika pathê* in this connection: 3.153); and the notion passes into the scholia, in which the dignity and elevation of tragedy are regularly contrasted with the vulgarity appropriate to comedy, and in which lapses are censured.[40] Not surprisingly, it is Euripides who comes in for most criticism; although his sensitivity to the audience is mentioned approvingly (for example, on *Tro.*1 or *Or.*128) the scholiasts disapprove when this leads him into artistic error: above all into the sacrifice of *semnotês*, of dignity (on S.*OT* 264), but also into implausibility and inconsistency of characterisation (*Med.*922),[41] and into irrelevance and the unnecessary dragging out of scenes (*Ph.*88: cf. the hypothesis to *Ph.*, on the *teikhoskopia*). Other dimensions of tragic restraint are brought into play here: and in subsequent chapters we will have to consider the principles of conviction (3.3) and coherence (2.4, 3.2); my purpose here, however, is simply to point out the existence of such restraints, and to introduce the most important of them, the principle of tragic dignity.

1.4 Review

The evidence surveyed in this chapter has provided a coherent and economical system of basic principles on which a general theory of Greek tragedy might be raised; let us review them.

(a) We have seen that throughout the tradition poetry is thought of in what are essentially *rhetorical* terms: the focus of interest is on the effects of poetry on its audience.[42]

(b) Poetry is also thought of *hedonistically*; its aim and value lie in the pleasure it gives to its audience.

(c) In the particular case of tragic poetry, we may speak of an *emotive* hedonism: the *primary pleasure* appropriate to tragedy is that which accompanies the excitation of an emotional response, characteristically in the range of horror, fear and pity, but more generally of those emotions which are ordinarily found distressing; the response is sufficiently intense to evoke physical symptoms – shuddering and weeping.

The main task of the tragedian, therefore, is to portray events to which a response of this kind is appropriate, and to do so in such a way that the emotive quality of those events is brought out and the response evoked in

[40] For example: (a) *to tês tragôidias axiôma*: S.*Aj.*74, cf. E.*Or.*1512. (b) the contrast between tragedy and comedy: S.*Aj.*1123, 1127; E.*Or.*1521; *Il.*2.478-9 ABT. (c) *semnotês*: S.*OT* 264; *Il.*2.478-9 ABT, cf. 6.474 BT, 24.162 T (*hêrôikê semnotês*).

[41] Euripides also provided Aristotle's example of inconsistent characterisation (1454a31-3), and his example of unnecessary depravity (54a28-9); this, too, is to be understood as a criticism of vulgar sensationalism detracting from tragic dignity.

[42] Cf. Russell 1967: 141-4, 1981: 2ff.

the most effective and satisfying way.

(d) However, the tragedian is expected to make the vehicle of this emotional stimulus interesting and attractive in other respects; to this end he has at his disposal *ancillary pleasures*: techniques and resources for attracting and holding the attention of the audience, and for diversifying its enjoyment.

(e) Finally, the nature of the tragic genre imposes certain *restraints* on the pursuit of the primary and ancillary pleasures; chief among them is the *dignity* of tragedy: as a serious and elevated form, tragedy should portray events involving characters of heroic status and quality, and the events and the characters involved in them must be portrayed in a way commensurate with their dignity.

In the following chapters, I plan to elaborate this outline of a theory; in the course of the discussion I will have occasion to explore somewhat further various aspects of the *Oresteia*, and I will naturally comment on other plays and passages from the corpus; *Ajax*, however, I will exclude from the discussion where possible, so that it is, as it were, virgin territory when I come to apply the elaborated theory in a more detailed illustrative study of that play in Chapter 5.

2. Meaning and Emotion

2.1 Introduction

According to Winnington-Ingram, *Persians* is perhaps the 'least great' of the extant plays of Aeschylus. It is not that he finds the play dramatically weak; on the contrary, he believes that 'in point of construction and dramatic craftsmanship, it is a finer piece of work than it is sometimes credited with being'. It is the play's *intellectual* poverty that Winnington-Ingram finds disappointing:[1]

> The interpretation of East-West relationships which it embodies is interesting, but does not seem to go much further than might be expected from an intelligent Greek of the time. Morally, it is a study in black and white, and so lacks subtlety. The theological doctrine is fundamentally the same as that of Aeschylus at his greatest, but it is not put to the severer tests – that is to say, it is not developed in a context which, like those of the *Oresteia* or the Danaid trilogy, raises well-nigh insoluble problems about the nature of Zeus and his justice.

These comments might seem surprising; why should we require of Aeschylus that he provide us, not only with the excellences of dramatic craftsmanship, but also with profound or original insight into international politics, ethics and theology? Winnington-Ingram begins the paper from which this passage is quoted with the claim that Aeschylus 'is a poet of ideas – of religious ideas'; and it is clear enough why, if one makes that assumption, these omissions will be found disappointing. But is this assumption itself not a surprising one, in the light of the account given in Chapter 1 of tragedy and its value to the poet and his audience of address?

As it happens, neither Winnington-Ingram's comments on the play nor the assumption on which they rest are such as to occasion widespread surprise. For it is the common practice of modern interpreters of tragedy to read the plays as vehicles of ideas: that is to say, the plays are commonly understood to embody some vision of the human condition or of the universal order, to explore or perhaps to commend opinions on issues in ethics and politics, in philosophy and religion. Buxton articulates the premise:[2]

> The tragedians were putting rival views of the world before an audience in the hope of being judged the best ... The aim of the dramatist was to persuade the spectators to accept his view ... of reality.

[1] Winnington-Ingram 1983: 1.
[2] Buxton 1982: 18.

The claim is rarely made so baldly, but the same premise can be seen working implicitly elsewhere. Knox, for example, in an influential study of Sophocles' *Ajax*, sees the play as examining the archaic moral code of helping friends and harming enemies:[3]

> The Sophoclean presentation of the old code in action makes the comparatively simple point that it is unworkable. The objective may be good, but in the world in which we live, it is unattainable. The old morality is exposed as a failure in practice.

When Knox writes 'comparatively simple' he means: by comparison with the points which Christ and Plato made; and this shows clearly enough what company Sophocles keeps in Knox's mind: he is a philosopher or moralist, who happens to work in a dramatic medium.

We shall see in Chapter 5 that Knox's reading of *Ajax* is in this respect quite wrong; at present we are concerned only with the *general* theory of tragedy underlying this and other such readings. And to the extent that the emotive theory of tragedy which I have urged would exclude such an intellectualising or moralising interest in the genre, it will seem to many substantially inadequate. But the two interests, the emotive and the intellectualising, are not in principle flatly irreconcilable: it may be that our concern with the ideas of tragedy too often becomes in practice a preoccupation overwhelming our awareness of tragedy as a vehicle of emotional stimulus; but it is certainly *possible* for a play to be the vehicle at once of ideas and of emotions – indeed, in some sense it must be so. Our task in this chapter, therefore, is to ask in what sense it must be, and in what sense it is, true that tragedy must, if we are adequately to grasp the tragedians' intentions, be read as a vehicle of ideas as well as of emotions.

2.2 The didactic theory

2.21 The tradition

The theory of tragedy that I adopted in Chapter 1 is essentially that of Aristotle concerning the *telos* of tragedy and its *oikeia hêdonê*; it is interesting, therefore, that Aristotle too has been criticised by modern interpreters of tragedy for his neglect of its intellectual dimension: consider, for example, these two passages:[4]

> Of tragedy as an interpretation of life he says but little. He nowhere refers to the great problems that give vitality to Greek tragedy, problems relating to man

[3] Knox 1979: 128.
[4] Atkins 1934: 117, Lucas 1968: 120. Cf. (e.g.) Schmid-Stählin 1934: 159: 'Dass die Tragödie des Aischylos und Sophokles im Kern eine religiöse Angelegenheit, dass ihre Aufführung den Hörern vor allen Dingen eine Erbauung war, darüber steht in der Poetik kein Wort ... Über Wesen und Wirkung der älteren attischen Tragödie, inbesondere der äschyleischen, sagt also der aristotelische Erörterung nichts aus.'

and his cosmic relations, to the works of Fate, human destiny and the like.

It is the statement that the things which happen are universals that arouses the attention of a modern reader. Surely the things which happen in tragedy raise all the great questions about pain and suffering and justice and the nature of the world in which the tragic event is allowed to happen ... It is remarkable that a work on tragedy should pass by such problems in silence.

It is at least possible that Aristotle passed by these problems in silence because the intellectual preoccupations which they imply were in fact foreign to tragedy as practised by and understood by his contemporaries; Plato would surely have agreed, and his belief that the tragic experience was inimical to the exercise of the rational faculties may look less tendentious when one recalls the intensity of that experience indicated in the sources we have surveyed. It could be objected, however, that my own survey was itself tendentious, passing over as it did in silence one important strand in the Greek tradition of thought about poetry. Our first task in this chapter, therefore, is to restore the balance by surveying the didactic theme in the contemporary and near-contemporary sources, and to assess its implications for the problem in hand.

The question of truth and falsehood in poetry emerged early in the Greek tradition. We saw in 1.11 that Hesiod's Muses already confess to mixing plausible falsehood with truth in the songs they sing and inspire (*Th.*26-8); the poet of the *Hymn to Dionysus* rejects as false variant accounts of the god's birth (*h.Hom.*1.1-7); and Solon, in an unknown context, made the point in a phrase that was to become proverbial: *polla pseudontai aoidoi* (fr.29 W). Pindar brings the question into close connection with poetic pleasure; as I suggested in my comments on Hesiod's lying Muses, it is the seductive embellishment of poetry which wins credence for the falsehoods it contains: *dedailmenoi pseudesi poikilois exapatônti muthoi*; it was the sweetness of Homer's words that inflated Odysseus' fame (*O.*1.28-32, *N.*7.20-3).[5]

Poetry was an important channel through which stories of gods and heroic ancestors were transmitted and disseminated in Greek society; in so far as these myths embodied the religious traditions and moral norms of the community, the poets could be seen as having a crucial formative influence on the beliefs and values of the Greeks at large.[6] So Xenophanes (DK 21B10), Heraclitus (DK 22B57) and Herodotus (2.53) can speak of Homer and Hesiod as teachers of Greece. But if people do learn from the poets, then the poets should tell them the truth; the element of persuasive falsehood that is mingled with the truth in poetry becomes an urgent moral problem, something either to condemn (as Xenophanes condemns the immorality of Homer's gods) or else to reconcile with truth and goodness by allegorisation (as Theagenes is reputed to have done, and as became common).[7] So far,

---

[5] Cf. Lanata 1963: 89-92.

[6] See (e.g.) Knox 1979: 3-24, Vickers 1973: 210-67.

[7] Xenophanes DK 21 B 11, 12; Heraclitus DK 22 B40, 42, 56, 57, 105, 106; see Pfeiffer 1968: 8-11, Russell 1981: 84-98.

then, we can see that the Greeks recognised that poetry has (so to speak) didactic effects, and believed that this confers on the poet a responsibility to ensure that those effects are proper ones by abstaining from the wicked, though entertaining, falsehoods by which they are apt to mislead and corrupt their audiences: a pessimistic wing accepts at face value the poets' apparent failure to meet that responsibility, and condemns them; the optimists assume that the poets must have intended to speak truly, and adjust their methods of interpretation accordingly.

Gorgias, so far as we can tell from the surviving fragments, took no part in this debate. He does indeed refer to the deception that tragedy works on its audience (DK 82B23); but he seems to be referring, not to its long-term educative effects, good or ill, but to the audience's temporary absorption in unreal events, as they are caught up in the pleasurable power of words. Such illusion, he says, is the aim of tragedy; therefore, the poet who manages to deceive his audience is honest (for he is doing his job, and not cheating the audience of their legitimate expectations of his craft), while the audience that allows itself to be taken in is clever (for it is responding appropriately, and not missing the delights that tragedy has to offer); Gorgias is evidently delighted with his paradox: it is usually dishonest to deceive and stupid to be taken in. Taplin offers a rather different interpretation of this fragment:[8]

> The member of the audience who succumbs to the spell of the play will through that experience be a better, wiser man than the member who resists and remains unmoved.

This restores a connection with long-term didactic or moral effect; but it ruins the paradox: in normal circumstances, being deceived would not naturally be regarded as a way of *becoming* less *sophos*, but as a sign that one *is* not *sophos*. Plutarch, in his citation of the fragment, confirms my reading: he explains that sensitivity is required if one is to be susceptible to the pleasures of words (*eualôton gar huph' hêdonês logôn to mê anaisthêton*: *Mor*.348c; cf. 15cd). The same ideas are taken up by the author of the *Dissoi Logoi*: does the legitimation of deceit in tragedy and in pictorial art tend to undermine the distinction in general between right and wrong? No: for questions of right and wrong do not arise in this context, the arts in question being concerned with pleasure, not with truth.[9] This, as we shall see, is a view which Aristotle endorsed.

The theme of the poet as teacher is, by contrast, most strongly emphasised in Aristophanes' *Frogs*. The poet, we are told, is to the adult as the schoolmaster is to the child (1053-6); and both the rival tragedians are made to agree that the criterion of the poet's value is the moral effect of his work on

---

[8] Taplin 1978: 167-9; cf. Halliwell 1986: 16.

[9] DK 90: see 3.10, 17. The treatise is dated *c*.400: cf. Guthrie 1969: 316-19, Lanata 1963: 224-5. Russell takes the last claim out of context when he writes that 'unless poets claimed truth, this particular sentence would not be worth uttering' (1981: 85-6): the author is not trying to establish the truth of this claim about poetry; he simply takes it for granted and unfolds its implications for a question in ethics. So the sentence would be the more worth uttering – the more persuasive as a premise – the less people would be inclined to dispute it.

the citizen-body: does it improve or corrupt them (1008-12: cf. 1031ff., 1419-21)?[10] Euripides might argue that he *has* improved the citizens by making them more intellectually acute (917ff.); but Aeschylus objects that, while he himself has inculcated martial virtues by the display of heroic exemplars, Euripides has put bad examples on stage, and so had a corrupting influence (1019ff., 1039-55). The 'teaching' which Aristophanes envisages seems to take two forms: models for imitation, such as we have just mentioned, and edifying maxims (1500ff., etc.). The first of these enables us to make a connection between the allegedly demoralising effects of Euripidean tragedy and the lapses from tragic dignity of which he was accused (1.3); by putting what is homely and familiar on stage, not only did he fall short of tragic elevation, but he provided the wrong kind of model for imitation: he should have given us heroic models, men 'better than ourselves', to whose excellence we could aspire.[11]

Plato provides further evidence for the widespread influence of this view of poetry. In *Lysis*, for example, Socrates is made to introduce a Homeric tag into the discussion of friendship (a tag which he will misinterpret and approve, before overturning it with some lines from Hesiod) with the explanation that the poets are teachers of wisdom (*houtoi gar hêmin hôsper pateres eisin kai hêgemones*: 213e-4a); in *Hipparchus* he attributes Peisistratus' sponsorship of Homeric recitations at the Panathenaea to a concern for the moral education of his people (228bc); in the *Republic* he refers slightingly to those who regard Homer as the teacher of Greece, providing a rounded education in all spheres of human life (606e). The attitude there criticised is attributed, in a more moderate form, to Protagoras in the dialogue named after him (325e-6a): when children study poetry, they are made to learn texts which contain both useful moral instruction (*nouthetêseis*) and narratives and encomia of outstanding men whom the children may be inspired to imitate (we see here again the maxims and models of Aristophanes). Evidently, Plato himself did not accept this view. First, he is dismissive of any idea that the poets have didactic intentions; as we have seen (1.11), he argues in *Gorgias* that poetry aims to give pleasure, and that it inevitably subordinates moral considerations to that end. But if he is sceptical of the educative intentions of poets, Plato does not deny that poetry has educative *effects*; this, in Plato's

[10] 686-7 should not be taken out of context: it is not denied that some forms of poetry required or permitted an overtly didactic stance: exhortatory elegy is the obvious example (e.g. Theognis 769-72, Solon fr.4.30 W), and the comic parabasis works with a similar convention (cf. Dover 1974: 29-30); that tells us nothing about tragedy. Taplin has recently pointed out (1983) the implication in *Ach.*500 that tragedy does have moral concerns; but since I am not intending to dismiss *Frogs* as anachronistic or unrepresentative (cf. 2.22), this point does not affect my argument materially. (I might also, with Taplin's note in mind, observe that in this chapter I am reacting, not against 'Victorian didacticism', but against *currently* influential tendencies in the interpretation of tragedy.)

[11] The contrast reminds us of the remark attributed to Sophocles, that he made characters as they ought to be made, while Euripides made them as people actually are: Ar.*Poet.*1460b33; for the interpretation, see Lanata 1963: 150-1.

view, is precisely the problem. First, the poets aim to give pleasure by stimulating emotion; this, in Plato's view, is necessarily inimical to moral health, since he believes that the emotional part of one's personality should be controlled. Moreover, poets (not being Platonists) are ignorant of the truth; therefore, they portray things (and it is above all the portrayal of virtue which worries Plato: *Rep*.600e) only in a shadowy and distorted way, as dim and misleading reflections of their transcendent originals. Consequently, the models which traditional education sought and found in poetry must be inadequate ones: hence the comprehensive censorship, in the earlier books of *Republic*, of stories in Homer and Hesiod that would tend to demoralise Plato's elite citizens, to erode their consciences and confuse their moral judgment (377b-392c: cf. *Laws*. 941c); we could also mention here the bitter passage about poets who praise tyranny or democracy, and so help to perpetuate those degenerate constitutions (*Rep*.568ad). Plato's conclusion is a radicalisation, one might say, of the view which Pindar expressed in passing; he argues that the more poetry succeeds in its own terms – the more attractive and pleasurable it is, holding our attention with its superficial charms while working on us insensibly at a deeper level – the more dangerous it is, and the more firmly it must be controlled (*Rep*.387b, 607a).

Aristotle is less disturbed by this complex of problems. He accepts that poetry has moral effects on the audience, and his theory of *katharsis* is presumably intended to show, in reply to Plato's attack on tragic emotivity, that the excitement of emotion can have beneficial consequences, actually helping us to keep our emotions in better order outside the theatre. (I take it that the process is a homeopathic restoration of emotional balance; but the details are of no consequence here.) But the idea of *katharsis* plays only a minor role in his theory of tragedy: *katharsis* is neither the aim of tragedy nor its positive justification (which resides in the *oikeia hêdonê*), but a by-product that helps to meet an objection to the genre. The primacy of *oikeia hêdonê* enables Aristotle to reject other moralistic criticisms in a way reminiscent of the *Dissoi Logoi*: moral error (that is, the portrayal of bad men, which might give us inappropriate examples to follow) and factual error are venial if they help the poet to achieve the *telos* of the poem more effectively: that is, if *ekplêxis* is enhanced (*Poet*.1460b20-23). One example of this usefulness in factual error would be the treatment of the gods; it will be more interesting and more convincing if the poet follows the falsehoods of popular myth than if he had adhered to the dry truth discovered by philosophy (cf. 60b35-61a1). And although Aristotle does lay some emphasis on the moral qualities appropriate to characters in tragedy, he does not (unlike Aristophanes) link his recommendations to any express concern for moral effects on the audience. His discussion centres rather on two points of tragic aesthetics: on the one hand, the seriousness and dignity of tragedy requires characters to be *spoudaioi*, a term which includes moral qualities as well as qualities of status and fortune (cf.1.3); on the other hand, the emotive aim of tragedy requires characters of such a moral character that pity will be an appropriate, and even a possible, response (52b30-3a17: cf. 2.5).

Chapter 9 of the *Poetics* might seem more promising.[12] Poetry, Aristotle observes parenthetically, is 'more philosophical and more serious' than history, because of its greater 'universality'. History is limited to portraying what actually happened on particular occasions; the poet must construct a plausible plot, and so is dealing with *hoia an genoito*, what *would* happen, probably or necessarily. Poetic narrative, therefore, has a greater universality and generality than historiography; its narrative accuracy is judged in terms of fidelity, not to a particular set of events, but to general truths about the ways in which things happen. By virtue of this generalising tendency, poetry is akin to philosophy; but that does not mean that it is philosophical in purpose or intent. To discover and exhibit general truths is the aim of the philosopher; the poet's aim is to construct a plausible (and therefore emotionally effective) plot, and he is concerned with generalisation only because it may help him to achieve that end: which is why, as we have seen, Aristotle subsequently argues that the poet can dispense with the truth altogether when falsehood is both plausible and conducive to *ekplêxis*. This is not to deny, of course, that in so far as poetry does deal in true generalisation it may be of use to the philosopher, and is worthy of his serious attention. We may recall here the way in which poetry is actually used in philosophical writing, by Aristotle himself, and even by Plato; both turn instinctively to the poets when in need of an illustration. This tendency is natural, and for precisely the reason that Aristotle gives. Neoptolemus' dilemma in *Philoctetes*, for example, is plausible: it is a specimen of a problem that does arise in life, it is the kind of thing that would happen; and it is uncluttered by the adventitious complications that tend to obscure such situations when they do occur in life; consequently, it is a readily intelligible and illuminating example of good *akrasia* (Ar. *EN* 1146a, 1151b). Aristotle's point, therefore, turns out to be uncontroversial, and does not throw much light on the didactic question.[13]

It is not only as a source of such illustrative situations that the philosophers turn to the poets. Plato and Aristotle frequently refer in passing to Homer and Hesiod when in need of some convenient and familiar formulation of a premise or conclusion; and the boundary between this use of the gnomic content of poetry and the use of it for informal substantiation of one's argument is thin: to clothe one's thought in a concise and familiar turn of phrase is inevitably to make it seem more intuitively acceptable. Even Plato is not above citing Homer in support of his argument, for example when he is condemning the demoralising effects of naval warfare (*Laws* 706de), as if the poet enjoyed some special authority. And, of course, in popular esteem the

---

[12] This passage should not be conflated (as Russell seems to do: 1981: 92) with Chapter 4 of the *Poetics*, where Aristotle is concerned with on that part of the pleasure of *mimêsis* that is afforded by recognition of the object imitated. (For a subtle defence of this conflation, see Halliwell 1986: 69-81; I remain unconvinced.)

[13] See Gulley 1971: but he is wrong to say that according to Aristotle the artist *aims* to regulate emotions (p.10): this is, as we have said, merely a beneficial side-effect; and he is wrong to imply that this effect is Aristotle's sole reason for valuing poetry (p.17): Aristotle also values the *oikeia hêdonê*.

poets, and above all Homer,[14] did enjoy such authority; this is presupposed by Plato's own polemics against poetry, and we can find further evidence in the orators. Isocrates, it is true, is willing when occasion demands to produce the standard denunciation of the poet's immoral lies about the gods (11.38-40), and once hints that Homer and the tragedians were, as Plato had argued in *Gorgias*, concerned only to give pleasure (2.48-9); but elsewhere he can assume that some at least of the older poets are reliable guides to the virtuous life (1.51-2; 2.3, 13, 43); he suggests that Homer showed the gods deliberating in order to warn us by an argument *a fortiori* of the limits of man's prescience (13.2); and he explains that Homer was given a place of honour in artistic festivals and in the education of youth so that repeated exposure to his works would inculcate a sense of the natural enmity between Greeks and foreigners and a desire to emulate the valour of the Homeric heroes (4.159). Lycurgus suggests that Euripides wrote *Erechtheus* to give the Athenians a model of patriotism (100: he wished to give the citizens a *paradeigma* by reference to which they would accustom themselves to love their native land); and he introduces a quotation from Homer by explaining that the poets, by imitating human life and selecting the noblest deeds, incite men to virtue more effectively than bare laws (102). Aeschines introduces a long exegesis of Homer by agreeing with his opponents that the poets are wise and useful (1.141-2); he represents Euripides (a poet second to none in wisdom, he claims) as trying to reform the practice of juries in some lines from *Phoenix* (1.151-3); he quotes Hesiod, claiming that the poet's aim was to educate and advise (*paideuôn ta plêthê kai sumbouleuôn tais polesi*: 3.134-5): as he says in the same place, people learn passages of poetry when they are children precisely so that they can make such use of them in later life (cf. Ar. *Frogs* 1054-6).[15]

We may note, finally, that the scholia sometimes attribute didactic intentions to the tragedians, and much more frequently to Homer; the attributions are often very naive.[16]

2.22 An assessment

My present concern, it should be emphasised, is with the interpretation of tragedy, and therefore with the *intentions* of tragedians; I do not yet wish to discuss either the *effects* of tragedy on its audience, or the possible *uses* to which tragedy could be put (its potential 'applications'), except in so far as these effects and uses are authorially intended (I will return to the questions

---

[14] See Verdenius 1970; his survey of the didactic tradition is useful, although I find his argument that Homer intended to instruct unpersuasive (compare, in more exaggerated form, Havelock 1963: 61ff.).

[15] Niceratus' father made him learn the Homeric poems by heart to make him an *anêr agathos*: but, objects Antisthenes, the rhapsodes know Homer and are fools (cf. Pl.*Ion*): Socrates explains ironically that this is because they are not familiar with the allegorical meanings (*huponoiai*): Xen. *Symp*.3.5-6 (cf. 4.6-8, 45; 8.1).

[16] See the scholia on A.*Eu*.95, Sc*T* 182-3, 224; S.*Aj*.118, 1036, 1093, 1318, *El*.23, *OT* 314, 946, *Ant*.75; on Homer, e.g. (all BT): 1.33, 194, 352, 416, 457, 523, 526, 566, 569, 611; 2.3, 10, 36, 53, 382, 596-600, 629, 774 etc ... etc ...; I find 1.611 and 11.89 particularly entertaining.

here excluded in 2.4). This limitation of my interest means that two strands of the didactic theme in the Greek tradition are not directly relevant to my present enquiry. First, it does not concern me that it was widely accepted that tragedy had important, long-term moral and intellectual effects on its audiences, for better or for worse; this may have been true, but its truth would not have depended on the tragedians' having written *in order* to have such an influence. Secondly, I am not concerned with the practice of using tragedy and other poetry as a quarry for edifying maxims or models; we know that this practice was fundamental to Greek education,[17] and the evidence surveyed in the last subsection shows that it continued to be important even for sophisticated adults (cf. Aeschines 3.135): but again, one can use poetry in this way whether or not it was intended to be so used.

If one believes that poetry does have moral and intellectual effects, then it is natural to believe also that poets have a responsibility to ensure that these effects are good: they must not, for example, corrupt their audiences by displaying gratuitous immorality, but should rather incite them to emulate paradigms of human virtue. Did the poets try to meet that responsibility? And did they write in order to be used as a source of edifying wisdom? If they did, then we are talking about a didactic *intention* in the making of tragedy, and that would be relevant to my present enquiry. But at this point, the tradition ceases to speak with anything like one voice. On the one hand, the line of thought represented by Gorgias and the *Dissoi Logoi* neglects the question of didactic intention, as does Aristotle; the poet, on this view, is not there to teach, but to arouse emotion and so give pleasure. Plato does not think that this *ought* to be so; but he has no doubt that it *is* so, and (as we have seen) he treats the notion of didactic intention as obviously false in *Gorgias*. The most vocal proponent of the didactic theory is Aristophanes: and that should give us pause, for Aristophanes is a comic poet, and his presentation cannot safely be taken at face value – it is astonishing how often his pronouncements on the moral purpose of tragedy are cited as impeccable evidence for the Greek understanding of the genre.

Nevertheless, however much Aristophanes may exaggerate and distort popular attitudes in his jokes, the jokes must have some root in those attitudes if they are to be at all intelligible or funny; and that there was a popular assumption that the poets ought to try and *did* try to edify and instruct is amply proved by the philosophers (in their more casual moments, and – in the case of Plato – in their polemics) and by the orators. Two considerations should give us pause, however. First, there is the fact that the assumption is contradicted, explicitly or implicitly, by the most sophisticated and reflective ancient analyses; and it is perhaps somewhat discredited by its applications, which are often astoundingly naive, and which often rest on very strained interpretations of the texts. Secondly, we should observe that the assumption is not applied in a theatrical context; that is, the didactic theory of the tragedians' intentions is not seriously invoked in descriptions of the experiences and responses of audiences in the theatre, as the emotive and

[17] Beck 1964: 117-22.

hedonist theory certainly is. But if the tragedians were writing for theatrical reception, then a theory of their intentions apparently divorced from theatrical experience is likely to prove misleading.

If, then, we were inclined on these grounds to discount the widespread assumption of didactic intention, how would we account for its being widespread? One possible line of argument is obvious. That the Greeks characteristically made a didactic *use* of poetry (of tragedy outside the theatre, or – to take a related example – of Homer outside the context of rhapsodic performance) is not in doubt; we have seen that poetry played a basic role in the education of school-children, and that it continued in adulthood to provide a way in which moral and other insights could be formulated, reflected on and transmitted. This suggests a simple confusion: in popular thought, although not in more sophisticated thinking, a familiar application has been uncritically referred back to the intentions of the author.[18] We could therefore explain the prominence of the didactic theme in Greek thinking about poetry without assuming that it accurately reflects either Greek experience in the theatre, or the intentions of Greek tragedians when writing for the theatre.

It might still be argued that a Greek tragedian of the fifth century would probably have shared in the common assumption that his work would have moral and educative effects on its audience, and would certainly have been aware of the didactic applications that the audience would be inclined to make outside the theatre; that he would therefore probably have recognised a responsibility to ensure that his work had a good effect and provided edifying material for didactic application; and that didactic intentions therefore cannot be excluded as rigorously as the foregoing argument implies. This seems to me correct; but three points should be noted. First, this was clearly far from being the tragedian's primary concern; he was writing for the theatre, where his overriding task – the one on which competitive success would depend – was to satisfy an audience that looked for emotional stimulus

[18] That the ancient sources do speak, rightly or wrongly, of poets' didactic intentions refutes Silk's claim (1974: 59-63, 223-4) that intentionalist interpretation was unusual in antiquity; note also that the scholia use interchangeably such phrases as 'The poet teaches ...' and 'The text teaches ...' – *didaskei ho poiêtês, didaskei ho logos*; and see Russell 1981: 96-7. I append some general considerations on Silk's anti-intentionalism. (i) Galen defines exegesis as the elucidation of difficulties in the text (Silk 1974: 61): but undoubted intentionalists (e.g. myself) habitually use such turns of phrase; one would have to show that Galen made a systematic distinction between authorial and textual meaning, and in the light of the evidence just mentioned one would be cautious in making that assumption about any classical author. (ii) Silk gives a very misleading picture of pre-Romantic interpretation when he suggests that intentionalism was a sporadic phenomenon; even a passing acquaintance with the history of seventeenth- and eighteenth-century hermeneutics would show that Hermann's view, so far from being a Romantic novelty (Silk 1974: 61), was rooted in an old and impressively consistent tradition. (iii) Silk is right to say that, e.g., alliteration can be present and aesthetically important irrespective of intention; it does not follow that the *meaning* of an alliteration is independent of intention. Silk fails to distinguish between interpretation, description and evaluation; my own approach, combining intentionalist interpretation with non-intentionalist criticism, is untroubled by his arguments. (iv) Silk's idea of intentionalism is in any case rather confused: e.g., p.60, where he fails to distinguish intention from articulate awareness or analysis of intention.

and aesthetic satisfaction. In this sense, Plato was right when he argued that the tragedian necessarily subordinated moral to hedonistic considerations: it is only that his somewhat eccentric moral outlook led him to infer from the priority of emotive interests that tragedy could have no moral concern or intent at all. That, on the present view, would be an exaggeration; but so would the view that assigned priority to didactic over hedonistic intentions. We might say, therefore, that it is not the presence of a didactic strand in the tradition that is misleading, but the prominence it is accorded in some parts of the tradition; and this can be explained away along the lines that I have suggested.

The second point to note is the ease with which the tragedian would have been able to meet his moral and didactic responsibilities. The use of poetry in education presupposes that it reflects the dominant values of the society; these values will therefore tend to be built into the conventions of the genres so used; and the texts of those genres will tend to embody, and so (as we said in 2.21) to transmit, to illustrate, and thereby to confirm and conserve, socially acceptable norms and shared wisdom. There are reasons why this tendency will be particularly acute in tragedy; as we saw in 1.3, one of the basic aesthetic principles of tragedy (that of tragic dignity) has a moral content, so that – quite independently of any specifically didactic purpose – there are pressures within the aesthetics of the genre which would impel tragedians towards writing in accordance with accepted and acceptable values. Consequently, the tragedian will not have to try at all hard to write in an edifying way; this will follow naturally from his writing within the generic conventions. Of course, Plato would not have agreed: but that is because his values were at odds with those of his society; eccentric positions like his or that of Xenophanes necessarily involved a rejection of the structures of the canonical genres themselves. But to accept and to work within the existing genres was to work within a system of conventions inherently edifying in tendency.

The third and final point to be made in connection with our qualified approval of the didactic theory is that it provides little or no support for the intellectual interests of modern tragic interpretation. As we have seen, when a Greek spoke of the poet as teacher he meant something that is, from a modern point of view, rather disappointing: that one could find in the poets moral exemplars, cautionary tales and formulations in gnomic utterance of moral, and indeed of technical, wisdom. One can indeed find such things, and we have conjectured that the tragedians wrote in some degree to that end; but such basic edification is a far cry from the intellectual depths which it is the habit of modern interpretation to sound. The idea that the tragedians wrote, in whole or in part, to explore or commend philosophical or religious opinions of any novelty or intellectual depth is not supported by this external evidence; whether the internal evidence compels us to believe that they did is another question, to which I turn in the subsequent sections.

2.3 Religion and politics

2.31 Introduction

It is sometimes argued that because tragedy was performed at a religious festival, it must have had some religious function or religious meaning; this would imply that the role of religious teacher was a natural or even a necessary one for the tragedian:[19]

> The religious function of the dramatist was implicit in the nature of the dramatic festivals themselves. If the vast majority of the words spoken on three days of a religious festival occurred in plays, then these words would have to carry religious significance.

The inference is mistaken. If a religious festival consists of, for example, athletic competitions, it does not follow that a boxing-match is inherently religious; it is the context as a whole – and *some* of its constituent activities, such as prayer and sacrifice – that carries religious significance in its own right; and the context confers on the other events, athletic, artistic or merely convivial, a derivative significance. They acquire their religious significance through being done in honour of the god, and this does not entail that they have in themselves cultic or theological content. It is the act of dedication, and not the thing dedicated, that is religiously significant.[20]

This is not, of course, to deny that tragedy does have theological content; we need only recall our discussion of the *Oresteia* (1.13) to see its importance: it would have been impossible to make sense of the action or to trace the poet's manipulation of his audience's emotions without a grasp of the theological premises of the plot at each stage. But to put it in this way makes it clear that the theological content derives, not from the requirements of a religious occasion, but from the nature of the material on which the tragic plots are based. The world of Greek heroic legend is a world in which the gods are everywhere at work; the narrative of events in which they are at work must of necessity have some theological structure, for if one is going to tell a story about gods, they must be gods of some particular kind, standing in a certain releation to the world and other characters, and so forth; if this is so, then certainly a grasp of the theological structure of the narrative will be essential for one's understanding the narrative simply as such.

How, then, would we go about identifying choices of theological structure in tragic narrative that have been influenced by a concern with theological reflection in its own right, by a desire to explore problems in religious thought or to commend answers to those problems? The assumption of such specifically intellectual interests will be superfluous: first, in so far as the poet conforms to the theological premises that are built into the genre and tradition within which he is working, and secondly, in so far as his treatment of the conventionalised religious premises can be explained by reference to

[19] McLeish 1980: 57.

[20] Tragedy, in the proverbial phrase, is 'nothing to do with Dionysus' (*ouden pros ton Dionuson*) – by contrast with satyric drama, to which critics are less prompt to attach theological significance.

the primary emotive *telos* of tragedy, or to some ancillary pleasure. As for Aeschylus, I find it hard to see him as a religious innovator. As Plato saw with alarm (*Rep.*380a, 381d, 383b), he purveys all the nasty old stories about the gods, and he does so for theatrical effect. So I would accept the conclusion reached by Lloyd-Jones in his study of Aeschylean theology:[21]

> That the moral background it provides has great importance, I am far from wishing to deny. What I do deny is that [Aeschylus' plays] contain an *advanced* morality ... This rude morality serves as an indispensable background to the action. But there is no reason for thinking that the dramatist's main purpose was to commend it to his audience. There was nothing new in it, and amongst most Athenians there will have been little disposition to deny it.

Therefore, I do not find the idea with which I began this chapter, that of Aeschylus as the poet of religious ideas, a very helpful one; there are religious ideas in his plays — it could not have been otherwise: but they are there for the sake of the play, and the play has its own, quite different *telos*. (This was our conclusion in 1.13.)

But if we are to say this about Aeschylus on the grounds of his conventionality, what are we to say about Euripides, in whose works the presence of unconventional modes of religious thought and expression is unmistakable? That this unconventionality is present is not merely a modern prejudice; the treatment he receives in contemporary comedy proves that he gave an appearance of unconventionality to his own contemporaries. To be sure, the normal cautions must apply here: we cannot safely take Aristophanes 'straight' (as many readers, ancient and modern, seem to have done), but must allow for a good deal of caricature and exaggeration. Since fourth-century orators could cite Euripides as a moral authority without fear of damaging their case (Lyc.100, Aesch.1.151-3: *ho oudenos hêtton sophos tôn poiêtôn*), we may safely assume that Euripides was not, in Greek eyes, so obviously subversive of all that is true and good as they were willing to pretend in the comic theatre. On the other hand, we must be able to give some account of the comedians' treatment of Euripides, of the connections, however tenuous, between their jokes and the perceived reality. The question is, then: can we account for the contemporary comic stereotype, and for the data of Euripides' own texts as they appear to us, in any way that does not require us to assume intellectualising intentions of the kind in question here? That is, can we account for these things solely by means of the apparatus erected in Chapter 1?

2.32 Euripides the traditionalist

If one took the Aristophanic caricature of Euripides without a precautionary pinch of salt, one would have to conclude that the tragedian was a determined sceptic bent in his plays on subverting traditional religious values

---

[21] Lloyd-Jones 1956: 67 (he assures me that he regrets the pejorative implications of 'rude'); also ibid. n.42: 'The "teaching" which the poets are said by the Aristophanic Aeschylus to

and assumptions, advancing in their place a somewhat confused assortment of ideas based on contemporary philosophical speculation; and something like this has indeed been widely held true. To be sure, the view that Euripides wrote, in part at least, as a commentator on and critic of traditional moral and religious beliefs has circulated in some wild and improbable forms, and still does: but this should not be held against it; a moderate statement is possible. It would be conceded that Euripides' plays on the whole presuppose internally the world-view of traditional mythology, and that his *dominant* concern in them was no doubt to exploit the emotive potential of that mythology. But it would then be pointed out, first, that the mythological world-view takes a relatively minor place in his work; in particular, he tends to secularise the stories, with the result that they are fundamentally intelligible without the mythological apparatus which he has taken over from the tradition. Indeed, it is sometimes clear that the overt mythological apparatus is to be understood as no more than a dramatic encoding of elements of a non-mythological view of the extradramatic world. Moreover, Euripides often puts into the mouths of his characters expressions of scepticism and moral protest by which he provides in his own person an implicit critique of the mythology with which he is working.

The first of these points need not imply any intention on Euripides' part to make a theological or philosophical comment on the primary world (it may be symptomatic of his beliefs: that is a different question); but the three points taken together do imply such an intention, and are therefore in apparent conflict with the general theory of tragedy advanced in Chapter 1. It would still, I think, be possible to accept the three points without doing fatal damage to my theory: for Euripides could plausibly be seen as exceptional in his critical tendency, and that tendency was evidently secondary even in his work (it was, after all, Euripides whom Aristotle thought 'most tragic' in point of emotional effect: *Poet.*1453a29-30); and I was at one stage sympathetic to some such view as this. Increasingly, however, I have found it hard to maintain even this moderate position; and I shall argue in this subsection that Euripides' plays will be better understood if we refer them to the established tradition of emotive dramaturgy that was Greek tragedy than if we appeal to the poet's supposed intellectualising intentions. Euripides' plays are indeed often striking and paradoxical in appearance: and it was this superficial unorthodoxy that gave rise to the Aristophanic caricature and its descendants; but I shall try to show that beneath a surface of rhetoric and sophistry Euripidean drama is far more traditionalist than is usually allowed. I shall also try to show how the preunderstanding which the popular image of Euripides encourages (and by which it has, since the time of Aristophanes, perpetuated itself) distorts our perception of the plays: this can be seen, I will maintain, in the way in which the *prima facie* implications of many passages are commonly discarded or inverted to fit the stereotype; from the way in which the dramatic and

provide ... was probably held to consist of "viva constantiae, fortitudinis, animi magnitudinis exempla" and not in the propagation of new religious or philosophical doctrine' (quoting Hermann); this is the conclusion that I reached in 2.22.

emotive intentions underlying various passages have often been obscured by the quest for polemical significance; and by the otherwise inexplicable tendency of interpreters to underestimate the integral role and importance of the traditional mythological apparatus in many of Euripides' plays.

I will begin by considering some examples of express or implied criticism of divine cruelty towards human characters; such criticism, implying at once a repudiation of the gods of traditional myth and a 'purified' ideal of the divine nature, might be thought obvious examples of Euripides' tendentious unconventionality. The first point that needs to be emphasised, however, is that it is not inconsistent with traditional attitudes towards the gods for men to protest at the way they have been treated. If a god acts against one's own interests or desires, it may be imprudent or unwise to register one's resentment, but for the Greek it is natural to do so, and admissible: in the *Iliad* Agamemnon complains that Zeus has deceived him (2.110-18; cf. 12.164-5); Menelaus that Zeus has cheated him of vengeance (3.365-8); Helen expresses her anger towards Aphrodite (3.399-412), Achilles towards Apollo (22.15-20); elsewhere, Theognis takes Zeus to task over the moral deficiencies of the order of things (373ff.; cf. *Od.*20.201-3); Aeschylus, to Plato's disgust, makes Thetis complain of Apollo's deceit and treachery (fr.350: cf. Pl.*Rep.*383b), while the Chorus of an unknown Aeschylean play complains of divine indifference to the fate of just men (fr.451h), and Cassandra protests in *Agamemnon* against her treatment by Apollo; in Sophocles, Tecmessa is bitter about the gods (*Aj.*950-4), and Hyllus complains of the divine cruelty displayed in the fate of Heracles (*Tr.*1264-74). On this last passage, Page comments:[22]

> If this were the work of Euripides, we should know what to make of it; in the context of the little we know about Sophocles, it has always been and still remains monstrous and incomprehensible.

This is not so: we have seen that it is entirely consistent with the mythological tradition for a mortal to lodge a complaint against the gods; and since that tradition did not consistently portray the gods as morally blameless, it is no surprise if a complaint of this kind takes the form of a moral rebuke. Hyllus' utterance is therefore natural on the lips of a character in his position; its bitterness and bewilderment aptly express the desolate sense of man's insecurity in the face of overwhelming and inscrutable powers with which Sophocles has chosen to provide the dominant tone of this coda. Sophocles himself has not corrected Hyllus' outlook, either because it did not offend his traditional piety, or because he did not think it his task as a tragedian to impair the emotional force of his work for the sake of theological precision; in either case, his use of these lines need not imply a tendentious or extradramatic intention on Sophocles' part. Nor, therefore, is it necessary to assume such an intention on the part of Euripides when he makes his characters speak in the same way (e.g., *Andr.*1161-5), although Page is surely

[22] *Gnomon* 32 (1960) 317.

right to observe that the assumption would readily have been made: my point about the dangerous influence of our preunderstanding of Euripides could not be more clearly illustrated.

When in *Bacchae* Cadmus complains to Dionysus of his excessive cruelty, the effect is more complex, for Euripides makes him articulate this complaint in terms of a 'progressive' theology: 'gods should not resemble mortals in their anger' (1348). From a traditional point of view, the truth of this claim is not at all clear: since, as we saw in 1.12, the Greeks saw vulnerability as an essential condition of pity, we would expect divine anger to be more terrible and uncompromising than human anger, precisely because it is exercised with impunity (cf. 5.1). However, it is not denied that Euripides is willing to make use of innovative patterns of thought; the question is: how and to what end does he make use of them? Here, the effect seems to be that of a foil; the counterfactual ideal emphasises by contrast the misery of man's actual state, at the mercy of harsh powers whose will cannot be turned aside or subjected to human postulates (1349-50). The effect of the foil is perhaps more clearly seen in the similar passage at *Hi*.120, where the servant appeals to Aphrodite by invoking an ideal of deity which, as the audience knows, the Aphrodite of this play conspicuously fails to satisfy. The very fact that the servant sees danger in Hippolytus' words shows that he knows the gods to be as the prologue has portrayed them, so that his resort to this enlightened ideal is futile and even (from Aphrodite's point of view) presumptuously unreasonable: she is, after all, only protecting her dignity and rights, her *timê*. But it is natural that the servant should, in these circumstances, feel that things would be better otherwise, and hope and pray that they will in fact prove to be otherwise. The lines are, therefore, in character; but they are also emotively apt. Hippolytus was introduced with a clear statement of what is to befall him (56-7), and this knowledge casts a tragic shadow over the following dialogue; his attitudes are, for the audience, painfully imprudent. It is right that Euripides should renew the note of sombre anticipation at the end of the scene, but the emotional effect would be rather flat if this were done by means of a bald prediction; the expression of a hope which the audience knows to be futile is more pregnant: it acts as a foil, and enhances the pathos. So Euripides' intention is not to juxtapose two theologies for polemical point, but to juxtapose two possible outcomes (one known to be illusory) for emotive point.

In his paper 'Euripides the Irrationalist' Dodds expresses himself rather oddly about Aphrodite's role in *Hippolytus*:[23]

> Mythologise the force which made the tragedy of Phaedra – turn Kypris into a person – and you get not a goddess but a petty fiend, whose motives are the meanest personal jealousies ... But from behind this transparent satire on the Olympians there emerges a deeper conception of Kypris and Artemis as eternal cosmic powers.

The oddity of this (to pass over the perhaps inappropriate assessment of

[23] Dodds 1973: 87.

divine jealousy, and the obscurity of the notion of a 'cosmic power') is that Dodds treats as an absurd hypothesis what has actually been done by Euripides, or (more precisely) by the tradition in which Euripides was working: in the play, Kypris *is* a person. It would be more accurate, therefore, to say: 'unless one *de*mythologises ...'; but this turn of phrase has the disadvantage of raising questions about the legitimacy, and indeed about the possibility, of the proposed demythologisation.[24] We are often told that Aphrodite is not to be understood as the fully mythological figure we see in the prologue, and that we are to read behind this symbol to the natural, even psychological, force which she represents; as Conacher has it:[25]

> The poet transforms a simple myth of divine vengeance (as it is represented in the prologue) by a goddess whose cult has been neglected into a tragedy explicable in terms of human psychology.

This view would perhaps be tenable, if it were a natural or psychological law that women of impeccable integrity fall in love with their stepsons whenever the latter are sexually abstemious; but if that absurd premise is not granted, then to direct attention in any degree away from the figure of Aphrodite as seen in the prologue is to render the play unintelligible. Unless there is a causal connection between Hippolytus' abstention from sexual intercourse and his fate, the whole action is turned into an odd, implausible and meaningless coincidence; and such a connection can only be provided by the machinations of the person we see in the prologue, an individual possessed of an intelligence which responds ruthlessly to slights on her personal honour. Aphrodite, therefore, precisely as we see her in the prologue, is absolutely necessary to the play as a whole;[26] and she is of a piece with the rest of the mythological apparatus of the play: with Poseidon, the curse, the bull, Artemis, none of which can be demythologised with even specious plausibility. The play is consistently and thoroughly entangled in myth, and demythologising interpretations cannot make proper sense of it.

Conacher does, in fact, recognise that Phaedra's passion can only be explained mythologically; this, with the episode of the bull, involves him in an unnecessarily complex account of the play in which the mythological element undergoes frequent changes of status. It is simpler and more plausible to admit that the play is, as I have said, consistently mythological. It is no argument against this that once Phaedra's passion has been excited the tragedy works itself out through the natural actions and reactions of the human characters; there is no reason why a goddess should not choose to

[24] Dodds takes it for granted that the mythological presentation is a 'transparent satire' because he believes that it gives an absurd picture of the gods; I do not find these gods absurd, even though I happen not to believe in their extradramatic existence: they are powerful dramatic fictions. If Dodds meant that Euripides could not have believed in such gods in the primary world, he may well be right; but that is irrelevant, unless we know already that Euripides was trying to express his extradramatic beliefs in his plays: which is part of the very point at issue.

[25] Conacher 1967: 27.

[26] Which is presumably why we are not allowed to forget her: 141ff., 236-7, 241, 359-61, 371-2, 401, 443ff., 522, 525ff., 725, 765ff.

exploit the normal behaviour of humans to work her revenge, *once* she has set up the abnormal situation in which this behaviour must result in disaster. Conacher also observes that Hippolytus' fault is not cultic, but is essentially the rejection of sex and marriage: therefore, he concludes, Aphrodite '*is* physical love, personified, not merely the goddess of it'; this dichotomy seems to me to be unintelligible in the context of Greek polytheism. The mythological view of Aphrodite is in fact the more comprehensive: since it embraces the goddess as object of cult, as personification, as natural force, it makes no sense to say 'merely' the goddess. And what I am stressing is that all these aspects are essential to an understanding of the play; one cannot understand the tragedy without retaining the personified goddess, in the strongest sense of 'personified'.[27] One may add that the alleged hints of a demythologised understanding of Aphrodite which some have found in the play do not stand up to scrutiny: 359-60 is a hyperbolic expression of the power of the goddess in a state of shock, while 443ff. occur in a thoroughly mythological context (451ff.): Dodds' citation of these lines in support of his own case is an astonishing lapse into an arbitrary 'proof-text' method of interpretation.

This discussion of *Hippolytus* tends to confirm my initial warning. The conclusion that Euripides is engaging in comment on or criticism of the traditional mythology depends on an inversion of the *prima facie* meaning of the text (the deities are dismissed as 'transparent satire', and we are urged to interpret away from them to natural and psychological 'forces') that is warranted solely by the expectation that Euripides would be critical of the material he is using; without that expectation, there is little opportunity and no reason to read the play in this way: rather, it can be seen as an unpolemical, uncritical exploitation of the traditional mythology for emotive purposes – that is, as a Greek tragedy consistent with the principles laid down in Chapter 1.

Another striking illustration of the power of the conventional view of Euripides to confirm its expectations in the face of *prima facie* discouraging evidence is to be found in discussions of *Ion*. To all appearances this play ends with a vindication of Apollo from the criticisms that have been directed against him in the course of the action; but since we know (of course) that Euripides was critical of the traditional mythology, it is assumed that these appearances are deceptive: if we look closely, we will be sure to find that the supposed vindication of the god is hollow, and the play will turn out to be a satire. The 'magic wand of irony' is an invaluable resource when one has to coerce a recalcitrant text into a preconceived mould, and interpreters of

---

[27] Conacher goes on: 'And her vengeance means the disaster which ensues when man ignores this force': yes – but only if one retains the fullest degree of personification, since (as I have argued) Hippolytus' fate cannot otherwise be explained as a causal consequence of his abstention from sex. Conacher dwells on the 'primitive' nature of the portrayal of Aphrodite (pp.28-9): it is scarcely more primitive than the gods of Aeschylus or Sophocles (e.g. *Ajax*); so this means only that Euripides is working with the traditional theology. In any case, the idea that such a portrayal would have the force of a *reductio* depends on the assumption that the play is to be read as an expression of extradramatic theological opinion: and this, as we have already observed (n.24), is question-begging.

Euripides make liberal use of it; but there are methodological problems: it is arbitrary to assume irony without compelling reason to relinquish the ostensible sense, and in the case of Euripides it is less the text than the preunderstanding which I am calling into question that has provided the supposedly compelling reason to make this move.[28]

Apollo has raped a woman: this is not unduly surprising, for that is how the gods do behave in the tradition; that he has done so leaves him open to Ion's rebuke (444ff.), but since we know very well what the gods are like there seems little point in making a great fuss about it. Nor, indeed, do the characters make a great fuss about it: the main thrust of their criticism of the god is rather that, having succumbed to natural passion, he has failed to do the decent thing by Creusa (355, 384, 437-9, 952); this is the main point of Creusa's most passionate complaint (881-922), uttered in the seeming nadir of abandonment, when the loss of her child is, in the light of Xuthus' apparent discovery of his, most galling. The audience knows this reproach to be false: the god has not abandoned her; consequently, the effect of her complaint on them is more to evoke a sense of gentle pathos and pity for the mortal than of outrage against the god. Once the reproach has been shown to the characters to have been made in ignorance of the facts, there is no further hint of disapproval: Ion is delighted to have a god for his father (1488: what has become of the principles of 444ff. now?), while Creusa is eager to defend his paternal care and for herself has nothing but praise for him. We may compare *Heracles*: for Amphitryon, the rape of Alcmene is a reproach against the gods in the depths of despair (344-5), but a source of pride elsewhere (1ff.); such utterances are not to be read as considered judgments *sub specie aeternitatis*, but as momentary responses to appearances, in which all the speaker's interests and sympathies are inextricably involved. In *Ion*, therefore, the rape is seen as a natural failing, about which a character might reasonably complain when the situation appears in one light, but which is soon forgotten about, and which is not in the end treated very seriously; the god's gratuitous cruelty would have been a more serious charge, but it turns out to have been illusory, since Apollo proves in the end to have made most satisfactory arrangements.

Apollo's route to these arrangements is, indeed, a circuitous one, and it might be argued that this results in unnecessary suffering; what right we have to argue this, however, when the characters involved come to quite different conclusions, is another question. Nothing is done to make us dwell on this point amidst the rejoicing at the end of the play; and arbitrarily to force the reflection onto the final scene is the last resort of a desperate preconception. Moreover, the complaint is on two grounds unreasonable: first, because it implies that the human principals should have been assured an untroubled life, whereas (as Creusa well knows: 969) it is the human lot to experience vicissitudes; and then, because (as Athene points out: 1615)

---

[28] Irony is often identifiable only in the light of external evidence (cf. Hirsch 1976: 23-5), so that the methodological problem is inescapable. My contention here is simply that the preunderstanding in question is unreliable; I do not object to its being a preunderstanding. The phrase 'the magic wand of irony' is lifted from Fraenkel 1950: 719.

divine plans characteristically come to fruition at length – a traditional motif.[29] These are familiar ideas; their familiarity should tend to discourage the kind of questioning that has led modern critics to feel dissatisfied with Apollo's handling of the problem. The circuitous route which he takes to the final settlement does, it is true, involve in addition the apparent oddity of an oracular god's plans going astray. There is, however, no mystery about why Euripides has made this happen: it is necessary if the plot is to be developed in an exciting and emotive way; need it also have satirical point? Zeus himself was deceived in the *Iliad*; in the *Odyssey* we find Menelaus using a trick to gain benefit from a god's omniscience – a paradoxical situation on reflection, but since the reflection is not one we are invited to entertain the paradox is unobtrusive and insignificant: similarly, I submit, in *Ion*. Once again, therefore, it proves to be only the conventional image of Euripides that makes us ferret out difficulties from an ostensibly traditional and unproblematic text; Euripides has not tried to bring the difficulties to our attention.

It should not need to be said that I am no more inclined to see in this vindication of Apollo a declaration of religious opinion than I am in the utterance of criticism without vindication in *Hippolytus*.[30] Sometimes Euripides wanted to achieve the emotional effect which comes from a resolution of conflicts and a happy ending (as Aeschylus did in the *Oresteia*); sometimes he wished to achieve a more uncompromisingly tragic effect without resolution. In both cases he writes as a Greek tragedian, and is interested primarily in the emotional effect of his play.

I argued in my discussion of *Hippolytus* that the importance of the mythological element had been seriously misjudged by some interpreters; but that is not the only play of which this is true. Consider, for example, this remark by Webster:[31]

> The *Electra* and the *Phoenissae* allow us to formulate crudely what Euripides did in his later period. He stripped away the Aeschylean divine machinery, and rethought the story as a situation in which ordinary people are involved.

I shall return to *Electra* shortly; of *Phoenissae* this claim is demonstrably untrue. In 17-20 we are introduced to the oracle given to Laius; in 66-8 to Oedipus' curse: the brief narrative that follows outlines a familiar irony, in which the very actions taken by those under a curse (*ordinary* people?) to avert its fulfilment precipitate their destruction (cf. 473-80). By means of the truce Euripides engineers a confrontation between the two brothers; this results in a powerful and emotive scene, in which the intense bitterness of their mutual hatred and the eagerness with which they set out to destroy each other is chilling: it is also quite clearly meant to be understood as the outworking of

---

[29] Cf. Dodds 1960: 188 (on *Ba*.882-7).

[30] With the vindication, cf. *IT* 711-23 and its sequel. Note also how the complaint in *Ion* 1312ff. is met with vindication: the 'bad' law is in fact restraining the complainant from unwitting matricide.

[31] Webster 1967: 13.

the curse (note 624: cf.765). Teiresias' speech at 867ff. goes over the same mythological ground (Laius' error and the curse of Oedipus), while at 931ff. he adds another layer of mythological causation (Cadmus' slaying of the dragon: which ties in with the stasima at 637ff. and 784ff., and with 1018-66). See further: 1306, 1424-5, 1503ff., 1556, 1593-4, 1595ff., 1611, 1726. The play is in fact saturated with allusions to the mythological causation of the events it narrates; it is hard to see how Euripides could have given the traditional mythology a more essential or emphatic role.

That is less obviously the case in *Medea*, but it is nevertheless true that the play works in an unobtrusively traditional way. Most obvious is the intervention of Helios to protect his grand-daughter (the moral indifference which this action displays should occasion no surprise: compare Poseidon and the Cyclops in *Odyssey*, for example). But we should not neglect either the recurrent references to Zeus, Themis and Dike, and to Jason's violation of his oath: cf. 21-3, 148, 158, 160-3, 168-70, 207-8, 410-13, 439f., 492-5, 764, 1352-3, 1392; see further 1231 (the Chorus attributes events to a *daimôn*: cf. 129-30), 1259-60 (an Erinys in the house),[32] 1333-5 (Jason sees the action of an *alastôr*), 1389-90; there is also a cult-aetiology in 1378ff. In fact, the play follows a familiar pattern: Medea's personal vengeance is also at once the action of Zeus *horkios* (although this does not mean that she herself is guiltless: compare Clytaemnestra); and she is protected at the end by a partisan god. The 'divine machinery' is less unobtrusive than is often made out; and, however unobtrusive, it is there, and the pattern of the plot cannot be understood without reference to it: so it should not be ignored. It is interesting, in any case, that Euripides' plots should fall so neatly into the patterns of traditional mythology even when he is not trying to bring this aspect into the fullest prominence.[33]

Another play in which the mythological component is often unjustly neglected is *Orestes*. Euripides carefully sets the action against the background of a family under curse (4ff., 807ff., 960-1012, 1547ff.); and the Furies are of great importance: 34ff., 238, 255-6 (with its immediate sequel), 316ff. (a powerful passage in dochmiacs), 408-10, 530ff., 836, 1646ff. The Furies do not appear to anyone but Orestes; but that is true also of Aeschylus' *Choephori*, and is no reason for denying their objective reality;[34] everyone in the play accepts without question that the psychological disturbance of Orestes is evidence of real demonic action. (259 might be thought to deny this, but Electra is simply trying to calm and restrain Orestes in his frenzy; nor can 396 be taken as an implicit demythologisation: it is uttered by Orestes who certainly, and in this very context, accepts their objective reality.)

[32] Not Medea: see Knox 1979: 320 n.54.

[33] Knox 1979: 301-2; he points out that the final lines are entirely appropriate in the light of this (against Page 1938: 181, Lesky 1972: 309 etc.); Lloyd-Jones 1971: 152. Grube (1941: 48) points to the role of Love (cf. 526-31, 627-41, 835-45); but this is much less prominent, and to claim that 'the drama is essentially of the same kind as *Hippolytus*, and a vindictive Aphrodite could easily have been introduced' is wild.

[34] Cf. also *IT*, where the Furies are invisible, but their pursuit of Orestes and the need for him to be freed from their persecution are entirely real, and are indeed indispensable presuppositions of the plot.

But what of the moral attitude to the matricide which is implied in the play? In the opening scenes Orestes, Electra and the Chorus are full of loathing for the act, and they condemn Apollo's command: cf. 28, 162ff., 191-4 (cf.819), 285ff. Menelaus is also shocked: 417. But this must, as always, be seen in the light of the emotional effect which Euripides was trying to achieve. He wants to present an appalling picture of abject misery and suffering; so he offers us an Orestes who is visually shocking (cf.385ff.), who is driven to frenzy by Furies (the action at this point is a striking stage-effect), and who is tormented by horror at what he has done. This horror is not to be read as a definitive, reflective judgment; it is an immediate, instinctive recoil from an act which, whether or not it was on balance justified, is loathsome. Subsequently, when Orestes has to defend himself against attack, his instinctive reaction gives way to a more balanced appraisal, one which takes account of all aspects of the case. So in 544ff., Orestes agrees that he is polluted *qua* matricide, but points out that he is by the same token pure *qua* avenger of his father; of these, the duty to the father is the more weighty, since the father is the more important parent, and also since his mother was an adultress and murderer; in addition, had he not acted, he would have been pursued by his father's Erinyes. All this is, of course, pure Aeschylus; the arguments were sound in *Eumenides* (1.13), and they are sound here. Nothing is said to detract from the horror of matricide (cf.807-43); but it is, in the final assessment, the act that was least bad; it was a wrong that was morally necessary.

We should observe that the audience does not approach the debate in which Orestes defends himself in a state of emotional neutrality. From the very beginning, Orestes and Electra have been the focus of our sympathetic attention; we are hardly permitted enthusiasm for their opponents. Indeed, Euripides reinforces this alignment by means of the contrast between Orestes' very proper respect, his *aidôs* before Tyndareus, and the latter's harsh and threatening manner: before the debate (485, 489; note 490), during it (536),[35] and after (607ff., 622ff.). It is clear, then, on which side of this argument the emotional scales are loaded; and we may observe that this trend of sympathy is sustained by Menelaus' desertion (we are surely meant to detect the hollowness of 692ff.);[36] Euripides has been careful to pin all their hopes on Menelaus' protection (52ff., 67ff., 241ff.), so that the failure of their appeal does indeed seem a devastating loss and a most cruel betrayal.

In the light of this manipulation of the audience's sympathies and prejudices, it would be foolish to place much weight on the arguments which Tyndareus uses against Orestes. In particular, one must agree with Grube, Steidle and Vickers[37] that the objection to Orestes' failure to proceed through

---

[35] This line must be retained, whatever else one does about the textual problem: cf. 564; see di Benedetto 1969 ad loc.

[36] Tyndareus' entry interrupted the climax of Orestes' appeal to Menelaus, and the warnings at 535 and 622ff. have also made clear what is at stake: the hesitation at 632-5 should alert us. Note also the significant juxtaposition of Menelaus' hollow offer of help with Pylades' conspicuous loyalty.

[37] Grube 1941: 384, Steidle 1968: 104-5 (the whole chapter is most useful), Vickers 1973: 579.

the courts is to be passed over as merely specious; it would not be the only occasion in tragedy on which an antipathetic character makes a specious appeal to legality. Moreover, in addition to the advantage of sympathy, Euripides has given Orestes the advantageous position in the debate; he speaks second, so that his reply has the dramatic force of a refutation.[38] For it is, of course, *dramatic* force that is the point here, and not logical force; interpretations which attempt to evaluate the opposing arguments judiciously, without fear or favour and from a timelessly synoptic point of vantage, fatally neglect the dynamics of the drama, its emotivity and sequentiality. In this connection, one must also add a warning against the common tendency to read into the earlier scenes impressions derived from the latter part of the play, in which the plot against Menelaus is being set in motion; the *initial* portrayal of Orestes and Electra, at any rate, is not that of a pair of abandoned desperadoes, but rather of pitiable sufferers compelled (this is the force of the recurrent emphasis on the divine command) to commit a crime from which, quite rightly, they recoil in horror. Whether the adverse reaction to Orestes and his sister is entirely appropriate even in the later scenes is another question; revenge, after all, is a perfectly respectable motive in Greek tragedy (see, for example, *Her.*732-3), as in Greek ethics in general: we should not import alien standards of judgment.[39]

In *Orestes*, the implicit moral judgment on the matricide is not strikingly novel; as before in the tradition, there is a recognition both of the utterly horrific character of the act, and of the factors which made it on balance morally necessary in this instance. It is not the dual attitude that is new, but the distribution of emphasis; Euripides wants to dwell more on the aspect of horror. But this is for evident dramatic and emotive reasons, and there is no need to assume that he is making an extradramatic point, or that he is registering a moral protest against earlier treatments of the story. The picture is very much the same in *Electra*. Before the matricide, Orestes recoils from what he is about to do (967ff.); but as in *Orestes*, what he says about Apollo's command in a state of shock should not be read as if it were a calm and definitive judgment: it is hyperbole, natural to the character and his situation. After the murder (1177-1232) Orestes and Electra dwell on the same theme in a state, once again, of shock, and are full of loathing at what they have done. This is, again, natural, since (as one must insist over and again) the horror of matricide is not in any way diminished by the judgment that it was, in the last analysis, justified; it is still the violation of a deeply-rooted prohibition, and so still has its peculiarly loathsome, repulsive quality. In this, then, there is nothing inconsistent with the tradition. As in *Orestes*, Euripides is seeking the emotional effect of shock at matricide, and to

[38] Dale 1954: 106 (on *Alc.* 697), Page 1938: 106 (on *Med.*465ff.).

[39] E.g. Ar.*EN* 1132b33-33a2, *Rhet.*1378b1-10; cf. Dover 1974: 181-4. Steidle comments: 'Zusammenfassend darf man feststellen, dass die Geschwister und Pylades ähnlich wie Medea, Hekabe oder die Kreusa des Ion sich in einer verzweifelten, ausweglosen Lage befinden, die den von ihnen geplanten Greueltaten für griechische Vorstellung ohne Frage eine gewisse Berechtigung verleiht, sie der Sympathie des Zuschauers jedenfalls nicht völlig verlustig lässt' (1968: 108-9).

that end he dwells on the aspect of horror; but this should not be thought to overturn the traditional judgment.

If one is predisposed to find religious criticism in Euripides, the appearance of the Dioscuri will seem to refute this assessment; the reality is not so simple. They say, first, that Clytaemnestra suffered punishment justly; it has in fact been made clear throughout the play that Dike is at work (cf. 771, 891-2, 953-6, 957-8, 1169-71, 1189): and we should not overlook the reminder here that Zeus and Fate are at work (1248-9, 1301).[40] On the other hand, Orestes' act was not just (since it was matricide), and so Apollo's oracle commanding him to do the deed was unwise. Like the similarly worded criticisms of Apollo in *Orestes*, these remarks need be no more than articulations of the natural shock and disgust evoked by the matricide. The Dioscuri also reflect that Apollo is their master, and temper their criticism; they yield, though not happily or with understanding, to the inscrutable will of higher powers (cf. Orestes at 986-7, and at *Or*.418). When Euripides makes minor deities (deities, moreover, related to the dead woman) acquiesce, in shocked incomprehension, in the will of the powers that uphold justice, and of their interpreter Apollo, it does not mean that he is thereby expressing his own condemnation of the myth; rather, he is carefully avoiding anything that might impair either his emphasis on the horror of matricide, or the emotional effect for which he has adopted that emphasis. To protect that, he *must* leave the justification for the murder unstated here, and he *must* leave the will of Zeus inscrutable; and he *may* do this, because his task as a tragedian is not to present moral assessments of stories, but to exploit their emotive potential.[41]

In *Heracles* the mortal characters suffer severely from the actions of the gods, and protest against their sufferings with bitterness; and the gods themselves do indeed act in a way which, though entirely in keeping with the tradition, would not be to the taste of an 'enlightened' theology. I have already had occasion to criticise the assumption that a dramatist who presents an unpleasant story about the gods, even if he includes within it explicit protests, and even if he is Euripides, must be moved by extradramatic *tendenz*; and it is clear enough here how Amphitryon's, and in more extreme form later Heracles', bitter protests against and challenges to the divine order intensify the desolate pathos of the situation. But what are

[40] This casts doubt on the judgment cited above from Webster in connection with *Ph*.

[41] It would take me too far from my theme to demolish the neurotic, morally insensitive Orestes and Electra found in the play by some interpreters: this is a fantasy based largely on psychological speculation, moral hypercriticism and a certain naïveté – Aegisthus is such a nice man at the sacrifice that all those nasty things they've been saying about him must be wrong. It must at least be emphasised that Clytaemnestra's expressions of regret are of little moral consequence: they cannot wipe out her guilt, and they certainly do not add anything to the horror of her murder – to suppose that they do is utterly to miss the horror of matricide simply as such; if, however, she were represented as utterly repugnant (if, for example, she were brought on talking as Aeschylus' Clytaemnestra does immediately after the killing of Agamemnon) this would tend to impair the effect: it would create complicating currents of feeling here unwanted. (There is, again, much to praise in Steidle's chapter on this play: 1968: 63-91; I concur with his view of the attribution of 1292-1307, pp.85ff.)

we to say when, in the course of these dramatically quite acceptable protests, Heracles is made to deny the truth of this kind of story and of the theology which it implies: and so also, it would appear, of the premises on which the plot of this very play is based?[42] Stinton argues, with a good deal of hesitancy, that the passage should be read as an expression of disapproval rather than of disbelief; in the other Euripidean passages which he cites, I find his careful exegeses convincing; but in this case one must conclude that the explanation does not fit. What Heracles says is, to be sure, rooted in disapproval: he is saying, under great emotional stress, that things cannot be so bad; but the denial is, nevertheless, explicit and emphatic.[43]

It will be said, therefore, that this passage, denying as it does the play's own premises, has a striking and paradoxical effect; it draws attention to the criticism of myth in an unmistakable and significant way. Perhaps so: but how striking is, or to the intended audience would be, the conflict with the play's premises? In context, the lines function intelligibly as a reply to 1314ff.; is it certain that we are meant to trace its implications further? I suggest that we should not: that the limited context of relevance is a conventional feature of tragic rhetoric; if so, then we should understand the lines as *locally* significant, and not worry about the possible polemical significance of a conflict that was not meant to be, and would not have been, remarked in theatrical reception. This is a point to which I shall return in 4.22; here I shall only emphasise that if we do not accept this limitation of relevance, we will be compelled to accept that Euripides was willing to destroy the effect of a scene of the highest tension and pathos by taking over a character in order to remind the audience – quite irrelevantly – that the story he has chosen to dramatise is in reality not credible. Whatever view one is inclined to take of Euripides' religious outlook and interests, this picture is surely difficult to swallow; certainly, it would do Euripides' dramaturgical skills little credit.

In the title of this subsection, I have called Euripides a 'traditionalist'. By this, of course, I do not mean to deny that he was an innovative and experimental dramatist who challenged and transformed the genre in which he worked; anyone turning from the work of Aeschylus or the work of Sophocles to a play of Euripides will be conscious of a distinctive style, tone and tragic manner. Euripides was a major artist, and naturally explored new

---

[42] I cannot accept Grube's argument (1941:58) that because only illicit unions between gods are denied, the premises of the play – involving an illicit union of god and mortal – are left untouched: 1345-6 go further than that.

[43] Cf. Brown 1978 (replying to Stinton 1976a: 82-4). Brown's paper is not without its own problems from my point of view. He accepts the 'detachment' of the gods in *Hi.*; he accepts that this passage is an expression of Euripides' own view, and suggests that he inserted it for fear that the audience would infer by paralogism that he endorsed the truth of the story he was telling (p.27: why on earth should they?); and he writes: 'If, finally, we ask why Euripides should have chosen to dramatise such morally difficult stories, a partial answer will be that they at least allowed him to present his own vision of the uncertainties and futilities of human life'; in fact, as Plato well knew, tragedy would be impossible without such stories; Euripides took them over from the tradition because they allowed him to write tragedies; and he was scarcely unusual in this: consider, for example, *Trachiniae*, *Antigone* and the prior *Oedipus*.

possibilities and new techniques in the practice of his art. It was, however, the same art as had been practised by Aeschylus before him, and was being practised by his contemporary Sophocles; his explorations sought out fresh ways of doing the same kind of thing: that is to say, they were new ways of exploiting the emotive potential of the same mythological tradition through the same dramatic form. So I have been arguing that it is often demonstrably mistaken, and never compelling, to interpret Euripides on the assumption that his writing was determined by 'intellectualising' purposes – by the intention to explore or commend religious or philosophical ideas for their own sakes; on the contrary, his treatment of the tradition can be accounted for purely in terms of the emotive intentions that were traditionally definitive of tragedy as a genre. This is true even when, as in the passages we have considered from *Bacchae* and *Heracles*, his innovations include the use of patterns of thought that are to some degree in conflict with the traditional mythology with which he is working: there are no sufficient grounds for concluding that Euripides designed these conflicts in order to subject the tradition to criticism; that he meant the audience to observe that there was a conflict; or that he was concerned with anything other than the enhancement of emotional effect.

The difference in tone and technique between Euripidean tragedy and the work of his colleagues is, as I have said, unmistakable, but it is not easy to give a satisfactory account of his distinctive characteristics; and until we have grasped accurately what he was really at, an accurate account must be impossible. Once we have cleared away the critical or polemical Euripides, at odds with the tradition and busy proclaiming his sophistic beliefs (or his rationalism, or irrationalism, or whatever it may be), and have begun to see him as a craftsman working within a particular tradition of emotive dramaturgy, then we can begin to enquire fruitfully into the nature of his craftsmanship: in what ways were the emotional effects at which he aimed, and the techniques by which he achieved them, innovative, distinctive? For example: we observed in our discussion of *Electra* and *Orestes* that he had shifted the traditional emphasis on the two aspects of the matricide in order to achieve an emotional effect rather different from that sought by Aeschylus: was it simply that he needed to find a fresh way of using this well-trodden material? Or was his innovation in some way characteristically Euripidean? Some features of these two plays do seem characteristic: for example, the highly rhetorical treatment (the encounters between Electra and Clytaemnestra, between Orestes and Tyndareus), and the introduction of elements unheroic in tone and 'realistically' treated (Electra's relegation to a peasant's hut, the madness of Orestes). Such characteristics would be worth pursuing: they are the truth behind the Aristophanic caricature of Euripides as a garrulous purveyor of ragged cripples who had degraded the tragic art.

It is not part of my present project to explore the particular characteristics of Euripides: but there is one aspect which it will be relevant to consider. Euripides is evidently caught up in the sophistic movement: so, indeed, is Sophocles, but less obtrusively so;[44] Euripides advertises his involvement, and

[44] Long 1968: 7-9, 166-7, Finley 1967: 77-88.

his use of sophistic material often seems contrived to force its paradoxical novelty on our attention. Take, for example, Euripides' lines on life and death:

τίς δ' οἶδεν εἰ τὸ ζῆν μέν ἐστι κατθανεῖν,
τὸ κατθανεῖν δὲ ζῆν κάτω νομίζεται;

Who knows if life might not be death,
and death below be considered life?   (fr.638)

This paradox achieved some notoriety among Euripides' contemporaries (Ar.*Frogs* 1082, 1478); but similar lines are found with a slightly fuller context in fr.833, and the parallel shows the point to be, in effect: 'Although we know very little about being dead, we know that the dead have escaped the misfortunes of life, and are in that respect to be envied': and this is an entirely traditional motif.[45] Euripides' character, then, is making a simple and traditional point; but the poet has sought out an arresting and paradoxical way of expressing it. Something similar occurs in Hecuba's prayer at *Tro*.884-9: the *form* of this prayer, even of the 'agnostic' formula of 885, is entirely conventional; but Euripides has given it a modern content, drawing on terms of contemporary philosophical speculation.[46] The effect is again arresting and paradoxical, as Euripides rather self-consciously points out. A taste for paradox and ingenuity is characteristic of the sophistic movement: one thinks most readily of Gorgias; and it is because he and at least part of his audience of address shared this taste that Euripides cultivated the novel and surprising in this way.[47] He exploits sophistic ideas to achieve these effects; this means that he must have been familiar with and interested in them, and that he may have accepted some of them; it does not mean, however, that his purpose in using them was philosophical or educative. His aim was rather stylistic; Euripides pursued paradox as an ancillary pleasure: a point which indeed qualifies my claim that his purposes were purely emotive, but in a way that is harmless, since it is anticipated and accounted for by the theory of tragedy outlined in Chapter 1.

The cultivation of this novel exterior was another factor that gave rise to the comic stereotype: when Aristophanes makes jokes about Euripides' devotion to peculiar gods (cf. *Frogs* 888-94), they are based on just such passages as Hecuba's prayer in *Trojan Women*. This kind of joke is made easier to devise, of course, by the Greek habit in the moral and didactic application of poetry of taking lines out of context and arbitrarily attributing their content to a didactic intention of the author. It is particularly important to bear this in mind when we read that Euripides persuaded people to disbelieve in the gods (*Th*.450-1).[48] This is worthless as evidence for

[45] A.fr.266.1-3, 255, 353; S.*OC* 955; in E., cf. fr.176, 816.6-11, *Alc*.937-8. Cf.4.44 below.

[46] Cf. Fraenkel 1950: 99-100 (on *Ag*.160).

[47] This is true also of the criticisms of Aeschylus which he makes in some plays: see the recognition-scene in *El.*, *Su*.846ff., *Ph*.751ff. Cf. Bond 1974; further, e.g., Winnington-Ingram 1969, Arnott 1973.

[48] The story of the prosecution for impiety in Satyrus is likely to be of comic origin: in the same context, *Thesmophoriazusae* is used as a historical source.

Euripides' intellectual purposes, his supposed concern to explore or propagate ideas, not just because it is a joke, but because it is a joke rooted in an interpretative practice which we know to have been unsound. The point is vividly illustrated by the use in Aristophanes of *Hi.*612 (*Th.*275, *Frogs* 101, 1471) – though the same example also shows clearly the fire without which the comic smoke-screen could never have been put up: for, like the prayer in *Trojan Women*, this memorable, aphoristic summary of the worse case is characteristic of the sophistic and rhetorical wit so distinctive of the surface of Euripides' writing.

2.33 Politics in tragedy

The scholia on a number of passages in tragedy claim that the poet has tried to secure the goodwill of his audience by appealing to their patriotic sentiments.[49] It is true that the scholia must be treated with caution, and that some of these interpretations are distressingly trivial; moreover, they are clearly influenced in this point by a specifically rhetorical concern with a speaker's *therapeia* of his audience. But we must (as always) ask whether the rhetorical bias of these critics has not enabled them to see more clearly the relationship between poet and audience. Certainly, there are several reasons why their suggestion should be taken seriously in principle. First, such a device would fit well into the general theory of tragedy outlined in Chapter 1. For we saw in 1.2 that the tragedian, who was a competitor and so dependent for success on the appreciation of his audience, had to secure their attention and goodwill by various means; the appeal to patriotic sentiment would therefore count as a kind of ancillary pleasure – if the tragedians used it: and it is reasonable to suppose that they did. As a competitor, the tragedian stood to the Athenian *dêmos* much as the Homeric bard did to his nobility, or as Pindar to his patrons. The aptness of this latter comparison is particularly clear if one thinks of the tragedians working outside Athens: compare Pindar's first *Pythian* with what is said in the *Life* of Aeschylus about his *Women of Etna*: that the play was an augury of prosperity for the city that Hiero was just then founding (*oiônizomenos bion agathon tois sunoikizousi tên polin*), and naturally won the favour of the patron it honoured. We might consider also Agathon and Euripides in their remove to Macedonia, recalling in particular that Euripides seems to have written an *Archelaus* in honour of his new patron. It is reasonable to suppose that a dramatist working for the Athenian *dêmos* would have exploited its patriotic and democratic sentiment in a similar way. This would have been particularly appropriate, since the dramatic festivals were civic occasions, and the Dionysia especially was something of a show-piece for the city;[50] glorification of Athens would therefore have been in place. This line of argument is, to be sure, speculative: but it is confirmed by the observation that the commonplaces of rhetorical encomium of Athens frequently recur in fifth-century tragedy, both in the

[49] A.*Per.*237, *Eu.*11 (cf.238); S.*Aj.*202, 861, 1221, *El.*707, 731, *OC* 92, 457, hyp.I (cf. on 712); E.*Su.*hyp., *Tro.*31, 209.

[50] Pickard-Cambridge 1968: 58-9.

form of passing allusions and in extended development; this coincidence of themes strongly suggests that the poets were engaged in deliberate glorification of the city.[51]

One of the most important themes in the praise of Athens is the reception and defence of suppliants and the oppressed: as the sun beneficently disposes all things for the best, says one orator, so Athens never ceases from punishing the wicked and helping the righteous; she disburses fairness in place of wrongdoing, and at her own risk and her own expense she ensures for the Greeks a common security (Hyp.6.5; cf. Gorg. fr.6: *therapontes men tôn adikôs dustukhountôn, kolastai de tôn adikôs eutukhountôn*); standard examples, the burial of the Seven against Thebes and the defence of the children of Heracles, receive frequent mention in the orators, and are said to be commonplace in the poets.[52] Euripides devoted a play to each (*Suppliants* and *Heraclidae*), and it is likely that Aeschylus also wrote plays on both of these stories (*Eleusinians* and *Heraclidae*).[53] The general theme is used in passing by Euripides in *Medea* and *Heracles*, and is the basis for Sophocles' second *Oedipus*. A recurrent pattern may be observed: Athens magnanimously receives a suppliant, and successfully defends his cause; in consequence, the city receives some benefit, so that the glorious deed becomes, by way of an aetiology, an affirmation of and celebration of the city's present well-being: an augury of prosperity for the city, in the words of the Aeschylean *Life* quoted earlier.

We should note in passing that cult-aetiology is combined with patriotic motifs in other ways as well;[54] and elsewhere religion and patriotism are combined, not by means of an aetiology, but by an affirmation of special divine favour.[55] Since state and cult were inextricably connected in fifth-century Greece, patriotism in tragedy inevitably takes on a religious aspect.

In this sense, therefore, tragedy may certainly be 'political': that is, it may be a celebration of the *polis*. But this is not the kind of political significance that has been of most interest to modern interpreters: these have looked, on the one hand for explorations of general political principles; and on the other,

---

[51] Schroeder 1914.

[52] (i) Burial of the Seven: Hdt.9.27; Pl.*Mnx*.239b; Xen.*Hell*.6.5.46; Lys.2.7-10; Isocr.4.54-65, 12.168-74. (ii) Heraclidae: Hdt.9.27; Pl.*Mnx*.239b; Xen. *Mem*.3.5.10, *Hell*.6.5.47; Ar.*Rhet*.1396a; Lys.2.11-16; Isocr.4.54-65, 5.33-4, 6.42, 12.194. Note Isocr.12.168: 'Who does not know, or who has not heard from the tragedians at the Dionysia ...' – this of (i); Pl.*Mnx*.239b claims that both (i) and (ii) are commonplaces in the poets, together with: (iii) Amazonian invasion: Hdt.9.27; Pl.*Mnx*.239b; Xen.*Mem*.3.5.10; Lys.2.4-6; Isocr.4.68, 6.42, 7.75, 12.193. (iv) Thracian invasion: Pl.*Mnx*.239b; Xen.*Mem*.3.5.10; Isocr.4.68, 6.42, 7.75, 12.193; Lyc.98-9. Also popular in the orators are: (v) Persian Wars: Hdt.9.27; Pl.*Mnx*.239d-41e; Xen.*Mem*.3.5.11; Ar.*Rhet*.1396a; Lys.2.20-47; Isocr.4.71-99, 6.42, 7.75, 12.195. (vi) Autochthony: Hdt.7.161.3; Th.2.36; Pl.*Mnx*.237bc; Xen.*Mem*.3.5.11; Lys.2.17; Isocr.4.23-5, 12.124-5; Hyp.6.7. (vii) Constitution: Pl.*Mnx*.238b-9a; Lys.2.18-19; Isocr.4.38-40, 10.35-7, 12.128ff. and 151-4.

[53] The subject of the former is not in doubt: the latter has been contested (Srebrny 1951), but I am not convinced that the title could have alluded to any other story when this one was so popular.

[54] E.*Erectheus* fr.65 Austin, *El*.1254-7, *IT* 958-60, 1448-67.

[55] A.*Eu*.916ff.; S.*OC* 668-719; E.*Ion* 1553-4, 1617: this (and not any satirical purpose) is why Athene is the *deus* in *Ion*, a play full of patriotic motifs.

for allusions to contemporary events, comments on specific issues, interventions in partisan controversy. I will not be concerned here with political interest of the former kind (I have already commented on one example in my discussion of *Eumenides* in 1.13, and I will look more carefully at Sophocles' *Antigone* from this point of view in 2.4); my interest will be the more direct and specific kind of engagement in the city's political life that has been alleged for some plays.

It should be conceded at once that the idea of covert contemporary allusion in tragedy finds some slight support in the scholia (although it should also be observed that they disapproved of it).[56] On the other hand, there are reasons for treating political interpretations with some caution. First, partisan political comment would risk the alienation of part of the audience, and this would not be desirable in a competitive festival; moreover, the civic nature of the festivals would in any case make patriotic and pan-Athenian sentiment more acceptable in tragedy than partisan politics.[57] Furthermore, when the tragedians do indulge in pan-Athenian politics, they make no secret of it; partisan politics in tragedy, by contrast, apparently works by stealth: it is to be discerned only, if at all, in oblique and cryptic hints; this should excite suspicion. In the light of these considerations, and given the lack of firm external evidence for the use of tragedy to commend political views that were not (as patriotic and democratic sentiments were) entirely uncontroversial in the mainstream of Athenian political life, we must be cautious in admitting political interpretations of tragedy. We must now consider some specific examples.

It might be helpful if we begin by considering an example which, since the play has not survived, is conveniently free from any distracting clutter of evidence. Forrest says of Phrynichus' *Sack of Miletus* that 'the only convincing explanation' of the play's purpose is that it was 'an attempt to shame the Athenians out of their appeasement policy'.[58] He exaggerates. It is, after all, conceivable that Phrynichus found the sack of a city an outstandingly moving subject in its own right, one most evocative of the tragic emotions (see, for example, *Od*.8.523ff., A.*ScT* 321-68), and that he felt that the treatment of an event so close to home would intensify the emotional effect: if so, he was right, although the experiment was an artistic misjudgment, since the intensification of emotion took a form that was unacceptable to the audience, and the play was a spectacular failure (1.11). So it is not necessary to postulate any political motive for the play at all; and, on any view of the matter, it is by means of its emotivity that such a purpose would have taken effect. Nevertheless, it is striking that Phrynichus chose to handle so politically charged a subject; and our suspicions can only be strengthened

[56] A.*Eu*.398; E.*Andr*.445, 734, *Or*.903, 1682; or (non-political) S.*El*.62, where it is criticised as more appropriate to comedy; anachronisms in general are disapproved of in the scholia.

[57] There is partisan political comment in Old Comedy (although the seriousness with which it is meant to be taken remains a matter of controversy); but what is acceptable given the licence and lack of restraint of the comic jester cannot necessarily be applied to the more restrained and decorous genre.

[58] Forrest 1960: 235.

when we recall that the play was sponsored by Themistocles. This will prompt the question: was the controversy which Herodotus records sparked off solely by Phrynichus' artistic misjudgment in using material too immediately painful to his audience, or was his putatively political motive somehow at issue? If so, what was it that was found objectionable: simply his political use of the tragic festival? or his backing the wrong party? In either case, the reasons which I gave for treating political interpretations with caution are strengthened: partisan politics in tragedy are dangerous or out of place. Consequently, even if we concede the likelihood of political motivation in this case, we have no reason for supposing it to be anything but an isolated and unsuccessful experiment.

Phrynichus and Aeschylus both wrote plays on the Persian War. Since Phrynichus' play is not extant, there is little that can usefully be said about it that is not an extrapolation from Aeschylus' *Persians* (certainly, we should attach no evidential weight to the possibility – it is no more – that the play was produced in 476, when Phrynichus' choregus was again Themistocles). As for Aeschylus' play, the element of patriotic (pan-Athenian and pan-Hellenic) celebration is obvious enough. Kitto, indeed, is inclined to play down this aspect; but he assumes an audience more resistant to flattery than we have any right to expect an Athenian audience to have been: as Plato observes, it is not difficult to praise Athens in Athens.[59] Moreover, some of Kitto's comments are obtuse: he professes, for example, an inability to see why the discovery of the mines at Laurium should have been a source of national pride and an object of celebration. On 231-45, he comments:

> Does it not look as if he was inviting his audience not to cheer but to think? At least, almost like a historian, he reminds us of three facts that help to explain the Persian defeat: one economic, one military, and one political.

That is surely too disengaged a description for this rehearsal of the city's military might and wealth, its democratic constitution (a *topos* of Athenian self-praise: n.52), and – in climactic position – its glorious victory at Marathon (243-4): the scholiast's remark ('Aeschylus says this wishing to praise Athens') is far more convincing. Forrest calls the 'patriotic' reading of the play into question in a very different way, claiming that Salamis itself 'in a sense was still a political issue': what sense? For this claim to be true in anything like a relevant sense, we would have to suppose that an Athenian audience would have responded to the recital of its achievements at Salamis with some emotion other than national pride: and that is incredible at any time; Pindar, at any rate, did not believe it (*P*.1.75-7). So the case for taking the play in a partisan sense dissolves: the achievement and the glory did not belong to any one party, and still less to the individual Themistocles (however important his role may have been), but to the Athenian *polis* as a whole. Of course, this is not to say that patriotic celebration is all there is to

---

[59] Kitto 1966: 74ff. (the quotation below is from p.84); against this, see Pl.*Mnx*.235d, cf. Ar.*Rhet*.1367b, 1415b: Aristophanes also makes fun of this Athenian propensity in *Ach*.636ff.

the play; it is not even the play's primary purpose: but it is present, as an ancillary pleasure.

It is when we come to *Eumenides* that the most impressive case for finding political significance in an extant tragedy can be made out; but precisely what this significance is, is a matter of controversy; and the problem is not eased by the fact that the play itself is prominent among our sketchy sources for the reconstruction of its political background, so that we run the risk of moving in very small circles. However, the attempt must be made. First of all, we can say with some confidence that the play adopts a favourable attitude to the Argive alliance. The references to the alliance are, to be sure, fully motivated within the play's internal economy: it is the natural expression of Orestes' gratitude; but the emphasis which the theme receives (289-91, 669-73, 762-77) makes it unreasonable to deny that Aeschylus intends to call to mind, and thereby to celebrate, the contemporary alliance by means of its mythological *aition*. It does not follow, however, that Aeschylus' point is partisan. The reversal of foreign policy which led up to the alliance was, it is true, bound up with the struggle between factions which culminated in the (ineptly so-called) 'democratic revolution' of 462/1; it was, therefore, in 462/1 a controversial part in the programme of one tendency in Athenian politics. But *Eumenides* was not produced in 462/1; and by 458 two factors had come into play which would have swung public opinion behind the alliance: the humiliation at Ithome had discredited the foreign policy of Cimon to which it was opposed; and the outbreak of war with the Peloponnesians, which had put the alliance to use, is likely to have promoted solidarity and inflamed patriotic feeling – as wars tend to do. It is most uncertain, therefore, whether a celebration of the Argive alliance would have had in 458 the partisan (and not pan-Athenian) significance that it would have had three or four years earlier.

The heart of the matter is the Areopagus. It seems clear, first of all, that the reforms of 462/1 are not being challenged: Athene in her speech of institution is quite content to found the Areopagus as a homicide court alone. (It might be argued that the more general references to *eunomia* imply a constitutional role; but in the light of the parallel with the Erinyes and their account of their own functions, it seems more probable that it is the anarchical consequence of a removal of *moral* restraint that is in question.) Does this imply a partisan position? In 461, clearly, it would; but again we must bear in mind that the play was not produced in the middle of the controversy over the reforms, but several years after the settlement: and the evidence that the issue of the Areopagus had *remained* controversial is non-existent. Certainly, the rout of the worsted faction was thorough: it lost the battle over domestic policy; its foreign policy was not only reversed but, as we have seen, discredited; its leader was ostracised. In so far as there did remain a coherent opposition, by 458 it had other issues to concern itself with, for Pericles had already embarked on a new series of radical reforms. There is one piece of evidence for active opposition to the constitutional settlement of 462/1 in 458: Thucydides records a conspiracy to betray the city and overthrow the democracy (1.107.4); and this is, in fact, the sole piece of evidence which Forrest could produce in the article already cited.[60] It is astonishingly feeble. First, we do not know that these conspirators objected specifically to the treatment of the Areopagus; on the contrary, it is clear that their discontents ran far deeper, for it was the democracy as such that they wanted to overthrow (their active opposition may have been triggered by the radical successes of 462/1: that is a different matter). Moreover, this conspiracy could not in any case tell us anything about the mainstream of Athenian politics: it was the work of a few extremists; if this is the best that can be done, therefore, it leaves the issue effectively non-controversial.

If we accept this reconstruction of the background to *Eumenides*, it follows that Aeschylus' acquiescence in the reformation of the Areopagus would not have been a *pointed* acquiescence; it would not even be correct to see the play as a plea for reconciliation between the conflicting parties based on acceptance of a *fait accompli*. Rather, Aeschylus is taking both the reforms and the new Athenian political consensus for granted, and is doing for it what came so naturally to the Greeks; he is using myth to furnish an aetiological charter for the political *status quo*. The significance of this is obviously pan-Athenian, not partisan; and it is a pan-Athenian interpretation of the play which best fits its whole structure. *Eumenides* is, in fact, the most splendidly elaborated example of the pattern of patriotic play described earlier: a suppliant is received and vindicated by the city, which in consequence receives great benefits: the alliance with Argos to secure its external safety, the court of the Areopagus to secure internal order, the blessings of the Eumenides (linked to their cult) to secure the fertility of the land and the well-being of its people. The best summary of the play's political significance is that which we have already seen applied to another of Aeschylus' plays: it is an augury of success for the state, *oiônizomenos bion agathon*; it is a confident, self-congratulatory celebration of the city, its institutions and cults, its prosperity and security. That Aeschylus should have written such a play in the wake of an internal crisis and in the face of external wars is doubtless no coincidence; but the political significance of his play is anything but partisan or controversial.

One other play of Aeschylus needs to be considered, his *Suppliants*. Attempts have been made to make connections between the Chorus of this play and Themistocles. This is fanciful and unnecessary: the suppliant-plot is too familiar for its use here to need an explanation of this kind; and the resemblances between a single aging democratic politician from Athens and fifty young barbarian women, with not the least comprehension of democracy (370-5) and in imminent danger of rape, are – to put it mildly – tenuous.[61] More worthy of serious attention is the manner in which Argos is portrayed: it appears to be a *democratic* monarchy (hence the perplexity of the barbarian maidens); and does not the benediction of the suppliants reflect a favourable attitude to Argos, as those in *Eumenides* reflect Athenian

---

[60] Forrest 1960: 236; we know of no attempt to revoke the reform of the Areopagus before 404.

[61] Cf. Garvie 1969: 155. (There are some good remarks on the political aspect of this play in Burian 1974.)

patriotism?[62] The first point to make is that the constitutional arrangements in this play are less surprising than is sometimes made out. The king does not deny that he has the authority to make the decision alone; on the contrary, he says that he will not make it alone, even though he has the power to do so (398-9). He takes this line in order to avoid the censure of the masses, who are disposed to criticise their rulers (399-401, 483-5). This is not essentially different from the conditions portrayed in *Ag*.455-7 (cf. *ScT*.1-9); and this in turn is not far removed from Homer. It is true that the 'democratic' aspects of this familiar constitution are given more emphasis than in *Agamemnon*, and that they are stated in terms reminiscent of fifth-century democracy (601, 604). But the king is, by virtue of his role as protector of the suppliants, a representative of the type 'good king'; and if one wants to portray a king as wise and good when writing for a democracy, how better than by stressing his concern both for the welfare and for the willing consent of his subjects? And when that consent has been won, how better to catch the exultant tone of the suppliants than by couching the report given to them in terms that would draw on the audience's enthusiasm, not for a putative Argive, but for its own democratic constitution?

As for the suppliants' blessing, it is of course fully motivated within the play; it is the natural response of gratitude. But the blessing differs in one crucial respect from those which are found in the plays exploiting Athenian patriotism: it fails; at any rate, it is most probable that in the subsequent course of the trilogy Argos is defeated in the war which its reception of the suppliants precipitates. The reception of the suppliants does not lead, as it does in genuinely encomiastic plays, to vindication and an assurance of the protector's future well-being, but to a much grimmer sequence of events. The blessing of Argos, therefore, does not foreshadow a celebratory climax, but is a mere episode in a continuing tragedy; so it would be unwise to look for an external, political motive to supplement the internal, dramatic motivation of the blessings. I conclude that there are no serious grounds for giving the play a political interpretation.

The case for finding intended political significance of any but an uncontroversial, pan-Athenian kind is nowhere stronger than in the plays I have examined here; if it fails in these cases, it will fail *a fortiori* in the more tenuous and elusive political interpretations that have been proposed for other plays. To be sure, if we knew on independent grounds that contemporary audiences came to the theatre disposed to ferret out covert allusions and to discern partisan meanings, then these interpretations would warrant more indulgent treatment; but we do not know that, and have (as I argued earlier) reason to doubt it. Given these doubts, the availability of non-political or non-partisan readings which accord with the dispositions which we do know that audiences brought with them to the tragic theatre must be decisive; the political readings are superfluous. Sometimes, indeed, they are worse than superfluous. Because (as I pointed out in connection with Phrynichus' *Sack of Miletus*) the fall of a city is such excellent tragic

---

[62] Cf. also S.*OC*688ff; Taplin 1977: 211.

material, there is no reason at all for assuming a political motive when Euripides ends a trilogy of plays on Trojan themes with a play about the sack of Troy. Both the misery of the vanquished and the dangers of victory (cf. A.*Ag*.472) are traditional themes; there is, therefore, no reason to look for connections with Melos or Sicily in *Trojan Women*. But if we did make such connections, we would find that the Athenians are in some sense cast in the role of the doomed Greeks (doomed, it is to be noted, for conspicuous acts of impiety, and not for the bloody sack as such); and this is flatly contrary to everything we know about the treatment of Athens in Athenian tragedy, and to everything that we might rationally expect. What the parallel would lead us to expect, and what we actually find, is the exact opposite: laudatory references exploiting patriotic feeling (204ff., 799ff.).

2.4 The intellectualisation of tragedy

I began this chapter by drawing attention to the intellectualising tendencies of modern interpretation of tragedy, to its preoccupation with tragedies as vehicles of ideas; this preoccupation did not seem easy to reconcile with the emotive and hedonist assumptions which, according to the survey made in Chapter 1, dominated ancient thinking about the genre, and my argument to this point suggests that we should not try to reconcile the two: rather, the intellectualism of modern interpretation should be relinquished. The obvious counter-arguments to this claim, based externally on the tradition of moral and didactic use of poetic texts, and internally on the religious and political content of tragedy, do not provide sufficient grounds for reaching any other conclusion. In this and the following section, I wish to explore these matters a little further.

To deplore the intellectualisation of tragedy is naturally not to deny that there is an intellectual element in our response to tragedy. To deny that would be absurd: an emotional response is always a response to something, and therefore presupposes the cognition of its object. What is presupposed in a response to tragedy is, first of all, the cognition of particular facts about a secondary or narrated world: for example, that Orestes killed his mother. But particulars would not, in any but the most rudimentary way, be intelligible unless we could set them in a broader context; that is to say, the narrated world must have some intelligible structure, which allows us to 'situate' the particular, to perceive its significance and implications. In the example of Orestes, the act of matricide would have relatively little significance for an audience that did not grasp the place of kinship in the moral world of the *Oresteia*; and its full significance can only be grasped in the light of the concept of Dike. The grasp of more general propositions about the narrated world is therefore also essential to the understanding of tragic action, and to the appreciation of its emotional force. Tragedy has intellectual (moral, theological, metaphysical) *content*, and this content must be understood.

The events and structures of a narrated world may or may not correspond to what the author or his audience believe about the primary world: *fiction*, we might say, is a narrative designedly false in particulars, though presenting a world broadly similar in structure to the primary world, while *fantasy* is marked by the structural dissimilarity of worlds. But whatever similarities and dissimilarities there may be between the structures of the two worlds, there must be some points of imaginative contact if the narrative is to be intelligible, and still more if it is to evoke close emotional engagement. Consequently, the narrative may well have implications for the primary world: the fictional narrative, that is to say, is potentially revealing about the primary world; the reception of and response to it may prompt us to reflect on, and may change our perception of and practice in, the primary world. This is true of narrative in general, but there are reasons why it might be especially so in the case of Greek tragedy. First, we have seen the fundamental importance of emotional engagement; and this, as has been said, requires a firm point of imaginative contact: tragedy is in some sense *peri ton homoion* (cf.1.12ii). Furthermore, the principle of tragic dignity (1.3) must encourage the tragedian to move in the vicinity of large issues of serious concern to us. If the conflict between (for example) Creon and Antigone is to become a matter of life and death, and so sufficiently grave to excite a strong emotional response, the antagonists must be motivated by principles of some gravity; if this were not so (if they were inflamed by some triviality, like the theft of a cock in Aristophanes' parody of Euripides), then the extremity of their conflict would be incongruous and unconvincing: this would in turn both ruin the emotional effect, and destroy tragic dignity. But this is not to say that serious issues are coherently formulated or purposefully explored in the play: the dramatist need do no more than is necessary to make his audience aware of their proximity; and certainly, he need have no interest in the issues as such, beyond their contribution to the emotive force of his play.

If a dramatist does allude to a moral or philosophical or religious issue for dramatic and emotive purposes, this may of course have the effect of prompting a member of his audience to reflect on the problem *as* a problem: to explore it, and perhaps to try to resolve it. It is helpful to distinguish between the interpretation and the application of a text. It is one thing to ask what the text is saying, another to explore the implications of what it says, its significance or value in the light of the interests which we have brought with us. What we have in the reflections prompted by the play is an intellectualising application of the tragic text. Of course, *any* text is in principle open to such, or to any other, application; but for most texts, intellectualising application would strike us as deliberately humorous, or else as strained and incongruous. What we have seen in the case of Greek tragedy, however, is that the nature of the genre tends to make such an application seem less strained: for it naturally moved in the vicinity of large and weighty issues, and seeks to portray a world that is (or may give the illusion of being) neither incoherent nor fantastic.

The *possibility* of an unstrained intellectualising application of tragedy does not imply that such an application was *intended*. If the tragedian, because of what tragedy was, could hardly have avoided writing in such a way that his plays would readily afford material for serious reflection, then the fact that they do so cannot in itself prove that the poet intended them to serve as the basis for serious reflection, or that he was concerned to prompt the audience to such reflection; still less can it prove that his aim was to guide their reflection on intellectual or moral issues in the extradramatic world, to explore or commend ideas. But in so far as we are trying to interpret tragedy (in an intentionalist sense) the question of whether the intellectualising application was intended is crucial.

I have argued in the previous sections that the external evidence does not support the view that Greek tragedians did as a rule intend intellectualising application of their plays; and we have not as yet seen any internal evidence for such a view. But the internal evidence will bear further consideration. Since, as we have said, the bare possibility of an unstrained application is insufficient evidence for its being intended, this internal evidence will have to take the form of evidence for a specific design. An author will choose and organise his material so as best to realise his intentions; so the choice of material that he has made and his treatment of it will provide us with evidence for his intentions. Therefore we must scrutinise particular plays, and ask whether their material and its organisation is such as to persuade us that the dramatist must have intended to prompt or to guide intellectualising application. The play I have chosen as a test-case is *Antigone*: for, as I have already said, this play does involve fundamental issues of a religious, moral and political nature; it has prompted reflection on such issues – that is, it has proved highly suitable for intellectualising application; and a large proportion of the modern work on the play has been dominated by this aspect.

The central issue in *Antigone* is easily stated: should Polyneices' corpse be buried? In normal circumstances, the answer to such a question would be an unhesitating 'Yes', and the responsibility for ensuring burial would lie with the nearest male relative: in this case, with Creon. But these are not normal circumstances. On the one hand, Polyneices was killed while leading a foreign army against his native city; his corpse, therefore, is that of a *polemios*, a public enemy – and, indeed, of a public enemy of that most nauseating kind, a traitor. On the other hand, Creon, the relative responsible, is now the ruler of the city that Polyneices' treason had threatened, so that he now bears the chief responsibility for the prosecution of the public enmity. This might be thought to confront Creon with a conflict of obligations; he reasons his way out of the conflict thus: an individual's obligations to his *polis* must override all other obligations, including those to his private *philoi*; so whatever obligations he may have had towards Polyneices *qua philos* have been cancelled by the treachery that made him *polemios*; in his private capacity, therefore, Creon need not accept his obligation to ensure burial, while in his public capacity as ruler he is obliged to forbid burial, thus inflicting on the traitor the penalty of *atimia* due to the city, and to its gods.

That Antigone responds more strongly than Creon to the claims of *philia* is natural: not, of course, because she is, in the English sense, of an especially 'loving' disposition; that would be hard to establish from the text, which portrays her rather as harsh and unyielding in temperament. But that is not what *philia* means in Greek: *philia* is not, at root, a subjective bond of affection and emotional warmth, but the entirely objective bond of reciprocal obligation; one's *philos* is the man one is obliged to help, and on whom one can (or ought to be able to) rely for help when oneself in need. The family, therefore, is a group, reinforced by special ethical and religious sanctions, the members of which are, to a greater or lesser extent, mutually dependent: dependent on each other for burial, above all, since burial is one thing which, by definition, no man can procure by himself for himself. It is loyalty to this group and its obligations that motivates Antigone.[63]

Antigone is a woman. The horizons of her action are therefore more constricted than those within which Creon acts. In Greek society a woman lives above all as part of a family (her father's first, and then her husband's), and far less directly than the male as an active part of the *polis*. For Creon, both as a man and as a ruler, political responsibilities are central to his definition of his own role and identity; for a woman, this cannot be so. Consequently, the civic obligations which allow Creon to rationalise his violation of *philia* are inevitably less potent for Antigone. It is for this reason that, as I have said, her greater sensitivity to the claims of her dead kin is natural. If her sensitivity is natural, however, her practical response is less so, and for precisely the same reason: she is a woman, and women are feeble creatures who sit at home and knit while the men are away fighting. This is, of course, a chief reason why women are not in so direct a way as men political animals; they are simply incapable of bearing the responsibilities that would entail. The same incapacity lies behind the taken-for-granted restriction when we said that the obligation to bury a corpse would normally fall on the nearest *male* relative. Of course, in the face of an edict such as Creon's, even a male might well hesitate; and if he went ahead it would be greatly to the credit of his courage, his *aretê*, his (significant word) *andreia*. For a woman to do this is something quite remarkable. Ismene illustrates the point. She, too, is a woman, and no less sensitive than her sister to the claims of kinship; but her disposition to act is more natural: she has the timidity and submissiveness that one would expect of a woman, and so she shrinks from an act of exceptional difficulty and danger. She approves of the principle of Antigone's resolution, but is alarmed by its suicidal folly: *anous men erkhêi, tois philois d' orthôs philê* (99).[64]

Antigone regards her action, and the sacrifice it entails, as *kalon*: and if she is right, the unwomanly hardness of her action will be justified and admirable. But if Creon is right, those same qualities will appear sinister and unnatural; her action will be 'daring' in a less favourable sense. So: to what

---

[63] There is no inconsistency between 450ff. and 905ff.: in the former passage she explains, in reply to a charge of sedition, what justified her act; in the latter passage (a more personal context, full of pathos: note especially the framing apostrophes) she speaks of the pressures which impelled her to do it. To equate these two, as if Antigone were a moral automaton, trivialises her act by underestimating the deterrents which faced her and the need for compelling personal reason if she were to overcome them.

[64] *Philê* is evidently active, despite Jebb.

extent is Creon right? We are left in no doubt by the end of the play that he is utterly and disastrously wrong; but there are some features of the dramatic technique of the play's earlier scenes that should make us reluctant to look too kindly on Creon, even before Teiresias' explicit denunciation of his edict. Antigone is established in the opening scene as the focus of sympathetic attention: to her focus, Creon plays adversary; he is the source of the threat to her – and that is an inherently antipathetic and alienating role. (I shall return to the terms 'focus' and 'adversary' in 3.1: their purport should be sufficiently clear without explanation here.) To offset that initial prejudice Sophocles would have had to work very hard, had he wished to win for Creon a fair hearing; and he has not done so. On the contrary, in spite of Creon's admittedly impressive opening rhesis (cited by Demosthenes as a paradigm of statesmanship: 19.247), he very soon displays the traits which we associate with a tragic tyrant; the impressiveness of his first speech serves as a foil to this development, and one function of the Guard's scene is to draw these traits out into the open (the often-remarked liveliness of the Guard's characterisation is designed in part to show up these traits as vividly as possible). So the audience's prejudice against Creon is well established and confirmed by the time that Antigone appears as a prisoner.

An audience ought not, therefore, to be disposed to give Creon the benefit of any doubt; but where, if anywhere, does his reasoning go wrong? The premise from which he begins (the overriding importance of loyalty to the *polis*) is impeccable; the conclusion he draws from this premise is a different matter, for it is a deep-rooted assumption in Greek literature – and, indeed, in Greek life – that the dead are not to be abused, that the pursuit of enmity beyond the grave is not *kalon*: to cite only the most obvious examples, recall *Iliad* 24, Sophocles' *Ajax* (which we shall be studying in Chapter 5), Euripides' *Suppliants*. Of course, we are often reminded that in Athenian law burial in Attic soil was forbidden to, among others, traitors; this, it is claimed, makes the impropriety of Creon's edict less clear-cut, given the circumstances in which it was issued. Even if this counter-example were strictly relevant, that blurring of the isues would not follow: for we are dealing here, not with an Athenian court of law, but with a tragedy; whenever the refusal of burial becomes an issue in tragedy, it is seen as an emotive wrong (for obvious reasons: were it not so, it would not be evocative of fear and pity, and so would probably never have become an issue in the play at all). It is this literary background that would most strongly have influenced an audience's response in the theatre, especially when reinforced (as we have seen) by prejudicial devices of dramatic technique. But in any case, the objection is not strictly relevant: for Creon is not simply forbidding burial in native soil (Sophocles has simply suppressed that more moderate alternative): he is forbidding burial as such; thus he is using the *atimia* of the traitor deliberately to mutilate the corpse, which is a different, and more serious, matter. Sophocles dwells with careful attention on the more repellent physical details of the exposure of the corpse, on the rot and the stench and the dirt, the scavenging birds and animals; these are forced on our attention precisely to make Creon's edict stand out as morally repulsive.

Creon, therefore, has simply made a mistake. He starts from fine principles, but overlooks the limits of their application; the overriding importance of the claims of the *polis* is irrelevant where the *polis* has no claim: and it has no claims against the established laws (*kathestôtes nomoi*) of burial. Having made this initial error, Creon is compelled to defend his position, and is thus drawn progressively into the arbitrary and tyrannical exercise of power. This development Sophocles uses to undermine his position still further; for not only is Creon trying to press the claims of the *polis* where the *polis* has no claims, but in doing so he ceases even to act as a valid representative of the *polis*, which repudiates his action, as we learn from Haemon. The 'one-man' theory of the state is never acceptable in Greek (or, more precisely and more revealingly, in democratic Athenian) tragedy: contrast the paradigmatically good rulers in the *Suppliants* of Aeschylus (cf. 2.33) and of Euripides (cf. 2.5); and this one-man theory is explicitly exposed and denounced in this play. If that theory of political authority is not accepted, then Creon's edict turns out to be politically, as well as morally and religiously, invalid. Thus the scene with Haemon completes the thorough overthrow of Creon's position.

One implication of this is that the play cannot, as some have supposed, dramatise a conflict between the authority of the state and that of the gods; because Creon's position collapses in purely political terms, his edict is not sustained *de jure* by the state's authority – even though he has the power *de facto* to enforce it. But such a conflict is in any case scarcely conceivable. It is not simply that it would be manifest folly for the state even to try to set its authority in competition with the known will of the gods; it is doubtful whether the Greek *polis* – which, as we have observed in 2.33, is a religious, not simply a secular entity – could have an authority that was not sustained by the favour of the gods. The real question at issue is far simpler: on which side do the gods stand? Antigone is sure from the beginning that the gods endorse her action, and Creon eventually discovers that she was right; I have argued that this issue could not at any stage have been in doubt for the audience.

This conclusion has a bearing on the question which brought us to the play. *Antigone* does indeed touch on matters of the utmost depth and seriousness: its characters are in dispute over matters concerning their loyalty and obligations to family, to state, to the gods, and these are for them questions of life and death; were this not so – were their conflict rooted in trivia only – the play would not call forth so profound an emotional response. Because of these associations, the play can and does prompt readers to serious reflection on moral and intellectual questions; but there is no sign that Sophocles has contrived the play with that end in view. Since he has made it clear from the beginning both that Creon is wrong and why Creon is wrong, the issues which are in dispute among the characters never appear as dilemmas posed for the audience's consideration; the answers are all there, pat. It seems, therefore, that Sophocles intended the play to be intellectually and morally straightforward and unproblematic. Indeed, its moral and intellectual purport could be reduced to a simple formula: impiety is a bad and dangerous thing; and this is, in effect, precisely the formula to which Sophocles himself does reduce the play at the end of Teiresias' scene and in the play's brief coda (1113-14, 1347-53). That is neither profound nor novel; and although one might entertain the hypothesis that Sophocles' rather disappointing aim was to commend this elementary moral and religious truth to his audience, the theory is not compelling. One *might* take the closing scene, with its carefully elaborated presentation of Creon's misery, as an extended object-lesson underlining the dangers of impiety; but it seems more plausible to suppose that Sophocles' artistic interests lay less in the moral implications of Creon's suffering than in its emotive potential. That is to say: his primary aim was to evoke an emotional response from his audience by the presentation of a moving picture of human misery. My conclusion, therefore, is that the internal evidence of *Antigone* does not suggest that Sophocles aimed to pose moral and intellectual issues for the consideration of his audience: rather, he presupposes a consensus on such issues; and his aim was to move and entertain them.

If Sophocles did not intend the intellectualising applications to which the play can (nevertheless) be put, intellectualisation fails as an approach to the interpretation of this play; that is not to say, however, that intellectualising applications are necessarily invalidated. First, I must stress that 'application' is not, in my usage, a derogatory term set in competition with 'interpretation'; an audience that responds to the emotive force of the play as Sophocles intended is as much applying it as a reader who is moved to moral reflection. Secondly, intended applications have no incontrovertible priority over unintended applications; application is free: it is not bound by authorial intention, and therefore cannot be invalidated by a disparity with the use for which the author intended the text. The validity of an application is determined by completely different factors: the context in which and the purpose for which the text is taken in hand, the interests and values of the interpreter and his audience. I am far from despising unintended intellectualising applications of tragedy; the development of my own philosophical and theological outlook was decisively influenced by my earliest encounters with the *Oresteia*. Nor do I want to say that the intellectualising application of tragedy can have no bearing on its *aesthetic* value, and that it is therefore irrelevant to literary criticism; it is obviously possible, indeed plausible, to hold that a text's intellectual richness or suggestiveness may render it aesthetically more appealing. My objections to the intellectualisation of tragedy are more modest. First, as an interpreter of tragedy I will insist that there is reason, whatever application we will in the end make of a text, first to have understood it; for this purpose, it is essential that we see clearly what the tragedians were really up to. Then, as a literary critic, I would argue that our aesthetic experience will be restricted and impoverished if we do not make the attempt to appropriate alien texts as they were intended; consequently, although I have no wish to outlaw intellectualising uses of tragedy, I would urge that we should *also* be willing to read and respond to the plays, and to subject them to critical scrutiny, without intellectualising preoccupations. To do so is, I believe, rewarding.

The eagerness of modern interpreters to exploit the, admittedly rich, potential of *Antigone* for intellectualising application without obvious encouragement from its author is striking evidence of the grip which this approach has on our reading of Greek tragedy. Why should this be so? There are doubtless many reasons. The prominence of the didactic view of literature in many ancient sources has, of course, fostered a misleading impression of the aims of the tragedians; and since classical scholarship is quite properly concerned with, among other things, the history of ideas, it is understandably eager to use ancient texts as evidence in this enquiry – just as ancient historians are more eager than literary scholars to find political meanings in tragedy. This is in principle legitimate; I have not denied that tragedy has intellectual content, and the content that it has will in some way be symptomatic of contemporary thought. But such reading is often naively done; it is fatally easy to work unthinkingly with the assumption – which reflection would expose as evidently foolish – that a text one has in hand was written for a purpose corresponding to the interest which we ourselves are taking in it (just as the Greeks themselves tended uncritically to refer to the author the didactic applications of texts it was their custom to make: cf. 2.22).

But it would be wrong to suppose that the fault is peculiar to classical scholars, or that it has its roots solely in their distinctive interests. Culler has rightly observed that one of the most powerful conventions in modern literary reading is a 'rule of significance': 'Read the poem as expressing a significant attitude to some problem concerning man and/or his relation to the universe.'[65] The tendency to intellectualisation in tragic criticism is therefore reinforced by the more pervasive intellectualism characteristic of modern criticism in general. 'Modern' requires some emphasis here, as is shown by an interesting study of the history of the interpretation of *Tom Jones* which Culler summarises elsewhere.[66] From this study it emerges that the preoccupations of this novel's interpreters have undergone a number of shifts, moving from plot to character to significance (in the sense of Culler's 'rule of significance'). The earliest readings of the novel saw character as a constituent of plot; in later readings, the emphasis is reversed, and 'incident is interpreted as a revelation of character':

> Most twentieth-century interpretations, however ... appear to be made possible by a different assumption: that the constituents of the novel must ultimately be interpreted in terms of a unifying vision of the world, so that *dianoia* or the thematic code has the supreme integrative function.

The parallels with the history of tragic interpretation are plain to see; and one may find a gloomy vision of our future in the most recent shift of emphasis which this study discerns in the interpretation of *Tom Jones*:

---

[65] Culler 1975: 115, cf. 175ff.
[66] Culler 1981: 63, citing an unpublished London Ph.D. thesis by Ivor Indyk.

There is yet one further reordering of codes that generates a different sort of interpretation: when it is assumed that works of art should account for themselves and that this is the uppermost level of structure, a code of irony and self-reflexivity becomes the integrative device, and the ultimate meaning of episodes and formulations is what they tell us about literary discourse and the novel itself.

Alarmist prognoses apart, this history should remind us of a simple truth: that the preoccupations of literary criticism, and the aesthetic preferences and intellectual fashions in which they are rooted, are historical and change in the course of history. It may be true that in our own literary culture, although we tend to despise overtly didactic or propagandist art, we do expect artists to have something serious to say, and tend to look down on texts that are not so designed. Modern critical procedure is largely geared to this assumption: reasonably so, for in such a culture it is likely to be true that the most artistically important texts will meet our intellectualised expectations. Equally (since the disappointment of an expectation tends to impair enjoyment), the absence of intellectual purpose may well appear to be an aesthetic demerit.

It would be parochial to assume, however, that the assumptions and preferences of our own literary culture are universally shared; and there are obvious counter-examples to such an assumption. Consider, for example, the theory of classical Indian drama, and the role in it of the concept of *rāsa*, introduced in Bharatamuni's *Nātyaśastra* (the earliest extant theoretical treatise) as the central critical principle of the genre, and later, after the decline of the classical drama, generalised as a universal aesthetic principle. *Rāsa* means literally 'taste' or 'flavour', and it is applied as a technical term for emotion experienced aesthetically; the evocation of *rāsa* was recognised as the preeminent aim of the dramatist.[67] I mention this, not because there is much similarity between Indian and Greek drama (there is not), but to illustrate my point that a concern with emotional effect apparently indifferent to our intellectualised preoccupations can sustain both a subtle and rewarding literary genre, and a sophisticated poetics. If we refuse to accept this, and continue to apply the unhistorical assumption that all literature must really be like ours, then our interpretations will inevitably be distorted, and our literary applications of texts – which means also: the range of our aesthetic experience and enjoyment – will be arbitrarily limited.

I have suggested that some of the traditional interests of classical studies and some of the current preoccupations of literary criticism in general have combined to foster the intellectualist bias of our approach to tragedy, our neglect of its emotive purposes. I suspect that there is also a certain prejudice

[67] A good summary account in Hiriyanna 1954: 29-42 (note p.21: 'Poetry then is to be regarded first and foremost as a means of securing a detachment from common life and not for any lessons or "criticism of life". There is no doubt that it has many lessons for us and that their value is great. But they are only the further good resulting from the poetic experience, and not the good which that experience itself is.') For a recent survey, with bibliography, see Gerow 1977; the best English translations of Indian drama are in van Buitenen 1968 and Coulson 1981: both have helpful short introductions. (See also Keith 1928.)

against emotion, as something of questionable worth: if not positively demoralising, as Plato thought, at any rate transient and trivial by comparison with the great questions of the human condition. Taplin provides an interesting illustration of this.[68] He demolishes with admirable efficiency a number of stock misconceptions about tragedy, and draws attention to the ancient evidence for the central importance of emotion to the genre. He is far from wishing to deny that 'tragedy is essentially the emotional experience of its audience'; but he nevertheless feels compelled to harness this emotion to some intellectual control, to a quest for order and significance in suffering (we saw in 2.21 that he misinterprets Gorgias to this end).

I find it strange, first of all, that Taplin seems to recognise only two possibilities: emotions aroused in a random and thoughtless way, and emotions ordered by a quest for significance. In shying away from mere sensationalism, he does no more than the Greeks themselves (cf.1.3); but there is a third possibility: intense but ordered emotion, controlled not by intellectual interests, but by the coherence of the whole simply *as* an emotional experience, by the aesthetic satisfaction which the audience receives through its experience of the emotions as an ordered sequence. The difference between an artistically satisfying meal and mere crude indulgence in delicacies does not lie in the subservience of the former to any intellectual end, but precisely in the meal's gustatory qualities: in the way in which various flavours and textures complement and supplement each other to provide a coherent and satisfying experience.[69] As for Taplin's claim that tragedy 'by creating a perspective on the misfortunes of human life, helps [us] to understand and cope with those misfortunes', this (like Aristotle's theory of *katharsis*) may or may not be true: it is no part of my case to deny it. What alarms me, even so, about Taplin's argument is the apparent implication that such an effect is necessary to justify and confer value on tragedy; but if the experience of tragic emotion is not, as Plato supposed, positively harmful or immoral, and if it is found aesthetically satisfying: is that not sufficient justification and sufficient value?

2.5 Morality and tragedy

In my comments on the agon of *Orestes* (2.32) I warned against the tendency to pay too much attention to the abstract intellectual strengths and weaknesses of the arguments advanced by tragic antagonists. Some interpreters of tragedy seem to feel duty-bound to adjudicate disputes with the strictest impartiality; and this is surely among the damaging

---

[68] Taplin 1978: 159-71.

[69] I have reservations in this regard concerning Stanford's references to football matches to illustrate the emotivity of tragedy (1983: 3, 7): this may be apt as to intensity of emotion, but the sporting event, unfolding in an unplanned manner, does not yield an *ordered* emotional experience. (To be sure, my own analogy with a meal is very imperfect, and should not be pressed beyond the strictly limited use I make of it here: though I note that the Greeks did themselves make use of it: cf. Chapter 3 n.24.)

consequences of the intellectualising approach to the genre, for if we give what I would regard as their proper relative weight to the emotional and intellectual aspects of tragedy, this even-handedness clearly could not be more misguided. When we are engaged emotionally in a situation, we tend not to assess issues and arguments with cool intellectual detachment, but are instead highly prone to prejudicial influence; I would claim that we must interpret tragedy in the same way. The consequences of neglecting this principle of prejudice can be seen very clearly in Fitton's study of Euripides' *Suppliants*. Of the debate between Theseus and the Theban Herald he writes that 'the debate that follows is energetic, but one can hardly say that it convinces us that Theseus is right'.[70] For my own part, I am less impressed by the case for autocracy than Fitton appears to be: but that is not to the point; rather, we must ask whether there is any doubt on which side the prejudices of the intended audience would lie. There can be no doubt: a good king answers an arrogant herald (these are both typical figures: 4.41); moreover, the good king is Theseus, and he is arguing before an Athenian audience; and he argues for democracy before democrats (it should not be forgotten that the democratic constitution was a *topos* of the praise of Athens: 2.33). Fitton's interpretation, therefore, which rests on his judgment of the opposing arguments in abstraction from their prejudicial context, is utterly worthless.

Prejudice, then, is vital to tragedy; this raises the question: to what extent and in what ways do the *moral* qualities of agents and actions in tragedy act as a prejudicial factor guiding the response of the intended audience? Presumably, the presentation of moral character is at least one means by which the tragedian can manipulate his audience's sympathies; for *ceteris paribus* an audience is more likely to be favourably disposed towards a character they can see as morally good than to a morally bad character. This is, in fact, the premise underlying Aristotle's discussion of the moral qualities of tragic characters in ch.13 of the *Poetics*, a discussion which I put to one side in 1.12 and must now take up again. The first point to notice is that the moral aspect is here entirely subordinated to the emotive end of tragedy; Aristotle makes his recommendations, not because tragedy has an autonomous moral purpose, but because various moral qualities promote or impede the audience's emotional response. But given this subordination, the moral qualities are in Aristotle's view of the utmost importance. First, sympathy is alienated by moral depravity (*mokhthêria*); therefore the tragic change of fortune from good to bad should not be due to *mokhthêria*, but to some error (*hamartia*).[71] On the other hand, if the moral excellence of the owner of the *hamartia* is too conspicuous and unqualified (*aretêi diapherôn kai dikaiosunêi*), the

---

[70] Fitton 1961: a similar view is taken in Chapter 4 of Greenwood 1953; far better is Collard 1972, 1975a.

[71] I cannot discuss this term in detail here: it would be methodologically most appropriate to allow the word the widest range of meaning permitted by the context; since it is defined only by the opposition to *mokhthêria*, this seems to leave open, as well as 'mistake of fact', misfortune and a range of moral errors with mitigating circumstances. See Stinton 1975 (with Moles 1979; note also Moles 1984), Sorabji 1980: 295-8.

change of fortune will be morally repulsive (*miaron*); therefore, the character's moral excellence must in some way be mitigated.[72] Thus the tragic character should be morally good (*khrêstos*, as Aristotle recommends in ch.15), but not outstandingly so, or his downfall will be repulsive; but he should certainly not fall short of being *khrêstos* (he should either be the kind of man already specified – neither depraved nor outstandingly good – or better, but not worse: *ê hoiou eirêtai ê beltionos mallon ê kheironos* 1453a16-17) or he will seem to deserve his suffering: it is only the man who suffers undeservedly (*anaxios dustukhôn*) who is pitiable.[73] This is at first sight a surprising conclusion, since in ch.2 Aristotle had required of tragic characters that they be 'better' than us, not 'like' us; but that seems to refer to high status and good fortune (as he says here: *tôn en megalêi doxêi ontôn kai eutukhiai* 53a10), and in general to the 'competitive' virtues more than to the 'cooperative' virtues in question in ch.13. Aristotle's position is consistent, therefore; but is it right?

Let us first ask whether Aristotle is right to insist that the tragic sufferer should be *anaxios dustukhôn*. An obvious counter-example is Aeschylus' *Persians*: so far from being *anaxios*, Xerxes has brought disaster on himself, as the play makes very clear, by his own culpable folly. Yet, although his downfall is deserved, the audience is invited to pity him.[74] Xerxes is pitiable, not because his suffering is undeserved, but because of the outstanding disparity between his good and bad fortune; he was a man of unique wealth and power, but has been utterly ruined: that contrast cannot be other than pitiable. That is to say: Xerxes is pitiable because he is *anaxios dustukhôn* only in a non-moral sense.[75] Adkins takes up this point, and argues that Aristotle's requirement that the sufferer be morally *anaxios* is anachronistic; it is unrepresentative of fifth-century values, in which the 'cooperative' virtues which Aristotle emphasises were of minor importance.[76] Stinton replies that, since he shares Aristotle's view, he cannot find it puzzling; but this is not to the point: one cannot prove the relevance of fourth-century values to fifth-century tragedy by showing that they persist in the twentieth century. More to the point is Adkins' gross exaggeration of the contrast between fifth-century and fourth-century values: the author of *ScT* 597-625 was by no means insensitive to the bearing of the cooperative virtues on pity.[77]

Stinton is right to remind us that in Aristotle's scheme, too, a character is pitiable *because* he is *anaxios dustukhôn* in this non-moral sense (*tôn en megalêi*

---

[72] The mitigation may, though it need not, be coincident with the *hamartia*: Stinton 1975: 238.

[73] Also, though Aristotle does not make the point here, the unnecessary *ponêria* would involve a lapse from dignity (cf. 1.3).

[74] This is the more striking, in that they are in the same play invited to indulge patriotic satisfaction at his defeat: it is, of course, possible to pity one's enemy, as Odysseus pities Ajax (5.1, 5.62).

[75] Cf. Schadewaldt 1955: 141: *anaxios* is 'nicht lediglich eine moralische Bewertung nach Verdienst und Unverdienst des Leidenden, sondern jedes Missverhältnis zwischen den objektiven Lebenumständen und dem, was ihn an Leiden trifft – so wie man wohl auch heute ergriffen sagt: Nein, dass gerade dieser junge, schöne, tuchtige Mensch auf so elende Weise umkommen musste!'

[76] Adkins 1966: cf. esp. pp.90-4 for documentation of the use of *anaxios* in the fifth century (e.g., Hdt.7.10: they perished *anaxiôs heautôn*).

[77] See further Stinton 1975: 243 n.3 (and p.238 for his failure to be puzzled).

doxêi ontôn kai eutukhiai); that the suffering is not morally deserved is only a *condition* of the suffering being pitiable. But the example of *Persians* seems to conflict even with this limited requirement of moral innocence as a condition of pity; and this is not an isolated example. The first case that springs to mind is that of Creon in *Antigone*, who clearly brings about his own downfall by acts which he himself recognises as culpable wrong-doing; it might be replied that the very fact of his coming to self-knowledge and repentance mitigates his moral fault, so that he fulfils the condition in another way. But is this true of Jason in *Medea*, or of Polymestor in *Hecuba*? This last case is perhaps the most striking; Hecuba's vengeance is, as everyone save Polymestor agrees, just:[78] the victim's sufferings are deserved, and certainly he is an *unrepentant* villain to the last. But is his agony not, even so, pitiable? To be sure, Euripides has contrived here an unusually complex and disturbing climax: he exposes us at once to the conflicting emotions of horror, moral satisfaction and pity. But the point I wish to make is that although these emotions coexist in tension, they do coexist; a straightforward opposition of moral desert and pitiable innocence is therefore an oversimplification.

It is true that there are characters who suffer justly, and for whom the audience is not invited to feel a moment's pity: for example, Lycus in *Heracles*. Stinton has suggested that if we feel 'nothing but satisfaction at the bloody end of Lycus', this is 'not so much because he is an enemy, but because he is evil'.[79] It is true that we can pity enemies (as we observed in the case of Xerxes above); but the case of Polymestor suggests that we can pity evil men as well. If we are not tempted to pity Lycus, it is because his sufferings are not exposed to our view in a shocking or heart-rending way, such as might excite our instinctive (and non-moral) pity for human suffering simply as such. I conclude, therefore, that Aristotle's requirement of moral innocence fails; for although the moral status of a character does influence our response, its influence is not overriding, and moral satisfaction need not outweigh other factors which conduce to pity. This conclusion is surely not surprising: for in life, too, we do not find it difficult to combine moral disapproval with intense and sympathetic emotional engagement; rightly so, for the alternative would be an inhumane moral fanaticism.

Let us turn now to the other side of Aristotle's moral requirement, the mitigation of the sufferer's virtue necessary to avoid a sense of repulsion; we may note that Aristotle himself seems less insistent on this point than on the other: *ê hoiou eirêtai ê beltionos mallon ê kheironos*. There is a problem here. Some defend Aristotle's view by arguing that he has in mind some truly unique example of human moral excellence, such as Socrates. It is not, in fact, clear that this is what Aristotle meant; his terms (*epieikês, aretêi diapherôn kai dikaiosunêi*) tolerate or even imply a less demanding standard. But the more the terms are pushed in this direction, the more vacuous the point becomes; for it is then increasingly unlikely that a dramatist would want to portray

[78] Note 1254; cf. Meridor 1978 (who however underestimates the element of pity); on the moral evaluation of revenge in tragedy, see my comments on *Orestes* in 2.32.

[79] Stinton 1975: 243.

such a figure, that he could do so convincingly, or that he could take sufficient precaution against the moral hair-splitting of a critic determined to protect his thesis: and in that case, it becomes increasingly difficult to claim the point as a significant one.

What one must ask, therefore, in considering a particular case is whether or not the innocence of 'a character who falls into misfortune by *hamartia* rather than by *mokhthêria* is mitigated in a way sufficiently significant for the claim to be plausible that this mitigation has made the decisive difference between an injustice that is pitiable and one that is morally intolerable. Moreover, the question must always be asked with the effect on an audience in mind: it is easy to survey a text from the artificial standpoint of the critic, and conclude that a certain character falls short of moral perfection in one way or another; but that shortfall is of little interest unless one can claim that it would so influence the intended audience's sympathies as to effect that degree of alienation crucial to Aristotle's theory. But here the point with which I began this chapter is again relevant; moral judgments are not to be made in abstraction from the other factors which prejudice us and sway sympathies. This is, again, a phenomenon familiar in life outside the theatre, and one which Aristotle himself was aware of; he formulates the point with characteristic clarity in the *Rhetoric*: 'the attitudes of those who are well- or ill-disposed, angry or calm, are not the same, but differ either absolutely or in degree; if one is well-disposed towards the man on whom one is passing judgment, one thinks he has done either no wrong or no serious wrong: but if ill-disposed, the opposite' (1377b31-8a1). This implies that when we are sympathetically disposed towards a dramatic character we are less prone (although not of course unable) to make adverse moral judgments, or to attach sufficient weight to those judgments for them to alienate our sympathy; but this is what is required by the theory of mitigated innocence.

A specific example is called for, and I shall discuss *Hippolytus*. First, Hippolytus himself; how is his virtue mitigated? He rejects Aphrodite;[80] but it is not convincing, when one reflects that the scene in which he is shown rejecting Aphrodite (88-120) is designed to place him at the centre of our sympathetic attention as imminent victim, to suppose that we are meant to register at the same time an alienating disapproval of his actions; it seems that we are to respond to his actions as imprudent, rather than as morally improper – an important distinction: for imprudence tends to intensify sympathy. Then he reacts to the Nurse's suggestion with 'violence and unnecessary cruelty';[81] but what else is one to expect of a Greek son of outstanding moral integrity (*aretêi diapherôn kai dikaiosunêi*) in such circumstances? An extreme reaction is precisely what is natural and appropriate to so perverse a deviation from sexual probity; it is indeed

---

[80] 'With contumely', Stinton adds (1975: 247); but Aphrodite's remark at 20-2 means that, although she does not resent Hippolytus' enthusiasm for Artemis, she does resent any exclusive enthusiasm; there is therefore no compromise: from her point of view, any rejection is rejection with contumely, since it is the rejection itself which deprives her of *timê*.

[81] Stinton 1975: 247; I should point out that Stinton is here talking about *hamartia*, not mitigation, so that my illustrative references to him are not meant as criticisms of his argument.

unfortunate that Hippolytus is reacting to a situation that does not in fact exist; but in the circumstances he could only have escaped from this illusion if he were morally less secure (so that the suggestion appalled him less), or if he were more calm and critical than we have any right to expect anyone, let alone a Greek, a hero, and a character in a tragedy, to be. Critics have also complained of his 'arrogant confidence in his own rectitude'; but this confidence is scarcely misplaced,[82] and superlative claims about oneself are by no means alien to the Greek heroic ethos; thus, they have no particular significance here. What, then, of Phaedra? The passion to which she falls victim is shameful, as she herself recognises, but the audience knows (as no one in the play can know before the intervention of Artemis) that it has been *imposed* on her by Aphrodite, without respect to, and indeed against, her own nature and integrity.[83] She is therefore seen as a victim in the strongest sense; and this must intensify sympathy. As for her slander of Hippolytus, it is not clear that the logic of her situation gives her any real alternative. She has fallen prey to a passion which she herself regards as loathsome; properly, she tries to conceal and overcome it; finding that she cannot resist, she resolves on suicide so as to maintain the concealment and avoid compounding her 'fault' by an act of infidelity. Hippolytus' response to the Nurse's indiscretion makes it clear to Phaedra that concealment is now impossible; her good name is lost, but with it the fortunes of her sons (717: cf. 305ff.) and the reputation of her family (719).[84] Something must be done to rescue the situation; so she takes a course of action that will destroy Hippolytus' credit if he accuses her. It will destroy more than his credit, but an action that harms an *ekhthros* (Hippolytus is such, not only because of his angry reaction in the previous scene, but because of the undeniable threat which he poses and always has posed to her sons and her family: cf. *Ion* 1291) is not, in a Greek context, so untoward.[85] Theseus is, at first sight, a promising candidate for blame; Artemis does indeed blame him (1316-24): but we must not neglect the terms of the following exoneration (1325-37). His 'error' is, in effect, analogous to Hippolytus': he reacts with a natural impulsiveness and

[82] Even his claim to unique status is perfectly justified, based as it is on his personal relationship with Artemis, which *is* unique.

[83] I do not attach much weight to the notion of an inherited disposition to sexual depravity (see Winnington-Ingram 1958: 175-6). It is natural that Phaedra should articulate her disgust by alluding (briefly) to these events; but we are better informed than her, having seen the prologue, and should not build much on the allusions. The hypothetical disposition is at any rate neither a sufficient condition of her passion (would it have occurred without the intervention of Aphrodite?) nor a necessary condition (would Aphrodite have been powerless in any other case?). Winnington-Ingram concludes from his understanding of causation in the play that the goddesses give an over-simplified account (pp.182-3); I conclude from what the goddesses tell us that Winnington-Ingram gives an over-ingenious one.

[84] Cf. Dover 1974: 228: 'The praise or blame which I earn by good or bad conduct affects not only the feelings of my family and friends but also their standing.'

[85] Phaedra has been severely criticised for an excessive concern with mere appearances (e.g. Vickers 1973: 286-95); but this misunderstands her words by neglecting the moral outlook which they presuppose (cf. Dover 1974: 226-9, 235-42). To make Phaedra's confession to the Nurse a point of criticism is desperately trivial, and neglects the force of the supplication: cf. 4.41.

appropriate extremity to a report which he can have no reason to doubt; that this reaction is in fact a disastrous mistake is due entirely to the illusory situation in which circumstances have boxed him. The only human character who acts with a tolerably clear vision of the situation is the Nurse; she is certainly blameworthy, but she is a slave, and so insignificant as a moral agent; and she is of course not a centre of emotional engagement in the play. Otherwise, Euripides is careful to avert blame from the human characters, and to throw all responsibility on to Aphrodite.

My claim is not that the principal characters of *Hippolytus* are irreproachable paragons of virtue; the play would hardly be plausible if that were so. But the point of view from which this fact might seem significant is inappropriate. No *reasonable* blame can attach to them; and nothing in their behaviour is so presented as to mitigate an audience's sympathies. In this case, at least, it does not seem plausible to claim that the characters are made to fall short of outstanding moral excellence in such a way as to make the difference between pitiable and morally repulsive injustice. The case is not unique; the same is true (for example) of Heracles (in *Heracles*), of the captives in *Trojan Women*, and so forth. Therefore, the other limb of Aristotle's moral requirement also fails.

Stinton accepts that Aristotle's recipe for avoiding the *miaron* is too limited in scope, but argues that a more flexible concept of 'moral redress' will save the essential insight:[86]

> The unworkable requirement, that morally faultless agents should not be portrayed falling from good fortune to bad, can be made to work ... by adding the clause, 'unless there is some compensating factor in the *praxis*'.

I cannot see how to refute this doctrine, and I am not sure that I want to; but it is at least worth raising the alternative possibility that Aristotle's concern over the *miaron* is simply mistaken. For why should moral outrage not itself be a tragic emotion, if (as I argued in 1.12) Aristotle's formula 'fear and pity' is too narrow, and other painful emotions are to be admitted? At any rate, a degree of moral outrage will presumably accompany any undeserved suffering, and it is not clear why we should postulate a degree of outrage that is too painful to be tolerated – unless (to adopt an Aristotelian phrase) we take into account the weakness of the audience. To explain such a weakness on Aristotle's part, one might point to the change of taste that seems to have occurred in fourth-century tragedy;[87] to a shift in emphasis in Greek ethics (that Adkins exaggerated his case does not exclude this possibility); and no doubt also to a certain defensiveness in the face of Plato's critique of poetry (cf. *Rep*.392a13-b6). However this may be, it is not self-evident that the suffering of a man of outstanding moral integrity would be untragic without moral redress, or (therefore) that Stinton's modification of Aristotle's theory is necessary.

I add two related points. First, something which has the effect of Stinton's

[86] Stinton 1975: 240.
[87] Haigh 1896: 430-1, Xanthakis-Karamanos 1980: 35-46.

moral redress may be worked into the play, not to avoid moral outrage, but for aesthetic reasons; the dramatist might seek a certain relief or relaxation of tragic intensity, as he does more decisively when he writes a 'happy ending' (cf. 1.12). Secondly, although (for example) Heracles' sufferings in *Trachiniae* are not deserved (ironically, they are the vengeance of a monster justly killed, and so are caused by one of Heracles' glorious achievements), they are, as it were, congruous with his person and role: violent death is the occupational hazard of professional monster-slayers. So too Hippolytus, though morally blameless, does bring about his own downfall by his imprudent attitude to the goddess; so his sufferings, too, are congruous. *Random* misfortune is unsuitable for tragedy, because it carries less conviction at the level of plot; we like things to 'hang together', to happen (or appear to happen) *di' allêla* (see 3.2); and if they do not, the plot, because it carries less conviction in the theatre, is also less emotionally powerful. Plots contrived to meet this requirement will naturally often meet the requirement of moral redress as well; but that is not the reason for their being contrived thus; and, as I have argued, it is not clear that they must be so contrived as to meet the requirement of moral redress in order to be acceptably tragic.

I have argued that Aristotle's account of the moral qualities of tragic characters is inadequate; can we draw some more general conclusions from this discovery in answer to the question which I posed initially? It follows from my rejection of the didactic theory that tragedy does not have a moral purpose (unless incidentally); but it necessarily has moral *content*;[88] that is, it portrays agents and actions which have moral qualities and which, explicitly or implicitly, are subject to moral evaluation. These moral qualities naturally influence response; it is probably impossible, and certainly inappropriate, to react to the Heracles of *Trachiniae* (a treacherous murderer, who has destroyed a city to satisfy his sexual appetite, insensitive to the feelings of Deianeira, and in the end savagely vengeful towards her) as we would to a fresh and innocent youth. The reason is simple: the object of an emotion always determines (or, since there are other factors, co-determines) the quality of the emotion. But a qualitative difference need not imply a quantitative difference; the nature of the pity which we feel for Heracles is different from the pity which we feel for Hippolytus: this does not mean that we are not to pity him, or that we are to pity him any less, or that we are in some way emotionally alienated from him. Of course, moral qualities may also have a quantitative effect on our emotional engagement with a character; but in either case, it is not the moral aspect alone that determines our engagement.[89] There are other factors which guide our sympathies, over which the moral factor will not always preponderate (for example, *Persians*); and indeed, our perception of and response to moral qualities are themselves swayed by these other determinants of sympathy and antipathy – as Aristotle observed in the *Rhetoric*. We should not even wish to limit these other factors

---

[88] This distinction is also made by Stinton 1975: 242.

[89] 'Manipulating the sympathies of the audience to achieve the desired tragic effect is an important part of the dramatist's art, and he does it by adjusting the moral terms of the action': Stinton 1975: 239; this is too narrow.

to determining *what* moral judgments we make: in life they determine also *whether* we are inclined to respond to a situation with moral evaluation at all; and since morality in tragedy can be no more than a means to the genre's emotive end, there is no reason to doubt that they may have the same effect here.

We will look at a main determinant of sympathetic engagement at the beginning of the next chapter; here it is necessary only to stress our cautionary conclusion. Since the tragedian is not obliged to invoke the moral dimension at all times, the audience should do so only when and as the dramatist invites. Moral evaluation is one resource in his repertoire of emotive devices, one means of manipulating our sympathies: but it is no more than that; it is not unique, or pre-eminent, or constantly applied.

2.6 Review

In this chapter I have tried to clarify the role of the intellectual and moral aspects of tragedy, and in particular to see whether they require any modification of the conclusions reached in Chapter 1.

(a) Tragedy necessarily has intellectual and moral *content*, for the tragic action must presuppose a world with a certain structure, a world, therefore, of which certain general propositions (moral, theological, metaphysical) are true; these propositions must be grasped if one is to understand and respond appropriately to the play. Tragedy also lends itself to intellectualising and moralising *applications*, the validity of which is independent of authorial intention; and it may have beneficial intellectual and moral *effects* on its audience, which would contribute to its overall value.

(b) However, neither external nor internal evidence permits us to conclude that the plays had an intellectual or moral *purpose*: that is, that the *intention* to encourage these applications or bring about these effects typically played a significant role in tragic composition. Therefore, the emotive-hedonist theory of Chapter 1 is not in need of substantial revision.

(c) Consequently, to *interpret* tragedy one must concentrate on its intended emotional force; interpretations preoccupied with the moral and intellectual aspects of tragedy, or assuming such a preoccupation on the part of the dramatist, will tend to be distorted.

(d) Tragedy is sufficiently justified by the aesthetic reward of the emotional experience it was designed to provide; it does not stand in need of such further value as may be conferred by unintended applications or effects. Since tragedy does offer aesthetic reward of this kind, it would be to our loss if in our reading or criticism we neglected this potential.

The older hermeneutic theorists used to include among the *adminicula hermeneutica* the writer's general object: the *scopus dicentis vel scribentis*. These two chapters constitute, as it were, the positive and negative aspects of an *exploratio scopi*, establishing what was and what was not the aim of the tragedian *qua* tragedian. In the next two chapters my attention will turn more to the ways in which the tragedian's aim could be realised in the dramatic text.

3. Person and Plot

3.1 Focus

3.11 Introduction

Critics sometimes ask what a given play is 'about', and would not welcome the obvious answer that *Bacchae* (for example) is about the death of Pentheus and its circumstances. Rather, the play is debated in such terms as these:[1]

> Those who think that Euripides is talking about orgiastic religions like that of Sabazius, or about mass hysteria like St. Vitus's dance, mistake the model for the concept, and miss the whole point of the play's universality. The *Bacchae* is about liberation and its containment.

And not, one is tempted to ask, about the dealings of a particular god with a particular man on a particular occasion? That rhetorical stroke would of course be unfair: the 'about' in this quotation and my 'about' cannot be incompatible in principle, since they work at different levels; and it is certainly true that there are many narrative texts that must be read at both levels, the overt subject being designed (in whole or in part) to serve as the vehicle of a latent subject or general application. But the conclusions which I have reached in the two preceding chapters will I hope have cast doubt on the assumption that a Greek tragedy is a text of this kind; the purpose of a tragedy was rather to realise in as effective a way as possible the emotive potential of a particular *praxis*. Herein lies the danger in our habit of asking what a tragedy might be 'about' at some deeper level. The *telos* of tragedy is emotional effect; and what carries the most concrete and powerful emotional charge is the *praxis* itself: the deeds and sufferings of the individuals portrayed on the stage. If we become preoccupied with the universal implications of the *praxis* (if our attention is generalised and not particularised), then it is likely that we shall fail to appreciate the full intensity of tragic emotion.

This is not to deny that general reflections may enhance the emotional effect of the particular action. The point is well illustrated by the fourth stasimon of *Oedipus Tyrannus* (1186-1222); the opening generalisation (*iô geneai brotôn*) comes with great force after the discovery of Oedipus' pollution but it is not the point to which the ode leads. The ode's structure makes it clear that Sophocles is not using Oedipus' case as a route to a universal truth; on the contrary, the universal truth is the route to the particular case: it is a

---

[1] Stinton 1975: 249 n.1.

preamble, creating a sombre and impressive context within which the appalled lament over Oedipus' downfall that fills three of the ode's four stanzas will move us more profoundly. The universal insecurity of mankind may lack in itself the emotive forcefulness of the individual's suffering, but it provides an apt backdrop against which to unfold the tragedy of an individual human being with deeper emotional resonance.[2] Similarly, when Cassandra suddenly turns just before her final exit from her personal fate to the condition of all mankind, the effect is profoundly moving (*Ag.*1322-30); in isolation, the lines might seem superficial and banal, but in context they take force from, and in turn reinforce, the emotions arising from the particular case; and that is why they are there. The general implications of a tragic *praxis*, therefore, although they are not the point of its representation, do contribute to the *oikeia hêdonê*; that is especially true of those which the poet articulates for us, but is doubtless also true in some degree of those that are left unspoken for our implicit recognition. But whatever force the *praxis* may take from its general implications, it remains the *praxis* itself that tragedy is truly 'about', and it is above all on this that the interpreter's interest must centre.

In fact, we can be more precise about the focus of the tragic audience's attention. We saw in 1.12 that the tragic emotions are to a large extent sympathetic emotions; this implies that tragedy has a *personal* focus. The audience is required to concentrate its attention on key figures in the action, and to do so sympathetically, that is, in such a way that they are involved with and respond to the fortunes and feelings of those characters. I shall use the term 'focus' henceforth in this technical sense, of any character who is serving as a centre of sympathetic attention.[3] The term has already appeared in this sense in our discussion of *Antigone* (2.4): because Antigone is exhibited to us in such a way as to invite pity, we are – or ought to be – inclined to respond to her with pity, and therefore to feel a corresponding antipathy towards the character cast as her persecutor; we saw the same effect in our discussion of the agon in *Orestes* (2.32, 2.5). By placing Antigone or Orestes or any other character in a focal position, the tragedian invites and encourages a competent and cooperative audience to distribute its emotional attachments accordingly; thus the structure of focal prejudices in a play or a scene becomes the fundamental determinant of appropriate evaluation of and

---

[2] Burton has curiously misjudged the force of this ode, finding in it a 'relaxation of tension' inducing in us a 'mood of acceptance' so as to prepare us to listen 'with some measure of calm' to the Messenger (1980: 178). This reading would have been plausible, had Sophocles developed the opening generalisation into a consolatory *topos*: 'All men are prey to misfortune, so your sufferings, Oedipus, are not unique'; but he has done the very opposite: 'All men are prey to misfortune, as one can see from this most extreme case; your fate, Oedipus, is so terrible that I wish I had never seen you.' Relaxation? Acceptance? And if Sophocles had meant us to hear the Messenger's speech with equanimity, why has he contrived that vivid and bloody climax? Not calm, but horror, is his aim; he wants his audience to squirm, to shudder, to weep: and this (as we saw in Chapter 1) is just what the audience want him to make them do.

[3] The nearest approach to this term which I have found in ancient criticism comes in a scholion on S.*OT* 1071, which describes Oedipus as 'the object of pathos with which the whole play is concerned' (*to gar hautou prosôpon esti to peripathes peri ho pasa hê diathesis tou dramatos*).

response to the characters: to their arguments and actions, to their moral qualities, and of course to their conflicts.

3.12 Mobility of focus

I have said that intense engagement with a focal figure is a characteristic of tragedy; but this engagement is not static. One need only consider, for example, the way in which characters are placed in focal position in *Agamemnon* only to be set aside again: Agamemnon himself is made the centre of expectation and anxiety at first, but his appearance on stage is brief; although he retains his importance in the plot after his departure, he ceases to dominate our emotional response; in the scene after his homecoming and defeat, Cassandra becomes the centre of sympathetic attention, but she in turn is dropped with scarcely a second thought, and certainly without a second thought of any sympathetic intensity. We might compare the abandonment of Electra in *Choephori*,[4] and also the way in which Orestes drops out of view at the end of *Eumenides*, to be succeeded as focus in effect by Athens.

This lack of enduring commitment to the focal figures of tragedy has caused difficulties for many modern interpreters. Waldock says clearly what others have felt; in his discussion of 'that slight but insistent trouble with unity that is so curious a feature of Greek drama' (I shall return to this 'trouble' in 3.2), he quotes W. Somerset Maugham as follows:[5]

> It is a psychological trait in human nature that interest is established in persons whom the playwright introduces at the beginning of his play so firmly that if the interest is then switched off to other persons who enter the scene later a sense of disappointment ensues.

Waldock finds this fault characteristic of tragedy, and explains that the technical resources of the genre were limited in such a way that the tragedian was always in danger of exhausting prematurely the material with which he began. If, however, the shift of focus is so common a feature of the work of mature and successful practitioners of the art of Greek tragedy, it is worth asking whether the phenomenon was not found entirely acceptable by its original audience; that is to say, the phenomenon may be a fault only from the point of view of an alien aesthetic. If so, then Greek tragedy will provide a counter-example, refuting the belief of Maugham and Waldock that the desire for static focus is a universal trait of human nature; it would instead be the product of habits encouraged by our own literary culture: an anachronistic distraction which could in principle, and should, be corrected.

Antigone is a useful example of the mobility of focus of which we are speaking. Up to 943, unquestionably, Antigone is the focus of emotional

---

[4] Taplin remarks, somewhat misleadingly, that 'this uncompromising abandonment of a named character is remarkable. While we are familiar with this kind of technique in Euripides, this is the only clear instance in Aeschylus, at least outside *Prom*' (1977: 340).

[5] Waldock 1951: 53.

engagement, and this is (as we saw in 2.4) a fact of some interpretative importance; but after her final exit, remarkably little attention is paid to her, and there is no attempt to foster close engagement: we are not, for example, invited to dwell sympathetically on her sufferings and death; she simply drops out of focus, and our attention is switched instead to Creon as he is crushed by the series of blows which follows in the wake of Antigone's death. The audience is obviously not expected to have any lingering preoccupations with the heroine (if it did, the later scenes of the play would certainly prove disappointing), but is expected to be able to lend ready and fully sympathetic attention to Creon. Creon, however, has hitherto played a relatively unsympathetic role; he is the adversary and persecutor of the focal character, marked by tyrannical traits, impiously dishonouring a corpse. Mobility of focus could not be more clearly demonstrated.

Some other examples are perhaps less clear-cut. In *Hippolytus*, for instance, Euripides has been careful to bring Hippolytus before our eyes at the beginning, and to establish an early emotional engagement with him; Phaedra, therefore, can never be more than a secondary focus. In saying that, as should be obvious from my insistence both on the readiness with which the tragic audience responds to the characters, and on the consequent mobility of their sympathetic attention, I am not trying to minimise the intensity of our response to Phaedra's suffering. What I do want to say is that she is, and is known to be, only an interim focus, so that she cannot usurp Hippolytus' central position in the play as a whole or detract from our response to him in the later scenes. We respond to her fully while she is there, but should be ready to switch our undivided attention to Hippolytus when she is not there.

In two other plays which Waldock mentions (I shall discuss *Ajax* separately in Chapter 5), the main focal character is not in this way displayed at the beginning of the play; but in *Heracles* and *Trachiniae* the hero and his return are, even so, at the centre of everyone's thoughts, so that the shift of focus towards him is well-prepared, and indeed dramatically necessary (the plays would be incomplete without the shift). The shifts of focus in *Andromache* are more violent. Neoptolemus is a significant figure in the background even in the early scenes, and, as in the two plays about the *nostos* of Heracles, his return is anticipated; nevertheless, he is less prominent than Heracles in the earlier parts of his plays. Clearly, it is Andromache who is focal throughout the first part. At 802ff., we are perhaps surprised to find Euripides apparently trying to switch focus to her persecutor Hermione; but if we read this in the light of the mobility of focus which, I am arguing, is characteristic of Greek tragedy, and if we recall how Creon moves from adversary to focus in *Antigone*, we will hesitate to explain this apparent shift of focus away: I do not think, for example, that Hermione's repentance is meant to seem obviously hollow; on the contrary, the image of her as an insecure young woman in a difficult situation, driven by fear into cruelty and now terrified about her own future, is both plausible and potentially effective. Nevertheless, the shift of focus is a kind of misdirection; it is not allowed to develop any great emotional intensity of its own, but instead is swiftly absorbed into a further movement of focus: first as we anticipate fearfully

Neoptolemus' death, and then as we respond to Peleus' grief (Euripides had brought Peleus to our attention earlier, but had not made us anticipate this shift of focus towards him).[6]

I have remarked that the later scenes of *Antigone* would fall flat if the audience were not responsive to a mobile focus; but for many modern readers the scenes do fall flat, and not simply because there is a shift of attention; rather, they object to *this* shift of attention, from Antigone to Creon, which they find anticlimactic. The first point to make is obvious: Creon suffers more harshly than Antigone. She goes to a noble death and reunion with her *philoi*; Creon, formerly so enviable for his good fortune (as the Messenger emphasises: 1161ff.), has been stripped of all that is dear to him, and is left to face a desolate life without compensation. A second point is that Creon's misery is given a correspondingly more intense portrayal. Antigone goes to her death with great dignity and self-control; her final scene of lamentation, which marks the play's first emotional climax, is highly pathetic, but it does not compare for intensity of expression with the play's second emotional climax, in which Creon is presented as a man utterly broken by his suffering. One has only to contrast the style of the two scenes (Antigone's eloquent, highly articulate stanzas with Creon's violent and broken dochmiacs) to see how the emotional pitch has been raised. In these two respects, therefore, the final scenes are offered to us as the emotional climax of the play.

Some would still feel that Creon is not a sufficiently gripping or impressive personality to sustain this climax; this would mean that his suffering, however intense, is less interesting than Antigone's, and that the emotional rhetoric of the closing scenes therefore remains a superficial attempt to work up inadequately rooted feeling. The distrust of and resistance to the power of rhetoric which this reaction displays is anachronistic and distracting; but I suspect that it is also inappropriate to be so much swayed by personality. There are two points to be made. First, it is what happens to a man, more than the kind of man that he is, that is emotive; Oedipus is pitiable because he has committed parricide and incest, because he must endure the agony of knowing that he has done these things, because he reacts to that knowledge by mutilating himself in a particularly painful and horrifying way; his personality is of relatively little weight besides these things. That, at any rate, was Aristotle's view: it is the *muthos* of tragedy that is most powerfully emotive, and *êthos* is entirely subordinate to this imitation of a *praxis* (1450a20-3, 29-35, 53b11-14); and this, I believe, was the common Greek view.[7] Moreover, if we are to be influenced at all by the kind of person

---

[6] One must consider the possible presence of Andromache in the closing scenes: I am very sceptical (cf. Steidle 1968: 119ff., although his reference of 1041 to Hermione is not convincing); it would, in any case do little to offset the shift of focus, unless one adopts a view such as Erbse's – against which, see Mastronarde 1979: 99-101; and that her presence would be thus inert is in itself a strong reason for doubting it. Once one has accepted the tragic mobility of focus, there is little reason to want Andromache reintroduced, or (if one felt compelled to reintroduce her by 1041 and 1246) to want to pay her much attention.

[7] I shall return to this in 3.4. It is interesting that Waldock, in the discussion mentioned earlier, should apparently have overlooked the fact that Hippolytus *is* the first character in whom interest is aroused; his remarks on pp.51-2 (and on pp.52-3, about *Ant.*) suggest that underlying

involved (which of course I do not intend to deny), we must still find the appropriate balance between personality and status; and this is the second point. In 1.3 we examined the importance of *semnotês* in tragedy; as Aristotle's definition shows, tragedy is *essentially* about the deeds of *spoudaioi*, men of high status and fortune. In 2.5 we observed that a man's moral innocence might have less bearing on our pity than the fact that his suffering is 'unworthy' of him, in the non-moral sense of contradicting his exalted status and great good fortune. We may add a technical observation: lyric utterance, the most emotively potent register in tragedy, is reserved for characters of higher status;[8] therefore, lowlier characters have a more restricted access to the devices by which pathos may be evoked. Status, then, is of great importance for tragic emotion; and Antigone is a woman, and therefore (cf.1.3) intrinsically less *spoudaios* than Creon, who is a male and a ruler. Of course, Antigone is a tragic figure in her own right, as (let us say) the Guard could never have been; she is an entirely successful incumbent of the focal position for more than half the play. My point is not meant to diminish Antigone's emotive potential, but to enhance Creon's; because of his status, the shift of attention from Antigone to Creon can and should be experienced as a genuinely climactic movement. It is worth noting that in other plays where there are shifts of focus that modern critics have found difficult, the movement is always similarly up the scale of status, and from a woman to a man: from Deianeira to Heracles, from Phaedra to Hippolytus, from Andromache to Peleus.

It should be obvious, finally, from what I have been saying here that the concept of a focal character is not equivalent to that of the 'hero' or 'main character' of a play; since an audience's sympathetic attention can be directed now in one way, now in another, focus is always focus in a given scene or other limited context. In a genre marked by mobility of focus, to search doggedly for a single hero or main character is pointless, and I would prefer to abandon these two terms.

3.13 Focal and non-focal roles

The Watchman who speaks the prologue of *Agamemnon* is a lively and attractive figure, to whose moods the audience is meant to be responsive; but he is clearly not a focal figure in the sense in which I have defined the term: he is not a major centre of emotional engagement. Indeed, in Greek tragedy he could not be, since, as we noted in 3.12, status is a determinant of tragic potential; this servant is too insignificant a figure to warrant tragic engagement. His dramatic function is rather to prepare the audience to respond appropriately to the tragedy that follows; and he does this by disclosing to them the situation and by setting a mood, or (more precisely, as

---

his unease with the switch of attention is a sense that Hippolytus is a less interesting and attractive personality than Phaedra; it is, then, a misleading *kind* of interest that is at fault, a preoccupation with the interiority of the *dramatis personae*, with their 'essential being' (p.52).

[8] Maas 1962: 53-4; cf. 4.21 below.

we saw in 1.13) by setting a pattern or sequence of moods.[9]

The technique of *Agamemnon* in its subsequent scenes is interesting, in that it makes relatively little use of focus in my sense. The character who dominates our attention for most of the time is Clytaemnestra: but by 'focus' I do not mean simply dominance of the stage; it requires that a character be the centre specifically of sympathetic attention, and we are not (until the final kommos, and even then in a complex and qualified way) invited to sympathetic engagement with Clytaemnestra, who is a sinister and threatening figure. In the parodos, Agamemnon himself is put into the focal position, as the character whose *nostos* is anticipated and about whose fate we are anxious; Clytaemnestra is seen as a threat to him. But Agamemnon's presence is brief, and he is dropped from focus after his exit, as we observed in 3.12; and there is no settled successor. Cassandra takes over for one powerful scene, but she too is soon dropped; and she is made focal partly in order to sustain her role as commentator, for in addition to the relative insignificance of focus, this play is marked by a great bulk of commentary and mood-setting (the quantity of choral lyric is the most obvious sign of this): the Cassandra scene is a way of inserting further commentary, and to be dramatically tolerable (to retain the audience's interest) the commentator must be slipped temporarily into emotional focus. It is clear, surely, why Aeschylus has worked in this way; we saw in 1.13 the importance of anxiety and despondency in the emotional pattern of the play, and the dominance of a threatening adversary, and similarly the bulk of sombre commentary, are ideal means of establishing that mood.[10] It follows that although it is apparently normal technique in Greek tragedy to have a focus of the kind that I have described, the technique can be varied for special emotional effect.

In some plays, the focus is sustained on a single figure throughout; in others, since focus is mobile, we must reckon both with provisional and with climactic foci: though I would emphasise again that provisional focus is no less focal while the character occupies that position. In other plays, we find more than one character occupying the focal position at the same time: sometimes because they are both in the same way victims (for example, Amphitryon and Megara in the first part of *Heracles*), and sometimes in more complex relationships (for example, that between Ion and Creusa in *Ion*). If *foci* mark one extreme of dramatic significance, the other is marked by what one might call *functionaries*; the limiting case is the silent extra, but the Nurse in *Hippolytus* (who, as we saw in 2.5, is there to ensure that things go wrong without blame attaching to the principals) may stand as a more substantial exhibit. Between these two extremes are ranged the more or less important characters used in various ways as sources of interaction with the focal characters; the most obvious kind is the *adversary* (exemplified by Creon in the first part of *Antigone*, or by Clytaemnestra), while the standard suppliant

---

[9] As we shall see in 3.4, the responsiveness of the audience which makes him a suitable instrument for this mood-setting depends on his *êthos*.

[10] It would be unwise to see here a characteristic of Aeschylus: *Per.*, *Su.*, and *ScT* do not encourage us to generalise from *Ag*.

plot (4.41) involves the confrontation of adversary and *assistant*. Another important dramatic role is that of *guide*; some characters are used to mould the audience's understanding and response, perhaps by expounding a situation, by commenting on the significance of events, by setting a mood, or in some other way providing a cue for the audience's reactions. We have seen that the Watchman in *Agamemnon* is a character of this kind.

One 'guide' at whom we might look more closely is Ismene. Her last line in the prologue of *Antigone* comes in a very emphatic position: it is spoken to Antigone's departing back at the very end of the opening scene; and it aptly summarises the implications of the preceding dialogue, the interplay of obligation (*orthôs philê*) and extreme peril (*anous*). But it is not only in the form of such explicit summary that her guidance is offered. The fears which she expresses throughout the argument with her sister underline the extremity of their position and the desperate nature of Antigone's undertaking; they show by contrast the exceptional traits of character that explain Antigone's bold action (the 'foil' is a species of guide); and they articulate, and so stir up and direct, the audience's own fearful engagement with Antigone's fortunes. Furthermore, her references to their family's inauspicious history (like those in the second stasimon) set Antigone's danger against a sombre background, and hint at sinister forces at work in the Labdacid household; this adds a dark, tragic depth to the emotions of the scene. Thus in various ways Ismene's presence is used to mould and direct the attention that Sophocles wishes to concentrate on the focal figure, Antigone. This does not mean, however, that the audience's assessment is identical with Ismene's; there are relevant differences in point of view: not least, that Antigone is a focal figure in a tragedy for the audience, but necessarily not for Ismene. Equally, we can appreciate, but do not fully share, Antigone's point of view. To her, in such a crisis, Ismene must appear a traitor to the family; so Antigone's harsh response is justified: no other response could reasonably be expected from her in these extreme circumstances. The audience, however, being less dominated by the immediate practical demands of the crisis, can make allowance for Ismene's natural weakness and take a more sympathetic view of her than does Antigone. So the audience is not alienated from either sister in this conflict between them; in terms of dramatic role Ismene is far from being an adversary: indeed, she is a subfocus, for her misery on being rejected is a real source of pathos.[11]

I hope that this brief analysis of Ismene's role will have done something at least to offset the impression of crude, schematic oversimplification that my rather breathless account of non-focal roles may have given. That account is obviously not meant to be detailed, nor do I regard it as exhaustive or definitive; but I have found it useful as a way of thinking about the work to which characters are put in the dramatic economy of a play. Of course, such a scheme is only helpful if it enables us to move from its categories towards a clearer perception of the details of a particular text, so that the very

---

[11] T. Wilamowitz (1917: 41) is too extreme in his account of Ismene's function; Winnington-Ingram 1980: 133ff. has some good observations.

vagueness and flexibility of my terms might be seen as an asset; and although it may be possible to devise a subtler and more effective set of categories for this purpose, it would still have to be remembered (as I have tried to remember here) that the dramatic economy of a Greek tragedy is above all an emotive economy, and that the dramatic functions of the characters must ultimately be related (and subordinated) to an emotive end.

3.2 Unity

We observed in 3.12 that the mobility of focus characteristic of tragedy has been felt by some critics to pose a threat to unity; if our attention is switched in the course of a play from one character to another, does this not threaten to break the play up into disjointed parts, or at least into parts with only a superficial connection? That last phrase is not my own; commenting on one of these problematic plays P.T. Stevens writes:[12]

> Is *Andromache*, then, merely a dramatisation of episodes traditional or invented, calculated to stir excitement, anger and pity, and linked together by a superficially adequate causal connection, or is there a character or a theme which inspired the choice of material and manner of presentation, and which gives to the play its own form of dramatic unity?

The account of the play which Stevens here rejects is, of course, threadbare, as any summary so compressed must be; it is also marred by prejudicial rhetoric.[13] But these faults aside, I would not have judged it a bad account; nor would I have thought the play thereby damned. Stevens, however, thinks that such a play would lack unity; and it is interesting to observe where he looks for possible sources of unity: to person and to theme.[14] The problem of unity is posed initially by the absence of any plausible candidate for the title of 'hero' or 'main character', in *Andromache* as in several other plays of the corpus. The conclusion of 3.12, however, was that such a figure is, in Greek tragedy, entirely dispensable. This suggests that person might not have been able to sustain the unifying role which modern critics expect: although some tragedies do focus on a single individual, the readiness with which unified focus is abandoned suggests that it might have been a matter of relative indifference for Greek taste; and the single focus would in that case be, aesthetically speaking, coincidental. On the other hand, Chapter 2 should have made us wary of reading tragedies as expositions of abstract themes; it is doubtful, therefore, whether a 'theme' could be any more successful a

---

[12] Stevens 1971: 8-9.

[13] 'Merely', 'superficially'; does this mean that the connection is at some profounder level inadequate? Inadequate for what? Not (as Stevens recognises) for emotional effect: and this is the *telos* of tragedy. Such 'nothing-buttery' is a common and insidious technique for the infiltration of unargued aesthetic principles; we will see more of it in 4.21-2.

[14] He is far from unique: compare (but one example out of many) Winnington-Ingram on *S.El.* (1980: 228): 'We would appear to be confronted with an interpretative dilemma. Is this a play of ideas or a play about a person?' Or a play about a *praxis* in which several persons appear?

unifying factor in tragedy than the personal focus. It is this approach which Stevens adopts to *Andromache*: the unifying theme, he suggests, is the evils of war. But this is a decidedly tenuous thread in the play, as Stevens concedes, and leaves much of the text unaccounted for; his suggestion is in fact a rather desperate attempt to salvage something from a play that he must regard as fundamentally flawed. It is possible, however, that the fault lies rather in Stevens' aesthetic presuppositions – which are not, of course, peculiar to him.

The notion of 'unity' figures prominently in modern discussion of Greek poetry; but it is an elusive concept, and must be handled with some caution. It is tempting to ask: one *what*? And even if we can answer this question, we will still have to ask: what reason have we to expect a Greek tragedy to be unified in *that* sense: to be a single so-and-so, and to be a single so-and-so by such-and-such a set of criteria? This is the crucial point. 'Unity', however we define it, is a term of aesthetic evaluation; as such it always presupposes and is always relative to some given aesthetic, to the standards of judgment which any given individual or community brings to the literary appreciation of texts. It should be obvious that we cannot afford simply to assume that these standards are historically or culturally invariant; rather, we must try to uncover the criteria of unity implicit in the aesthetics of Greek tragedy itself: that is, in the standards of judgment presupposed in the composition and reception of tragedy in its native environment. Therefore, the elucidation of the notion of 'unity' is a task, not for philosophy or the theory of art, but for historical scholarship.

We have remarked on the prominence of the notion of unity in modern criticism of Greek poetry: no less remarkable is its comparative lack of prominence in ancient criticism. This is a point which we shall have to weigh in due course, but it might be sensible to begin by examining what is certainly the *locus classicus* for dramatic unity in ancient literary criticism, the *Poetics*. Aristotle's is a name frequently invoked in this connection; Stevens, immediately before the passage already cited, casually includes *Andromache* among the plays which 'in varying degrees and in different ways lack unity on Aristotelian canons'. A closer look at what Aristotle actually has to say on the subject, however, will show that his requirements are more modest and more flexible than is widely supposed.

Aristotle is interested in the *sustasis* of a play. His use of this term echoes a passage in Plato's *Phaedrus* to which we shall return shortly, but with one significant difference: unlike Plato, he applies it, not to the ordering of the segments of a text, but to the ordering of events in the story which the text narrates; this is a point which should be borne in mind in what follows. A play, in Aristotle's analysis, has a *muthos* (plot), and this is the *sustasis* (or *sunthesis*) *pragmatôn* – that is, the ordering of the actions which make up the *praxis* which the play narrates or 'imitates' (for all these terms, see 1450a4-5, 32-3, 54a14). The *muthos* is unified if it represents a unified (that is, a single) *praxis* (51a16-19, 31-2, 59a19); and for singleness of *praxis* Aristotle has two criteria. First, causal continuity: the events which make up the *praxis* should follow in due causal consequence one from another (50b27-8, 51b34-5, etc.). Secondly, completeness: the causally continuous sequence of events narrated in the play should have a beginning, a middle (more precisely, middle parts, in the plural: *mesa* 59a20, cf. Pl.*Phdr*.264c4), and an end; these terms, too, he defines with reference to causal sequence (50b26-33, 59a19-20). These two causally based criteria allow Aristotle to reject two devices for securing unity of *muthos* which he regards as inadequate, though widely employed. A *muthos*, he argues, is not unified simply because it narrates events drawn from a single man's career (50b16-19), nor simply because it narrates events that occurred within a single span of time (59a21-30). For neither principle guarantees a causal connection between the events which it gathers together; a 'middle part' selected might contribute nothing to the bringing about of the final event of the *praxis* (cf. 59a24-9).

It is interesting to note that in his comments on plots based on the experiences of a single figure, Aristotle shows no sign of anything like the modern sensitivity to personal interest, and does not expect it of his opponents; the argument ignores considerations of persisting personal focus, and turns solely on causal continuity. Aristotle makes the reasonable point that the causal continuity of a sequence of events is not secured by their befalling one man; many unrelated things happen in the course of a man's life. Conversely, we might add, two events do not necessarily fail of causal connection simply because they befall different people; and this observation is highly relevant to the unity of plays with mobile focus. If the original audience of tragedy found Aristotle's criteria of continuity and completeness of *praxis* sufficient conditions of unity, then it would be no surprise that we find certain plays resistant to the kinds of personal and thematic integration favoured by modern criticism. It seems, then, that Aristotle's 'causal' theory of unity does help us to explain certain features of the tragic corpus that we would otherwise find problematic; and this is a strong argument in favour of accepting that theory as an essentially correct account of the underlying aesthetics of Greek tragedy. If, like Stevens, we find the resultant unity 'superficial', that is our loss.

It is widely believed that Aristotle would have applied his criteria of unity in a highly restrictive way; if so, then it is clear from the practice of the tragedians that his view was in this respect exaggerated and unrepresentative of Greek taste in general. But a more permissive reading is possible. First of all, we may note that Aristotle accepted as satisfying his criteria of unity a *praxis* as long and involved as the Trojan War in its entirety; this, he suggests, could have been treated as a single *praxis*, although with the disadvantage that the result would be either too long for an audience to assimilate, or else (if compressed within a narrower compass) too complex for them to follow (59a29-35).[15] Furthermore, he apparently regards it as a virtue in Homer's

---

[15] This passage may be paraphrased: 'Most other poets write (single-figure or) single-period plots, and so fail completely to achieve unity of *praxis*. Homer is far better: he does not treat even the Trojan War in its entirety (legitimate though this would have been so far as unity of *praxis* is concerned; but it would have laboured under the disadvantage of being either *ouk eusunoptos* or *katapeplegmenos*); instead, he has selected one part of that story.' Lucas is therefore wrong to comment on 59b1: 'The first *kai* ... must be rendered 'or', the second could as well be explanatory' (1968: 217); both must be rendered 'or': the *mian praxin polumerê* refers to something

treatment of his more restricted *muthos* that he intersperses it with passages (such as the Catalogue of Ships) which do not narrate events drawn from the causally connected sequence constituting the *praxis* of which his *muthos* is an imitation (59a35-7). This is a controversial point, and there is (as often in the *Poetics*) a source of confusion in Aristotle's use of his terms; I believe that he applies the term *epeisodion* to two different kinds of scene (I am not concerned with the further technical sense defined in 52b16, 20-1). The *epeisodia* in 55b1-16 are parts of the main *muthos*; for example, the escape of Orestes and Iphigeneia in Euripides' first *Iphigeneia* is mentioned in Aristotle's universalised abstract of that play's *muthos* (*sôtêria* 55b12): and it becomes an *epeisodion* when elaborated for dramatic representation with circumstantial detail appropriate to the particularised *muthos* (in this case, the involvement of Orestes suggests the device by which the escape is effected: *hê sôtêria dia tês katharseôs* 55b14-15).[16] But this does not seem to be the sense in the passage about Homer: for one cannot use parts of a *muthos* to interrupt (*dialambanein*) the narrative of that same *muthos*; these *epeisodia* therefore, must be insertions that are not part of the main *muthos*.[17] There will naturally be less scope for such intrusions in tragedy than in epic, since it is a less expansive form (cf. 55b15-16, 59b17-22); the point stands nevertheless that Aristotle is not compelled by his theory of unity to demand an exclusive concern with that sequence of events that is the unified and unifying *praxis* of the play.

The obvious objection to this 'permissive' reading of Aristotle is the apparently strict attitude which he adopts in 51a30-5; but there is in fact no conflict. He there reiterates his insistence that the *muthos*, to be unified, must be the imitation of a single, complete *praxis*, that is, of one closed, causally connected sequence of events. Because such a series is causally connected, no part of it can be removed or transposed without disruption of the sequence; an event which could be removed or transposed without such disruption is not part of the single complete *praxis* (such events one might well find in the defective *muthos* of a single-figure play, the events of which are not necessarily related causally to each other: 51a16-30). Aristotle could quite consistently adopt this strict attitude to *muthos* while being tolerant of episodes that are not part of the *muthos*. That is to say, he could require that a play represent at least and predominantly a single connected series of events; and since this

---

like the Trojan War *praxis* (from which Homer took a single *meros*), and is therefore in contrast with the single-figure and single-period plots which Aristotle flatly rejects.

[16] For this passage, see Nickau 1966: 160-5.

[17] Aristotle is saying: 'Homer could have treated the whole Trojan War, a single *praxis* with many parts (*merê*); but he does not: instead he has taken one *meros* and used many other *merê* to break up the main narrative.' Nickau interprets this passage in conformity with the other sense of *epeisodion*, but I do not find his argument convincing (the example of the Catalogue would, I think, be decisive, but Nickau deletes this phrase, following the Arabic: since the omission can be explained palaeographically, this is hazardous). His reference to the papyrus scholion on *Il*.21.240 is unavailing: it is true that Achilles' battle with the river is an essential transition to the battle of the gods; but that itself is an episode in the second sense – it has neither antecedent nor consequence in the *praxis* of the *Iliad*, and does not advance the *muthos* at all.

series would have a crucial structural role, holding the play together as its core or backbone, he could reasonably take a strict view of it; but he need not impose the more stringent requirement that the play represent *only* events of that series. If he did refrain from imposing that further requirement, his objection to plays based on a single person or a single period of time would still stand; for in such plays it would be impossible to discern the backbone of a single *praxis* within the mass of causally inessential episodes. The inclusion of such episodes within a play that did possess a causal backbone might be justified by some other contribution that it made to the play: for example, it might enhance (let us say, by contrast) the emotional effect of some part of the *muthos* proper; and this is a form of justification to which Aristotle would surely have been sympathetic, since (as we saw in 1.11) he recognised that pleasurable emotional effect was the *telos* of tragedy, and that the *muthos* was only the most important of the means to that end.

I have said that Aristotle's causal theory, permissively interpreted, is essentially correct; but some qualifications are necessary. Aristotle concentrates on the unity of the *muthos*, as something that can be abstracted from the dramatic text and analysed for its coherence; but there is a danger both in the abstraction and in the analysis of distorting the theatrical reality of drama. In the theatre, the audience does not analyse; it is therefore the *impression* of continuity and completeness that is essential, and this does not depend solely on such continuity and completeness as analysis might find (I shall return to this point in 3.3). Aristotle would have no difficulty with this qualification, since he himself gives an example of two events that give an impression of happening *di' allêla*, although analysis would show that they are not causally connected, and he observes that this is as effective as occurrence actually *di' allêla* (52a4-10). That example covers continuity; but the qualification is even more clearly necessary in the case of completeness: for there are in fact no closed causal sequences such as are required by Aristotle's definition of beginning and end (50b27-30). What is essential about the beginning of a plot is not that it should have no causal antecedents (which is impossible), but that the audience should not be left asking unanswered questions about the causal antecedents of the plot; and they will not be inclined to ask such questions if they are given enough information in the course of the play to understand what is being played out before them. Similarly, the end of the plot need not be an event without consequences; but it can and, by the modified Aristotelian requirement, should be such as to leave the audience free of unanswered questions about possible consequences.

The abstraction from the dramatic text, too, is dangerous; in the theatre it is not the pure *muthos* that creates an impression of continuity and completeness, but the *muthos* as realised in the dramatic text – that is, in the words spoken and the deeds done on stage. There are formal devices which may reinforce, or indeed create, an impression of continuity; for example, our sense of the continuity of *Andromache* in its transition from the rescue of Andromache to the intrigue against Neoptolemus is enhanced by the fact that the actions both arise out of Neoptolemus' marriage to Hermione – who is the pivotal figure (cf. 3.12).[18] In this context, we should note that various kinds of echo or interconnection between the parts of a play can help to reinforce the impression of continuity; and here the personal and thematic factors which I criticised earlier may find a unifying role, although a subordinate one. As for the impression of completeness, the element of formal closure is of considerable importance. The brief choral tags with which most plays end have often been assailed for their banality, but this is to miss their point; they are there, not to say something of importance, but to bring the plays to a marked and formally satisfying end. Euripides' use of the *deus* and of concluding *aitia* can be viewed in the same way: 'It is clear that when an *aition* turns up the play is over. It reinforces our feeling of finality.'[19]

Euripides' *deus* speeches also, and more obviously, contribute to the completion of the narrative by expounding the course of events consequent on the last action of the play (it is because Euripides often gives more information than is necessary for this purpose that one looks for additional functions, such as the formal or – as in 2.33 – the patriotic and religious). We must recall here that the Aristotelian beginning, middle and end are parts of the *praxis*, not of the play. The *praxis* may include events outside the span of time in which the actions staged in the play fall; and these events must be represented obliquely in the play, just as some events concurrent with the stage-action are made known only by report (for example, in a Messenger-speech: 4.43). The beginning of the *praxis* might be narrated in a prologue speech of the kind that Euripides favours, or in some other kind of retrospective passage; in *Agamemnon*, for example, Aeschylus reveals by stages more and more of the past: the sacrifice of Iphigeneia in the parados, the Thyestean banquet in Cassandra's scene. Similarly the end of a *praxis* may be reported in a prophetic speech analogous to the retrospective prologue (the *deus* is a case in point), or may be disclosed in a less formal way: the *praxis* of *Trachiniae*, for example, is carried beyond the final *exeunt* by the series of instructions which Heracles gives his son. There is, of course, considerable disagreement about how far the *praxis* of this play is in fact carried: the pyre is beyond doubt, and the marriage of Hyllus to Iole, but what of the apotheosis of Heracles? I cannot answer this question with any confidence, but would offer a word of caution. An audience expecting completeness would not be inclined to press unanswered questions on a play by thinking beyond what is given in it; they will not (to take an extreme example) be inclined to worry as they come away from *Ion* about what was to happen to poor old Xuthus.[20] One might doubt, therefore, whether such an audience could be expected to think forward even to so familiar an event as the apotheosis without more decisive prompting than can be found in the text of *Trachiniae*.[21]

[18] Cf. Steidle 1968: 118-31 (who, however, overestimates the *relative* importance of this as against simple continuity of plot); a premature impression of completeness is avoided in this play by the *nostos* plot: cf. 4.41.

[19] Kitto 1961: 286.

[20] 'We are bound to feel sorry at what is in store for him': Owen 1939: xxx.

[21] One could probably make sense of the emotional effect of the apotheosis if one recalls the possibility of a slight final relief of tragic intensity (cf. 2.5); but I find no sign of such relief in the

I would distinguish this technique of prospective completion of the *praxis* from the device I term 'foreshadowing'. A number of plays in the corpus achieve impressive emotional effects by alluding to an unnarrated sequel: *Trojan Women*, in which the destruction of the Greek fleet is predicted, is a good example,[22] and the second *Oedipus*, foreboding the fatal conflict of the two brothers and Antigone's consequent death, perhaps the supreme example. It would, I think, be strained to include these events in the *praxis* of either play, for their function is not to bring the sequence of events narrated in the play to a point of rest; in both plays, the *praxis* has an ending, and the foreshadowing points beyond this, lifting a little the veil which the illusion of completeness would normally drape over the causal consequences of the events of that *praxis*. This means that the principle of completeness must be further qualified, but not that it is destroyed: in each case, the *praxis* does come to a natural point of rest, and the text is formally closed; the foreshadowing does not leave the audience perplexed by unanswered questions about the future, but does significantly add to the emotional force of some part of the play. Thus the mild violation of closure which the foreshadowing entails is justified by the contribution it makes to the *oîkeia hêdonê* of tragedy.

I have argued that the tendency of modern criticism to look for unity in focus or in theme is mistaken; rather, we should look to causal continuity of *praxis*, since in the aesthetics of tragedy it is this which, with certain qualifications, supplies the necessary and sufficient condition of dramatic unity. One might go on to ask: why does unity of this kind seem to modern critics to be, in Stevens' word, 'superficial'? I am not sure that I can supply the answer to this question; but one possible approach would be to consider the place which a unifying element is expected to occupy in the functional hierarchy of its text. It could be argued that modern critics look for a unifying element at the top of this hierarchy: that is, something is sought to which every other element in the text is, in the last analysis, functionally subordinate; something which will explain what those elements are there for. A causal criterion of unity does not meet this requirement. The causally continuous *praxis* is not ultimately the *telos* of the play, but exists to serve a purpose beyond itself: in the view of tragedy that I have proposed, it exists to sustain emotive and ancillary effects; and these may constitute in any given play a disparate array of otherwise unrelated ends. A metaphor might help to illustrate the point: modern criticism looks for the unity of an umbrella (a single covering formula or function, under which all the elements of the text are gathered); continuity of *praxis* offers only a platform which may accommodate a variety of guests who need not all be there for the same

---

text of *Tr.* – for example, in Hyllus' last spech; the weight would have to rest entirely on the unmentioned apotheosis: and this should excite suspicion. (The closing lines of the Chorus cannot do anything to alter the mood, since such tags tend not to carry much weight, being formal in function: cf. 4.21iii.)

[22] J.R. Wilson (1967) believes that the relevant part of this prologue is interpolated; this is absurd, and his arguments mostly carry little weight; but Athene's opening is certainly abrupt: a lacuna? (For the foreshadowing, see Meridor 1984: 209-11.)

reason. Euripides' *Suppliants* is a case in point. The *praxis* of this play is causally continuous (one might feel, and precisely on causal grounds, that the episode of Iphis and Evadne is inadequately motivated: but this is not part of the main structure); but this continuity is used as the base on which a sequence of diverse emotional effects is constructed: the pathos of the supplication and initial rebuff; the patriotic celebration of their acceptance and vindication (cf. 2.33); the grief of lamentation over the recovered corpses. The 'umbrella' instincts of modern criticism are rather clearly displayed in recent discussion of this play: where it has not been simply downgraded as a piece deficient in unity, 'defences' have sought an integrating formula that would assign to the divergent emotional movements converging point.[23]

That this integrating instinct is misplaced in the criticism of Greek poetry might become clearer if we look for a further principle that would govern the treatment of material within the unified frame established by the principles of continuity and closure; a survey of Greek criticism would reveal as the prime candidate *poikilia*, diversity. That this is a concept of great importance in Greek literary aesthetics from an early period no reader of Pindar will doubt; and in a fragment of the fourth-century tragedian Astydamas one finds the claim that the poet should furnish for his audience a varied feast (*poikilên euôkhian*).[24] The term occurs very frequently indeed in Greek critical writing: often it is applied to stylistic variation and embellishment;[25] but it is also freely used of the structural diversity that comes through the use of digression and contrasting material.[26] It is found in this latter application in the scholia,[27] and also in Aristotle. He regards an excess of *poikilia*, such as might result from compressing a great deal of material into too narrow a compass, as a fault (59a34); but he accepts that the quality is in itself a desirable one, and regrets that the scope for it is more limited in tragedy than in epic (59b26-31). The reason which Aristotle gives here for valuing *poikilia* is an obvious one: uniformity is dull, variety is pleasant, refreshing, retentive of interest and attention (cf. *Rhet.* 1371a25-6). The attractiveness of diversity allows us to class it as a kind of ancillary pleasure (cf. 1.2); so Dionysius, commenting with approval on the *poikilia* which Herodotus cultivated (he says) in emulation of Homer, observes that change is a source of variety and pleasure in historiography (*hêdu khrêma ... hê metabolê kai poikilon: ad Pomp.*3.11, U-R II 236.9-15). But *poikilia* may also contribute directly to the primary

---

[23] E.g. Fitton 1961 (who makes liberal use of irony to bring the play's diversity of moods under one heading) or Shaw 1982.

[24] Cf. Pi. *O*.3.8, 4.2, 6.84; *P*.9.77; *N*.4.14, 5.42; fr.179, 194; see Maehler 1963: 70, 90. Astydamas fr.4.1; the *euôkhia* metaphor appears also in Metagenes fr.14 K, where too it arguably implies *poikilia*: but this depends on one's understanding of the controversial phrase *kat' epeisodion metaballô ton logon* (discussed in Norwood 1930). It is unfortunate that the implications of this and of Cratinus fr.195 K, the earliest extant uses of the term 'episode', are so uncertain.

[25] E.g. Isocr. 5.27, 9.9; D.H. *Comp.* 19 (U-R II 84.7-12, cf. 87.12-16 etc.).

[26] E.g. D.H. *Thuc.* 7 (U-R I 333.22-4), *ad Pomp.*3.11 (U-R II 236.9-15) etc. I hope to undertake elsewhere a more systematic study of ancient theories of unity, diversity and digression in literary works.

[27] Cf. Chapter 1 n.38; see also Bywater 1909: 307 (on *Poet.*1459a37). We may note in passing that, as usual, Plato disapproved on moral grounds of *poikilia* in music (*Rep.*399e, *Laws* 812de) and in the *mimêsis* of character (*Rep.*604d-5a); cf. also *Mnx.*812d.

pleasure of tragedy: I have already mentioned the possibility that contrasting episodes (not integral to the *muthos*) may be used to enhance the emotional effect of the main narrative; but it is also emotionally effective if the poet builds the *muthos* itself out of contrasting episodes. A scholion on the *Iliad* (21.34 BT), after commenting on Homer's way of varying his narrative, mentions *peripeteia* as an emotive use of *poikilia* (*poikilon on kai theatrikon kai kinêtikon*); and Plutarch explains that poetry makes especial use of *to poikilon* because change and surprise produce the greatest *ekplêxis*, and therefore the greatest pleasure (*kharis: Mor.* 25d).

This emphasis in ancient criticism on the virtues of diversity corresponds to the relative lack of interest in the notion of unity. To the best of my knowledge, the scholia on Homer and on tragedy make no use of the concept at all; they are concerned with what they call *oikonomia*, but mean by this simply dramatic or narrative management, the effective ordering of incidents and episodes.[28] A similar concern is found in Plato. He observes that tragedy is not just a random concatenation of speeches of varying emotional tones, but their appropriate relative disposition (*hê toutôn sustasis prepousa allêlois kai tôi holôi sunistamenê: Phdr.* 269ce, cf. 264ae); he illustrates the point by quoting an epigram, the four end-stopped lines of which could without loss be shuffled around into any order (264d). Thus he suggests that the construction of a speech should resemble the physical constitution of an animal: it should have all the necessary parts, and they should all be appropriately placed, so that one could in each case explain by reference to its function why a particular section – or limb – ought to be just where it is (264bc). This image is taken up by Aristotle, of course, and brought into more immediate contact with the concept of unity (59a20; cf. 50b34-51a6). He is followed by 'Longinus', who uses the image twice, though without developing the idea (10.1, 40.1); and the image is also found in connection with historiography: but even here it is closely linked to the concern for *poikilia*.[29] This is a strikingly meagre haul; and if one wishes to find a Greek critical term for that constancy of theme and focus so admired by modern critics, one might (with pardonable exaggeration) choose *homoeideia*: the vice of dull uniformity antithetical to the prized virtue of *poikilia*.

The value placed on *poikilia* is not more than permissive: that is, *poikilia* is not the only thing valued, so that a dramatist is always free if he sees fit to neglect it in pursuit of some compensating virtue. For example, the intensity of a play might be heightened by concentrating on a single effect, if only the pitfall of *to homoeides* is avoided. Nevertheless, *poikilia* is valued, and is an important principle of artistic construction in Greek tragedy; and for that reason we should be particularly wary of attempts to press on the plays more stringent criteria of unity than the two derived from our permissive reading of Aristotle. For *poikilia* is a centrifugal principle; it tends to promote divergence from any single unifying element that might be seized upon by those seeking some stricter kind of unity than that endorsed by Aristotle.

[28] Cf. Richardson 1980: 269 & n.9.
[29] E.g. D.H. *ad Pomp.*3.14 (U-R II 238.8-11); Polybius 1.3.3, 14.12.5; D.S. 20.1.5 (with 20.2.1 for *poikilia*).

Nevertheless, some restraint on the pursuit of diversity clearly is needed. As Plato would say, the parts of a tragedy, however diverse and divergent, should not be put together chaotically, but should sit appropriately with each other and with the whole which they together form. But how are we to judge what is 'appropriate'? Clearly, this must be determined in the light of the *telos* of tragedy, and we must therefore consult the theory of tragedy developed in Chapter 1. Tragedy aims to produce an aesthetically satisfying sequence of emotional experiences, supplemented by ancillary pleasures, under the restraint of tragic dignity. What we must ask of any segment of a play, therefore, of its selection, its placing and its treatment, is first of all: does it provide (or is it causally antecedent to) some emotional or ancillary effect? Then: does it do so without detracting materially from the primary or ancillary pleasure afforded by any other segment? And finally: does it, when combined with these other segments, contribute towards a sequence of emotional and ancillary experiences that is, as a whole, aesthetically satisfying? (In asking this last question we have not, as it might at first sight appear, reverted to an 'umbrella' concept of unity: for it may still be that no integrated account could be given of the play's end, save the trivial one: the conjunction of this and this and this effect; except in this trivial sense, to ask whether such a sequence of effects is for a given audience aesthetically satisfying is not necessarily also to ask whether they subserve a shared higher-order end.) If for all parts of a tragedy the answer to each of these questions is 'Yes', and if no part violates the principle of dignity (or some other relevant constraint), then we have in the highest degree *hê toutôn sustasis prepousa allêlois kai tôi holôi sunistamenê*.

Two points must be added, however. First, that this judgment would be one only of structural excellence. It would still be possible to say that the structurally flawless play was inferior to some other and structurally imperfect play: for its effects might individually or conjointly prove less profound or less rewarding; the question of coherence, as we might call it, is distinct from the question of quality. Secondly, the principle of coherence is in one sense empty; it raises but leaves unanswered the questions: what for the audience of Greek tragedy constituted a rewarding experience of tragic emotion? In what ways could emotional effect be enhanced? When would ancillary pleasures conflict with or distract from each other or the primary tragic pleasure? For there is still a danger of misunderstanding if we use our own tastes uncritically in the interpretation (I do not say: the evaluation) of plays that presuppose a different aesthetic. To answer these questions would require an exploration in greater depth and detail of the practice of the Greek tragedians than is possible in this volume: this and the subsequent chapter offer some suggestions on a handful of points; but naturally the scope of this study will not permit the exploration to be taken very far. The principle of coherence, then, does not answer all the questions which it raises; but it does at least raise some tolerably clear and demonstrably relevant questions: and this, it might be argued, is an improvement on the notion of 'unity' from which we began.

I have in this section proposed four principles of tragic construction:

continuity, closure, diversity and coherence. It might be helpful now to consider briefly how these principles would apply to some problematic cases from the tragic corpus. I have chosen two plays by Euripides. First, *Heracles*. The structure of this play has often been criticised on the grounds that the 'second reversal' – Heracles' madness and his killing of his children – is causally inconsequent and introduces a second action unrelated to the drama of supplication and rescue with which the play begins. So, for example, Stinton:[30]

> The *Heracles* is evidently nothing like the kind of play Aristotle regarded as essentially tragic ... Its peculiarity, apart from some apparent structural weaknesses and lack of cohesion, is that the visitation of Lyssa which causes the tragic act is not grounded in any part of the previous action, and it has no kind of moral justification. Its only motive as given in the play is the malign jealousy of Hera, a datum of the myth from Homer on.

As Stinton says, the jealousy of Hera is a datum of the myth: therefore, the second reversal is causally grounded in the previous action at least to this extent, that it was an action involving Heracles and leading to his winning glory and good fortune; for, given that Hera is his enemy, it is certainly in accordance with probability, if not with necessity, that his success will provoke a counter-stroke from her. Moreover, since Heracles' good fortune is in part the rescue of his children, it is quite reasonable of Hera to choose the children as the point of her attack; and although it would, from an analytical point of view, have been no less causally connected had Heracles been pitched into some other misfortune by Hera's counter-attack, by staying with the children Euripides has enhanced the impression of continuity (compare the use of the marriage in *Andromache*, discussed earlier). To be sure, the audience is not directed to recall Hera's enmity in the earlier scenes (there is one incidental reference): but Euripides must be allowed to achieve a surprise without preemptively weakening its effect of *ekplêxis*; as Aristotle was aware, surprise is a powerful emotive device (52a2-4: cf. 1.12iv). The point is that when the attack does occur, the audience will not find it an unintelligible *non sequitur*, but at once understands it as a natural consequence in the light of a familiar mythological datum. The play, then, has an adequate causal frame, securing unity; and the diversity of the *praxis* within that frame needs no argument: an action of pathos and cliff-hanging tension passes into jubilant triumph; that is at once shattered by an unexpected and calamitous assault on the victor; and the play continues with the desolate aftermath. The emotive use of *poikilia* (derived here from sudden reversal) could not be more clearly displayed: and the diverse elements surely combine to form a sequence that is *ekplêktikôtaton*, both exciting and moving.[31]

Trojan Women is a more complex case. Its construction is perfectly

[30] Stinton 1975: 249-50.

[31] It will be obvious, after Chapter 2, that I have no time at all for Chalk's discussion of unity in this play: he finds in the action of the play 'a coherent abstract argument' about 'theories of *aretê*' (1962: 8, 10); a quaint example of intellectualisation.

consistent with my own, rather flexible adaptation of Aristotle's theory; indeed, the play from this point of view appears very finely made. With Aristotle's own account as it stands in *Poetics*, the play cannot be reconciled, although its incompatibility is not so straightforward as is sometimes supposed. Grube, for example, finds in this play clear evidence that Euripides would not have accepted Aristotle's views:[32]

> The *Trojan Women* ... has no action or plot in the Aristotelian sense. A number of incidents are chosen, from a great number that could have been chosen, to illustrate the sufferings of the vanquished, but there is not between them that inevitable connection which Aristotle declared to be essential. If unity of plot is to be the criterion, the play must be condemned out of hand. Nevertheless, these incidents have complete dramatic relevance and together form a simple and clear emotional pattern.

It is admirable that Grube recognises and emphasises the importance of the play's emotional economy; but there is more to be said about the plot. The play's point of departure is the last group of captive women awaiting distribution to Greek masters after the fall of Troy (32-44); it comes to rest when those of them still left are taken away to their assigned masters, while the city is finally razed (1260-71). This is a fair beginning and end by Aristotelian standards, and secures closure; is there a suitable middle to give continuity? Yes: for what would necessarily or probably occur as the consequence of this beginning and the antecedent of this end? What does occur: the women would be assigned their various fates. So the play does have a plot which is unified, that is, which imitates a single *praxis*, a closed and causally connected series of events. And yet there is something odd about this middle: the incidents which together constitute it are causally related to the beginning and end, but they are not causally dependent on each other; this means that the play satisfies Aristotle's definition of an 'episodic' plot (51b33-5), and we must therefore assume that he would not have approved. But in that case, he is open to criticism. He himself implies elsewhere that the beginning and end of a *praxis* need not be linked by a *single* line of causal connection; if an epic narrates two simultaneous events, then necessarily it will have episodes that do not follow each other in necessary or probable sequence: and Aristotle admires epic for being able to do just that (59b22-6). It is possible, therefore, that Aristotle has defined the episodic plot in a way more restrictive than he might have wished. One would hope so: his position as stated neglects the middle ground between plays with a unilinear causal structure, and plays lacking causal structure altogether (such as single-figure and single-period plots). And this middle ground ought not to have been neglected; for there is a most substantial difference between the episodes of *Trojan Women*, which together make up a causally integrated middle, and an episode like Io's in *Prometheus*: a causally irrelevant occurrence usurping a disproportionately large place in a play already decidedly weak in causal structure. This, surely, and not the more careful construction of Euripides'

[32] Grube 1941: 80.

play, is what warrants condemnation as episodic.[33]

If there is no causal dependence between the various incidents which constitute the play's middle, another principle is required to determine the arrangement of episodes within that series; and this principle is, as Grube saw, provided by the emotional *telos* of tragedy.[34] The lament over the corpse is a natural tragic climax (as in *Andr.*) because of its intrinsically intense pathos; its position at the end of the medial series is therefore secure, which means in turn that Andromache's scene should not be too far separated from this, its sequel. Cassandra's scene is most apt in first place, both because her foreknowledge takes up the ironical foreshadowing of the victors' fate in the prologue, and because the spectacular entry of the raving prophetess initiates the series most strikingly, but would perhaps have been disruptive at any later point. This gives the order: Cassandra-Andromache-corpse. Polyxena is reasonably deprived of a scene to avoid a repetitive sequence of scenes with a similar structure; her fate is represented obliquely, therefore, and (as we shall see) used as a binding device. Helen, however, is anything but repetitive. She is not out of place in this *praxis*, for we have been warned that she is among the captive women whose fate remains to be decided (34-5); but her fate will be rather different from that of the Trojans, so that the structure and tone of her scene will inevitably provide a contrast. The principle of diversity recommends her, therefore, and Euripides enhances the contrast by turning the scene into a rhetorical debate, affording its own kind of ancillary pleasure (cf. 4.22); this contrast with the pathos of the other scenes, and the mockery of the captives' sufferings when the guilty woman escapes with obvious impunity, intensify in turn the emotional effect (and primary pleasure) of the surrounding misery: and this effect will be most striking if the contrast is inserted between the two causally sequential scenes (Andromache and the corpse) that are also the most brutal and tragic parts of the play's middle.

So much for the order of scenes; we should now observe how Euripides has contrived to give to this sequence of episodes an *impression* of continuity and movement. Consider first the prologue, parodos and first two scenes: Cassandra is mentioned by Poseidon (41-4), and her entry is anticipated in the parodos (168-72); then comes her scene; and this is followed by a retrospective allusion in the following scene (616-19). Poseidon also reveals to the audience Polyxena's fate (39-40); at the beginning of the first scene, then, we see that Hecuba is deceived (260-71), and when she takes up the theme later (502) we pity her ignorance and the pain of the coming disclosure; this disclosure occurs at the beginning of the following scene (622-30), and it

---

[33] *PV* is, I think, the only play in the extant tragic corpus that is fundamentally flawed by the standards of my structural criteria; this I find reassuring, for it does seem to me (despite some fine writing) an uncommonly feeble play. The weakness in plot-construction is quite unlike anything else that we find in Aeschylus: which does not, of course, prove that it is not by him, but does make one sympathetic to arguments to that effect (cf. Introduction n.4).

[34] Grube is mistaken, however, when he suggests that the episodes have been chosen from a wide field of possibilities: could one recall any other incidents that involved well-known Trojan women of high status in this span of time?

provides Andromache with the theme of her rhesis (636-83: esp. 641-2, 679-80). Here, then, we have two developing sequences of allusion that bind these episodes together and suggest an unfolding pattern of events. By this stage, of course, we are already in the Andromache-sequence, and continuity is no longer a problem: Hecuba will find some consolation in thinking of the child's future (701-5), an illusory hope at once shattered by Talthybius' cruel news (709-25); and the scene with the child's body is in every sense a necessary or probable sequel to this development. So Euripides has ordered and connected the episodes of his play with craft to avoid the potential weaknesses of a play the middle parts of which, though causally integral as a group, are causally independent of each other. The result, in my view, is flawless: *hê toutôn sustasis prepousa allêlois te kai tôi holôi sunistamenê.*

3.3 Conviction

If we look closely at what is said in *Trachiniae* about oracles, a number of difficulties come to light; for ease, I enumerate the references:

(i) 43-8: Heracles left a tablet with some reference to the fifteenth month from his departure (I believe these lines to be genuine).
(ii) 74-82: Heracles left oracles about Euboea (if *khôras* is right: the emendations are not convincing) saying that he will either die or else live the rest of his life happy (*ton loipon êdê bioton euaiôn' ekhein*).
(iii) 157-74: the tablet, the 15-month period and the alternative of death or an untroubled life (*to loipon êdê zên alupêtôi biôi*) are here brought together; it is added that the oracle came from Dodona.
(iv) 821-31: the 'old oracle' of which the Chorus speaks here has some surprises: a twelve-year period is mentioned; and instead of the alternatives of (ii) and (iii) we have a simple prediction of rest from toil, ironically interpreted as death.
(v) 1159-1163: a previously unmentioned oracle from Zeus (origin unspecified, but old) riddling about the agent of death.
(vi) 1164-73: the Dodona oracle ('new') predicting release from toil at this time.

Minor loose ends need not delay us long: the isolated local reference of (i), the vagueness of the chronology (how do the fifteen months of (i) and (iii) relate to the twelve years of (iv)? note also the reference in 648 to a twelve-month absence; (iv) is 'old', but (vi) is 'new' – but perhaps only by contrast with (v)), the unheralded appearance of (v); it is the fluid content of the oracle that is of most interest: in (ii) and (iii) an open conditional, in (iv) and (vi) a riddling categorical. Is Sophocles inconsistent? One might try to rationalise by claiming that Deianeira has misremembered the content; but that is merely to substitute an implausibility: why should she have dreamed up out of nothing this reference to her husband's death?

Criticism of inconsistencies and implausibilities was, we know, a staple of

Greek literary scholarship. In the scholia, the comment that something is 'unconvincing' (*apithanon*) is common enough. For example, in *Hecuba* Euripides has the story of Odysseus' infiltration of Troy so that it is Hecuba herself, and not Helen (as in *Od*.4), who recognises and protects him; this is evidently implausible, and is condemned as such in the note on 241: the charge is repeated at 281, with the extenuating plea that the implausibility is useful for the supplication of Odysseus by Hecuba in this scene.[35] This kind of defence is recommended by Aristotle in the section of the *Poetics* that deals with Homeric problems: 'If a poem contains an impossibility, this is a fault; but it is justified if it achieves the *telos* [sc. of *poiêtikê*]'; we know that he regards pleasurable emotion as the *telos* of the art of poetry, and accordingly he goes on to explain: 'if that or another passage is thereby rendered *ekplêktikôteron*' (1460b22-6: this is the model for my 'Aristotelian' defence of causally inessential episodes in 3.2). The application of this defence to the fluid oracle of *Trachiniae* is clear enough. In the early scenes of the play the characters must be uncertain of the future and anxious: the apparently unqualified optimism of the oracle in its later form would have interfered with this, but the openness of its earlier form promotes it; in retrospect on the disaster, however, the irony of the oracle in its later form enhances the pathos, and is therefore preferred.

This device and the defence of it we have borrowed from Aristotle inevitably recall the thesis of the younger Wilamowitz, that Sophocles aimed to make the most of each scene in his plays, and was willing to sacrifice strict consistency of plot and character to that end. That is certainly true, and not only of Sophocles; to take but one case from Aeschylus: I argued in 4.13 that coherent and satisfying sense can be made of the course of the trial in *Eumenides*, but it must also be recognised that Aeschylus has achieved this apparent result by tacitly suppressing some awkward considerations – for example, the fact that the Erinyes had no father; the Erinyes' claim that they pursue only the murders of blood-relations (605) is convenient in this context, but quite inconsistent with the rest of the trilogy (see, e.g., *Ag*.59, *Ch*.651, *Eu*.312-20, 421, 546); and the difficulties connected with Orestes' purification are notorious.[36] But we must proceed cautiously. It is one thing to say that a tragedian would sacrifice consistency to *ekplêxis*; it does not by any means follow that the effect of individual scenes in isolation was the tragedian's only or highest concern, to the neglect of their conjoint effect in proper sequence. This further step would conflict with the principle of coherence proposed in 3.2 (which in turn is a restatement of the point we made in 2.4 concerning tragedy as an ordered sequence of emotional experience); but in some at least of his formulations this step does seem to

[35] The note on *Hec*.521 finds an inconsistency: Achilles' tomb is at Troy, and the army has crossed to the Chersonese, so how could the sacrifice be offered at his tomb in the presence of the whole army? The terminology is already current in the fifth century: Arph. *Thesmo*.266-8. See further Bywater 1909: 191 (on *Poet*.1451b16).

[36] See Taplin 1977: 381-4, who I think worries too much about the problems, although he eventually reaches the right conclusion: 'it seems more likely that they were meant to coexist without this kind of close scrutiny.' (Now see also Parker 1983: 386-8.)

have been taken by Wilamowitz,[37] and in this one more recent critic has followed him. Dawe, in rejecting one account of the overall emotional economy of *Agamemnon*, comments:[38]

> It appears to me ... that it is precisely in the *Agamemnon* that there appears for the first time in really pronounced form the desire to make the utmost out of each successive scene, and to pile different kinds of dramatic thrill one upon the other in such a way that the audience is constantly being presented with a variety of spectacle and situation.

I am far from wanting to deny that Aeschylus has cultivated the *poikilia* of which Dawe speaks; but I do not see that this is inconsistent with a coherent economy: I would not, as it happens, subscribe willingly to the account which Dawe is rejecting, but I hope that 1.13 will have shown that rather more can be said about the overall coherence and design of this play than he allows. Aeschylus has followed the principle of diversity, to be sure; but he has also followed that of coherence.

The Greek tragedian was restrained, therefore, in his use of inconsistency and implausibility by the principle of coherence; he was also restrained by the need to maintain dramatic conviction – I dislike the term 'illusion', although a Greek would happily have spoken of *apatê* here.[39] When an audience, or at any rate an audience that expects *apatê*, becomes conscious of something in a play as implausible or inconsistent then they are distracted and disappointed, and the force of the play is diminished. If the audience do not register an implausibility or inconsistency, then of course it is quite irrelevant that there is a difficulty that might have been uncovered by careful reflection. This takes up a point made in 3.2: it is the *impression* that an audience receives, whether of continuity and completeness or of plausibility and consistency, that is important, and the impression that an *audience* receives: for the audience has neither the opportunity nor the inclination to apply the precise, not to say pedantic, analysis that is available to the scholar or critic.

If, then, a dramatist does sacrifice strict plausibility or consistency for dramatic effect, he must conceal the fact from his audience; what factors promote such concealment? First, the conventions of dramatic practice to which the audience is used may so naturalise some highly implausible things that the oddity is never registered as such. We could say that *Trachiniae* begins with Deianeira behaving most strangely; how are we to explain her unmotivated soliloquy? what psychological quirk does it betray? Of course, we would not say such things, because we are entirely familiar with the theatrical convention involved, and happy to acquiesce in it. In the same way, there is nothing 'implausible' in a fluid treatment of time and space for

---

[37] T. Wilamowitz 1917: 39-40 (e.g.).
[38] Dawe 1963: 51.
[39] A fact which makes it perplexing that we should so often be assured that 'dramatic illusion' is a concept inapplicable to Greek tragedy: e.g. Sifakis 1971: 7-14 (a very muddled chapter.)

an audience used to such treatment,[40] and nothing 'grotesque' in the use of the eccyclema to an audience that expects it.[41] When the devices of tragedy are taken outside their naturalising context, then they do seem strange and unconvincing: hence paratragedy in comedy.

So some things which might appear implausible to analysis will not obtrude themselves as such in the theatre because they conform to normal theatrical practice; a second factor we might sum up as 'prominence' – a factor of little consequence to analysis, the whole point of which is that it has the leisure and inclination to attend with equal care to any detail of the text. Aristotle is perhaps looking in this direction when he suggests that irrationalities should be confined 'outside the play' (1454b7, 60a29). It is certainly true that what happens in a play's prehistory will be less prominent than what occurs in the course of its action; to return to the beginning of *Trachiniae*, it is highly implausible that Deianeira and Hyllus have not conferred or communicated before, but an audience will not notice this, giving more attention to the unfolding *praxis* than to the prehistory from which it unfolds where explicit mention is not made. But there are other points to consider: what happens off-stage is less prominent than what happens in our presence; what receives no visual emphasis than what is foregrounded by movement or gesture on stage (cf. 4.3); what involves a functionary than what involves a focal character (3.13). In Euripides' *Phoenissae* (to illustrate this last point) Teiresias' strange shift from reticence (891ff.) to insistent publication of the truth (922-8) should not attract our attention, since it is on Creon that our attention is focussed; Teiresias is a device for turning the screw on Creon, and we accord him only such attention as befits that function: his fluidity, therefore, is not prominent.[42]

A third factor we may call 'definition': the more clearly defined something is in a play, the easier it will be for an audience to detect inconsistencies. If a trait of character (for example) is brought home to us, perhaps because it is vividly presented or heavily emphasised, or because the character is essentially a stereotype with few marked traits, then uncharacteristic action will more readily obtrude as such. The dramatist's chief ally here is the underdetermination of fictions, which allows him to leave things vague, so that it is usually impossible to say with certainty that this or that is strictly speaking inconsistent. An illustration of this factor might be found in the prophecy in *Philoctetes*; Sophocles never needs to tell us clearly and unequivocally the terms of the prophecy, so he leaves it ill-defined and draws on it in unobtrusively inconsistent ways at different points in the play: its vagueness makes possible its fluidity.

Finally, we must take into account the disposition of the audience. An audience that sat alert on the edge of its seats eager to detect 'flaws' of construction is more likely to find them than an audience content to refrain

[40] Cf. Dale 1969: 119ff., 260ff., Taplin 1977: 290-4, 377-9.

[41] Contrast the reaction of a reader not used to the convention: Pickard-Cambridge 1946: 109-10.

[42] Interestingly, Sophocles treats Teiresias in a similar way in *OT*: contrast 316ff. and 432 with 447ff.

from such sceptical scrutiny. The extent to which the tragedians were willing to make use of implausibilities and inconsistencies which they evidently wished and expected to remain unobtrusive shows that they were writing for an audience highly cooperative in this respect. This makes sense: the poets were offering, on condition of this passivity, an aesthetic reward which the audiences wanted; the man who is deceived is wiser than the man who is not, as Gorgias says (cf.3.21). This is a fact of some importance: if the tragedies presuppose an audience that would not register the relatively obvious difficulties of which *Oedipus Tyrannus* (to take a spectacular example) is made it is vain to propound, as so many critics do, interpretations of tragedy that depend on subtle juggling with slight discrepancies. I do not say that Greek audiences were in this respect abnormal by comparison with audiences in other theatres; but their dispositions were certainly far removed from those of many modern interpreters of tragedy.[43]

The general point that I have been making in this section is this: that a thorough distinction has to be made between analytical plausibility and theatrical conviction. Only the latter is of real interest to interpretation and criticism; and if we come upon a problem in analysis, before we yield to the temptation to castigate the author or emend his text, to rationalise the inconcinnity or find significance in it, we should ask whether it is a violation of theatrical conviction. The test is essentially negative: it convinces unless it obtrudes upon the audience's attention in such a way as to disturb or perplex them; and since there are various factors, including the audience's disinclination to notice, which act against such obtrusiveness, we should hesitate to discover a fault. I should emphasise that it is only the *basic* test of theatrical conviction that is negative; there are also positive degrees of conviction: of two things that pass this minimal test, one may carry more conviction in the theatre than the other. But here, too, there is no simple correlation between theatrical conviction and analytical plausibility; positive conviction depends not on abstract verisimilitude, but on the liveliness, variety, *êthos* and emotion which (as the Greeks well knew) engage the interest of and excite an audience, which distract them from mere analysis, and which give the play a grip on their imaginations and feelings.

3.4 Character

In Chapter 6 of the *Poetics*, Aristotle argues for the priority of *muthos* (plot) among the 'parts' of tragedy, and concludes that tragedy is primarily the representation of an action (*mimêsis praxeôs*), and only derivatively the representation of agents (*kai dia tautên malista tôn prattontôn*: 1450b3-4). The *praxis* is the chief thing: what is done, rather than those who do it. But this

---

[43] Bain 1979 discusses *OT*, with a splendid treatment of the realism/conviction question (cf. esp. pp.141-4); see also the – somewhat imbalanced – introduction to Dawe's edition (1982: 6-22). Dawe also cites the fragment of Gorgias (p.22); but his disparaging references to Aristotle (pp.7, 14) suggest that he has not noticed how Goethe's comment (p.22) was anticipated in the *Poetics* (60b22-6).

can hardly be meant to exclude an interest in the agents of the *praxis*, and an interest in them precisely for their own sakes: as we saw in 3.11, a close interest in the agents as centres of emotional engagement is essential if tragedy is to achieve its *telos* of exciting pleasurable emotion. But even in 3.1 we observed that the persons of tragedy are meant to be of interest to the audience only as they feature in the emotive economy of the *praxis*; they are not objects of interest in abstraction from or in a way that goes beyond their specific role in the *praxis*: hence the phenomenon of mobile focus. Moreover, we have established that the emotive force of the *praxis* depends more on what happens to the persons than on their personalities (what kind of persons they are); so tragedy is emphatically not a *mimêsis prattontôn* in the sense of being designed to display the personalities, rather than the experiences, of men. That is to say: the representation of character is not the *telos* of tragedy (in the sense: that part for which the other parts are there), but is there to facilitate the representation of events: *oukoun hopôs ta êthê mimêsontai prattousin, alla ta êthê sumperilambanousin dia tas praxeis* (50a20-2). This is the point that Aristotle wished to make.

This conclusion does not imply that the representation of character, the representation of an agent as being a certain kind of man with respect to his dispositions, is irrelevant to or unimportant in tragedy; on the contrary, Aristotle assigns it the second most important place in his account of the genre, and devotes considerable space to his discussion of it.[44] The scholia, too, are much concerned with *êthos*; and that this is not radically unrepresentative of fifth-century attitudes is shown by Aristophanes' jokes about tragedians throwing themselves with excessive literalness into their parts, and (if it is genuine) by the statement concerning his own practice attributed to Sophocles.[45] It will be as well, then, to give some thought to this matter.

The tragedian devises a *praxis*, a causally connected series of events. In this *praxis*, various persons (I avoid using the ambiguous term 'character' in this sense henceforth, despite the problem of idiom) play an active role: the events of the series are either their acts or the consequences of their acts. The role a person plays in the *praxis* imposes certain constraints on everything that the person is made to do or say; for if they are to do so-and-so (their doing that being an event in the *praxis*), then they must be such as to do so-and-so, and

---

[44] 1449b36-50a14, 50a20-b12, 54a16-36, b8-15; cf. 60a8-11 on Homer; see also Pl. *Ion* 540b3-5, *Laws* 719c3-e3.

[45] Arph. *Thesmo.*148ff. (note *mimêsis* in 156), cf. *Ach.*410-3, fr.59b Austin; for Sophocles see n.47 below. In the scholia: (i) *êthos* is attacked or defended against attack, e.g.: S.*OC* 1725; E.*Or.*71, *Med.*972 (Euripides pandering to the audience), *Andr.*229, 330, 362. (ii) *êthos* is applauded, e.g.: S.*Aj.*572, 750, *OT* 9, 118, *El.*126; E.*Ph.*446, *Hi.*433; cf. *Il.*5.667 BT, 6.467 BT, 6.474 BT etc. (iii) typical terms in the discussion of *êthos* are: *prepon*: e.g. S.*OT* 126; this criterion is used to (mis)attribute disputed lines at S.*Aj.*354, *El.*1178; *prosêkon*: E.*Or.*71; *axion*: A.*PV* 175 (cf.345); *harmozon*: S.*El.*126, *OT* 58; *oikeion*: S.*El.*1236, 1406; E.*Or.*176; *Med.*922; *pithanon*: S.*Aj.*572, *OC* 1725; E.*Med.*910, 972, *Or.*176; *axiopiston*: S.*Aj.*750, 780; *eikos* (and cognates): e.g. S.*OT* 1 (frequent); *êthikon*: S.*El.*126 (*êthikon kai harmozon gunaixin*), *Ant.*940, *OT* 958; *aêthôs*: S.*El.*86; E.*Or.*71. For *êthos* in the Homeric scholia, see Richardson 1980: 272-5 (and 272, 278 on *pithanotês*); and Griffin 1980: 50-80 on characterisation in Homer.

as their role is worked out in the dramatic text, the dramatist must try to make them act and react in word and deed in ways consistent with their being that kind of person. So Aristotle observes that in matters of *êthos* as in the *sustasis pragmatôn* (that is, *muthos*) one must always adhere to the standard of necessity and probability, 'so that for such a man to say or do such a thing is either necessary or probable' (*hôste ton toiouton ta toiauta legein ê prattein ê anankaion ê eikos*: 54a33-6, cf. 51b8-9).

Here, as in discussions of plot, Aristotle has emphasised analytical plausibility, whereas we should be looking at theatrical conviction. As we saw in 3.3, the basic test here is negative: if the audience is not disturbed by a sense of incongruity or improbability, then the characterisation is up to standard; the dramatist has kept safe the impression of plausibility and consistency. And, again as we saw before, the sense of incongruity or improbability is impeded by various factors which tend to make what would, to an analytical approach, seem implausible not obtrude its implausibility under theatrical conditions; and one of these factors is the audience's willingness to be persuaded. Is the behaviour attributed to Pentheus in *Ba.*1316ff. incongruous with his treatment of Cadmus earlier in the play? The latter passage is a report, not something thrust on our attention by enactment on the stage; and perhaps the character of Pentheus has not been drawn with sufficient fullness or depth for a decision to be possible (one might attempt to explain away the apparent difficulty): lack of prominence and definition together hide the incongruity, therefore. And the passages are in any case far apart: a cooperative audience will not at 1316ff. be thinking back to earlier scenes with sceptical intent; its interests lie elsewhere, in the emotion of the present scene, to which the mention of Pentheus' former kindness makes a definite contribution.[46]

In addition to the negative test, there are positive degrees of conviction, in character as in plot. A person, we have said, has a basic role in the *praxis*; he has to perform certain actions, and these imply a basic character: he is such as to do so-and-so. Now, for any of his acts, there will be various ways in which it could be realised at successively less abstract levels until one reaches the particulars of the dramatic text: Ismene must decline to help her sister, but Sophocles could have made her do this in many different ways; when he had decided that she would do so broadly speaking as she does, he need not have given her just the speeches that he has; and given that he has done so, he need not have used those very words. An action in the *praxis*, therefore, may be realised in many different ways; the particular way that is chosen will be causally essential, in so far as it is the realisation of an integral part of the *praxis*, but causally contingent, in that it is only one of many causally adequate possibilities of realisation. The options which the dramatist selects in realising the *praxis* may but need not be suggestive of some particular

---

[46] I do not understand what Garton says on this passage (1957: 252): 'When Euripides bespeaks sympathy for Pentheus at the end of *Bacchae*, he does so less by inventing, by calling up virtues hitherto undisclosed, than by revealing the old character from a different viewpoint ... The effect is one of unexpected subtlety.' (Garton has returned to the question of character in tragedy: 1972.)

disposition or trait of character. If a person acceding to a request says 'Yes, I will do it', this tells us nothing about the kind of person he is; if he says 'Yes, since it is a noble deed', this tells us one thing about him; if 'Yes, since I am afraid of you', it tells us something different. The dramatist can with relative ease avoid obtrusive incongruity, and so pass the minimal test of conviction, simply by choosing ethically colourless options in his realisation of the *praxis*. But he may choose options that are actively suggestive of some trait of character such that a person who possessed it would indeed necessarily or probably do in that situation what the *praxis* requires that he do. Then we have a form of positive conviction: not just the absence of any sense that something is wrong, but a lively sense that something is right, a welcoming recognition that this is how it *would* be.

A dramatist, then, may achieve conviction by working out the character implied by a person's role in the *praxis* in an ethically coloured realisation of that role: the ethical colour, we may add, is bound to be less indeterminate than the basic implied character ('such as to do so-and-so' is a vague phrase, that would probably be satisfied by mutually inconsistent accounts of the person's character). The level of detail to which this process of individualisation is carried is obviously variable; it is always appropriate to ask: at what point has the dramatist ceased to be guided by a conception of this person in particular, and begun to draw more on stock, on a less differentiated or indeed on an individually undifferentiated tragic manner? Or rather, it is inappropriate to ask that, in so far as it misleadingly implies a sharp division: there is instead a gradual shift from the more to the less specifically differentiated; and about this we may ask.

The process of individualisation may be sustained to the most detailed level of textual choice, that of individual words; there is in particular ancient testimony to Sophocles' powers of stylistic characterisation at this level. Plutarch quotes Sophocles as saying of his own work that in its third phase he had achieved the style (*eidos lexeôs*) that is most expressive of character (*êthikôtaton*);[47] so the *Life* remarks that he could portray a whole character in half a line or a single phrase (*hôst' ek mikrou hêmistikhiou ê lexeôs mias holon êthopoiein prosôpon*).[48] An ancient commentator on *Ant.*42 offers an example: 'observe the *êthos* expressed even here in the fact that she calls the deed a *kinduneuma*'; that Ismene uses *kinduneuma* ('hazard') and not some other, more neutral word (*ergon* or *ponos* or *khreos*) is suggestive of a particular disposition, and one that is consistent with her role in the *praxis*. At the other extreme, the attempt to individualise might be abandoned altogether. It has disturbed many commentators that Aristotle apparently envisaged tragedies without *êthos* (50a24-5), and there is a tendency to moderate the claim: *aêtheis tragôidiai*, we are told are not 'without' but 'deficient in' *êthos*.[49] This interpretation is not encouraged by the context (*aneu de êthôn genoit' an*: cf.

---

[47] Plut.*Mor.*79b: cf. Bowra 1953: 108-25 (with Lloyd-Jones *JHS* 75 (1955) 158-9), Lanata 1963: 146ff.

[48] Compare the D-scholion on *Il.*8.85: 'Homer's skill is such that he can disclose a man's whole character through eve a single word (*kai dia mias lexeôs holon ton andra sêmainein*)'.

[49] E.g. Bywater 1909: 167, Lucas 1968: 103; *contra* Janko 1984: 230-1.

50a28-9 *ouden ekhei êthos*), nor by Aristotle's later comment on Homer's characters (*ouden aêthê all' ekhonta êthos*: 60a11). Moreover, in his main discussion of character, he explicitly treats *êthos* as conditional, and therefore as dispensable: *êthos* will be involved *if* the speech or action makes clear the nature of some moral choice (*prohairesis*: 54a17-19, with Vahlen's supplement: cf. 50b8-10). *Prohairesis* here is too narrow;[50] but the point is essentially that which I made in the previous paragraph. A person's role in the *praxis* will give some indication of character, though it may be highly indeterminate; beyond that there is no necessity for the words and actions given to him in the realisation of the *praxis* to indicate what kind of a person he is. There was, in fact, a manner of tragic composition from which such indications were naturally excluded, the rhetorical; for in this style, what is said does not depend on the personality of the speaker (I shall return to this point in 4.22). This manner – which was characteristic of the 'modern poets' whose plays Aristotle describes as 'without *êthos*' (50a25-6, 50b7-8) – sacrifices positive ethical conviction, but offers as compensation (unless one's taste is set against it) rhetorical interest.

I have been speaking of individualisation; but we should be cautious here. Such Sophoclean characters as Electra or Philoctetes carry great dramatic conviction, because their individuality has been worked out in the details of the text; but the individuality that is thus worked out is not in itself detailed or subtly nuanced: it consists rather of a few basic traits, clearly and consistently delineated. Commentary on *êthos* in the scholia is in keeping with this; the commentators think in generic terms, not focussing on the individual as the possessor of a complex of personal traits that uniquely defines his or her individuality, but on the behaviour typical of or appropriate to a class to which the individual can be assigned.[51] It may not be immediately obvious that so distinctive and impressive a character as (let us say) Aeschylus' Clytaemnestra can be reduced to a few basic traits; but, as Winnington-Ingram justly observes, Aeschylus has given us the key to her character in the prologue, and his real triumph is to have found for her a 'tone of voice' that is both distinctive and persuasively expressive of that core.[52] Subtlety of characterisation, then, should be conceived less in terms of refinement of underlying conception than of the success – the vividness and conviction – with which a simple and easily grasped conception has been realised in textual details.

It is possible to criticise Easterling's use of the notion of 'human intelligibility' for its neglect of the filters which, by naturalising unrealistic behaviour, make it seem intelligible: the conventions by which characters are conceived and translated into dramatic text in *Greek* theatre, and in Greek

---

[50] A tendency to act *kata pathos* would presumably also be relevant to dramatic *êthos*; but this point reflects a deep-rooted problem in Aristotle's moral philosophy.

[51] For a 'generic' view of character in the scholia, see (e.g.): A.*ScT* 158; S.*Aj*.340, 596, 916, *OT* 118, 173; E.*Ph*.267, 766, 1605, *Med*.57, *Or*.823. See Russell 1981: 131. The tendency seems to be characteristic of Greek thinking about *êthos*: cf., e.g., Pl.*Ion* 540b; Ar.*Poet*.1454a19-23, *Rhet*.1408a25ff.; D.H. *Lys*.9 (U-R I 16.22-17.2); Plut.*Mor*.853cd.

[52] Winnington-Ingram 1980: 7 n.13.

theatre. But in one respect, at least, her discussion is admirable; for the apparently vague and elusive notion of human intelligibility turns out not to be far removed from the generic conception of character found in the scholia. Easterling insists on a distinction between 'human intelligibility' and 'character':[53]

> The claim that I have been making for the human intelligibility of the carpet scene is not at all the same thing as attributing motives to Agamemnon in terms of his character.

Accordingly, when she dismisses the question 'What sort of a person is Agamemnon?' as 'distracting', she still defends the human intelligibility of his words and actions: 'It is easy enough to imagine a highly successful person in his moment of triumph being simplistic in this sort of way.' This is the kind of observation which one could readily imagine a scholiast making: *pithanon to tou Agamemnonos prosôpon; êthos gar tôn sphodra eutukhountôn* – and so forth. The claim is, of course, true, and so the action carries dramatic conviction; and the audience, being convinced, is unlikely to begin a speculative enquiry into Agamemnon's motivations (or, for that matter, into the reasons why his actions seem natural). This vindicates Easterling's distinction, and disposes of much modern scholarship. In sum: human intelligibility seems, reasonably, to rest on the availability of an implicit assimilation of a character's behaviour to some ready generalisation about the way people (or people of such-and-such a kind) act (or would act in such a situation); this intelligibility conveys a dramatic conviction that discourages speculative exploration and analysis of motive and character.

This must at once be qualified in the light of the more general point which I think can be made against Easterling's position. The generalisations in question are those which are ready to hand for a competent audience and in the theatrical context; these may include conventional stereotypes, or principles of psychological causation that are entertained only in fictive contexts, but which are, in such contexts, felt as entirely natural. It is of no consequence, therefore, how actively a given fifth-century Athenian believed in such a phenomenon as *atê* outside the theatre, how readily he would have resorted to that concept to explain behaviour in life; inside the theatre, it is clear that he was expected (there is no reason to believe mistakenly) to have ready resort to it. Nor will it be of great consequence, given that the concept of *atê* is accepted in the theatre, if a character's behaviour is not such as could be met with in life; if it can be brought under the concept of *atê*, this will explain it sufficiently to safeguard conviction.[54] *A fortiori*, it will not matter

[53] Easterling 1973: 15 (her later contribution, 1977, seems to me less significant). She is obviously not using the term 'character' in quite the same way as myself; she rejects the term, as implying analytical plausibility, while I would wish to transfer it to dramatic conviction. (On Agamemnon's actions in the tapestry-scene, see also Buxton 1982: 106-8.)

[54] 'What we must remember is that such an explanation is a diagnosis of something actually observed in human behaviour, and not a piece of mumbo-jumbo independent of observed phenomena' (Easterling 1973: 6). True, the explanation draws on a theory which exists to account for observed phenomena; but the theory might be too powerful, capable of explaining

whether the behaviour in question can be explained in terms of a modern psychological theory; and even where it could be so explained, it would be risky to exploit the coincidence: in applying these alien categories of explanation there is an inevitable irrelevance, and a real danger of misunderstanding.[55]

It would be easy to illustrate the ready availability of such concepts as *atê* for psychological explanation in tragedy from Aeschylus or Sophocles; we might think, for example, of Eteocles' decision to fight his brother in the *Seven*,[56] or of his brother's decision to fight him in the second *Oedipus*. Since I was concerned in 2.32 to emphasise Euripides' participation in the tradition, it might be more interesting to take our illustration from him. We can at once complete the series which the other two poets began: in *Phoenissae*, Euripides shows the two brothers meeting face to face, and falling to the same perturbation of mind. A more revealing case, perhaps, is that of Pentheus in *Bacchae*. After Dionysus' enigmatic exclamation (810), he succumbs to the god's trick with a rapidity that demands explanation; and there can be no doubt that the explanation most readily available to Euripides' audience would have worked with the notion of *atê*: Dionysus has made his victim mad. Those for whom Euripides is axiomatically above such things must find a more sophisticated psychology to explain it; and so some have professed to discover signs in Pentheus' earlier behaviour of repressions and obsessions, of unconscious desires that make him vulnerable to persuasion: Dionysus' seductive question 'has touched a hidden spring in Pentheus' mind'.[57] There are several difficulties in this view. One is that the evidence for it consists entirely of fanciful misreadings of the text.[58] Another is that it is theologically

---

things not to be met with in life, but perhaps to be met with in dramatic fictions; then, because there is an explanatory category available, the unlifelike behaviour will be to some degree naturalised and so unobtrusive.

[55] There may be some too unimaginitive to respond where they cannot apply the categories they habitually use in life (or in literature other than Greek tragedy); this is their misfortune. The rest of us would be more profitably employed learning to understand and respond to the relevant categories.

[56] It is wrong to talk of an inconsistency here (e.g., Dawe 1963: 31ff.), since this causal explanation for Eteocles' behaviour in the latter part of the play is available. But Dawe exaggerates even the *prima facie* difficulty when he describes 653ff. as a 'violent outburst' (p.39): Eteocles exclaims in grief and horror, and then makes a calm and reasoned judgment that he is the most appropriate opponent for his brother; all that needs explaining is the moral blindness that made him able to reach such a depraved conclusion.

[57] Dodds 1960: 175; cf. Winnington-Ingram 1948: 45-7, 159-61. Pentheus' submission is no better motivated, in terms acceptable to a modern psychology, than Heracles' madness; Dodds was, of course, under the influence of a theory which did find traces of advancing insanity in Heracles – but this has worn less well than the parallel theory about *Ba.* (see Bond 1981: xix, 206-7). It is interesting that Dodds contrasted these two plays with *Eum.*, in which the conversion of the Erinyes is 'a bare act of god' (1960: 172): this, though Aeschylus has been at pains to portray the hard struggle which Athene has in reconciling them by persuasion; once again, we see clearly the power of errant preunderstandings to distort our perception of the text.

[58] Some examples: (i) 215ff. are 'far too vivid and detailed' (Winnington-Ingram 1948: 46); but there is nothing here that is not an expression of two basic prejudices of Greek males about women: their propensity to alcohol, and their propensity to illicit sex; so Pentheus' suspicions are 'inevitable' (Winnington-Ingram's word); they are voiced at some length because outrage cannot be worked up in a passing phrase: this is simply the disapproval of impetuous moral

superfluous: the gods do not need a 'traitor within', having sufficient power without; nothing predisposed Io to turn into a cow. A third objection to this view, and perhaps the most far-reaching, is its tendency to cohabit with a thoroughly distorted conception both of the god and of the reasons for Pentheus' downfall.

In several parts of the play – by Teiresias, by the Chorus in the first stasimon, by the Herdsman at the end of his report – Dionysus is presented as a mild and beneficent god; his gift is not ecstatic frenzy but joy and relaxation. Is this a misleading picture of him? There is more to Dionysus, as Pentheus' demise makes clear; but what is there to set against the claim that the milder picture is also the more typical? Obviously, the Chorus and the Theban women: but the Chorus is the special entourage of the god (the Pythia's psychological state was not typical of the worshippers of Apollo); and the women of Thebes are maddened to give a spectacular warning, a display of power by a god whose deity has already been slighted. Both groups, then, are entirely untypical; and there is no reason to suppose that if the Thebans had accepted the god's cult at once there would have been any disruptive frenzy. There would, perhaps, have been some undignified revelry (of the kind for which Teiresias and Cadmus are, alas, too old), and there would above all have been the gift of 'joy through wine and feast and music'.[59] Dionysus, therefore, is in this play not *typically* a god of irrational extremes: he is quite content to be 'the genial wine-god of the Attic festivals';[60] but his geniality will fade away if he is crossed, and he will, like any god in Greek tradition, use his beneficent powers in an extreme and no longer beneficent way to punish those who deny him *timê*. That, the god's honour, is the crucial point. The sole cause of Pentheus' downfall was his refusal to honour Dionysus as a god. He refused to pay this honour, not because of any repression or inhibition, but because the facts spoke against the truth of Semele's claim (26-35, 242-5): and his unconscious, if one admitted its existence, would be causally quite as irrelevant as that of Hippolytus (cf.2.32); for it was not that which drove the women of his city in frenzy from their homes.

This discussion of *Bacchae* has taken us some way beyond the question of characterisation in tragedy; but it does serve to illustrate some dangers of imposing on the plays concepts of psychological explanation other than those

orthodoxy. (ii) 343-5 are misread as 'violent horror', and this is then praised as a 'fine psychological stroke' – for horror of such violence must imply a secret fascination (Dodds 1960: 114; cf. Winnington-Ingram 1948: 55 n.3); this ignores the tone of deliberate sarcastic contempt: the point is rhetorical, not psychological. In general, the extremity and violence of Pentheus' reactions do not argue any particular instability of psyche: they manifest a pattern of behaviour familiar from other plays, a tyrant stereotype that raises no problems (cf. 4.41). (iii) Dodds finds evidence in 475 of the god's working on Pentheus' psychological weak point (1960: 172): absurdly; to hint at a secret is a device by which to excite curiosity that needs no help from abnormal instabilities.

[59] Winnington-Ingram 1948: 61. I register a passing protest against the habit of finding sinister significance in *misei* (424: cf. Winnington-Ingram 1948: 68); it means merely that Dionysus does not associate with such people: cf. Hes.*WD* 299-300.

[60] Dodds 1960: 117.

which they presuppose: if we talk about character at all, we must be willing to employ appropriate categories. Let us now conclude this discussion of character by reminding ourselves why its representation is important to the tragedian. The minimal level, that degree of apparent coherence and plausibility which lets a character pass the negative test by evoking no adverse reaction, is necessary to protect the conviction of the play. The positive levels of dramatic conviction can be seen as advantageous in two ways. First, a lively and convincing representation is inherently interesting and enjoyable; *êthos*, therefore, can be counted as an ancillary pleasure. But it also contributes to the primary pleasure, tragic emotion; for we are more likely to be closely and responsively engaged with characters who carry great conviction in the theatre. We may recall here the beginning of 3.12; the Watchman in the prologue to *Agamemnon* does not have the status to be focal: but because he is presented with convincing *êthos* he is able to evoke an emotional response, and so set a mood. An expository prologue in the Euripidean manner, without *êthos*, could not work in the same way.[61] And there are other ways in which *êthos* can contribute to the emotional tone of a scene; for example, Deianeira's tenderness towards the captives in *Trachiniae* is not required by her basic role in the plot: but it is not gratuitous, since it is used to enhance the pathos and irony of her situation. This brings us to the final point: that his character does necessarily have some bearing on the degree and nature of our response to a person in tragedy; though we were right to warn against an overestimate of its importance as a factor determining response, it would be wrong to deny it all weight.

[61] S. *Tr.* has an expository prologue formally similar to those of Euripides, but with *êthos*; Deianeira also has status, and therefore can be focal.

4. The Tragic Text

4.1 Introduction

If I were asked to reduce my account of Greek tragedy to the barest of its essentials, I might propose a summary along these lines:

> A Greek tragedy is (a) narrative in dramatic form (b) treated seriously and with dignity in an elaborated poetic manner (c) of painful events (d) in the careers of men of high status and fortune (e) drawn from heroic legend (f) told to evoke in the audience painful emotions such as fear and pity (g) for the sake of the pleasure which accompanies such emotional excitation under fictively and aesthetically controlled conditions.

Comparison with Wilamowitz's well-known definition may help to bring out my special emphases:[1]

> An Attic tragedy is a self-contained portion of heroic saga, treated poetically in an elevated style for presentation by a chorus of Athenian citizens and two or three actors, and designed to be produced as part of the public act of worship in the sanctuary of Dionysus.

This covers my (a), (b) and (e). It elaborates on the occasion and circumstances of performance: rather more, perhaps, than is necessary or proportionate in such a brief formula (after all, we found in 2.31 that the religious aspect of the occasion had no particular influence on the content of tragedy); but with this concentration on externals there goes a neglect of the essential questions of function – that is, of meaning – that I have tried to cover in (f) and (g): in mentioning (e), Wilamowitz tells us a little of what tragedy is *about*, but of the *point* of the narrative we are told nothing.

Another famous definition of tragedy, that of Aristotle, is closer to mine (a fact which, of course, I would regard as corroboration of my approach). Aristotle defines tragedy thus (1449b24-8):

> ἔστιν οὖν τραγῳδία μίμησις πράξεως σπουδαίας καὶ τελείας μέγεθος ἐχούσης, ἡδυσμένῳ λόγῳ χωρὶς ἑκάστῳ τῶν εἰδῶν ἐν τοῖς μορίοις, δρώντων καὶ οὐ δι' ἀπαγγελίας, δι' ἐλέου καὶ φόβου περαίνουσα τὴν τῶν τοιούτων παθημάτων κάθαρσιν.

> A tragedy, then, is a representation of an action that is serious, complete and possesses magnitude; in language pleasurably enhanced, using each of its kinds

[1] U. Wilamowitz 1910: 108.

in separate parts of the play; in a dramatic rather than a narrative medium; effecting through pity and fear a *katharsis* of such emotions.

This covers (a), (b), (d) and (f); (c) and (e) are implied, at least; the prominence of *katharsis* does not reflect its intrinsic importance in Aristotle's general presentation of tragedy (it is the only occurrence of the notion in the extant *Poetics*), and is perhaps determined by polemical needs: I have replaced it with the equally Aristotelian notion of tragedy's *oikeia hêdonê*, and would argue that this does better justice than Aristotle's own formulation to his overall view (see 1453b11-13, etc.). Aristotle also alludes in this definition to the structure of the tragic *praxis* (requiring completeness and magnitude); this brings us on from the questions which I examined in Chapters 1 and 2 to the matter of Chapter 3; and when he mentions also the disposition of the various kinds of poetry in tragedy, he comes into contact with the kind of question I wish to look at in the present chapter. Here, I shall be dealing with some more detailed aspects of the tragic text: with portions of the 'grammar' of tragedy, to recall the image of Fraenkel which I mentioned in the introduction. Obviously, we cannot work from the script offered by manuscripts and editions to the dramatic text, and thence to an understanding of that text – that is, to a grasp of the particular course which a play charts through the field of meaning which we have been delineating in general terms – without a working knowledge of the media and forms through which tragic meaning is realised. Of course, this opens up too vast a realm of detailed technical study; I shall only be touching on a few of its provinces, so as to bring the broad 'semantic' enquiry of the preceding three chapters closer to a point from which it would be able to take over freely the results of more detailed 'syntactic' studies.

4.2 The verbal text

4.21 Some formal conventions

The easiest dimension of the dramatic text to recover is its verbal component: it seems to stare out at us from printed copies of the plays. But to read and understand this, in a relatively superficial sense of 'understand' – to know the meaning of the words and perceive their syntactical relations – falls far short of understanding what the words are doing: why these words have been chosen and placed in this order, the function or point of their use. This (a more realistic sense of 'understand') depends on less immediately apparent features of the verbal text. There are, for example, the conventional forms within which the words are organised: the moulds, so to speak, into which they have been poured; these forms already (that is, irrespective of the particular words that fill them) have a meaning of their own, which will guide a competent audience in its understanding of the particular words. Let us consider some examples.

(i) *Lyric-iambic sequence:* There is a well-documented tendency for a monody or lyric dialogue within a scene to be followed by a parallel monologue or dialogue in iambic trimeters; the reprise does not advance the thought or plot, so much as cover the same ground in a different register, the iambics generally being of a calmer, more reflective character than the lyrics. The shift of register does not represent a corresponding change in the speaker's mental state; rather, his reaction is explored under two different aspects.[2] Here is an obvious case in which the failure to grasp a formal convention would, in spite of an 'understanding' of the words at the more basic level, encourage serious misunderstandings (such as irrelevant psychologising). Once the convention has been grasped, however, one is free to enjoy, without such worrying distractions, both the special excellences of each mode of presentation, and the *poikilia* of their juxtaposition.

(ii) *Texture:* The iambic reprise of lyric is only one striking illustration of a more general feature of the verbal text of tragedy, its varied metrical texture (the mode of delivery was covariant). At one level, this variation enriches the aesthetic interest of the text through *poikilia*; but the variation also has expressive functions, as in the correlation of the two registers of (i) with different emotional tones. Aristotle suggests that the iambic trimeter was found most suitable as the standard metre for tragic dialogue because it was most akin to the rhythms of everyday speech: that is, it is the least marked of the available forms;[3] and on the whole, a shift from spoken to 'recitative' metre reflects a rise in tension or excitement: Fraenkel comments thus on *Ag.*1649ff.:[4]

> Even if neither Aristotle nor anyone else had told us anything about the difference in character between iambic trimeters and trochaic tetrameters, we should probably be conscious here of the jerk with which the rhythm changes to greater excitement.

We may compare the difference between an iambic and an anapaestic entry-announcement: in nearly every case of the latter, Taplin observes, 'there is some way in which the entry is slow or stately'.[5] On the whole, one could say that trochaics are treated as dialogue at a higher pitch, and anapaests as an approximation to lyric (with which, indeed, the boundary – between *Marsch-* and *Klaganapäste* – is fluid). The shift to lyric proper represents a still higher pitch. It is presumably the increasingly obtrusive and complex rhythmic patterning at each of these levels that makes them apt

---

[2] Cf. Fraenkel 1950: 623-7 (on *Ag.*1178-1330); Greenwood 1953: 131-8; Dale 1954: 74 (on *Alc.*280ff.); Kannicht 1969: 85 (on *Hel.* 253-329).

[3] *Poet.* 1449a24ff., 59a11ff., *Rhet.* 1404a30, 08b33ff.; obviously, this is meant only relative to other verse-forms. The comic trimeter, being more flexible, is even closer to ordinary speech than the tragic; but the elevating effect and aesthetic attractiveness of the stricter metrical form were not to be lost.

[4] Fraenkel 1950: 780; but this does not seem to apply to the use of trochaics in *Per.* See further Imhof 1956, Drew-Bear 1968, Michelini 1982: 41-64.

[5] Taplin 1977: 73.

vehicles for the increasing emotional pitch.

One illustration of the difference between iambic and lyric can be found in Cassandra's kommos in *Agamemnon* (1072ff.). At first the Chorus responds to Cassandra's lyrical exclamations in trimeter couplets, but these interventions do not rise above the trivial and banal; when, however, they are drawn into her excitement and become lyrically involved, their contributions acquire more substance. (It is worth observing that this change of pitch coincides with the first mention of the Erinys in this section: 1119.) In this lyric context, iambics simply do not have enough force to be the vehicle of significant remarks; on the other hand, when Cassandra has to give a clearer exposition, she switches to iambics (1178ff.), which (as we have seen) are calmer and more rational, less emotional in tone.

(iii) *Choral tags:* The rather trivial iambic interjections in the first part of Cassandra's kommos are there, not for their content, but to punctuate the lyric exclamations and to retain the structure of a dialogue. That is, their function is purely formal and structural; it would be foolish, therefore, to attach much interpretative weight to what is actually said in those lines. A rather extreme parallel can be found in E.*Ph*.335-6; Iocaste's long and emotionally intense monody is followed by a couplet of astounding banality from the Chorus. If the audience did not find this intolerably bathetic, it is presumably because they were not inclined to pay close attention to this kind of choral utterance. Bland choral tags rounding off a monody or rhesis in this way are common: it has been suggested that they were designed to be no loss if drowned by applause, which might be true;[6] but whether or not that is so, they serve a function in the elucidation of structure. They may mark a transition, such as that here from a lyrical virtuoso-piece to dialogue of more normal pitch, or they may mark off distinct sections in a formally structured scene such as an agon. For example, E.*Ph*.443-5 announce the entry of Eteocles, and thereby (as well as identifying him for the audience) mark the beginning of a new dramatic situation; and then the three rheseis are each 'tagged' by the Chorus. We may observe that in the following tetrameter scene, the Chorus does not contribute such tags; the raised pitch indicated by the metrical shift dissolves the formality of structure which such tags are designed to highlight.[7]

The habitual blandness and evidently formal purpose of these tags should dissuade us from attaching too much weight to the nuances of their content. They do have content, and it is not always neutral: in the tags from *Phoenissae* just mentioned, the Chorus declares itself in favour of Polyneices and against Eteocles; but, then, who needs the Chorus to tell him that in this play Eteocles is in the wrong and his brother in the right? Or that Phaedra was right and the Nurse wrong in *Hippolytus* (431-2, 482-5)? The term 'guide' (3.13) would surely be an inflated account of their dramatic function; such

---

[6] Cf. Pickard-Cambridge 1968: 272-3 for active displays of approval and disapproval by the tragic audience.

[7] For this task of emphasising structure, compare the recitative codas that provide formal closure: cf. 3.2.

guidance is totally redundant. Euripides has simply used the moral contrast to supply the tags with content (given that they must have *some* content); their function does not really differ from that of more neutral pairs (for example, E.*Hi*.981-2, 1036-7; S.*Ant*.681-2, 724-8;[8] E.*Alc*.673-4, 706-7 – this last a fine example of the bland conciliatory manner habitual with choruses in tragedy).

That such tags are usually bland, their content of no great importance, naturally does not mean that they can never take on greater significance; it does mean that we should not expect them to do so, and that we will therefore require clear contextual cues before attaching particular weight to the contents of such a tag. An obvious example is *Ant*.278-9, which surely is meant to suggest to the audience that Creon is acting against the will of the gods; but it gains the prominence which makes it able to suggest such a thing only because of the violence of Creon's reaction, which draws unexpected attention to it and highlights its content. The recognition of this principle imposes on modern critics, schooled in 'close reading', an unfamiliar discipline of restraint in interpretation.

(iv) *Stichomythia:* This is a conventional form which still causes considerable difficulty. Collard, for example, writes:[9]

> The longest Euripidean stichomythia remain the most severe problem for both audience and reader: so often the virtuoso command of form seems more important to the poet than a more plausible (dare one say, 'realistic'?) variety to the dramatist.

'Euripides' practice often defies apparent dramatic reason,' he complains, though he adds that it would be unreasonable to look for 'near-perfection in conception and realisation', and that some allowance must be made for 'individual foible':

> A measure of self-indulgence should not be denied to Euripides, or any artist, especially if Euripides' experience in the theatre showed him that the audience – if not the jury – appreciated his skill with stichomythia.

This last suggestion does indeed seem very plausible; but why, if that was the case, is Euripides described as *self*-indulgent? And why is the practice said to defy dramatic reason? What could be more reasonable for a dramatist than to write in a style appreciated both by himself and by his audience? There is an astonishing complacency in Collard's assumption that Euripides would have been an artist more nearly perfect *sub specie aeternitatis* had he written to satisfy twentieth-century, rather than fifth-century, taste.

Euripides wrote stichomythia of this kind, presumably, because he and his

---

[8] We are not to be dissuaded by this from backing Haemon's judgment against Creon's; nor *pace* Coleman 1972: 14, are we meant to be struck by the fact that Creon's supporters are now admitting that there is a case against him.

[9] Collard 1980: 85.

audience, or at least part of it, shared a taste for the form; but what, more precisely, was that taste a taste for? Why did they like the form, and what dramatic and artistic functions did it serve? Let us consider, as an example, *Ion* 264-368; at 105 lines, this is the longest passage of continuous stichomythia in extant tragedy: what is there about it to appreciate? First of all, it is clear that to sustain the rigid form at this length is to display a virtuosity that is in its own right impressive and interesting; in addition, symmetry and strict form are pleasant *per se* – the rhythm of the dialogue is, as it were, another system of poetical patterning superimposed on the metrical patterning of the trimeters. (Euripides achieves variety, not by breaking the rhythm of the form, but by working in switches of initiative: Ion takes the lead up to 307, then Creusa takes over, and Ion resumes the lead in 330.) Secondly, the taut dialogue brings the two characters into close interaction with each other; when, as here, the two are mutually unrecognised *philoi*, this closeness of interaction presents opportunities for pathos, and Euripides stretches the dialogue here partly in order to exploit these opportunities to the full. (Compare E.*El.*220ff. and S.*El.*1176ff. – this is the longest Sophoclean stichomythia, although characteristically less strictly regular than Euripides' examples; both passages bring together unrecognised *philoi* for pathetic effect, as does E.*IT* 494ff.) Third, the tight form produces a tension that enhances the emotive potency of the exchange. This same tension also makes stichomythia ideal for scenes of plotting (e.g., E.*Ion* 933ff., *El.*612ff., *Or.*1100ff.).

Stichomythia is strangest for modern readers when it is used to convey information between characters, as at A.*Su.*293ff. or E.*Med.*662ff. (This is not the same as the brief 'abstracting' dialogues that usually precede a Messenger's rhesis: cf.4.43.) But if the information is too important to be thrown off in a brief speech, and is on the other hand not to be given the lavish treatment of an elaborated rhesis, some artistic form is needed to enhance its effect; and stichomythia is the obvious form for such a purpose.[10] In such cases, the strict symmetry of form is 'unrealistic', and it is from a prosaic point of view extremely inefficient; in life, such information would be given more concisely in a brief exposition, with more strategic questioning from the recipient. But the question of 'realism' is irrelevant here, since the convention naturalises the 'unrealistic' form. On this question of 'realism', Collard remarks:

> The contrast between Comedy and Tragedy ... in their use of stichomythia may seem ... to support the argument that the ancient theatre was less insensitive to 'realistic' dialogue than is commonly held.

But 'insensitivity' is not the point; lack of 'realism' is not registered as such in a context in which the form is, because of convention, expected and accepted; one may compare the treatment of stage-machinery in tragedy and comedy

---

[10] In the case of A.*Su.*, a rhesis is out of the question, since the informant is the Chorus (Dale 1969: 211-14); Danaus, their patron, could have spoken for them, but this would have entailed the loss of the emotive kommos (on the suppression of Danaus, see Taplin 1977: 204-6). I note in

(cf. 3.3). Of course, if anything like this occurred in life, it would be indicative perhaps of unusual reticence on the part of the informant, or of signal impatience on the part of the recipient of the information; the form would reflect the character or mood of those involved. But that would obviously be a ruinous way to read tragic stichomythia.[11]

This set of examples is of course not meant to be exhaustive, nor have I treated any of them in depth; I merely cite them to illustrate my basic point: that interpretation of the words cannot proceed successfully unless one has grasped the distinctive characteristics of the conventional forms into which the words have been poured before they are set before us.

4.22 Rhetoric

The use of formal rhetorical techniques for the composition of dramatic speeches is one feature of the verbal text of tragedy that causes recurrent problems. I want here to comment on two areas of difficulty in particular: first, on the frigidity which is often felt to result, especially when rhetorical composition leads to a 'suspension' of *êthos*, and especially when this happens in a passage of high pathos; and then on the frustration that is often felt at the apparent irrelevance of many rhetorical set-pieces, especially with those that develop abstract or general arguments far beyond the demands of the dramatic context.

(i) *Frigidity:* The first kind of problem is well illustrated by a comment which Lee makes on *Trojan Women:*[12]

> Unfortunately, her [Hecuba's] character suffers in the *agôn*. She argues too coherently for a grief-stricken old woman and we are scarcely able to recognise the Hecuba of a hundred lines before.

Lee evidently brings with him an expectation of consistent portrayal of character, and is disconcerted when the dramatist apparently invites him to suspend this expectation for a scene wrought in the rhetorical manner. But we observed in 3.4 that it was open to a tragedian to compose *rhêtorikôs* rather than *êthikôs*. This style was not to everyone's taste, even in the ancient world: Sophocles is quoted as speaking of a style that is *êthikôtaton* and *best* (cf. Chapter 3, n.47), and the scholia are unenthusiastic. But it was approved by some: by Euripides, evidently, and increasingly in the fourth century;[13]

---

passing that 455-67, in which the threat to hang themselves is made, is an excellent use of the tenseness of stichomythia; cf. 916ff., where stichomythia is used for the tensest moment of the confrontation between King and Herald, relaxing into irregular blocks after the crisis has passed.

[11] Regrettably, one still finds critics who do read in this way: e.g. Fitton, who includes in his list of Theseus' vices 'punctiliousness' on the grounds of E.*Su*.129, 143 (1961: 430). Or consider Dawe on *OT* 559 (1982: 149).

[12] Lee 1976: 220; cf. xxi-ii.

[13] Cf. Xanthakis-Karamanos 1980: 59-80.

Aristotle comments: 'The older poets made their characters speak *politikôs*, contemporary ones *rhêtorikôs*' (1450b7-8). This contrast between the 'political' and the 'rhetorical' manners of composition is not directly equivalent to that between the 'ethical' and the 'rhetorical'; but it must refer to the ability to speak as the situation required with or without the artifices of rhetorical *tekhnê*: and one would expect *êthos* to be more apparent in the less 'technical' or artificial manner, so that the two distinctions do run parallel.[14]

It might be objected that presentation of character was itself an element of rhetorical technique; but it was so in a sense rather different from that normally in question in dramatic criticism. In drama, as we saw in 3.4, *êthos* depends on the impression of an intelligibly consistent and credible personality; but Aristotle explicitly denies that rhetorical *êthopoiia* depends on maintaining consistency with a previously established impression of character: 'This [persuasion based on the *êthos* of the speaker] should be achieved by means of the speech, and not through a prior opinion that the speaker is a certain kind of man' (*dia tou logou alla mê dia tou prodedoxasthai poion tina einai ton legonta: Rhet.*1356a8-10). Rhetorical *êthos* is a matter of assuming in a given speech the *persona* which best suits and supports the thought there expressed; and this is why composition in the rhetorical manner tends to expel dramatic *êthos*. We may note that *dianoia*, which Aristole regards as the part of tragedy that falls within the province of rhetoric (55b34-6), is explained as *to legein dunasthai ta enonta kai ta harmottonta* (50b4ff.); that is, although it is a quality of the person (namely, his ability), it is defined in relation to the situation (*ta enonta* – 'what the situation requires': cf. *Rhet.* 1355b10 *ta huparkhonta pithana*),[15] rather than in relation to the individual speaker: it is impersonally conceived.

The consequences can be illustrated (to take but one example) by Hecuba's denunciation of Polymestor in *Hecuba* (1187ff.). In her lengthy exordium she adopts the pose of the plain man, unskilled in rhetoric and contemptuous of fine speaking allied to moral depravity; this is itself an obvious rhetorical ploy, and fully accords with Aristotelian precepts for rhetorical *êthos* ('persuasion is achieved by means of *êthos* when the speech is such as to inspire confidence in the speaker; for we place more confidence in decent men, and do so more readily': *Rhet.*1356a4-7; cf. D.H.*Lys.* 8, 19). But just because it is an evident rhetorical ploy, it seems (if one is looking for dramatic characterisation) incongruous; what business has Hecuba speaking as if she had employed a professional speech-writer? What business has she with the professional's tricks and his self-conscious concern with form (1195-6)? But once we have recognised the dramatist's willingness to suspend *êthos* in rhetorical contexts and accepted the naturalising convention, we will no longer be inclined to look for it there, and will therefore not find its absence disturbing; and conversely, we will hesitate to trust our

[14] Cf. *Rhet.*1417a23 for a contrast between speaking *apo dianoias* and *apo prohaireseôs* (i.e., *êthikôs*).

[15] Cf. Thuc.1.22.1 *peri tôn aei parontôn ta deonta*; this kind of language is frequent in the rhetoricians: e.g., D.H. *Lys.* 15 (U-R I 25.11-12: Lysias is *heuretikos ... tôn en tois pragmasin enontôn logôn*), *Th.*15, 34 (U-R I 347.6-8, 382.1-3). (See also Macleod 1983: 68-9.)

anachronistic intuitions when we think we can recognise welcome and familiar touches of characterisation in rhetorical commonplaces, such as the opening of Hippolytus' self-defence before Theseus.[16]

Significantly, rhetorical composition is most accessible to modern readers in narrative speeches, and especially in those of Messengers; for these are obvious set-pieces, and the comparative lack of individuality in the speakers means that readers do not bring to their speeches expectations of character which will be disappointed. By contrast, when rhetoric is used in more personal contexts, in self-assertion, self-explanation or self-defence, in appeal or in persuasion, then the speaker, being a major figure, does carry definite expectations of character, while the speech itself, being of a more personal nature, awakens in us a presumption that the treatment will also be personal, and therefore characterised. Moreover, the pathos that is often intended in such passages also makes modern readers look for manifestation of character; for we are not used to the evocation of emotion by the relatively impersonal techniques of rhetoric, and look for the sensitive delineation of individuality responding to circumstance. But one conclusion of 3.12 and 3.4 was that Greek audiences were not in the same degree intent on the personality of a dramatic *persona*; this was reflected in the subordination of person to *praxis*, a subordination which seemed to us not unreasonable, since it is to a large extent what happens to a person that is emotive, and not what kind of a person it happens to. Thus there is a limited independence of pathos and character (limited, because emotional response may still be qualified by the personality of its object); it is therefore not absurd in principle that pathos should be sought in the rhetorical, rather than in the ethical, style.

In sum: there are factors in such contexts which, for a modern reader, create strong expectations that will not in fact be fulfilled; this leaves us with a sense of disappointment: and frigidity is above all an effect of such disappointment. It is only by learning not to expect what will not be offered, and by learning to see the logic of the taste that refrained from offering it, that we will begin to make this style aesthetically accessible to ourselves.

(ii) *Irrelevance:* Let us start once more with some examples of modern unease. Having mentioned the impression which Euripides sometimes gives of 'presenting and matching debating points for their own sake', Collard goes on:[17]

> Older critics of Euripides told us that our instinct is right, and that the poet is guilty of self-indulgent digression for the sake of rhetorical display, at the cost of dramatic continuity and relevance.

Or, again, Lee on *Trojan Women*:[18]

---

[16] Well treated by Gould 1978: 57-8.

[17] Collard 1975b: 59.

[18] Lee 1976: xxii. Lee's treatment of this agon is further vitiated by his strange belief that Helen's 'determinism' is Homeric, and that Hecuba is, on Euripides' behalf, a champion of 'free will' (p.xxiii).

We should not dismiss the *agôn* as nothing more than an interlude which provided Euripides with the opportunity to show off his wit and cleverness. The *agôn* has important functions ... The subject of the debate, though not entirely relevant to the play, is intrinsically important and is far more than the basis for an idle exercise in logic-chopping.

The prejudicial choice of terms should not escape notice: guilty, self-indulgent (a term which we met in Collard's discussion of stichomythia as well: 4.21iv), nothing more than, show off, cleverness, important, idle, logic-chopping.[19] The assumption is obviously that if Euripides were convicted of an interest in rhetorical display 'for its own sake', this would be an indisputable artistic flaw: and therefore that we should charitably seek out and emphasise redeeming features.

This task is one which Conacher undertakes; he sets out to 'defend' some speeches that have been 'assailed' for irrelevance, and concludes:[20]

Generally speaking, Euripidean rhetoric is not as dramatically inorganic as many scholars have argued, and ... many passages which have been assessed simply as set pieces of sophistic debate also contain much that is relevant to major themes and even significant revelations of character ... in the plays to which they belong.

The prejudicial expression – 'simply': as if sophistic debate were self-evidently of no interest or value – is by now familiar; it is interesting, and perhaps disquieting, to note that the two forms of defence which Conacher offers – theme and character – reproduce the pair to which we found modern scholars making instinctive but misguided appeal in discussions of unity (3.2). What Conacher is doing – and, of course, he is not alone – is trying to show that Euripides' dramaturgy really does conform to modern standards and tastes; what is alarming is his apparent failure to consider seriously the possibility that they are precisely *modern* tastes, which would not have been shared by Euripides: to Euripides and his audience, if not to Conacher and his, sophistic debate might indeed have had interest and value as a literary form. When Euripidean rhetoric can be redeemed with some show of plausibility for modern taste, this is as welcome to such critics as rain to parched soil, and they duly make as much of it as they can; but this is a most hazardous procedure. For if Euripides did *not* share our tastes and did *not* set out to satisfy them, then the apparent plausibility of the reconciliation is likely to be an illusory coincidence. And if we insist on trying to make sense of and defend what is written in terms of our alien aesthetic, rather than seeking to elicit and apply the aesthetic which in fact determined its writing, then this can only lead to two things: to the *interpolation* of alien and inappropriate

---

[19] See Haigh 1896: 235-6 for some other harsh phrases: 'contagion ... evil ... baneful ... mere forensic display ... blemishes and symptoms of decay'; but Haigh does allow that the rhetorical tendency suited the taste of Euripides' audience (p.237).
[20] Conacher 1981: 25.

meanings; and to the *loss* of the meanings intended by the author and apt to the genre.[21]

In many cases (although not in all) Conacher's attempt to 'defend' Euripides' rhetoric does indeed achieve a most respectable show of plausibility; but Conacher himself concedes that one could not without special pleading defend all instances. He offers as an example E.*Su*.232-45, lines which are 'nothing more than political *topoi* based on contemporary circumstances'; this is also, he believes, the case with the debate between tyranny and democracy in the second agon of the same play:[22]

> This passage, which reads almost like a set piece from a rhetorician's school, has only the most general kind of connection with the dramatic situation ... and contains various rhetorical criticisms of each constitution which are quite irrelevant to it.

This is certainly correct; and Conacher has here made a crucial point. Speeches of this kind have always at least some very general connection with their context; their theme is in some way suggested by the context, and the speeches themselves could not simply be swopped from play to play. But the theme, once suggested, is often developed to an extent or in a way that is not required by or functional within the dramatic context as such. The contextual integration is sometimes a perfunctory and transparent excuse for introducing the passage; there are hooks by which it may be attached, but these plainly do not show *why* the passage is there, and so do not indicate its function or meaning. Thus the passages in question are valued always *also*, and sometimes *only*, in themselves. So while it is legitimate to look for more intricate and organic links, we must not by any means assume that they are a necessary virtue; to make that assumption would encourage forced, interpolating explanations.

In the case of the political debates from Euripides' *Suppliants* to which Conacher points as examples of tenuously integrated rhetoric, it is easy to see what context-free value they might have add for a fifth-century audience, quite apart from any love of sophistic argument and rhetorical technique; we commented in 2.33 on the element of patriotic – and this necessarily includes: democratic – appeal to the audience in tragedy, and observed in 2.5 that these speeches had to be understood in this light. But another notorious example cannot be explained in this way: the argument between Amphitryon

---

[21] These considerations apply also to cases like that of Hippolytus' self-defence mentioned under (i). The two problems are not quite equivalent: in (i) we considered a (to us) unfamiliar way of writing, where the end was on the whole perfectly clear (the framing of a statement, appeal, evocation of pathos, and so on); the problem was that we were baffled and alienated by the unfamiliarity of the form. Here it is the end itself that is obscure; if digressive speeches cannot be given dramatic point of an 'organic' or 'unified' kind, then they must have been valued either in themselves or for some other centrifugal, ancillary pleasure which they afforded; and it is precisely the nature of this value that is in question. But naturally, there is a connection between the two problems: if rhetorical technique was found an interesting and rewarding way of reaching the organically intelligible ends of (i), that is presumably by virtue of qualities which could also contribute to rhetorical digression's being an end in itself under (ii).

[22] Conacher 1981: 25.

and Lycus in *Heracles*. Bond, in his discussion of this passage, cites approvingly Wilamowitz's judgment that Euripides has sacrificed drama for rhetoric; he points out that Lycus' 'epideixis on the theme "Heracles was not brave" ' is a deliberately paradoxical display, of the kind which occurs frequently in Euripides (Bond mentions some other examples), and which were inspired by contemporary rhetorical training (again, he gives non-tragic examples), and concludes:[23]

> The debate about archery is long and not particularly appropriate ... Why did Euripides insert the debate? ... Euripides is examining and criticising two traditional views, (a) that Heracles was brave; (b) that bravery means standing up to the enemy.

That Euripides is examining these views is in one sense obviously true; but to offer it as an explanation of the debate, and not simply as a description of its content, is to imply a seriousness of purpose on Euripides' part that it would be rash to assume. Gorgias called his *Helen* (a supreme example of the genre with which we are dealing) a *jeu d' esprit* (*paignion*); and clearly, its purpose is not to establish the case for which it argues as true; its point lies rather in the paradoxicality and cleverness of the argument, and in the effectiveness and beauty of the words used in presenting that argument. The masterly conduct of argument, with skilful use of all its dialectical and linguistic resources, is being treated as something to admire and savour in its own right, as one might admire and relish the metrical and linguistic resources of a poetic text. This taste (which I, for one, do not find inaccessible or contemptible) evidently existed in the fifth century; and Euripides shared it (we commented on his attachment to the sophistic movement in 2.32). It is this taste that provided both the point and the artistic justification of his digressive rhetoric. The work by Gorgias is one which Bond strangely does not cite; but it has an obvious tragic parallel in the agon of *Trojan Women*, where Helen offers her own self-defence. I quoted Lee's uncomfortable remarks on this agon earlier; if one accepts that the sophistic display has, or would at any rate have had for at least part of its contemporary audience, its own aesthetic value, then the logic-chopping would not have been, as Lee supposed, 'idle'.

The examples here have been taken from Euripides, for obvious reasons; the sophistic taste for rhetorical display and paradox is characteristic of his work. But the tendency to digressive set-pieces which is most fully developed, and most overtly allied to formal rhetoric, in Euripides among the extant tragedians, is in fact common in some measure to them all. This one might expect, in view of the importance of *poikilia* in Greek literary aesthetics; as we said in 3.2, this is an inherently centrifugal principle, one that defies our demands for a tidy integration of content. We might consider here the beacon-speech in *Agamemnon*, or the Messenger-speech in Sophocles' *Electra*; true, the overwhelming verisimilitude of the latter report has emotive force, enhancing as it does the effect on Electra, and therefore her desolation, but one should not underestimate the autonomous value of its narrative and

[23] Bond 1981: 102, 106, 109.

descriptive skill.[24] In the same play, Sophocles rather clearly engineers the debate between Clytaemnestra and her daughter to a large extent because of his interest in such set-piece confrontations. It is true that he is less epideictic than Euripides: 'The decks, we might say, are less ostentatiously cleared for this sort of display';[25] nevertheless, the speeches are efficient rhetorical performances.[26] This point has not escaped the notice of Kells, who remarks that 'there is something curiously legalistic and unreal about Electra's pleading on behalf of Agamemnon'.[27] In other commentators, this might simply have been an adverse aesthetic judgment (a loss of meaning); but in Kells it is taken as corroboration of his jaundiced view of Electra and Orestes – an interpolation of an alien meaning. This is a fair example of the disastrous consequences that can follow from misunderstanding the point of rhetoric in Greek tragedy.[28]

Kells' reading of *Electra* exploits, in addition to this general misunderstanding of its rhetoric, a particular misunderstanding. A number of critics have felt that there is a difficulty in Electra's contribution to this debate: is not the *lex talionis* 'an awkward principle for a person intent on murder'?[29] Kells comments:

> In these lines we have the crux of the whole ethical situation of the play; if retributive killing is wrong ... then Electra's and Orestes' killing of their mother is going to be just as wrong as was Clytaemnestra's killing of Agamemnon. Electra condemns herself out of her own mouth.

But if we accept that rhetoric in tragedy has a centrifugal, self-contained tendency, then it is arguable that these unwelcome implications (unwelcome since they belong with a reading of the play that is irretrievably faulty)[30] are

---

[24] Cf. Reinhardt 1979: 151-2.

[25] Dale 1969: 152.

[26] Cf. Navarre 1900: 74-5, Schmalzriedt 1980.

[27] Kells 1973: 127 (on 566ff.).

[28] Another example, this time from Euripides, is the belief that E.*Su.*857ff. (the *epitaphios*) is meant satirically (e.g. Fitton 1961; against this, Collard 1972). There is, of course, a certain piquant paradox in the fact that it is *these* men who are being praised; but paradox is, as we have seen, the point of many of these pieces of rhetoric, and it is not at all the same thing as satire or irony.

[29] Gellie 1972: 110; cf. Winnington-Ingram 1980: 220-1 & n.19. The next quotation is from Kells 1973: 128.

[30] Kells is following Sheppard 1927; there is a cogent critique in Stevens 1978 (cf. also Szlezák 1981). I comment briefly: (i) The ingenious interpretation which Kells offers of Orestes' question to the oracle convicts Sophocles of carelessness, since the (on this view) *suggestio falsi* in *endikous* (37) would be an unnecessary hindrance to the audience's perception of the subtlety. Apollo's command is, in any case, so well-entrenched a part of the tradition that a clearer counter-indication would be needed; it is vain to point out that Sophocles has departed from tradition by suppressing the Erinyes (pp.5-6): for that is not a point which must, on pain of a total misunderstanding of the play, be gleaned by the audience from the subtlest of hints. (ii) Kells offers us a simple dilemma: the matricide was *either* justified *or* abhorrent; this is too simple, since in all the tragedians (cf. 2.32) the matricide is seen as justified *and* abhorrent. (iii) Kells attaches great importance to Clytaemnestra's maternal grief (pp.7, 9; contrast Reinhardt 1979: 261 & n.19); but Aeschylus' Clytaemnestra also expresses (sincere) grief for her son (cf. 1.13). (iv) Kells neglects the implications of the juxtaposition of Clytaemnestra's prayer (636ff.)

controlled; an audience used to the conventions of tragic rhetoric would receive them as making a case against Clytaemnestra, but would not be inclined to explore their implications beyond this limited context. In the same way, those interpreters of *Orestes* who see far-reaching consequences for our understanding of the play as a whole in Tyndareus' appeal to due process of law are not only (as I suggested in 2.32) swallowing rather naively a debating-point that is to be passed over as merely specious; they are also at fault in neglecting the limited context of relevance that such debating-points in tragedy possess. This is true also, I believe, of some notoriously problematic lines in *Heracles* (1341-6). To see in this passage, as many interpreters have done, an open denunciation of the play's very premises is dramatically ruinous: I pointed out in 2.32 that this would destroy what we know a Greek tragedian would have valued most highly, emotional effect; and we may add (in the light of 3.3) that it would violate the principle of conviction, an important tragic restraint (cf. 1.3). But if we read this passage as a retort to Theseus, and accept that its implications are restricted and controlled by that limited context, such interpretations are unnecessary. Theseus has used a standard form of *consolatio*: 'Others, too ...', giving it an *a fortiori* twist: 'Even the gods ...'; but Heracles is unwilling to accept any lessening of his guilt and grief, and must therefore reject the premises of Theseus' attempted consolation before going on to explain his own and quite different reason for accepting Theseus' offer of sanctuary: not because his situation is, as Theseus claims, not really so bad as it appears, but because it is so bad, and because it is not consistent with his heroism to shrink even from such extreme suffering. His rejection of Theseus' premises is, to be sure, inconsistent with the presuppositions of the play, and indeed with what Heracles himself says before and after: but it is, to adopt the terminology of 3.3, an analytical inconsistency, deprived of dramatic significance by convention; because the implications of rhetorical points in tragedy are controlled, the conflict need not and ought not to become apparent to the audience.

4.23 Act-dividing lyric

A Greek tragedy is a narrative presented in a series of formally separated acts; the sequence of these acts is articulated by the exit and entry of actors in conjunction with the alternation of speech and song. This is the basis of Taplin's theory of the formal structure of tragedy.[31] It is, on reflection, difficult to see how things could have been otherwise, given the course of the genre's development; when the tragedian's personnel consisted of a single actor (himself) and the Chorus, the only way in which plays could be put

with the arrival of the Tutor: an apparently propitious answer, which the audience knows to be the first stage in her destruction; does not Apollo approve the killing? (v) He also neglects the emphasis throughout, not only on the horror of what Clytaemnestra has done, but on justice, the gods, retribution, the Erinyes (cf. Winnington-Ingram 1980: 217ff., Burton 1980: 224 and his whole chapter).

[31] Taplin 1977: 49-60.

together is this: the actor enters, makes a speech or engages the Chorus in dialogue, and leaves; and the Chorus sings a song while he changes costume before returning as another character. This basic pattern can be varied: even in the earliest stages of development lyric utterance (by the actor or by the Chorus) can be introduced into the predominantly spoken texture of the acts, while the act-dividing lyric may shrink to an astrophic or anapaestic residue when a swift re-entry is desired; and with the multiplication of actors, more complex permutations of exit and entry become possible; but the basic pattern is not thereby destroyed.[32]

This structural analysis suggests that the function of the tragic Chorus cannot be discussed as a *single* problem: we must distinguish between its function (or functions) within acts, and its act-dividing function. I will return to the Chorus within the act in 4.42; here I wish to consider briefly the nature of act-dividing lyric. For this, like digressive rhetoric (4.22ii), has provoked vigorous discussion; and here, as there, there are dangers in a premature application of evaluative criteria: the interpreter must test the appropriateness of such criteria against the function of the feature in question within the genre's own poetics.

The basic function of act-dividing lyric is, not surprisingly, to divide acts: to keep the successive units of predominantly spoken texture apart, and to fill in the gap left by their being kept apart with words that will keep the audience entertained (my use of this word is not derisory); this is in keeping with Aristotle's view of lyric as a *hēdusma* (cf. 1.2; and note the scholion on S.*Aj*.693). It performs this basic task primarily by contrast. The metrical texture (and also its musical and choreographical accompaniment) contrasts with the predominant texture of the verbal text within the acts: and along with this change of texture there is a corresponding change of dialect colouring and poetical vocabulary; in both respects, therefore, act-dividing lyric advertises itself as an obviously different kind of poetry. There is also a contrast of tone and content; the lyric interludes tend to range more widely, and are usually more emotional in tone. Act-dividing lyric is therefore set apart from what is contained within the acts, and because of this contrast it is capable of marking the structural break clearly. But the differences which set it apart from the act also tend to heighten its autonomous aesthetic qualities, thereby making it more entertaining: for example, the shift from iambic to lyric metres, in which the rhythmical patterning is more distinctive, more obtrusive and therefore – since patterning is inherently a source of aesthetic pleasure – poetically more rewarding.

Act-dividing lyric therefore performs its basic function by diversifying the main narrative text with contrasting and aesthetically heightened material. This is to say that it follows the aesthetic principle of *poikilia*; and, as we have

[32] This pattern is not followed in Old Comedy, a genre of which we may be sure that it did *not* develop from a Chorus and single actor: for its characteristic scenes, the agon (Gelzer 1960) and the episodic scenes which typically follow the parabasis, require at least two actors – 'hero' and opponent or interloper. (The Chorus cannot take on these roles, of course, but needs an actor as spokesman: in *Ach.*, where the spokesman Lamachus arrives only at the last minute, the agon is one-sided and wholly untypical.)

observed before (3.2, 4.22ii), the tendency of this principle is centrifugal. Consequently, we may say that the basic function of act-dividing lyric, if it does not strictly demand 'irrelevance', certainly tolerates, and perhaps encourages, it: irrelevance is no hindrance to act-dividing lyric's achieving its fundamental purpose. It is true that the dramatist may wish to use a particular ode in a more complex way; he may, for example, wish not simply to create a gap and entertain us during it, but to carry us across the gap that he has created in a particular way – perhaps by creating a certain mood, moulding our expectations, preparing (or misleading) us in readiness for a new development. But two points must be made. First, we must not make of these possible extensions of the basic function of act-dividing lyric a norm against which functionally simple odes will be judged; it would be unreasonable to find fault with an ode for doing no more than the dramatic context required. The second point is that there is no necessary connection between this kind of functional complexity and the 'relevance' of an ode: it is relatively easy to compose odes that are 'relevant', in that their themes are part of or arise directly out of the play's *praxis*; but such an ode may do no more than fill a gap, while an ode more tenuously connected with the *praxis* might be functionally important in one of the ways suggested above.

Let us consider a simple example. At S. *Tr.*496, Deianeira and Lichas enter the palace to prepare gifts to be sent to Heracles; there is a brief interval before their reappearance, which the first stasimon is designed to fill (497-530). It opens with an acclamation of the power of love,[33] an appropriate response to the revelations made in the previous scene; but this acclamation does not add to our understanding of the theme (already stated by Deianeira in 441-4), and the point is not developed: in the main body of the ode, the goddess of love appears not as victor, but as umpire of the battle between Heracles and Achelous. The thematic opening, then, is used to ease the transition from the act to the lyric narrative that is the ode's chief point, the means by which Sophocles proposes to entertain us during this interval. This narrative is 'relevant', in the sense that it pictures an event from the prehistory of the play; but Deianeira's account in the prologue (18-27) would suffice for our understanding of the *praxis*, and its elaboration here is for the autonomous aesthetic value of the short but vivid description which the event is given here. The management of the transition between the two acts which this lyric divides is particularly skilful: we have seen how the *hêdusma* is introduced by an acclamation that arises from the act preceding; towards its end, the narrative focusses on the frightened girl who was there as a prize: and this note of pathos about Deianeira (*hôste portis erêma* 530) aptly introduces her entry as she seeks pity for her present plight (535).

A clear example of 'irrelevance' that is nevertheless functional can be found in the opening of the second stasimon of *Hippolytus* (732-75): the Chorus' escapist longings intensify the effect on us of the painful and inescapable reality with which they are juxtaposed. Similarly in the first

---

[33] I agree with Stinton (1976b: 136ff.) in finding Wakefield's punctuation after *Kupris* attractive.

stasimon of Euripides' *Electra* (432-86), the song's initial movement is away from the harshness of present reality into a distant and more splendid world: *kleinai naes, hai pot' ebate*. The lavishly poetical style of the lyrics; the magical presence of the Nereids; the heroic glory of Achilles (a goddess's son) and the magnificence of his arms (a god's craftsmanship): these are images of a vanished splendour in the starkest contrast to Electra's degraded status, and they enhance its pathos. In both odes, we are returned in the end to the grim reality, the effect of which has been enhanced by the contrast: to the murderous daughter of Tyndareus and the pressing need for vengeance, to Phaedra's ill-omened marriage and her sinister passion.[34]

And yet there is act-dividing lyric that cannot be accounted for in this way; in the third stasimon of the Taurian *Iphigeneia*, for example, the interval between the deception of Thoas and departure of Orestes and Electra, and the return of the Messenger to report their abscondence, is filled by an account of Apollo's seizure of Delphi (1234-83). This does have a rather tenuous contextual motivation, in that Apollo has been a prominent figure in the background of this play; but the emphasis must be on 'tenuous', and it is hard to discern any functional complexity in this ode. If this fact perplexes us, it is because we have approached act-dividing lyric from the wrong direction. The first thing we must ask about act-dividing lyric is: With what success does it perform its basic task? That is, does it separate two acts in a way that provides autonomous aesthetic reward? Only then should we go on to ask whether and in what ways it has been put to further use in its dramatic context: Is it used to enhance the emotional effect of the *praxis*? To manage a transition? To guide us by means of commentary? These and other possibilities exist: for the Chorus is above all, as Vickers says, a 'flexible dramatic instrument';[35] but where (as in this example from *IT*) there is no more than divide acts that an act-dividing lyric could helpfully do, it would be foolish to expect it do more than that: especially when it has done it so pleasantly.

4.3 The non-verbal text

Our discussion of act-dividing lyric (4.23) has brought us to the limits of the merely verbal component of the Greek tragic text: for in origin these were not simply words lyrically textured, but words designed for performance accompanied by specially composed music and dance. These accompaniments are irrecoverably lost to us; and we must therefore accept that our knowledge of the dramatic text is inevitably partial – no less so than where a lacuna has deprived us of part of the verbal text. How serious is this loss? The music and dance would of course have enhanced the aesthetic reward of the odes – an important consideration, since we have emphasised their role as intercalary *hêdusmata*; they would also have reinforced the

[34] These two odes are also discussed by Vickers 1973: 19-22 (see also Padel 1974).
[35] Vickers 1973: 10; the discussion that follows is excellent.

representational and expressive meaning of the odes, for we know that both dance and music were regarded as mimetic.[36] But if (as we have no reason to doubt) the mimetic element of the accompaniment supported, rather than qualifying or contradicting, the verbal text, then its loss will threaten no severe distortion in our understanding; if we may distinguish between substantive and subsidiary channels of communication, and we would be talking here of a subsidiary channel. The loss, then, is mainly one of aesthetic richness; a tract of the genre's ancillary pleasure has been removed, and we will therefore be unable to judge with full appreciation the aspect of *poikilia* and *hêdusma* in act-dividing lyric.

There is, then, reason to deplore our loss of the non-verbal dimension of the act-dividing text, since it restricts our appreciation of the plays; but we have no reason to fear that this loss will decisively distort our overall understanding of the plays. What of the non-verbal component of the text within the acts? I shall consider as a test-case a short sequence from Euripides' *Hypsipyle* (fr.60.5ff. in Bond 1963). Hypsipyle has just made a long speech pleading for her life, which the Chorus conventionally tags (fr.22.9-10: cf. 4.21iii); Eurydice, however, contemptuously rejects the plea, forcing Hypsipyle to make one last and desperate appeal before she accepts the inevitable. Note first that Hypsipyle is bound (fr.60.29); this visual expression of her helplessness augments the pathos. Secondly, the opening lines of her appeal are met by obdurate silence (60.7); the verbal text points here to a perceptible pause in performance, a space empty of words which enacts the failure of the appeal more eloquently than anything Eurydice could have said. Hypsipyle's speech continues, therefore, more as a lament than an appeal, and culminates in an emotional apostrophe of her absent protector. Again, perhaps, the futility of the appeal is emphasised by a slight but perceptible pause, in which no rescuer appears from the eisodoi; so at 60.20 she turns to her guards and offers herself to be lead away: here the contrast in delivery between the climactic apostrophe and the quiet submission must be important and effective in performance; and the submission could be expressed also in movement towards the guards and by some simple gesture (such as offering her bound hands to them). At this moment, however, the last moment, the rescuer does enter, in haste and with an urgent address to Eurydice. At once, however, Hypsipyle breaks in with a further plea; so Euripides continues to exploit the pathos of her position, and he enhances this visually by making her adopt the posture of a suppliant (60.25-6, 29-30; cf. 4.41). The appeal she now makes evokes a tender response from Amphiaraus before he turns back to Eurydice to resume his interrupted address. She, however, had modestly veiled herself on his entry (60.43, 52; cf. *Hec.*974-5). This action has the effect of withdrawing her temporarily from contact, and so facilitates the brief and pathetic exchange between Hypsipyle and Amphiaraus; it also means that when Amphiaraus wishes to re-establish contact with her, he must begin by asking her to remove the veil; when she does so, therefore, the action marks visually her

---

[36] See esp. Pl.*Rep.* 398a-9d, *Laws* 655d-6b, 668a-71a, 814d-6d; Ar. *Pol.* 1339-42b.

new accessibility: it enacts her making herself open to Amphiaraus' plea on behalf of her prisoner.

A comparable situation occurs at *Andr.*501ff. Andromache is brought on, bound; the fact that she is bound is used here, and again when Peleus releases her at the end of the rescue action, to excite both pity for the victim and indignation against her persecutor. When Peleus her rescuer arrives, Andromache strikes the suppliant posture; and in this instance Euripides exploits her bonds to give a new twist to the pathos (573-4). The pose is maintained during the debate, and provides a tacit source of pathos and outrage throughout; and when Peleus finally helps her up (717ff.), this action provides a visual enactment of his success in rescuing her.

These examples are slight: they contain no exceptional devices of performance; but they serve to illustrate how, even in technically unexceptional passages, the Greek dramatist is constantly aware of his verbal text as only one part of a complex dramatic text. Therefore, we must read his words at all times with an eye and ear to the total orchestration of sound and silence, and of visual media, of costume, posture, action and movement, if the full force and meaning of the drama is to be perceived. This consideration has had increasing influence in recent criticism of tragedy, and rightly so;[37] but it raises an obvious question: how far is it possible to reconstruct the non-verbal dimensions of the dramatic text when only a verbal script remains to us? This question in turn has two sides. First, is it safe to make inferences, as I did in my two examples, from what is said in the verbal text to accompanying stage-action? Secondly, can we be sure that there is no stage-action to be supplied of which the verbal text tells us nothing?

In an important discussion, Taplin answers the first of these questions positively: we may assume that actions mentioned in the verbal text were (where practicable) visibly performed; and this surely right.[38] On the one hand, there are details of the verbal text which would perhaps seem pointless, even frigid, if they were not enacted (for example, the play with Andromache's bonds in the passage mentioned above); and the positive advantages of enactment to the dramatist, above all in reinforcing emotional effect, make it inconceivable that the resource was not exploited. This claim is not purely speculative; ancient evidence makes it clear that the value of the resource was appreciated, and that it was not neglected in the theatre. Aristotle's reserved attitude to *opsis* is, to be sure, notorious;[39] but this was forced on him by critics who regarded it as *phaulon* (the defensiveness of ch.26 of the *Poetics* is obvious). That such criticism was possible in itself sugests that the visual dimension was important in tragic practice; and in spite of his reservations, Aristotle does show signs of appreciating the force of what is seen on stage: he describes it as *psukhagôgikon* – that is, as contributing to the emotional impact of tragedy (1450b15ff.: cf. 1.12 and 53b1ff.) – and perhaps mentions it as a source of pleasure alongside *mousikê* (62a16: but this may be an interpolation), while he recommends that a dramatist visualise the action

[37] E.g. Steidle 1968: 9-32, Taplin 1977: 12-39 and *passim* (further references 488-9), 1978.

[38] Taplin 1977: 31-9.

[39] Taplin 1977: 477-9; cf. Janko 1984: 228-9; Halliwell 1986: 66-7, 337-43.

as it would occur on stage (55a22ff.). He appreciated the same principle in rhetoric: 'inevitably, those who contribute to the effect by gesture, voice and costume, and in general by performance (*hupokrisei*) are more pitiable' (*Rhet.* 1386a32ff.).[40] Also relevant is Aristophanes' reaction (or affected reaction) to Euripides' 'rags' (cf. 1.3); it would be unintelligible unless Euripides were exploiting, perhaps in a new or extreme way, a channel of communication integral to the dramatic text. If he were merely tampering with a piece of decoration of no great significance or force, and still more if such things were not made visible at all, these jokes would be pointless. It is, of course, another question how fair the jokes were to Euripides; it would seem not very fair at all, for Aeschylus had exploited rags – and a king dressed in them – in *Persians*,[41] as had Sophocles in *Philoctetes*, while Sophocles' Electra was at least poorly dressed (*S.El.*191, cf. 452). One assumes that there was some basis for the joke; but it may have been very tenuous: and once a joke had started, it would tend to perpetuate itself and exaggerate itself. The point here, however, is as always not the fairness of the joke, but the implications of its very possibility for the poetics of tragedy.

There are some relevant observations in the scholia as well. A commentator on the opening scene of *Ajax* well observes that the appearance of Ajax on stage enhances the pathos of his madness (scholion on S.*Aj.*57); and a note on *Aj.*346 explains the use of the eccyclema by pointing out that *ekplêxis* may be achieved when *ta peripathestera* – objects of pathos – are made visible. One may add to this external evidence internal evidence that the dramatists appreciated the point, observing, for example, the way in which they liked to follow up a Messenger with a visual presentation that made the emotional force of his news more concrete – 'the dying, the dead, the mourners, the victors'.[42]

As for the other side of the question – was there nothing in the non-verbal text that is not recoverable from the script? – I am again in broad agreement with Taplin;[43] but this is the more difficult issue. Obviously, there is a great deal about the visual presentation of a tragedy that is not specified in the words: for example, each character must have some costume, but not every character's costume is described at all in the verbal text, and none is described in exhaustive detail. It is possible to say, with Taplin, that no *significant* visual effect is left unsignalled; but 'significant' is ambiguous: do we mean simply 'meaningful'? Then the claim is certainly false, for many details of costume will have signified, for example, a minor character's status and occupation, but receive no explicit mention. But if we mean 'important', we must also ask: by what criteria?

The problems can best be illustrated if we look at what is (as Taplin sees)

[40] On *hupokrisis* see Rutherford 1905: 87-156.
[41] Taplin 1977: 121-3, Thalmann 1980.
[42] Taplin 1977: 172; cf. Dingel 1967: 106-12 ('Botenbericht mit nachfolgender Demonstration'). Elsewhere Dingel speaks aptly of 'die vergegenwärtigende Kraft des Requisits' (Jens 1971: 362) – he is there discussing the urn-scene in S.*El.*, where the object gives the scene's emotions a concrete centre.
[43] Taplin 1977: 28ff.

the most weighty counter-example to his (and my) position, the Queen's ceremonious entry in *Persians*. Taplin argues that this only *becomes* significant retrospectively, and that it is signalled precisely where it does become significant. But the entry can only acquire this added and retrospective significance because it was already meaningful in its own context; the entry displayed the wealth and power of the Persian Queen, and was *therefore* able to display its loss retrospectively. But this meaning is abundantly signalled in the immediate context of the original entry: in the anapaestic announcement (cf. 1.21ii), the greeting ('a more unusual and attention-catching device', as Taplin says;[44] and note how its use is emphasised by 153-4, which add to the ceremonious effect), the lavish oriental flattery (150-1), the act of prostration, and (as a constant background) the emphasis on the wealth and power of Persia. Moreover, the chariot-borne entry is, as Taplin shows in the first part of his discussion, a natural visual exponent of this meaning. But clearly, if we are dealing with a standard visual realisation of a meaning that is already clear from the verbal text, the fact that it is not explicitly mentioned cannot justly be used to defend the interpolation of stage-business with a meaning that is not already implicit in the words: and it is only then that the question of unmentioned stage-action becomes crucial in interpretation. We may conclude, therefore, that the further an alleged visual effect is from the subsidiary or interpretative end of the substantive/subsidiary scale mentioned earlier – the further it is from being an unexceptional device used to support the words without adding to or amending the meaning which they already bear – the more reluctant we should be to accept it into the dramatic text without explicit indication in the verbal text.

The more important it is for us to recognise some non-verbal device, then, the more likely it is to be signalled in the words; why should this be so? The obvious reason is that if a point is important enough to warrant special emphasis by means of an unusual non-verbal effect, it is important enough to be made emphatic in the words as well: for the words do constitute the dominant medium of tragedy. This principle must be qualified when applied to states, as distinct from events, on stage. States are of value to the dramatist precisely as constant and tacit sources of emphasis: so Andromache's suppliant posture is before us and still influencing our response even between the passages in which it receives explicit attention; and the shabby costume of Electra in Sophocles' play would constantly bring to the fore her degraded status, even though little effort is made to draw attention to her clothing verbally. Events, however, depend for their effect on a brief span of time; and it is reasonable, therefore, that they should need reinforcement in the dominant medium.

It should be stressed that in saying that the non-verbal aspects of performance are in need of verbal support we have not reduced them once more to the merely subsidiary role assigned to the 'standard' effects that are not explicitly signalled. The contrast still stands: in the one case, a point is made in the words in a substantially adequate way, and its non-verbal

---

[44] Taplin 1977: 74; see also Sider 1983.

realisation merely illustrates or echoes the verbal text: in the other case, although the point is made in the words, its full force or weight cannot be appreciated unless the performance is either seen and heard or else imagined, so that the non-verbal text does significantly amplify or extend the point as made in the verbal text alone. (Of course, we are dealing here with a graduated distinction, and not, as this convenient idealisation implies, with a sharp dichotomy.) In the sequence from *Hypsipyle*, for example, or in the urn-scene from Sophocles' *Electra* (to take a more unusual and striking device), our appreciation of the force and meaning of what is said depends on our reconstruction of the text as stage-event; as Taplin says, 'these techniques do not work on the printed page; it is only in performance or in the theatre of the mind's eye that they come to life'.[45]

4.4 The repertoire

4.41 Types

Any act of communication depends on a body of presupposed knowledge that is assumed to be shared by the utterer and his addressee. By the 'repertoire' of tragedy in a broad sense I mean that whole corpus of data which is the content of the knowledge that a tragedian can assume to be shared with the audience and to be available in this generic context. Within this corpus it may be possible to identify a smaller repertoire of 'types', that is, of recurrent though optional configurations of features which, being recognisable as such, are potentially communicative – more richly and more economically so than comparable *ad hoc* configurations: for these, since they are not recognised as conforming to a familiar pattern, do not bring with them the same wealth of expectations and preunderstandings. Such conventional configurations need not, of course, be explicitly recognised on either side of the transaction; implicit familiarity will suffice. Nor need they be exhaustively specific, nor inflexible; it is necessary only that there be some recognisable, recurrent pattern which, when invoked, will bring with it expectations of at least a general kind: these the dramatist may then fill out or modify, and indeed he may wish to exploit the communicative potential of the type by thwarting its expectations. In this section, I wish to look briefly at some illustrative aspects of the tragic repertoire of types.

Let us begin with an obvious example, that of supplication, which we have already met in the passage from *Hypsipyle* examined in 4.3. Suppliancy consists in a system of roles and obligations which may be engaged by certain conventional forms of action (kneeling, touching the protector's chin and knees, and so forth) and by the accompanying verbal formula; it is a distinctive situation, recurrent in tragedy and entirely familiar to the audience, whose understanding of and response to everything that happens in the context is conditioned by that familiarity. In *Hippolytus*, for example,

[45] Taplin 1971: 44.

Euripides exploits his audience's familiarity with supplication to resolve a problem in the plot: how is Phaedra's illicit passion for Hippolytus to be disclosed *ad intra*? On pain of compromised integrity Phaedra herself must keep silent; but if she does keep silent, the plot will grind to a halt: she will die with her secret intact. The Nurse is employed to resolve the dilemma: we understand her supplication as a form of moral pressure which, even though unscrupulously used in this case, takes away from Phaedra the initiative in revealing the truth; she is rendered relatively passive, and can therefore break her silence without appearing forward. Those interpreters who have criticised Phaedra for revealing her secret have failed to weigh the force of this device, designed precisely to deflect such moralistic scrutiny.[46]

When Odysseus comes to fetch Polyxena in *Hecuba*, Hecuba pleads for the life of her daughter by reminding him of the earlier occasion on which he was her suppliant (245); she uses this reminder to establish a claim on his gratitude, and so to urge repayment of the debt: life for life (*antidounai* 272). Hecuba herself does not make a formal supplication at this point (that she does not is implied by 334-45); but she does use the language of supplication figuratively in order to keep vividly in mind the debt on which she rests her claim (272-8). This evocation of suppliant motifs makes the audience sensitive to the type, and tends perhaps to excite some expectation of a supplication as the climax to her appeal; and when Hecuba is rebuffed and urges her daughter to supplicate, it does seem that we are to have an appeal in two stages, in which the pathos of the second stage is heightened by the ritual performance (cf. E.*IA* 1146-1254). But Odysseus takes evasive action (342-4), and the climax is an unexpected one: not the pathos of intensified appeal, but the pathos of Polyxena's nobility in the face of death (345-78); our expectations have been misdirected, and the actual climax gains force from its unexpectedness.[47] The type appears again later in the play. When Agamemnon enters, Hecuba (who wishes to avenge her son's death on Polymestor) asks herself whether to seek his aid by supplication; this long deliberative build-up (736-51) leads to a climax in which she adopts the ritual posture of the suppliant and begins her appeal (752-3). Agamemnon, misreading her object, interrupts and too lightly promises satisfaction. The ensuing stichomythia (used partly because a formal contrast to the rhesis of the appeal itself is desirable, and partly for the heightened tensions of the form: 4.21iv) initiates him into a shocked understanding of the true situation. At 787 Hecuba resumes the speech begun in 752-3, and rises towards an

---

[46] This is not to deny that Euripides could have evaded the problem: if he had simply brought on a slave distraught at the knowledge of her mistress's passion, would we have been inclined to ask how he or she knew? But once Euripides had decided to make an issue of the secret, the dilemma stands; and this he did, I take it, because he valued the opportunity it afforded of giving emphasis to Phaedra's integrity in attempting to keep silence. I note in passing that Winnington-Ingram's interpretation of Phaedra's submission (1958: 179: 'Why does Phaedra yield? There can be no doubt that the fundamental reason is the deep longing she has to make the revelation') has not a scrap of support in the text; we have met this kind of thing before (3.4).

[47] Note how the evasiveness of Odysseus (visually realised in his movements) acts as a foil to this nobility: which also itself touches on, and draws power from, another Euripidean type, the noble self-sacrifice (cf. Strohm 1957: 50-63).

emotional climax at 811; but there is a second interruption, for Agamemnon has now realised what is being asked of him and tries to extricate himself from the role of supplicated (the contrast between the two interruptions is striking and effective). Hecuba persists with her appeal, and at last at 850 Agamemnon gives way; a turning-point has been reached, the more effective for the tension created by a formal supplication sustained across two interruptions and for almost a hundred lines of text: sustained in the visual text also, since the suppliant's posture keeps before us always the formal context of the appeal.[48]

Supplication is an established ritual outside the theatre, as is (to take a less obvious example) the *boêdromia* discussed by Taplin;[49] the dramatic repertoire naturally draws on the conventional forms of life. On the other hand, types may have a more purely dramatic existence. For example, the agon is not an established ritual outside the theatre (although, of course, comparable situations do exist outside the theatre); and although it is less clearly defined as a form in tragedy than in comedy, it does nevertheless display in tragedy a tendency to fall into a regular and relatively predictable form.[50] The existence of this as an identifiable, if loosely defined, type means that once its presence is clear to the audience in a given context, various expectations are brought into play: for example, the restricted context of relevance (4.22) or the convention governing the order of speakers (a factor in our discussion of *Orestes* in 2.32). It is worth noting that the latter convention is manifested only by a tendency, and is not without exception (there is an exception in *Medea*, although the departure from the norm is even there clearly signalled in a choral tag: *Med.*576-9); types, as I said initially, are flexible, and they must not be used mechanically in interpretation.

We have looked at supplication as providing a local pattern for an action or situation; it can also be used on a larger scale to provide the overall pattern of a plot, its basic framework or logic: as, for example, in Aeschylus' *Suppliants*. (We may recall how in 2.33 our interpretation of the play was swayed by its failure to conform to the identifiable sub-type in which patriotic motifs are combined with the suppliant-plot; the fact that *Eumenides* did conform to that sub-type was found no less significant.) Another such plot-type is the *nostos*-pattern; Euripides' *Heracles*, for example, takes a suppliant-situation as its point of departure, but uses this to anticipate the return of Heracles: a return rather like that of Odysseus, with the hero coming home to find and

---

[48] Gould 1973: 84-5 reconstructs this scene somewhat differently: 752f. and 787 are figurative; 811 leads up to a formal supplication, but Agamemnon evades; contact is made at 841ff., acknowledged at 851. But that the action should not be performed when verbally signalled, and should be performed when not so signalled, goes against the conclusions of 4.3; and the deliberative build-up would be flat if the supplication were not to occur for another 100 lines; in any case – would a suppliant make an appeal before pinning the victim down ritually? Capturing the protector is the precondition, not the climax, of one's appeal. Gould's article remains fundamental; see also Kopperschmidt 1966, Vickers 1973: 438-94.

[49] Taplin 1977: 218-20 (with further references).

[50] Cf. Duchemin 1968; the 'tags' discussed in 4.21iii are one device which emphasises the formal regularity of these confrontations. For comedy, see Pickard-Cambridge 1962: 200-4, Gelzer 1960.

set right a threat to his dependants and status by enemies who assume him dead, except that in this case the return is flawed by the divine assault which turns the rescue into a slaughter of the suppliants. Not surprisingly, the souring of the return is typical of tragic *nostoi*: for example, *Agamemnon*, in which a powerful emotional effect is achieved by the anticipatory concentration on the adversary who will spoil the return (cf. 1.13, 3.13).[51] Sophocles' *Trachiniae* illustrates the bearing of this plot-type on the question of 'unity': by bringing the hero's *nostos* so firmly within the audience's horizon of expectation from the beginning of the play, Sophocles ensures that his audience will not respond to Deianeira's tragedy, formally self-contained though it is (even to the extent of ring-composition: 1ff. is recalled in 943-6), with a premature sense that the *praxis* has achieved completion; the audience still has unsatisfied expectations which will carry them across the death of Deianeira without the dislocation of a premature sense of closure. Euripides uses the same device in *Andromache*; the anticipated return of Neoptolemus helps to smooth the transition from the action of supplication and rescue to the intrigue against Neoptolemus; and this in turn leads to a more tragic homecoming for him than had been anticipated.

Typical situations and typical plots require typical roles: for example, a suppliant-plot implies a victim, a persecutor and a protector; if one constructs such a plot, these 'slots' must be filled. These three roles are not directly equivalent to the typical roles in tragedy's emotional economy, discussed in 3.1; but for obvious reasons, when superimposed the two patterns will tend to correspond: victim to focus, persecutor to adversary, protector to assistant. There is, however, yet another level of typing in the personnel of tragedy, the level at which we may properly begin to speak of typical characters, rather than simply typical roles. For instance (to take an example which can easily be correlated with our example of type-roles), there are recognisable types of the good ruler and of the bad ruler or tyrant; the one is a natural filler for the 'protector/assistant' slot, the other for the 'persecutor/adversary' slot. These, being patterns familiar to the audience, provide the dramatist with an easy way of prompting moral judgments and guiding reactions of sympathy and antipathy; we saw, for example, in 2.4 that Creon's being typed as a tyrant is one means by which Sophocles reinforces our alignment against him in his conflict with Antigone.

Here, once again, a warning against the mechanical application of the concept of types is needed; this will be clear if one considers Sophocles' use of the tyrant-type in *Oedipus Tyrannus*. Oedipus at the beginning fits well into the type of the good king, by virtue of his solicitous concern for his people's well-being and perhaps also of the openness of his government (91-3: an adumbration of the democratic inclinations of the typical good king); but he is soon indulging in the violent suspiciousness which we associate with a Creon or a Pentheus. In fact, Sophocles has taken some care to motivate Oedipus' reaction: Teiresias goads him to fury, first by his apparently

---

[51] Fränkel observed that the bath traditionally marked the wanderer's true homecoming (1960: 97-9); the manner of Agamemnon's death therefore underlines the flaw in his *nostos*. (A.*Ch.* also contains a flawed *nostos*.)

treasonous refusal to disclose his knowledge, then by his obscure and seemingly gratuitous accusations; the recollection of his silence at the time of Laius' murder also raises doubts (390ff., 558-73), and there are circumstances which suggest Creon's complicity (287-9 with 555-6; cf. the scholia on 287, 326); it is also true that Oedipus is effectively insulated from the truth at this stage by what he thinks he knows.[52] Although Sophocles thus motivates and mitigates Oedipus' tyrannical reaction, the type is clearly evoked; but this should not, as the type normally would, have a substantially adverse effect on our response to him. Rather, we see him pursuing false trails, oblivious to his true situation; and the vigour and impetuosity of his reactions, expressed through the tyrannical traits, make this pursuit seem more futile and more pathetic. This variation on the tyrannical theme is possible, essentially, because it is Oedipus who is victim and focus, and who is therefore so placed that the audience is naturally disposed to see him as pitiable. The same is true, perhaps, of Pentheus, whose tyrannical traits in *Bacchae* are more uncompromising: his apparent power is illusory, and the audience must see through that illusion and identify him as the true victim.[53] Thus no type can properly be read in isolation; the context in which a type occurs and communicates is complex, and one must always consider other factors in the context – above all, one must consider its focal structure.

The ruler may be represented on stage by a proxy; the Herald is a decidedly bad type in tragedy, mainly because of his frequent use as a tyrant-proxy, which leads to his association with the role of adversary and with generally unpleasant traits.[54] But this type, too, is used flexibly; Talthybius is admirably presented in *Hecuba* and *Trojan Women*, where his sympathy and reluctance are used to show up more clearly the grimness of the orders which he must implement.[55] Once again, we see that we must not use types mechanically as an aid to interpretation; the 'mould' may have its own meaning, but this does not necessarily prevail in the interaction with the meaning of the specific content that has been poured into the mould in a given case, any more than it necessarily prevails over the meaning of the mould's own context.

This emphasis on the flexibility of types might suggest that the notion is too weak to be of any use; it may be helpful, therefore, if we look briefly at one clear instance in which character-types are used. The Messenger's speech in *Orestes* is a good example. First, the Messenger who brings the bad news breaks it to Electra with evident sympathy and reluctance; this solidarity with the focal figures must recommend him to the audience. But

---

[52] Cf. Vickers 1973: 500ff., Bain 1979: 132ff.

[53] It is sometimes supposed that the audience's sympathies in *Ba.* lie initially with Dionysus, and shift towards Pentheus as the roles of victim and persecutor are exchanged. But since Dionysus' identity was disclosed to the audience in the opening scene, they ought not to fall prey to this misconception of the real relationship between the two characters, nor miss the pathos of Pentheus' illusion of power.

[54] In A.*Su.*, *PV* (Hermes), E.*Held.*; cf. *Tro.*424-6, *Or.*888ff., fr.1012.

[55] Gilmartin compares Hephaestus in *PV* and Lyssa in *Her.* (1970: 218 n.30); so perhaps we are dealing here with another recognisable type. The very fact that it is a *herald* who is sympathetic, being unexpected, enhances the effect; this is true also of Lyssa.

there is more: he is introduced as a loyal retainer of the Atreid house, poor but *gennaios* (868-70); this attaches him at once to two sympathetic types.[56] The first speaker in the debate on which he reports is Talthybius, the herald; the adverse elements of the herald-type, on which we have already commented, are invoked here (889-97). A little later we are offered the demagogic rascal, an alien, paid, glib, trouble-making; against him is set the sturdy farmer, backbone of the land, unimpressive to look at, but *andreios* (917ff.).[57] Thus the sympathetically typed speakers defend Orestes, the antipathetically typed speakers are hostile to him. The Messenger's own prejudices are natural in his position, of course, but the audience shares them, and the use of these prejudicial types gives expression to and reinforces those natural inclinations.

In that illustration, we saw that the Messenger was individualised by means of two loaded types, the loyal retainer and the poor but noble man. But his functional role of delivering a report is itself highly typical; indeed, the Messenger is a notable type of Greek tragedy, intelligible only in the light of the naturalising conventions. I will return to this type, and to another of like kind (the Chorus in its role within acts), in the next two subsections.

Before we leave this discussion of character-types, however, one further level should be mentioned, that deriving from the mythological tradition that was the tragedian's main source of material. In fact, the predetermination of a given figure's presentation by the tradition is very flexible indeed: contrast, for example, the treatment of Odysseus in *Ajax* and *Philoctetes*.[58] And this question is complicated by the opposed evidence of Antiphanes (fr.191 K) and Aristotle (*Poet*.1451b25) on how familiar the myths actually were, at least to fourth-century audiences. But clearly, there were some limits to the flexibility of traditional figures; one could not, in a tragedy at any rate, portray Achilles as a feeble coward. And the data of myth were in some degree available to the tragedian as a communicative resource; we saw in 3.2, for example, how the audience's familiarity with the jealousy of Hera rendered intelligible to them her unexpected intervention in *Heracles*. There is in this respect some difference between tragedy and a genre like New Comedy, in which persons and events were completely invented, and only conventionalised formal structures and plot- and character-types were available. The mythological tradition exercised some constraint over the tragedians, and was therefore in far greater measure a communicative *resource* for them; how important either the constraint or the resource were is a matter of dispute: but the question should be kept in mind.

[56] (i) Loyal retainer: E.*Andr*.726ff., *Hel*.1640-1 etc.; the type goes back to *Od*., of course – and recall the Nurse in A.*Ch*. (ii) Poor but noble: S.fr.836; E.*El*.253 etc., *Andr*.640, fr.326.7, 362.27 etc. Commentators stress Euripides' progressive social attitudes; but the type itself, which is independent of Euripides' sententious elaborations, depends only on aristocratic condescension – which is ages old.

[57] (i) Glib town-dweller: E.*Ba*.717; for the contrast of glib townsman and sturdy countryman, see Dover 1974: 112-14. (ii) Uncomely but brave: cf. E.fr.842; Archilochus fr.114W, with Lloyd-Jones 1971: 39-40 (& nn. 59-62) for discussion and further references.

[58] A number of writers have recently protested, with justice, against the view that plot and treatment in tragedy are fixed by myth; e.g. Taplin 1978: 162-4.

4.42 The Chorus

In 4.23 I discussed act-dividing lyric; this is one aspect of the Chorus as a type, for obviously the acceptability and intelligibility to an audience of the Chorus as they fulfil this function is heavily dependent on the naturalising convention. But as I pointed out in the earlier discussion, the question of the Chorus' function within the act is a separate one – although the key phrase of 4.23, that the Chorus is a 'flexible dramatic instrument', is again essential.

We commented in 4.21iii on one purely functional role of the Chorus within the act ('functional' here precisely in the sense of 'functionary' introduced in 3.13): its provision of brief and rather bland comments, significant not so much for their content as for the contribution they make to the structure of a scene – highlighting structural regularity, marking transitions, punctuating actors' lyrics, and so forth. Not far removed from this is their provision of entry announcements and the like.[59] These two examples suggest that the Chorus is used essentially as an all-purpose convenience, giving whatever assistance is needed within a scene to ensure its smooth running. This can be illustrated further if we look at the Chorus' more integral contributions to the dialogue. Drama depends on speech; and given that the use of soliloquy is to be relatively sparing, it is useful to have a flexible presence to hand throughout, to be talked to (or at) by anyone that the dramatist needs to make talk: this presence makes it easier for the dramatist to get his characters to think, react, makes plans and so forth in the only way that will be accessible to the audience – aloud. This is seen clearly when the Chorus, in default of an appropriate principal, serves as audience *ad intra* for a Messenger – a point to which I shall return (4.43). Meanwhile, let us survey *Hippolytus* quickly: when Phaedra lapses into silence, the Chorus is there for the Nurse to talk to while Euripides sets up her assault on Phaedra's resistance; when the Nurse is off-stage interfering with Hippolytus, the Chorus is there, so that Phaedra can report to them what she hears within (thereby allowing Euripides to report it to us); when the Nurse has been dismissed, the Chorus is still there, so that Phaedra has someone to whom she can outline her plan; when Theseus arrives, it is the Chorus who tells him of his wife's death, and it is the Chorus who acts as partner in his laments. Thus the Chorus is always at hand, to act as a convenient ear or to provide an impromptu reaction or simply to oil the workings of the scene; this medley of oddjobmanship is neatly summed up by *Hi*.362ff., where the stanza in which the Chorus reacts to Phaedra's revelation is of chiefly structural importance: it serves to keep separate the Nurse's reaction and the beginning of Phaedra's rhesis, addressed (of course) to the Chorus in their role as available listener (*Trozêniai gunaikes*).

The Chorus is used within the act, therefore, as an all-purpose ear and source of interaction with the actors. If, as in 4.23, we look back to the earliest stages of tragedy, we will see the inevitability of this role; when there is only one actor, it must be the Chorus which greets, addresses, listens to and reacts to him as he acts out a succession of different roles; and as the number of

[59] For a detailed study of entrance-announcements, see Hamilton 1978.

actors increases, the dramatist will still have the Chorus at his disposal for these purposes, although he will be less dependent on them. So I am inclined to agree with Taplin that the Chorus of early tragedy must have played an important and active role within the acts.[60] *Persians* is a good example: the Chorus of this play may be 'anonymous and colourless',[61] but hardly more so than many principals in Aeschylus; and although it does not itself play a principal's role, its supporting role is large and important. Indeed, *Persians* is a better example than Taplin will allow. He says that A.*Su.*418-37 is the 'only mid-act ... choral strophic song in surviving tragedy', but conjectures that 'such songs may not have been uncommon in archaic tragedy'.[62] This is a plausible conjecture; but it is not plausible to exclude from this category *Per.*623-80, which Taplin treats elsewhere as an act-dividing song and an exception to his theory of formal structure.[63] The decisive point is not the lack of a preceding exit, so much as the integration of the song with a continuing action; like the mid-act astrophic song at *Ch.*152-63, it is sung at a principal's request while the principal herself performs ritual acts; and although the song is in this case followed by an entry, the continuity of action is nevertheless more marked than with the song from *Choephori*, since the entry is a direct response to the combination of song and ritual (in *Choephori*, the song is followed simply by a transition to another topic).

We can now see more clearly the importance of distinguishing the Chorus' role within the act from the Chorus' act-dividing role. The Chorus is important in *Persians*, and it is important in *Agamemnon*, but not in the same way. Its importance in the latter play depends most of all on the length and functional complexity of the act-dividing songs: its role within the act, though still larger than we would expect to find in Sophocles or Euripides, has shrunk by comparison with *Persians*; in *Persians*, though the Chorus is important within the acts, its two act-dividing songs are functionally very simple (the parodos is more elaborate, however, since it has taken over – or retained – the functions of a prologue).[64] It would seem, then, that the reduction of the choral element which Aristotle ascribes to Aeschylus must antedate *Persians*, as does the development of the trimeter as the main dialogue metre which accompanied the shift of emphasis to *logos* or *lexis* (Ar.*Poet.*1449a16-25); this would suggest that the use of complex lyrics essential to the understanding of the *praxis* that we find in *Agamemnon* is an experimental or innovative technique of his later work. Certainly, in other late plays he seems to be experimenting with the Chorus in another way; for

[60] Taplin 1977: 87, 206-9; I wish, however, that he had not used 'cantata' as a term of derision.
[61] Garvie 1969: 106.
[62] Taplin 1977: 208-9.
[63] Taplin 1977: 108-14.
[64] I say 'or retained' in view of Themistius' claim that the spoken prologue was an innovation of Thespis. The difference that I have mentioned between *Per.* and *Ag.* is obscured by most quantitative estimates of the Chorus' function: e.g., Griffith 1977: 123, who gives choral lyric + anapaests and choral total as percentages of the total number of lines in the play, but does not distinguish act-dividing lyric. The figure for *Per.* would be: parodos 14 per cent, act-dividing lyric 11 per cent; for *Ag.*, 13 per cent and 18 per cent – a marked contrast. But, of course, all such calculations are highly artificial.

the Chorus of *Suppliants* and *Eumenides* has been promoted within the act from a supporting to a principal role, as a focal character in *Suppliants*, and as a rather unusual kind of adversary in *Eumenides* (where the uniquely flexible structural technique also suggests bold innovation).[65] With so few plays of Aeschylus, and with those we possess so eccentrically distributed over his career, such speculation about the development of technique is hazardous; but I am prepared to believe that Aeschylus' choral technique in both *Agamemnon* and *Eumenides* is (in diverse ways) innovative. Certainly, it ran counter to the historical trend, which was to retain the relative simplicity of act-dividing lyric found in *Persians* while reducing the role of the Chorus within the act: Aeschylus made his Chorus of suppliants focal; Euripides, when he had a Chorus of suppliants, had simply to limit the important of the suppliant-plot, and gave us in his *Suppliants* a wealth of other things to take an interest in, exploiting to the full the principle of *poikilia*.

4.43 The Messenger

The visible stage is, inevitably, the focal point of drama, and what happens on it, before the audience's eyes, will have the most powerful effect on them, other things being equal. But we have seen that the verbal text was dominant in Greek tragedy (4.3); and the highly 'oral' nature of fifth-century culture gives us some reason to assume a high degree of responsiveness to the spoken word in the original audience.[66] This gives the Greek dramatist perhaps greater scope than the modern for overcoming the potential limitations of the dramatic focus on the stage; by spoken narration, he can extend his field of operation much further and handle events of a kind that could not be narrated directly.[67] To be sure, there is sufficient violence and death on the stage in extant tragedy to scotch any notion that a convention existed preventing the open display of violent action;[68] but technical problems limit the possibility of direct presentation, and the more spectacular kinds of violent action – pitched battles, supernatural bulls, human sacrifices – seem to be technically impossible. If his descriptive and narrative rhetoric is powerful enough, the dramatist can overcome these technical limitations, extending his field of operation without loss of emotive and dramatic force.

There is, therefore, scope for, and even a need for, a means of oblique dramatisation in Greek tragic theatre; and it is natural that, instead of being met on an *ad hoc* basis in each play, the need should encourage the development of a relatively stable conventionalised form: hence that recognisable, if loose, type, the tragic *angelos*.[69] That there is a convention at work here is clear enough: one has only to consider how odd it would seem, were it not for the naturalising effect of a convention and its concomitant

[65] On the structural technique of *Eu.*, see Taplin 1977: 362ff., 368ff., 377ff., 384ff., 407ff.

[66] Cf. Walcot 1976: 22ff.: but not all his conclusions are acceptable, and the argument is marred by some nonsense from McLuhan.

[67] Aristotle compares tragedy unfavourably with epic in this respect: 1460a11-17.

[68] On deaths in tragedy, see Pathmanathan 1965.

[69] Cf. (e.g.) Taplin 1977: 80-5.

expectations, when an anonymous figure suddenly appears to give a long and elaborate report of events off-stage, often in a situation of some urgency, and often to people who have no pressing need to know (that is, to the Chorus, acting in one of its typical roles: 4.42). The conventionalised type is recognisable also in the relatively predictable form; there are divergences, such as the use of a principal character (such as Hyllus in *Trachiniae*) or the Phrygian's monody in *Orestes*, but these are in pursuit of identifiable special effects, and they depend for their effect precisely on their divergence from a norm; and therefore they presuppose the convention.

The Messenger could be treated as a mere functionary (3.13), a neutral vehicle for oblique dramatisation; this is implied by the apparently widespread view of the Messenger as an unengaged, unindividualised figure. Barlow, for example, speaks of the Messenger in Euripides as a 'detached observer' conveying a 'rational account of objective fact, the existence of which has nothing to do with him personally';[70] were this really so, one would be baffled by the dramatists' neglect of so fine an opportunity to sway and stir and guide their audiences – 'detached', 'rational', 'objective' are not epithets richly suggestive of the attractiveness and force of skilful narrative rhetoric. But it is not true: the Messenger 'usually has an occupational identity, a reason for being involved, and some personal reaction to the events he reports'.[71] One example which we considered in 4.41 was the Messenger-speech from *Orestes*, where the speaker's involvement, together with a prejudicial use of types, gave the speech a definite and persuasive slant. In the rest of this subsection I propose to examine rather more carefully the Messenger-speech from *Hippolytus*. The speech is not a particularly complex one – it shares the high degree of formalisation typical of Euripidean Messenger-scenes; but I hope to show that Euripides exploits this simple narrative form in subtle and effective ways.

The Messenger-scene in *Hippolytus* begins with the entry of a servant, introduced and identified by the Chorus (in their familiar role) as an attendant of Hippolytus (1151-2); an audience, familiar with the convention, will at once infer his identity, and the two features of his entry to which the Chorus draw specific attention (he is urgent and grim-faced: 1152) indicate the tenor of the news he is to impart. The opening couplet gives the audience all the necessary orientation for the following scene; the striking economy of this is made possible by the presupposed familiarity with the earlier scenes of the play and with the conventions of tragedy. But these presuppositions hold in full only for the audience in the theatre, who are allowed a (certainly, very general) preview of the Messenger's news before any of the figures on-stage; this puts them into a privileged position from which to monitor, not only the news as it is imparted, but also the reaction of the other characters as they learn what the audience has anticipated.

The dialogue between the Messenger and Theseus, and the rhesis which

---

[70] Barlow 1971: 60; so Bremer speaks of the 'impersonal presence' of the Euripidean Messenger, who gives a 'factual assessment of all that has happened'; he contrasts this with Sophocles' use of *ēthopoiia* in Messenger-scenes (1976: 46).

[71] Taplin 1978: 82.

follows, constitute the 'complicating action' of the scene thus introduced. At this point, we must shift the analysis to another level. Since the complicating action of the embedding narrative (that is, of the scene in the play) is itself an embedded narrative (the Messenger's report) the further development of the scene *ad extra* will not be properly intelligible without reference to the unfolding of the narrative *ad intra*. In what follows, therefore, I will concentrate on the inner system of communication, the exchange between the Messenger and Theseus.

The dialogue which begins this exchange provides an abstract of the Messenger's narrative, as he lets his information out in small doses which prompt Theseus to draw him out by further questioning. What the Messenger says first of all is utterly vague: he indicates only that his news is disturbing and important – worthy of the concern of the whole political body (1157-9). That manner of expression naturally makes Theseus jump to the conclusion that an affair of state is in question, and he expresses his disquiet by an apprehensive use of the particle *môn* (1160). The Messenger bluntly states the real burden of his news, and Theseus' relief is signalled by an echo of the particle, now in an ironical sense; the shift from apprehension to irony reflects the relaxation of tension on Theseus' part. His attitude to the affair is shown by the sarcasm of his request for further details, and at this point a significant conflict of attitudes emerges. The Messenger regards the death of Hippolytus as a serious blow, damaging to both Troezen and Athens; Theseus' reaction contraverts this. So the insistence with which the Messenger lays the responsibility with Theseus (*sou ... su sôi*) acquires an accusing tone: not just '*your* fault', but 'your *fault*'. Theseus persists; he picks up the Messenger's *sôi patri* exultantly, and in his request for a yet more detailed account puts a highly tedentious interpretation on Hippolytus' demise.

This dialogue abstracts the factual content of the following speech: we know now that we are to hear how Hippolytus has been brought to the verge of death by an accident involving his own chariot, as a result of his father's curse. But the Messenger's evaluative stance has been made quite clear: he regards what has happened as a disaster of great import, as something pitiful (*oikeios* in 1166 is pathetic, and foreshadows the line he will take later), and as a matter of admittedly delicate reproach to Theseus. Theseus' rejection of that view has also been made clear; he puts a completely contrary interpretation on the facts: justice has been executed on a peculiarly despicable criminal, giving cause for satisfaction and gratitude. This challenge to his view presents the Messenger with the specific evaluative task which he will have to face in the main body of his report: to present Hippolytus' integrity and undeserved suffering in such a way that it will break down Theseus' hard-hearted satisfaction.

The main narrative speech is made more complex by the development of the orientation into a substantial subnarrative; to get Hippolytus onto the beach where he will come to grief, it is necessary first to get him started on his journey into exile. But it is not necessary to do so at such length, so far as the story to be told is concerned; the whole course of events would be fully intelligible if it began at 1198 with only a few words of introduction. The preliminaries are elaborated to serve the Messenger's evaluative *tendenz*, and are designed to bring about in readiness for his account of the disaster itself a properly disposed frame of mind.

This orientation, therefore, begins with a slanted narrative of Hippolytus' departure for exile (1173-87). It is itself briefly oriented (1173-7) by the picture of the servants' grief, and the reason for it (note the emotive *tlêmonas*). It then issues into the main action: Hippolytus arrives, with a following of loyal friends and contemporaries; their tearfulness and loyalty are dwelt on simply to load sympathies. At 1181, Hippolytus brings himself under control, and offers a prayer: the quotation of his words introduces, as it were, a further level of communication embedded in the scene. Hippolytus' words *per se* are free of the tendentiousness of the Messenger's account in which they are embedded; they express only resignation and respect, with no hint of reproach for Theseus, but a simple acceptance of the need to obey. But this very fact makes them highly tendentious when embedded in the Messenger's account; the attitudes and qualities which these words express are eloquent of Hippolytus' innocence of the charge brought against him in 1172. The speech is followed by a flurry of eager obedience on the part of his followers; then Hippolytus speaks again, asserting his innocence in appeal to Zeus; his words are again followed by a display of his followers' loyalty. The repeated pattern of utterance and reaction is not fortuitous; the touching loyalty of Hippolytus' friends shows him in a flattering light, and attracts sympathy and admiration.

The resolution of the introductory subnarrative completes the Messenger's preparations; by a number of devices, he has placed Hippolytus in focal position – at the centre of sympathetic attention; and he has implicitly portrayed him as an admirable man (must he not be so to command such devotion?) and as an innocent man. The main narrative opens with a brief orientation (1198-1200); its complicating action is the appearance of the bull. The lines in which this is described effectively convey the terrifying weirdness of the apparition (note the crescendo: the noise – terror – wave – and finally the bull itself, *agrion teras*); then Hippolytus' horses bolt (1218). Thus the elaborate evocation of the horror of the apparition is turned to enhance the fearfulness, and so the pitifulness, of Hippolytus' plight. But Hippolytus does not give way to terror; he reacts with a cool-headed use of his expertise with horses. This attempt to bring the horses under control has two rhetorical points. First, by casting Hippolytus in the role of the capable hero of the story, it reinforces the story's referential and emotive focus on him; but the sequence of attempted recovery and failure is itself more forceful than immediate disaster: it extends the tension, and also, by evoking for us the prospect of success, it intensifies the emotional impact of the actual failure. The bull's mysterious ubiquity adds to the sense of horror, and renders Hippolytus helpless, for all his skill and capacity; the hopeless flight delays the disaster, again enhancing its effect; its hopelessness makes the victim even more pitiable.

When the disaster strikes, it is reflected in the syntax. The dramatic action of the flight, related in complex sentences, is brought to an abrupt halt in one curt sentence (1234); this serves as a kind of interim result: but the narrative resumes, in a manner still more painful for the victim (*autos d' ho tlêmôn* 1236), adding another turn to the screw. For the third time Hippolytus' words are quoted: a pathetic appeal to his horses, and an appeal for help that again protests his innocence. Once again, Hippolytus' words are followed by a movement of support, but one which cannot succeed (again the pattern of attempt and failure, with intensifying effect). The action is then brought to its conclusion abruptly, the result interwoven with the end of the main action (1246, recapitulating the main abstract – cf. 1163 – but with added emotional colour: *dê* is pathetic, as Barrett notes). The Messenger adds a coda (1249-50) which, with due deference, for the first time explicitly disputes his master's judgment; deference is, of course, a rhetorical device of emphasis: to begin 'It is not my place to say that you are wrong, but ...' is to imply that one has compelling reason to commit the impropriety, and therefore that the error is gross.

The Messenger spoke in response to Theseus' request for a detailed account of events; and, as I observed earlier, the conflict of attitudes to those events which became evident in the preliminary dialogue determined the precise evaluative slant which the Messenger would have to give to his account. He has performed his task extremely well. We have seen how Hippolytus is set at the centre of the speech's emotional structure: he is the focus of the loyalty of the narrator and of all others involved in the story; his misfortunes are met with universal grief; he is the hero of the story, the one who is admirably competent, and who would – if anyone could – be in control; but he is not, a discrepancy which enhances the pitiable helplessness of the innocent victim in the face of a terrifying, and terrifyingly inexorable, supernatural power. And Hippolytus is certainly the *innocent* victim: the whole tendency of the speech's sympathies assumes his innocence, and that tacit presupposition is made explicit at the very end, when our sympathies have been elicited for the victim. Thus, the speech has definite presuppositions, adopts definite attitudes, and expects an appropriate response: if you will, it defines very clearly the role of the implied audience. Theseus' position is not allowed for; the rhetorical strategy is simple and effective: because a limited range of response is allowed for in the speech, one must either enter fully into its attitudes, or else deliberately hold aloof, maintaining a contrary set of attitudes while absorbing the referential content of the report. To do that, one must contrive to resist the psychagogic power of skilful and vivid narrative. Theseus does not entirely manage this feat of self-control, and he is left with sympathies torn; he has been offered no hard evidence of his son's innocence, so that his resentment cannot be broken down entirely (1265-7); but his final indecisiveness is in marked contrast to the attitude with which he began the scene, intransigent and harsh.

4.44 Tragic wisdom

I tried to make clear in 2.4 that although I am sceptical of the intellectualising tendencies of much modern interpretation of tragedy, I would not wish to deny that there is intellectual content in tragedy; such a denial, I pointed out, would in fact be unintelligible, since even our emotional response to tragedy presupposes the cognition of events in a structured secondary world. There are, then, 'ideas' in tragedy, and I will be looking for some of them in this subsection. I begin the search in a speech from *Trachiniae*.

At one point in that play, Lichas turns in desperation to Deianeira in the hope that she will dismiss the old man whose awkwardly persistent questioning threatens to expose the deception he has worked on her. She already knows the truth, however, and in her reply she explains to Lichas why he should give up his attempt to deceive her.[72] She says first that Lichas is not speaking to a bad woman (or wife: 438). The implications of this claim are unfolded later in the speech when she explains that she will not be hurt or resentful if she learns that Heracles is in love with Iole; she has never before objected to his promiscuous affairs (459-62). In saying this, she upholds the traditional concept of wifely virtue, which requires of the woman submission in all things, not excluding the tolerance of infidelities.[73] Deianeira adds that she is not unaware that human affairs are subject to change (439-40); the instability of all things human is, of course, a very frequent motif in tragedy.[74] It has a corollary: men must learn to think and act accordingly. We have been shown in an earlier scene that Deianeira does indeed think and act accordingly; her response to Lichas' good news was guarded: 'Certainly I must rejoice – and yet: I must also be afraid lest (God forbid!) Heracles should fall from his present good fortune' (293-306). This fear (which proves only too well-founded) is not by any means characterising Deianeira as timid and vulnerable;[75] it shows, rather, her clear perception of the human condition. In tragic thought, it is a characteristic human failing to be swept away by good fortune into an impetuous confidence that is forgetful of human insecurity;[76] this fault Deianeira avoids when she hears of Heracles' success. So, too, in 439-40 she accepts the decline of her own fortunes, recognising its human inevitability.[77] So much for her introduction: she is a submissive wife, and accepts the inevitable changes of fortune; she now goes into more detail. First, she recognises the power of Love (441-6), another tragic commonplace;[78] since love holds sway even over the gods, it would be

---

[72] The absence of *Dreigesprach* in this scene is sometimes (e.g. Reinhardt 1979: 41, 113-14) seen as evidence of immature technique (contrast *OT* 1110ff.); but obviously, Deianeira's withdrawal from the argument between Lichas and the old man is contrived to add weight to her rhesis when she does break her silence.

[73] The most telling parallel is E.*Andr*.222-7; but see also *Alc*.150-5, *Hi*.420, *Andr*.207-34, *Su*.40-1, 1063, *El*.1052-3, *Tro*.645-56, fr.545, 909.

[74] E.g. A.*Ag*.1327-9. fr.399; S.*Aj*.125-6, 646-9, *OT* 1186-96, *Ant*.1156-60, *Tr*.126-31, *OC* 607-15, fr.13, 945, 954; E.*Her*.101-4, *Ion* 969, 1510-11, *IA* 31-2, fr.45, 304, 415, 661, 1074.

[75] Easterling is right to reject the view that Deianeira is timid and irresolute in the prologue: her manner is 'queenly and dignified' (1977: 122-3, 1982: 84).

[76] E.g. A.fr.154a.17-20; E.*Su*.463-4, *IA* 919-23, fr.409, 437.

[77] This seems to me the more plausible interpretation of this passage; it can also be read as a recognition and acceptance of the instability of Heracles' affections (so Easterling 1982: 128).

[78] A.fr.44; S.*Tr*.497ff., fr.941; E.*Hi*.359-61, 443-58, 1266-81, fr.136, 269, 430, 431, 898. I retain *men nun* in 441 (*contra* Dawe), and find the deletion of 444 (after Wunder) tempting, though resistably.

absurd for her to be angry with Heracles if he has succumbed. Secondly, for Lichas to lie is disgraceful (449-54);[79] she adds the prudential point that he cannot hope to get away with the lie (455-6). Thirdly, if he tells her the truth she will not be hurt or resentful; we have already considered these lines as an expansion of her claim to be a virtuous wife, but we should note that she goes on to say that, so far from resenting Iole, she pities her (462-7). This further illustrates her accommodation to the conditions of human life, for it is again a commonplace that the man who is aware of human – and therefore of his own – insecurity is compassionate: hence the linkage between the prudent fear for herself and Heracles and the pity which she feels for the captives who exemplify the danger in which they, too, stand (296-306).[80]

We have identified the themes of Deianeira's appeal, and pursued them into the tragic corpus. In doing so we have sought parallels mainly in gnomic form, but that is merely for convenience; it is when thus articulated that the ideas are most manifest. But they also permeate the tragic corpus implicitly. It is fair to say that the ideas of this speech are commonplaces of tragic wisdom, recurrent motifs drawn from that way of thinking about the world that is characteristic of tragedy. The term 'commonplace' should not be taken pejoratively here. Given that the purpose of tragedy is emotive, rather than intellectual, it is precisely from the traditional ideas and conventional wisdom of the *polis* that the tragedians should be expected to draw the theological and moral structure of their dramatic worlds; for these ideas by their familiarity are readily comprehended, and so carry conviction to a high degree. That is to say, a narrated world built on this foundation will speak most directly to the intended audience, and will have the most potent emotional effect. So commonplace wisdom of the kind we have studied here provides another element in the tragedian's repertoire, another resource for dramatic communication. Of course, there is no question of stating dogmatically that the intellectual content of tragedy is drawn exclusively from this pool of typical ideas; we insisted in 4.41 that types are flexible, a resource rather than a straitjacket, and in 2.32 we found some innovative patterns of thought in Euripides. Nevertheless, the pool does form the basis for the tragic world, the source of its predominant and characteristic ideas.

Let us pursue this enquiry into the following scene of *Trachiniae*, and try to build up a fuller picture of womanhood in the tragic world (on the intervening ode, see 4.23). We find that Deianeira has not entirely retreated from the virtuous attitudes expressed in her earlier speech: she still harbours no anger against her husband (543-4, 552-3), and she resorts to her device with evident reluctance and hesitancy (582-7). But there has been a crucial, and in the end a disastrous, weakening.[81] First, the prospect of sharing

[79] Cf. the prologue of S.*Ph.* (with Odysseus' attitude, cf. fr.833: *contra* fr.834); also *OC* 1125-7 (cf.1145-6), fr.955; E.*Hcld.*890-1, fr.206; Chaeremon fr.27.

[80] Note the specific point of contact between Deianeira and Iole here: 465 echoes 25. For the linkage of fear and pity, cf. S.*Aj.*121-6, *Ph.*501-6, *OC* 560-8, 1334-7; E.*Med.*344-5, *Su.*55-6, fr.130.

[81] It should be noted that our reading of her earlier rhesis rules out any interpretation of it as deliberate deception (e.g. Reinhardt 1979: 23, 45-7): she appears in it as a paradigm of wifely and human virtue, and if this were a mere facade it would imply a studied hypocrisy impossible

Heracles' bed with Iole, or (more probably, in view of her advancing age) of being ousted altogether by the newcomer, has become intolerable to her (536-40, 545-51). It is a commonplace that the marriage-bed is a woman's most vulnerable point, the thing she will fight most vigorously to protect.[82] Certainly, for a woman to give way to this innate weakness of her sex is usually regarded as a sign of depravity; Deianeira, however, is a focal character, and so we are invited to respond to her more sympathetically. Nevertheless, she does weaken, and this leads to a compromise of her wifely virtue; she decides to cross her husband's will. To this end, she devises a *mêkhanê* (534, 553-4); again, this corresponds to the commonplace of tragic womanhood, for women are cunning – and their cunning exercised in defiance of the male is typically ruinous.[83] Furthermore, when she has this dangerous idea, she at once shares it with other women (531-5), and gives them an opportunity to dissuade her from what she knows to be wrong (582-7); the Chorus, however, only encourages her (588-93). Again, the notions of female solidarity and the corrupting influence of women on women are commonplace.[84]

It would be easy to find other references to balance against these, which would give a more favourable estimate of women; even the dangerous cleverness of women can be fruitful, if rightly exercised (see, for example, E.*Su*.294). But this is not really inconsistent with the views we have surveyed already; these do not say (except hyperbolically) that there are no virtuous women, but that female virtue is a rare and fragile thing (because of the sex's moral weakness), and that its absence is fraught with danger (because of their cunning). So the typical image of womanhood in tragedy is essentially consistent. Nevertheless, the pool of commonplace ideas that underlies tragedy is not in the strictest sense a *system* of thought; ideas that are incompatible, or at least in unresolved tension, happily coexist in the pool. This is to be expected from what is essentially folk-wisdom. A body of thought that tells us *both* that too many cooks spoil the broth *and* that many

---

to reconcile either with her response earlier in the play to the news of Heracles' success and the plight of the captives, or with her manner in this following act. It is also true that the earlier speech cannot, in dramatic terms, be read as a deception; for there is nothing in the context to undermine the image of herself which Deianeira presents, and nothing at her subsequent appearance to prompt a retrospective re-evaluation of the speech. The natural assumption is simply that she has changed her mind.

[82] Cf. A.*Ag*.1338-47; E.*Med*.263-6, 569-73, 1367-9, *Andr*.177-82, 370-3, 465-70, 904-5, *El*.1032-5, fr.914. We must admire the cunning with which the Centaur has chosen this weak spot to seize his opportunity for vengeance.

[83] Women's cunning: E.*Med*.407-9, *Hi*.481, *Andr*.85, 911, *Ion* 616-17, 843, *IT* 1032, fr.276, 321, 464; as will be observed, the destructive tendency of women's cunning is apparent in most of these examples; cf. S. fr.189; E.*Andr*.269-72 (del.273), 353; Carcinus fr.3. It is worth noting that the references about women are mainly from Euripides: this is simply because the Euripidean manner, being more sententious, is easier to extract in this way; the same view is implicit in the work of other tragedians, if less often made explicit. It was presumably because he articulates the common view most clearly that Euripides acquired the comic stereotype reputation as a misogynist; once again (cf. 2.32) the Greek didactic habit of application out of context contributes to a distorted view of the poet.

[84] E.g. E.*Hel*.329, *Andr*.930-1, 943-53, *Tro*.651-3, fr.108, 410.

hands make light work, *both* that fools rush in where angels fear to tread *and* that he who hesitates is lost, might on reflection seem unhelpful; but if one reflects more carefully, it will be obvious that this body of proverbial wisdom would be less efficient in the purposes for which we actually use it, were it less vacuous.

As an example of this kind of unresolved tension in the wisdom of tragedy, we might consider attitudes to the prolongation of a life irrecoverably ruined: death is horrible and life sweet, so that it would be mere folly to die;[85] but on the other hand, death is a blessed release, so that one might well seek it;[86] but if one would choose to die, courage and honour will call on one to endure life;[87] although, equally, if one would choose to live courage and honour may call on one to die.[88] So Hecuba and Andromache oppose commonplaces: Polyxena's death is terrible – no, she is more fortunate than the living – but death is nothing, while in life there is at least hope – if the dead know nothing, they are freed from suffering (E.*Tro*.628-83).[89]

The best known confrontation of these two attitudes is in Euripides' *Heracles*; but even in saying that, one begins to give a misleading impression of the debate, which is not really a conflict of 'attitudes' or 'philosophies of life' at all. Consider the parallel I used earlier. If you offer me help in some task, saying 'Many hands ...'. and I decline your offer with 'Too many cooks', we are not really disagreeing about a *general* issue at all; rather, we differ about the specific requirements of this particular situation, and we merely articulate our perception of the needs of the situation by means of generalisations to hand in received, proverbial wisdom. Tomorrow, perhaps, I will need your help in another task, and I will just as readily use the proverb 'Many hands ...'; different circumstances will prompt appeal to different parts of the same, conveniently flexible, proverbial pool. So here, the disagreement between Amphitryon and Megara is not really one of moral principle, but concerns their assessment of the immediate situation. Megara can see no hope, and hints that to prolong a hopeless life is a cowardly flinching from death (80-1, 90, 92). Amphitryon has no concrete hope to offer; but he wants to hold out longer, and so offers some encouraging general reflections: human affairs are unstable, so there may be a change for the better even now (101-4); true courage is never to despair (105-6). The question of the reality of the suppliants' hope is the point at which Lycus attacks (143-4); and Megara takes up the theme again, presenting the acceptance of inevitable death as an act of courage and good sense (278-311). Amphitryon at once gives way; but it is not that he has been converted to a new understanding of true courage (as accepting the inevitable, rather than

[85] E.*Alc*.691-3, 722, *IA* 1218-19. 1250-2, fr.533, 534, 854.

[86] A.fr.466, *PV* 747-51; S.*Ant*.463-4; E.*Hcld*.593-6 (though she is not certain what comes after death: a thought which deters the Nurse *Hi*.191-7), *Hi*.599-60, 1047, *Hec*.377-8, *Tro*.271.

[87] See esp. Agathon fr.7: for the necessity to endure in general, A.*Per*.293; S.fr.319; E.fr.37, 98, 505, 572.

[88] S.*Aj*.473-80, *El*.989, fr.488, 952; E.*Alc*.723 (actually retorted to Admetus' praise of life).

[89] Helen is apparently in two minds on the point: Ajax must have been mad to commit suicide (*Hel*.97); but she herself thinks that she has nothing to live for (56, 293ff.), contemplates suicide in lyric excitement (348-59), and enters into a suicide pact (835ff.).

as holding on to hope come what may). Rather, he has been persuaded that rescue is indeed beyond hope; and this new perception of the particular situation has made a different set of generalisations seem relevant, as expressing the appropriate response to the situation. It may, perhaps, seem perverse to claim that in uttering generalisations Amphitryon and Megara are debating particulars; but the meaning of a piece of language does not always appear on its surface:[90]

> Honestly,
> some people's manners
>   repel you.
> Ask how they are
> and, godammit,
>   they tell you.

4.5 Review

I began this chapter with a brief summary of my theory of Greek tragedy designed for comparison with those of Wilamowitz and Aristotle; it might be helpful if the chapter closes with a more elaborate epitome. This will serve both as a review of the last two chapters, showing how the material contained in them is related to the basic theory of tragedy outlined in Chapter 1 and defended against intellectualising distortions in Chapter 2, and also as a general review of my poetics of Greek tragedy.

It is tempting to begin by asking what tragedy is *about*; but the range of referential meaning available in tragedy is determined by the point or purpose of tragic narrative. So it would be better to begin by asking what tragedy is *for* – this will constitute the decisive core of any theory of tragedy.

1.1 The fundamental tenet here is what I have labelled the *emotive-hedonist* theory; that is to say, the point or purpose of tragic narrative was to give to its audience aesthetic pleasure through the excitation of an intense emotional response (1.11). This response was most typically in the range of horror, anxiety, sympathetic fear and pity; but it ranges more widely, embracing even joy: the distinctively or definitively tragic emotions, however, are those which are ordinarily found distressing (1.12). This emotional experience is the *primary pleasure* of tragedy.

1.2 Tragedy is the source also of *ancillary pleasures* (1.2). These (for example, the pleasure taken in the poetic qualities of the text) are not as such part of the primary pleasure, but they may be used to enhance it, whether directly (e.g., to intensify the emotivity of some passage) or indirectly (e.g., to retain interest so that the audience is receptive to the play's emotive force). They may also be used in an autonomous or digressive way (as, for example, when rhetoric is cultivated for its own sake: 4.22;

[90] Hein 1973:16.

cf. 2.33 on patriotism);.this is licensed by the value set on the centrifugal principle of *diversity* (*poikilia*: 3.2).

1.3 The pursuit of primary and ancillary pleasures is subject to certain *restraints*. For example, the principle of *coherence* restrains the cultivation of diversity where it would (for an audience with appropriate aesthetic dispositions) detract from the emotivity of the play; the same principle requires that tragedy seek, not a random excitation of emotions, but a coherently ordered and aesthetically satisfying sequence of emotional experience (3.2; cf. 2.4). The principle of *conviction* is also important (3.3); but most fundamental to the nature of tragedy is the principle of *dignity*: tragedy is a serious and elevated form, and must portray weighty events involving men of high status in a way commensurate with their dignity (1.3).

We can now return to the deferred question of what tragedy is about.

2.1 In view of the primary pleasure of tragedy and the principle of dignity, it is not surprising that tragedy typically is a narrative of painful events in the careers of men and women of high status, drawn from heroic legend.

2.2 The narrated worlds of tragedies necessarily have a certain structure, and it is possible to trace certain generic norms: since the events which tragedy narrates are typically drawn from heroic legend, it is from the traditional wisdom of the *polis* as embodied and transmitted in those legends that the structure of the tragic world is drawn (4.44; cf. 2.22, 2.31). But this basic pool of wisdom can be varied for emotive or ancillary point (cf. 2.32).

We come finally to consider the ways in which tragedy is organised as a text that is coherent and apt to its purposes.

3.1 The play as narrative depends on a core of *praxis* (a series of narrated events) which must satisfy, or must when ordered into plot and realised in the text give the appearance of satisfying, the requirements of *continuity* and *closure*. The satisfaction of these two requirements suffices to give a play unity, and more stringent demands should not be made; nor should the unifying *praxis* be seen as exclusive of material that is causally inessential, providing that the principle of coherence is observed (3.2).

3.2 The *praxis* is narrated in a series of formally distinct *acts*, in which the verbal text is predominantly spoken, although there are significant variations of texture among the conventional forms of the verbal text within the act (4.21). The series of acts is articulated by the exit and entry of actors, together with the alternation of the mainly spoken verbal text of the acts with the mainly sung verbal text of the sections that are *act-dividing*; this material is essentially of an intercalary nature, although it may be used in functionally more complex ways (4.23; cf. 4.42).

3.3 Both act and intercalary matter must be understood not simply as structures of words, but as words written to be delivered in particular ways and within particular visual contexts, with these non-verbal aspects themselves being meaningful components of the dramatic text (4.3). But the verbal component is the *dominant* medium of tragedy; therefore the probability that a meaning realised in the non-verbal text will also be expressed verbally is proportional to the importance of that meaning being grasped by the audience.

3.4 Since the primary pleasure of tragedy depends to a large extent on emotional engagement with the persons involved in the *praxis*, a scene will in general be designed to evoke from the audience a system of sympathetic and antipathetic responses; typically, there is a concentration of sympathetic attention on one or more *focal* figures, in relation to whom the role of the other characters in the emotive economy of the scene is defined (3.1). But focus in tragedy is *mobile* (it is no more than focus in a given scene), and should not be used as a criterion of unity (3.12; cf. 3.2). The focal structure of a scene is the single most important prejudicial device available to the tragedian, and no interpretation of the contents of a scene should proceed without reference to it (2.5; cf. 4.41).

It will be clear from this summary that what is being summarised is itself not an exhaustive or detailed treatment of the subject: as I indicated in the Introduction, my aim has been only to lay the foundations for a poetics of Greek tragedy. I do not propose now to attempt any more detailed study; rather, my next task will be to consider in a more sustained and concentrated way than has been possible for the illustrations used in the course of my argument how this foundational theory will apply to a specific example. The example that I have chosen is Sophocles' *Ajax*. This was the play which I was studying when the project of research embodied in this book imposed itself on me: moreover, the play contains at least one intriguing interpretative crux (the 'deception-speech'); and the function and artistic integrity of the closing scenes constitute a standing problem which might – and if I am on the right lines in my thinking about the poetics of the genre, which ought – to respond to reassessment in the light of my account of the purpose and structure of Greek tragedy.

5. Sophocles: *Ajax*

5.1 Prologue (1-133)

The opening of the play confronts us with a problem of staging. Odysseus enters from one of the eisodoi and hunts about cautiously (5-6, 19); when he is near the central door of the scene (11) Athene addresses him. These are the first words of the play: where does their speaker stand, and in what relation to the actor playing Odysseus? And how does the latter react? Analogy suggests that the goddess should be visible to the audience and at ground-level; this seems to be the case with the deities who appear in the prologues of *Alcestis* (where access is needed to the scene door), *Ion*, *Bacchae*, *Hippolytus* (in these three cases the movements of the deity are coordinated to avoid an encounter with a human character; this implies that they are at ground level, where such an encounter could occur; the same is true of the ghost in *Hecuba*, which, coming from the underworld, must be at ground level) and *Trojan Women* (Poseidon's deictics imply proximity to Hecuba). The problem in *Ajax* would then be to explain Odysseus' reference to the invisibility of Athene: to be sure, the lines (14-19) do not say explicitly that she is invisible on this occasion;[1] but it has been argued (for example, by Jebb) that they would be pointless if this were not implied.

When a god intervenes in tragedy, he or she almost always identifies himself for the human characters. One exception occurs in *Rhesus*, where Athene does not identify herself, but Odysseus, being a familiar associate of the goddess, is able to recognise her (she does later identify herself to Alexander, falsely). In *Hippolytus* Artemis does identify herself on entry; but Hippolytus arrives after this, and he too is able to recognise her because of their familiar association. In both these passages we find an emphasis on non-visual means of recognition (*Rh*.608-10, *Hi*.1391-3) that has been held by some to imply the invisibility of the intervening deity; but this interpretation is in neither case attractive: there is no hint of invisibility in Theseus' response to Artemis or in Alexander's to Athene, and it is hard to see why the goddesses should be selectively invisible to their favourites (though see *Hi*. 86) or – more importantly – how this would be represented on stage. It seems rather that the emphasis on non-visual means of recognition is a conventional motif when a god is identified by a mortal intimate to whom no explicit profession of identity has been made. (It is worth noting that at the end of *Philoctetes*, where Heracles is certainly – and explicitly – visible, Philoctetes

---

[1] Cf. Taplin 1977: 116 n.1.

lays some stress on the god's familiar voice; he is, of course, an old intimate.)[2] The prologue of *Ajax* fits this pattern: Athene does not name herself, and Odysseus' familiarity with her is (as we shall see) of some importance in this scene. There is no reason, therefore, to suppose that Odysseus' greeting here implies that the goddess is invisible to him on this occasion.

In *Hippolytus*, Artemis probably appeared above ground level, as is usual for concluding theophanies; but in *Rhesus* Athene should be at ground level, since this would facilitate her rather complex interaction with the human characters and express more clearly in terms of theatrical space the controlling presence which enables her to direct the sequence of human movements. Both of these considerations apply also to the prologue of *Ajax*; and the conclusion that Athene is at ground level is made certain by the analogous prologue theophanies cited earlier; there are no cogent objections to this arrangement.[3] We must assume, therefore, that Athene follows Odysseus onto the stage, and stands aside for a while, watching him; her first words arrest his searching, and he turns to face her; they converse, standing in front of the central door.

It is the presence of the goddess that gives rise to this problem of staging; and this presence is (if we may generalise from his meagre remains) a departure from Sophocles' normal practice. He regularly constructs his opening scenes in the form of a dialogue, so that the exposition *ad extra* is unobtrusively conveyed through utterances fully motivated *ad intra* (the

---

[2] There is no self-identification at A.*Eu*.64ff., perhaps because Orestes is familiar with Apollo: but there is also no recognition-formula. This might be thought to confirm suspicions of the text (cf. Taplin 1977: 363-4), but I doubt it; after all, Apollo hardly needs to be identified or recognised when he appears at Delphi.

[3] Calder offers six arguments (1965): (i) 'A sudden and majestic entrance onto the *theologeion* avoids the awkwardness of the goddess entering into the orchestra': there is no awkwardness; prologue deities regularly appear in the orchestra. (ii) 'There is no possible reason for the invisibility of the goddess except that she is on the *theologeion* and Odysseus is in the orchestra where ... he would have difficulty seeing her': she is not invisible; even if she were, it would be absurd to suppose that a mechanical explanation of this kind is necessary: she is a goddess. (iii) 'The famous fear of Odysseus is reasonable if he is alone in the orchestra with Ajax ... while his protectress is high above on the *theologeion*': I hope that my comments on the relevant passage will make it seem plausible enough without this. (iv) 'Because Athene is on the *theologeion*, Ajax emerges from the hut, partially turns, and looks towards the roof, not Odysseus ... it is what Athene means by her promise, "I will turn away the vision of his eyes and keep them from beholding thy face" (69-70). If Athene is on the ground and Odysseus "fairly close to her", the effect could only be absurd or magical if Ajax looked straight at Athene and Odysseus but saw only Athene': Athene says not only 'I will turn away ...', but also 'I will darken ...' (85); the effect is not 'magical', but an exercise of divine power: again, it is absurd to make a deity dependent on simple mechanical expedients (cf. 86). (v) 'Tecmessa's assertion that Ajax addressed words "to a hallucination of his frenzied mind" ... is immediately explicable if the goddess were on the roof': Tecmessa actually says (301) that Ajax spoke to a 'shadow' or 'phantom', which if anything suggests that she *could* see the goddess, but only dimly. The 'hallucination' (quoted from Stanford), like Jebb's 'some creature of his brain', is fanciful. (vi) 'A goddess who has just uttered such godlike sentiments must retire from the *theologeion* while the mortal who has heard them exits on the ground ... They would not walk together out of the orchestra': a deity leaves the orchestra after concluding a prologue in a godlike way at E.*Tro*.97. Athene and Ajax need not go together: they could use separate eisodoi; such simultaneous exits are rare (Taplin 1977: 90), but there is one in the closest parallel to this prologue, A.*Eu*.93.

contrast with Euripides is obvious; *Trachiniae* is in point of form an exception: cf. Chapter 3, n.61); but the presence of a god as a partner in such an expository dialogue is unique in extant Sophocles. The reason for it is obvious: no human character is or, in the circumstances, could be in possession of all the relevant facts, and it is Athene, Odysseus' patron and architect of Ajax's downfall, who must be on hand to explain what has happened. As Odysseus is progressively enlightened, so too is the audience, and his reaction is (as we shall see) a cue for the audience's own; so prepared, the audience will be in a position to watch with sympathetic distress Ajax's anguish and despair as he in turn uncovers the truth.

A scholion on these lines rightly admires the conciseness of the exposition in them, and notes that in the words *peiran tina* (2) there is already an adumbration of the plot; the phrase establishes at once the air of hostility which is to pervade the play. Stanford's comment on this is somewhat naive:[4]

Odysseus has no intention of attacking Ajax: he is primarily looking for information, and it is characteristic of him to put knowledge before action.

But information is potentially a weapon, and Odysseus is in this scene gathering intelligence with hostile intent; *peira*, qualified as it is by *ekhthrôn*, must denote a hostile act. (Stanford is nevertheless right to deny that these lines give an unfavourable impression of Odysseus.) So the first thing we learn about Odysseus in this play is that he is always to be found watching for a chance to assail his enemies, and that his present actions are part of just such a campaign against Ajax. That, at any rate, is Athene's reading of his motives, and Odysseus does not deny it; indeed, he confirms it (18-19).

This point is worth emphasising, since Odysseus is widely regarded as an ethically enlightened figure; this is indeed the case, but not in quite the way that is generally supposed. Knox, in one of the most influential modern studies of the play, speaks of his 'abandoning' the traditional moral code of helping one's friends and harming one's enemies; Burton speaks of 'a conflict between two worlds, the world of the Homeric warrior and a more compassionate world to which Odysseus belongs and in which Ajax is an alien'; Winnington-Ingram concurs: 'Odysseus ... belongs to a world that has passed beyond the primitive heroism of an Ajax. A more modern world ...'[5] But Odysseus' initial attitude, at least, belongs entirely to the traditional world and its morality; he is trying to harm his enemy. The question is, therefore: does his attitude change? Knox's claim is that Odysseus '*abandons* the traditional morality at the moment of victory and exultation' – in effect that he passes from one world to another in the course of this scene; is this claim true?

Odysseus is looking – with hostile intent – for information: he wants a clear account of and explanation for the night's strange events, in which (it seems) Ajax mounted a lone attack on the army's livestock. Athene explains

[4] Stanford's commentary (1963) is cited by author's name alone for notes *ad loc.*, as are: Campbell 1881, Jebb 1896, Radermacher 1913, Kamerbeek 1953, Fraenkel 1977.

[5] Knox 1979: 130 (cf. 2.1 above), Burton 1980:11, Winnington-Ingram 1980: 62.

that the attack was directed against the army's leaders, and miscarried by her sole agency; she imposed on Ajax the delusion that the animals he was slaughtering were the generals. At the end of her explanation she says that she will show to Odysseus his enemy's delusion (66-70),[6] and turns to the door to summon Ajax from his tent (71-3); Odysseus objects, but he is beaten down in argument and stands aside to watch. Ajax enters from the scene (perhaps carrying a whip),[7] and converses with the goddess; after a brief dialogue, he retires. Athene turns back to Odysseus; they converse; Odysseus leaves by the entrance through which he arrived, Athene presumably by the opposite eisodos.

When Athene invites him to inspect and gloat over the plight of his fallen enemy, Odysseus protests (74ff.). But we are given no reason to suppose that this protest springs from compassion; Odysseus is quite simply afraid. When Athene makes the point (which a scholiast regarded as 'harsh': *sklêron*) that to gloat over the fall of one's enemies is a source of unequalled pleasure (79), Odysseus does not repudiate the maxim so much as evade it; his reply is no more than a lame repetition of the request he has already made in 76. The lameness of this reponse is evident to Athene, who offers a scornful assessment of his motives (81); and Odysseus cannot deny her assessment, although he seizes defensively on the opportunity it contains to mitigate the charge of cowardice: this response (82) implicitly concedes that it is fear that moves him. In Odysseus' defence, we may agree that what he has already learnt of Ajax's intentions and state of mind does make his alarm reasonable.

It is fear, then, rather than pity which makes Odysseus reluctant to confront his enemy; nevertheless, it is pity, and not exultation, that results from the unwelcome encounter: does this not mean that Odysseus has *now* abandoned the traditional ethic? It does not. Odysseus concurs with Athene's judgment that before the onset of the delusion in which he is now disastrously trapped Ajax was all that one might require of a man: there was no one to surpass him in judgment or in timely action (no one *ê pronousteros ê dran ameinôn ... ta kairia* 119-20). 'An archaic mode of indicating that a man was all that a man should be confined itself to two aspects of his character,

---

[6] Fraenkel (1963, after Reichard) deletes 68-70 (cf. Taplin 1977: 146 n.1); but the linguistic arguments are not conclusive (Long 1964), and Mastronarde's defence (1979: 80-1) has persuaded me that the lines are genuine: it is Odysseus' fear that prevents him from relying on her assurances. (Note also the defence of the parallel for the alleged interpolation cited by Taplin: Mastronarde 1979: 31-2, on S. *Tr*.336.)

[7] The play's ancient subtitle (*Mastigophoros*) records a tradition that Ajax was carrying a whip at his first entry; but the title as recorded in the didascalia was simply *Ajax*, and the hypothesis shows that more than one way of distinguishing it from *Locrian Ajax* was current; there is no reason, therefore, to trust the tradition reflected in the subtitle as evidence for the *original* performance. Nothing in the text requires the whip (110 alludes only to a planned action); but it would be unobjectionable, underlining 110 and displaying Ajax's state of mind more vividly; so it is possible that Sophocles intended it, or at least would have been happy with it. The same cannot be said for an alternative proposal, that Ajax is carrying his sword (Taplin 1978: 85); this has no textual foundation and no clear function; it would be a gratuitous distraction and (most important) would anticipate and blunt the effect of the sword's appearance at 646 (cf. 5.32).

his valour on the battlefield and his wisdom in discussion';[8] critics hostile to Ajax have tended to discount this high estimation of his character and abilities, but when one reflects on how close he has come to success in so audacious a plan (cf. 45, 447ff.), and that single-handedly, this grudging scepticism seems unreasonable. Because he recognises Ajax's outstanding prowess, Odysseus can see the fall of Ajax as a paradigm of the frailty and vulnerability of mankind: and that means also, of his own frailty and vulnerability. It is to this vision that he responds: thinking, he says, of his own lot no less than of that of Ajax (*ouden to toutou mallon ê toumon skopôn* 124). That Odysseus reacts in this way does not alter his personal relationship with the fallen individual; in 121ff., he expresses his pity of Ajax as man of man, without prejudice to the hostility between them, which is still taken as an unquestioned presupposition: 'Although he is my foe' (*kaiper onta dusmenê* 122; cf. 18). Enmity is compatible with the kind of pity that Odysseus displays, because human antagonists are always united at a more fundamental level by their shared humanity, so that the demise of a foe, as well as being a possible source of satisfaction and pleasure, is always potentially a reminder of one's own insecurity. This attitude is by no means untraditional; we saw in 4.44 that it is built into the tragic world, and it is present already in Homer. There, the heroic world is seen as one of constant competition, and hence of constant enmity; but the competitors are, on the whole, aware that their rivalries are played out in the face of the mortality that is the common lot of all men. Pity (*eleos, aidôs*) is a recognised virtue in the Homeric world; and the consciousness of shared humanity is the basis of that pity. To be sure, the virtue is more often praised than practised: the pressures of a competitive ethic naturally tend to make men forgetful of the compassion that is demanded by their common humanity; but it is nevertheless praised. Odysseus' reaction in the prologue of *Ajax*, therefore, does not imply an 'abandonment' of the traditional ethic, but on the contrary is in the fullest accord with its ideals.

Odysseus is aware of the limitations of human existence, and in his reaction to Ajax's downfall he responds appropriately to the exhibition of these limits. The same humane and prudent restraint is evident in his dealings with Athene. In the first part of the scene he is elaborately respectful and deferential (14, 34-5, 38); the scholia on these lines rightly explain them as *therapeia* designed to secure her continued goodwill. (This deferential manner contrasts starkly with the abruptness of 74, 76; the change of tone reflects Odysseus' alarm at the prospect of an encounter with Ajax.)[9] This is

---

[8] Dover 1974: 161 (cf., e.g., *Od.*11.510ff.). Athene's parting words (*kai stugousi tous kakous* 133) have caused consternation among interpreters: *kakos* is 'an astonishing word to apply (even by implication) to a supreme example of heroic *aretê*' (Winnington-Ingram 1980: 55). But *kakos* in tragedy is a term of rather wide range, and its precise implications in any given passage are determined by the context. Here the general term is set in antithesis to and controlled by the more specific *sôphrôn*; and the sense of the latter is fixed by 127-30. (*Kakos* is given a similar sense by antithesis with *eusebês* in E.*Hi.*1339ff.; cf. S.*Ant.*288, where the substance of the fault is given by the preceding lines.)

[9] The present tense of the imperative in 74 reflects Odysseus' urgency and alarm: see Moorhouse 1982: 218-19.

the proper bearing of a mortal towards a god, as Athene confirms in her final remarks (127-33), and Odysseus is rewarded with her favour. But this intimacy does not make the goddess an altogether comfortable companion for Odysseus. In such a relationship, the mortal is of necessity subordinate, and Athene dwells on and exults in her divine power in such a way as to emphasise this divide. Her reply to Odysseus' first speech establishes the point: she had known perfectly well what Odysseus was about before he spoke, and indeed had been supervising his activity all along (36-7). This reply hands the initiative in the following stichomythia back to Odysseus; he must adopt the role of questioner to her superior knowledge, while she is reticent, disclosing a little, enigmatic information in each answer: in this way she compels Odysseus to probe further, and leads him through eager enquiry to surprise, perplexity and at the last to helpless alarm at a situation from which no escape seems humanly possible.[10] It is only when he has been brought to this aporia that Athene grants a full account, breaking out of the stichomythia with an imperious assertion of her own power (51ff.). Odysseus is again disconcerted by his divine patron when she proposes to display to him Ajax; and again in the stichomythia she leads him into a perplexity only to be resolved by recalling the ease with which a god can perform what is humanly impossible (84-6). The ease with which Athene can delude and mock even so great a man as Ajax is the crowning illustration of her divine power (118-20); and here, too, Odysseus' association with such power is far from comfortable for him.

If the goddess is formidable and disturbing to her favourite, she is far more terrible to her enemy, whom she breaks and mocks without pity.[11] It is widely assumed that Athene has some more elevated motive than personal resentment for her attitude towards Ajax: that she is 'the merciless but just

[10] The sequence of particles in 38-50 well reflects Odysseus' changing reaction: in 38, *ê kai* 'inquires with a certain eagerness' (Jebb, quoted by Denniston 1954: 285); in 40, *kai* introduces a request for further information with a note of surprise (Denniston 309-10); in 42, *ti dêta* – 'the question springs out of something which another person ... has just said' (Denniston 269) – with the emphatic position of *poimnais*, gives the perplexed, 'Then, if that is so, why was it the *sheep* that he attacked?'; in 44 and 48, a note of surprise or shock has entered the *ê kai*; and at 50 the tone of surprise in *kai pôs* is very strong (Denniston 310).

[11] The asyndeton in 60 implies vehemence: Athene is capable of passion in her enmities. (Certainly she is not so sedate as Hermann and Jebb supposed: 'Hermann supported his conjecture ... by the remark that the asyndeton ... implies an agitation of mind unsuitable to the goddess. But it rather expresses the vehemence with which the frenzy drove Ajax forward.') This is reflected in the mockery of Ajax (already apparent in *eukerôn agran* in 64): observe the cruel irony in 90 (Jebb, followed by Kamerbeek and Stanford, refers this to 770ff.: but how could an audience take that point? Since we know that Athene has been working the ruin of Ajax, the irony is more immediate – and more chilling); the response in 94, 'ironical, with perhaps a hint of refusal' (Stanford, comparing *Frogs* 888); the pose of eager questioner in 97 (*ê kai* again: but contrast the distribution of roles in 36ff.; since she knows the truth, and has ensured that Ajax does not, the pose is mocking here); the provocative question asked (with an eye to the observer of the exchange) in a tone of mock innocence (the opening exclamation is 'a colloquial expression ... used here ... to introduce a new topic non-committally': Stanford); the assumed eagerness with which she interrupts in 107 and 109; the perfunctory mock-protest of 111, followed by a dismissal which in fact is designed to incite him (114-15: 'The asyndeton adds vigour to the command': Jebb). Athene is playing with her victim.

divinity who punishes the wrongdoer' – the wrongdoing in this case being the 'crime' of his 'murderous onslaught' against the other Greek leaders.[12] We shall assess these descriptions of Ajax's plot shortly; here I wish only to emphasise that there is no evidence to support such an assumption about Athene's motives. Athene's summing up at the end of the scene makes it clear that Ajax has incurred her displeasure by some slighting of her personal honour: the moral which she draws from Ajax's downfall is to speak no arrogant word to the gods (127-8); and the inference from this advice is inevitable, that Ajax has brought ruin on himself by just such an arrogant provocation as Athene warns against (this inference will, of course, be confirmed later in the play by Calchas). Neither here nor anywhere else in the play is there any hint that Athene was moved in any degree by a concern to oversee impartial justice *inter homines*; it is with her own rights and her own honour that she is concerned. This should not be thought discreditable to her. In the heroic world, honour is the most precious commodity, among gods as well as among men; one not only may, one must react to insults and to actions which detract from one's status. Among men such reaction is (in principle) constrained by what we have already identified as the limitations of human existence; but for a god, immortal and overwhelmingly mighty, these constraints do not apply. Athene's actions are therefore entirely appropriate to a Greek deity (she *is* just, then: but not for the reason Knox gives), and they should raise no moral or theological qualms. This point was well appreciated by a scholiast; a note on 79 admits (as I mentioned earlier) that the saying is 'harsh', but explains that as a goddess Athene need not fear *to nemesêton*; a note on 82 warns us against contrasting Athene's attitude unfavourably with that of Odysseus, arguing that the attitude assigned to each character is appropriate to that character: 'She, being divine, speaks freely; he, as a mortal, guardedly considers what is opportune' (*hê men meta parrêsias dialegetai hôs theos, ho de hupestalmenôs hôs thnêtos ton kairon horai*).

The inference which, I have argued, we should draw from Athene's concluding remarks is rendered the more natural, in that the central panel of the scene has already shown us Ajax speaking a 'haughty word' (*huperkopon epos* 127-8) to the goddess. In rejecting her plea on Odysseus' behalf (112-13), and in the arrogant tone of his parting words (116-17), he shows no awareness of the submissiveness proper to a man in his dealings with the gods; the contrast with Odysseus' deferential manner earlier in the scene highlights the impropriety. It is true that Ajax is still in the grip of madness, and some have thought that his actions in the prologue must therefore be discounted as a 'distortion'.[13] But in what does the madness consist? Certainly not – Knox is right to insist on this[14] – in the intention to kill the commanders; there is no hint of *mania* before Athene's intervention: the plot is clear-headed (as its near success shows), and Tecmessa's account points to a calm, grim state of mind. Essentially, the *mania* is the delusion which made Ajax mistake his victims: I think also we are given to understand that this

[12] Knox 1979: 131.
[13] E.g. Burton 1980: 11.
[14] Knox 1979: 129.

delusion was frenzied;[15] but this is not the decisive component of *mania*, the point of which is the magnitude of the folly of what Ajax did, objectively observed: the absurdity of the misdirected attack. This gives us no clear warrant for discounting the attitude he displays towards the goddess in this scene; and even if one were inclined to make allowances, Ajax's words would surely add psychological, if not logical, force to what is implied about him by Athene's words in the coda.

Although it is clear that in this respect, as in others, there is a contrast between Odysseus and Ajax, it would be wrong to interpret the contrast as if the two characters were of equal dramatic weight. It is certainly Ajax who is at the centre of attention: he dominates the opening discussion, which is about *his* whereabouts, *his* actions, *his* intentions; his appearance is the centre-piece of the scene, prepared for and retarded by Odysseus' protests, so that it comes as a kind of suspenseful climax; and the brief coda to the scene is entirely devoted to reaction to his apearance and to reflection on its implications. Thus Ajax is at the centre of attention throughout the scene; and since this attention is clearly, and indeed explicitly, sympathetic, Ajax occupies what I have called the focal position in the scene (3.1). To this focus, Odysseus is guide; he is there as a source of implicit and explicit commentary, directing our attention towards Ajax in a particular way.

How, then, are we invited to see and respond to Ajax? He is clearly a great man; Athene and Odysseus testify to this, as we have seen, and Odysseus' fear of a confrontation with him points to the same conclusion. His bearing when he does appear on stage reinforces this impression of formidable power; but in that apearance, we see that this unmistakably powerful man is also helplessly trapped in a grotesque delusion, from which he can escape only at the cost of learning of his utter humiliation. This makes him pitiable in the extreme; the scholia are (again) right to explain the appearance of Ajax on stage as a means of emphasising the pathos of his position: we might say that it reinforces the focus (see scholia on 57 and 66; cf. 4.3). Ajax, then, is both a formidable, magnificent figure, and at the same time a pitiable one; and he is the more pitiable, the more magnificent he appears, for the contradiction between his inherent worth and the condition in which he now finds himself makes the pathos of his degradation harsher and more intense. The scene therefore demands implicitly from the audience a paradoxical emotional response to Ajax, a mixture of admiration for his greatness and of pity for his helplessness. That response is the one to which they are also explicitly directed in the reflective coda; Odysseus testifies to Ajax's prowess, and articulates for the audience their shock and distress at his miserable condition.

I have argued that we should not see Athene's intervention as an impartial upholding of the rules of competition between men; but the question

---

[15] It is generally assumed (without argument) that *maniasin nosois* (59) is to be taken with *phoitônt'* rather than *ôtrunon*; that does not seem to me the most natural reading, and certainly Stanford's argument ('Athene was not the cause of his madness, only of his delusion') will not do: for the delusion essentially *is* the madness. (452 implies that Athene was the source of a certain degree of frenzy in the delusion also.)

remains: is Ajax's plot against the Greek leaders a violation of those rules? And is it a 'criminal' act, such as might tend to alienate or impede the sympathetic response of which we have spoken? The answer to the first question is: yes; the obvious parallel is in *Trachiniae*, where we are told that Zeus condemned Heracles to a year's degrading slavery for his use of guileful treachery in a feud (269-80). But we should observe that it is only the *means* to which Zeus objected; and clearly we must be careful not to exaggerate Ajax's fault by forgetting that in the heroic world to avenge slighted honour is in principle praiseworthy. Achilles' first impulse in *Il.*1 is to kill the man who has insulted him (and Athene, when she intervenes to prevent this, does not suggest that it would be *wrong*: only that restraint will in this case promise a more effective restitution); and later in this play we hear how easily a quarrel among the chieftains will escalate towards a murderous sword-fight (719-32). If Ajax believes that he has been the victim of a treacherous plot to slight his honour and deny his status as the foremost warrior among the Greeks by means of a corrupt adjudication in the contest for Achilles' weapons, then his reaction, though extreme and certainly open to criticism, is less untoward than we, outside the heroic world, might naturally suppose.

Moreover – and this is a point to which morally censorious critics should pay more careful attention – Sophocles has done nothing in the prologue to invite an adverse moral judgment on the plot. In the tense stichomythia in which the plot is disclosed to him, Odysseus reacts (as we have seen) with perplexity, amazement and terror; but neither here nor elsewhere in the scene is the planned vengeance treated as a 'crime' deserving 'punishment'. Sophocles has, in fact, suppressed this aspect of the affair entirely; he does not allow it to come to expression until Menelaus raises it: and by that time, our sympathetic engagement with Ajax has been long and firmly established, while (as I will argue) the audience should not be disposed to take too favourable a view of anything that Menelaus says. If, then, we persist at this point in the play in making an issue of the adverse moral aspect of Ajax's plot, we do so perversely: in the face of heroic ethics, in despite of Sophocles' silence, and – above all – against the grain of the focal structure of the scene: 'for the attitudes of those who are well- or ill-disposed are not the same ...; if one is well-disposed towards the man on whom one is passing judgment, one thinks that he has done either no wrong or no serious wrong: but if ill-disposed, the opposite' (Ar. *Rhet.* 1377b31-8a1; cf. 2.5).

Ajax's reaction to the adjudication of the arms, whether justifiable or not, is extreme; and the extremity of temperament which governs Ajax's dealings with his fellow-men spills over, as it was always likely to do, into his dealings with gods: this we have observed already. I would emphasise that it is here, in temperament rather than in adherence to an ethical code, that Ajax differs from Odysseus. I have argued that Odysseus does not abandon the traditional morality, but that in this scene he comes upon, and respects, one of the limits which that morality set to the prosecution of enmity, a point beyond which it would be improper and unsafe for a man (although not for a god) to go. Odysseus is balanced and restrained; he willingly acquiesces in the conditions of human existence. But such acquiescence (his *sôphrosunê*) is a constitutional impossibility for Ajax's more extreme temper. It is this temperamental incapacity that prompts Ajax to transgress the prudent and proper limits which the traditional ethic sets to human conduct; and attitudes which are always, for a man, dangerous become ineluctably fatal when they impinge on his dealings with the gods: for with the rules governing relations between men and gods, Athene is very much concerned.

The traits of character which lead Ajax into his violation of the traditional code, and therefore also the violation itself, are thus inseparable from his heroic greatness; Odysseus, though of sounder temperament, is not so great a man as Ajax. We have said already that there are pressures in a competitive ethic which impel a man to transgress the limits which that ethic seeks to impose on the competition which it enjoins; Ajax illustrates this point. His faults, one might say, are just those into which a man of outstanding competitive excellence is likely to fall, proceeding as they do from an excess of those very qualities which, in a competitive system, make a man enviable and admirable. Consequently, Ajax's violation of the traditional code does not make him contemptible; his faults should not provoke contempt or alienation, because they are the faults of a great man, and as such will tend not to compromise, but rather to enhance, our mingled admiration and sympathy. The contrast with the Atreidae later in the play is instructive here; their violations of the conventional ethical norms are portrayed as proceeding from traits that are otherwise despicable and alienating, from their deficiencies in *aretê*, their weakness, their jealousy of and disloyalty towards a comrade; and for this very reason, they do (as we shall see) evoke contempt.

5.2. Parodos and First Act (134-645)

5.21 Parodos (134-200)

The parodos, with its long anapaestic prelude, is of a form unique in extant Sophocles, although familiar from Aeschylus (we find it in *Persians, Suppliants* and *Agamemnon*); consequently, it has often been regarded as a sign of early technique. But even if anapaestic preludes were exclusively 'early' (which it would be rash to assume with confidence, with evidence so sparse), the development of tragic technique is clearly not *sufficient* to explain Sophocles' use of the pattern here, since Aeschylus had already shown how to dispense with an anapaestic prelude. Burton observes that the Aeschylean anapaestic preludes are 'predominantly narrative', but argues that this does not account for the anapaests in *Ajax*, which are not narrative but 'in the strictest sense dramatic'.[16] The Aeschylean anapaests (and the Chorus' anapaests in the parodos of *Hecuba*) are indeed predominantly narrative: but so are the following lyrics in *Agamemnon*; the essential point is that, while the anapaests

---

[16] Burton 1980: 9: but what *is* the strictest sense of 'dramatic'? Burton's own solution is *ad hoc*: it will not account for the Aeschylean examples; and his comparison with *ScT* is invalid, since the specific association of dochmiacs – a marked form in this position, as anapaests are unmarked – is independently established.

in that play are used for relatively subdued exposition, the lyric narrative is a carefully contrived vehicle of high pathos (cf. 1.13). This reflects the characteristic contrast of tone between recitative and lyric textures (4.21ii); and the difference between the expository and the emotionally charge styles is particularly clear in the interwoven anapaests and lyrics of the parodos of *Antigone*.[17] In *Ajax*, although not narrative in form, the introductory anapaests are expository in function (this is true also of Aeschylus' *Suppliants*); they tell us about the spread of Odysseus' report through the Greek camp and about reactions to it, while the lyric stanzas move to a more speculative and emotional level. This expository opening to the parodos seems to be necessary. In the prologue the action has been 'frozen' to show Ajax at a particular moment which, although essential to the plot (*muthos* or *sustasis pragmatôn*), is of no great consequence for the story (*praxis*): the prologue portrays events of little importance in the referential component of the play's narrative, but essential for establishing its evaluative slant (cf. 3.2, 4.43); Sophocles must now set the *praxis* in motion again. Furthermore, while in the prologue we see Ajax under the relatively detached guidance of his equal and rival, in the following scenes he is to be surrounded by loyal dependents; the Chorus' slanted exposition achieves this shift of perspective.

This shift is evident when the Chorus opens with an emphatic statement of allegiance to Ajax: they rejoice in his prosperity; but the anaphora, with antithetic particles, emphasises the contrast as well: when his prosperity is under threat, they are terrified; this antithesis deepens the notion of allegiance into that of dependence (as the scholion on 134 notes). The Chorus mentions two possible threats, a divine blow and slander, and these serve as a transition to the specifically expository section of the anapaests; it becomes clear in 141 that the generalised form of 137-40 contained an implicit reference to circumstances that do now obtain. The lines that follow inform us of developments since the prologue; they describe (in loaded language)[18] the spread of the hostile rumour, emphasising the malicious glee which contributes to the rapid credence which it gains, and explaining this reaction in terms of envy (*phthonos*);[19] as in epinician lyric, this motif throws light on the greatness of the object of envy. The Chorus round on the jealous, insisting on the interdependence of small and great; here the theme of dependence is enlarged to embrace not only the family and followers of Ajax but the whole Greek army;[20] and while in the former case it has a pathetic

---

[17] Cf. Burton 1980: 90-5: but despite his caution about developmental theories (pp.8-9), he regards this as a 'transitional' stage. This is odd: for it is later than A.*Ch.* and (probably) than S.*Tr.*; and it is in any case difficult to see why the interweaving of anapaests should count as a step towards dispensing with them altogether.

[18] As the scholion on 148 observes, *psithuros logous* ('whispered words') well suggests the malicious, furtive, insidious nature of the process: note also *eis ôta* (149), *plassôn* (148), *eupeista* (151: implying 'specious'), *khairei kathubrizôn* (152-3: cf. Hes. *WD* 196f.. for malicious joy among the evils of mankind); *mallon* (152) is a nice touch, saying much concisely: 'As it spreads and gains strength, the spiteful joy of each new hearer is greater than that of his informant' (Jebb).

[19] 157: cf. Pi. *N*.8.21 (on Ajax, as *N*.7.20ff.); tr.adesp.fr.547.12; E.fr.294.

[20] 159 must be taken as 'protecting rampart' (Kamerbeek, against Jebb), in view of the Homeric parallels (*herkos* and *purgos Akhaiôn* of Ajax, *herkos polemoio* of Achilles: recall also Ajax's

effect, in the latter it displays the folly and ingratitude of Ajax's enemies. For the attitude of Ajax's enemies is (in the eyes of the Chorus) both mean and foolish; the beginning of the last section of the anapaests sums them up with contempt: *toioutôn andrôn* (164). But (and here they return to the original theme of their own dependence, given precision now by the contrast of great and small) they are too weak to defend him themselves; it is for Ajax, the great man, to take action: he has only to show himself for his enemies to fall into a cowed silence.[21]

In 137-8 the Chorus mentioned two possible threats, but the anapaests have developed only one of them; this is natural: the spread of the rumour is all that they know for certain, and the expository section concentrates on that. In the lyrics, which can be more exploratory and more emotional, the Chorus recalls the darker possibility: that the rumour is true, and that some divine attack has been launched against their hero – for (rightly) they think that there could be no other explanation, should the rumour prove to be true (183-6). But this thought remains speculative: they go on to pray that Zeus and Apollo will avert, not the putative *theia nosos*, but the rumour; the correct alternative is unwelcome, and therefore not worthy of credit. Having thus returned to the assumption of a malicious rumour, the Chorus expands the appeal with which the anapaests closed. If the Atreidae or Odysseus (observe the abusive periphrasis) are spreading lies, Ajax should not encourage these rumours by staying in his tent; it was in his absence that the birds chattered, and they were to fall silent when he appeared. The epode develops this into a more elaborate summons; by staying in his tent Ajax fuels the rumour: *kakan phatin arêi* (192) is now developed metaphorically: he inflames the *atê*, so that his enemies' *hubris* spreads like a forest-fire fanned by the wind. The end of the epode sets off the Chorus' loyalty and grief against the abusive enemy with poignant brevity (200).

5.22 First Act: First Scene (201-332)

It is Tecmessa, not Ajax, who emerges from the tent in response to the Chorus' appeal: since she is to be the main representative of Ajax's dependents in this part of the play, Sophocles has to introduce her before Ajax reappears; and since she and the Chorus have complementary areas of ignorance (scholia on 201, 233) their meeting serves to complete the exposition – the Chorus has told us what has happened in the camp since the prologue, and Tecmessa can now review for us the whole story of the night's events as they appeared from Ajax's tents.

---

shield *êute purgos*; see further Alcaeus fr.112.10, Callinus 1.20, A.*Per*.349). But I agree with Campbell that the alleged architectural metaphor is 'fanciful'.

[21] The Chorus envisages a situation modelled on Achilles' withdrawal from the battle (this, surely, is the correct interpretation of *agôniai skholai* in 194): so that the appeal in 168ff. might be compared with *Il*.18.197ff. (I cannot imagine why Jebb insists on taking *exaiphnês* in 170 with *ptêxeian* against the parallel from Alcaeus.) The very Homeric (cf. esp. *Od*.22.302ff.) image of the birds brings us back to the beginning of the anapaests in terms of imagery as well as theme (note *omma* in 140, 167). For the dove, cf. (e.g.) *Il*.21.493, A.*ScT* 294, *Su*.223.

Her opening paragraph (201-7) is vague: she merely adumbrates the theme and sets the tone of the following dialogue; her vagueness prompts the Chorus' request for further information (Sophocles needs this response before proceeding to the substance of the exchange in order to identify the new character: 208-13). It is only with the third set of anapaests that the substance of the scene is introduced; her reply to their question confirms what the Chorus had chosen not to believe in the parodos (214-20: especially 216 with 182). The unwelcome revelation changes the emotional pitch of the dialogue, and the Chorus shift into lyric (221-32) to work out the implications of what they have heard – both what must have happened, and what will result from it: they see at once that the hostility to Ajax of which they spoke in the parodos must now harden into a threat to his life. Their last words indicate in passing the content of the rumour which Tecmessa's report has confirmed for them; from this hint, she in turn is able to fill in the gaps in her knowledge (233-44). The Chorus' second lyric exclamation widens the scope of the perceived threat; in the parodos they had spoken of their dependence on Ajax, and they now see that the danger which threatens him threatens them also.

In her last recitative paragraph (256-62) Tecmessa tells us that the frenzy has left Ajax. The Chorus is relieved (Sophocles chooses this moment of relaxation for the shift down to spoken metre); but Tecmessa insists that the recovery has made the situation worse, since they must now reckon with Ajax's reaction to what he has done. (This dialogue, 265-81, has been criticised for dullness and frigidity, perhaps rather unjustly: for the point about Ajax's reaction is one which, in preparation for the scenes which are to follow, merits emphasis; and if the exchange is stretched out more than is strictly necessary for this purpose, considerations of pace suggest that a relatively 'slack' interlude is desirable between the high-points of kommos and rhesis.) The same point provides the climax of Tecmessa's fine narrative of the night's events: on his recovery, Ajax forced her to tell him what had happened, and on hearing the truth he was overwhelmed by grief before settling into an ominous silence. She ends her speech (which is conventionally tagged by the Chorus) by asking his comrades to intervene: for where they had recognised a threat to Ajax from without, she perceives the threat which Ajax in despair poses to himself.[22]

5.23 First Act: Second Scene (333-595)

(i) *Kommos (333-429):* Tecmessa has introduced the idea that Ajax poses a threat to himself. The scholarly reader, being familiar with what is to come, is apt to take the suicide too much for granted; for the audience intended, this

---

[22] An inconsistency (if one were interested in such things) could be found between the order of events given here (Ajax tortures the animals, leaves the tent, returns, recovers) and that implied in the prologue (the torture of Odysseus is separated from that of the others by Ajax's excursion); obviously, Sophocles has chosen the most effective arrangement at each point: it is more dramatic for Ajax to be in the middle of his cruel activity when he appears on stage, but that would make Tecmessa's narrative unnecessarily untidy.

is a new idea in the play, and if Ajax's decision to commit suicide is to carry full dramatic conviction, Sophocles must first make clear to them the extremity of his situation. To this end he turns the entry of Ajax into a visual coup displaying his degradation; and in the lyrical part of the scene that follows he allows Ajax to express in an emotionally charged medium his bitterness, humiliation and despair. First, as soon as Tecmessa has directed our attention back to the tent which holds Ajax, we hear his cries from within; this renewal of outspoken grief concerns and alarms those who overhear, and their consternation allows Sophocles to build up towards the entry itself: of course, we can only conjecture about the precise staging of this, but it is reasonable to suppose that Sophocles could count on an arresting and shocking visual display as the climax of this preparation.[23]

The dialogue after Tecmessa's entry was evenly distributed between her and the Chorus, and her lines were in a recitative metre: that is, not too far in pitch from the Chorus' more emotional lyrics. By contrast, Ajax on his entry dominates our attention entirely: it is he, the actor, who is given the emotionally charged lyrics (the strong dochmiac element further raises the emotional pitch), while the others are allowed only the briefest interjections, and these merely spoken.

Ajax begins with an appeal to the Chorus, as his sole remaining friends (349-50: the theme of treachery again); he shows them the bloody evidence of the disaster that has overtaken him, and calls on their loyalty for the only thing that can now help him: let them kill him. This last clause is curt, unexpected and emphatic;[24] its incisive form is deliberately (on Sophocles' part) shocking, and the Chorus is duly shocked. But the thought against which they protest (and which Tecmessa foresaw) will become the dominant theme of the lyrics. In the second strophe, Ajax becomes more precise about

---

[23] It is generally assumed that at 346ff. Ajax appears on the eccyclema 'garnished with woolly deaths': and if one accepts that the eccyclema was used at all in the fifth century, this case seems secure, for 346-7 look very much like the introductions to other putative eccyclema-borne discoveries. (That this kind of flourish occurs when some striking discovery is made is itself evidence for the eccyclema: for the habit would not have been acquired if there were not a theatrical coup to hand.) Pickard-Cambridge's objection (1946: 109-10) is based on his general scepticism about the device: which boils down, in effect, to a feeling that it would be absurdly unnatural to have such tableaux trundling in and out of scene, and that the inconsistency of an internal scene displayed externally is intolerable (1946: 112, on E.*Her*.1028ff.: contrast Bond 1981: 329-30; Pickard-Cambridge also argues that Theseus' failure to notice at once the corpses on display supports his view: a frivolous point; such delayed reactions are conventional: e.g. E.*Ba*.215-48ff.). This is a very parochial approach to drama (cf. 3.3, and 5.41 below). In discussions of the eccyclema here, *ouk ektos* (369) has often been taken very precisely as referring to the interior and exterior of the tent (e.g. Hourmouziades 1965: 103): it is of course simply 'go away' (cf. S.*OT* 676) – Tecmessa has approached Ajax to make her appeal, and is rebuffed. But this does illustrate Hourmouziades' excellent discussion of the division of the acting area (pp.65-74; cf. p.99, on Tecmessa as a character 'linking' the eccyclema-tableau to the Chorus).

[24] Commentators interpret the compound in 381 either as 'kill me with those animals' (scholiast, Jebb) or as 'join in killing me' (Kamerbeek, Stanford): both are pointless, the latter silly (why should it require a collaborative effort?). The prefix is rather intensive (LSJ s.v. *sun* DI2), adding to the shock of the sudden demand.

his troubles (of which he speaks in a bitterly sarcastic manner);[25] but he also begins to withdraw into himself. Tecmessa tries to make an appeal, but is curtly rebuffed; henceforth Ajax pays no attention to the others on stage (he apostrophises his enemies, Zeus, the underworld, the Trojan countryside; in 430ff. he speaks to and for himself). Having met incomprehension, he breaks off the initial contact; the interlocutors now protest helplessly, but cannot break into Ajax's intense concentration: the Chorus' last couplet in this section is simply a confession of helplessness.

Ajax's position is even worse when he considers it in relation to his enemies; not only have they escaped him (373), but the grotesque and humiliating circumstances of his failure invite mocking laughter (382): if only he could kill them! Then he could die – thus his thoughts in the last pair of stanzas return to the central theme of these lyrics. Tecmessa is horrified, using the theme of dependence to convey her protest (392-3: she will elaborate on this later). But Ajax ignores the protest, and dwells on the idea of death: the apostrophe, the paradoxical imagery, the emotional verbal repetitions, indicate the intensity of feeling. He reviews his options: he can look for help neither from the gods nor from men (397-400); not from the gods, in view of Athene's opposition (401-3); not from men, in view of the hostility of the army (404ff.);[26] there is, therefore, no alternative to death. In the final stanza he calls on the Trojan landscape, the place where his greatness has been displayed and where he has at last fallen into dishonour: he calls on the land in order to take leave of it; thus the final stanza binds together the dominant themes, loss of honour (cf. 426-7) and the death which this demands. Such a conclusion aptly summarises Ajax's outlook.[27]

(ii) *Ajax's rhesis (430-484):* As in the first part of the act, Sophocles makes use of the lyric/iambic sequence (7.21i). The material of Ajax's lyrics is reworked in a spoken section, more measured and discursive; in it, Ajax offers a systematic and conclusive exposition of the reasons for his intended suicide. This exposition is given a careful structure:

(A) (i) The opening of the speech is an arresting cry of distress: by means of a conventional *figura etymologica*, Sophocles uses this cry to introduce a

---

[25] In 364-7 Ajax sardonically sets his greatness against the absurdity of what he has done: so *aphobois* is 'not formidable' (scholiast), pointedly in contrast with *deinon*; the 'pathos' of Jebb's view is not to the point.

[26] On the text and colometry of 404ff., see Stinton 1977: 127-8; I am not convinced, however, by his treatment of 408-9, especially by the argument that the sense is improved if we remove *an*, since Ajax wants to die: does he want to die at the hands of his enemies? The position of the particle is a problem; but until a better solution appears, we will have to live with it.

[27] 422ff. should be compared with the boasting of epic heroes: e.g. *Il.*18.105-6. It will be objected that those lines are appropriate to Achilles, who *is* the best: Ajax is second best, so this is evidence of megalomania (e.g. Winnington-Ingram 1980: 14-15). This is too literal-minded: the use of superlative expressions is not so jealously calculated in Homer (e.g. *Il.*7.289, 18.80, 689). The scholiast on 421 gets this passage right: and he is right to point out the intensification of pathos; much attention has been devoted to this contrast between the greatness of Ajax and his ruin (118ff., 205-7, 364ff., 410-11), and the same idea is being pursued here: an effect that is entirely spoilt if one is obsessed with Ajax's 'state of mind' and constantly tutting over his exaggerations.

statement of the speech's first theme, Ajax's ill-fortune (*kaka:* 429-33); this statement flows by means of the connecting relative *hotou* in 434 into a review of those *kaka*.

(*ii*) This review takes the form of a contrast between Ajax and his father; this is inherently pathetic (a scholion on *Il*.17.194 observes that there is a pleasantly pathetic effect – *hêdu kai peripathes* – when a son is found to be more unfortunate than his father), and prepares for the latter part of the speech, in which Telamon is to function as the focus of Ajax's sense of public disgrace, and as the main constraint on his choice of action. Hence this part of the speech is cast as a carefully balanced antithesis: 'my father ... but I his son' (*patêr men* 434; *egô d' ho keinou pais* 437); the contrast is emphasised by the preliminary elaboration of the points of similarity (*ton auton eis topon* 437, cf. 434; *ouk elassoni sthenei* 438; *oud' erga meiô* etc. 439, cf. *aristeusas* 435), and reaches its climax in the crucial point of contrast: glory (*eukleia* 436) against disgrace (*atimia* 440) – the most important value in Ajax's world. (Note in 440 the echo of the end of the lyrics, 426-7.)

(*iii*) With the adversative *kaitoi* (441: 'There is usually a certain combative tone in *kaitoi*')[28] the third section begins: Ajax passes from a review of the actual situation to a review of unrealised possibilities. The calling to mind of desirable might-have-beens is, of course, a way of enhancing one's bitterness at misfortune or failure; the rhetorical effect here is comparable. Two unrealised possibilities are considered, in closely parallel form (*ei ... ouk an tis ... nun de; kei mê ... ouk an pote ... nun de*). Ajax asserts that he *should* have been awarded the arms of Achilles, and *would* have been, if the adjudication had not been corrupt: but he was not, being cheated of his due by the Atreidae, his enemies;[29] and he *should*, having been cheated, have restored his honour by taking vengeance, and *would* have done so, if he had not been misled: but he did not, being foiled by Athene at the last moment. *Hôste* (453) brings us back to the actual situation, the consequences of the failure of his project; these consequences are intolerable – mockery (454). The whole excursion into might-have-beens is, in effect, an elaboration of the *atimos* of 440: Ajax is dishonoured by the unjust adjudication, and now far more by the mocking triumph of his enemies. This sums up his *kaka*, and sums up the whole situation as it poses to him the question of what he is to do.

(*B*) *kai nun ti khrê dran* (457). This – 'And now what must I do?' – states the

---

[28] Denniston 1954: 556.

[29] 'Is there not something vaguely unpleasant about Ajax, even in hypothesis, seizing greedily upon the arms of a living Achilles?' (Winnington-Ingram 1980: 28, on 442-4). This is one of the many points at which Winnington-Ingram's animus against Ajax leads him into absurdity; 'seizing greedily' is a wholly gratuitous substitute for 'being awarded'. (He was perhaps confused by the verb in 444: but that refers to the action of the interloper who, in Ajax's view, seized what was rightfully the prize of his own valour.) There is a mild paradox in that while Achilles was alive there could have been no occasion for such a decision; but the paradox makes a point: that a real hero, like Achilles, would not have stood for the conspiracy which (in Ajax's view) turned the adjudication against him – and since they were his arms, his putative wishes are highly relevant. (One may note that, on the same page, Winnington-Ingram's obsession with Ajax's 'state of mind' has induced him to treat the conventional tag at the end of the speech – 481-4 – as 'most significant': against this, see 4.21iii.)

second theme, which is again developed by way of a connecting relative (*hostis*). In addition to *atimia*, Ajax must reckon in choosing a course of action with the enmity of the gods (457-8: cf. 398, 401ff., 450ff.), of the Greek army (458: cf. 408-9, 440, 445ff.), of the Trojans (459) – Greeks and Trojans together making up, in effect, the whole of Ajax's human world (cf. 399-400). He considers two possibilities, again using parallel form: the option is stated as a question (460, 466: *alla dêt'*: 'The commonest use is in questions which follow a rejected suggestion'),[30] an objection raised (*kai poion ... pôs* 462; *alla hôde g'* 469), and the idea is repudiated (466, 470). The first option is to go home, withdrawing his support from the army; but the contrast with his father's glorious achievements (*Aii*) makes that intolerable. The second option is a single-handed assault on the Trojans, leading to glorious death; but that would help his Greek enemies, and is therefore not to be contemplated.

Peira tis zêtêtea (470): the peculiar awkwardness of Ajax's troubles is the contradiction between his inherent worth and the situation in which he finds himself. His problem, in the face of the *atimia* which ostensibly belies his worth, is to establish the truth in his father's eyes (his father being, as I have said, the focus of his sense of shame); yet his relationship with the Greek army rules out the most obvious field for such a demonstration: therefore another option is required. *Aiskhron gar ...* (472): at once he starts talking about the extension and curtailment of life; the particle ('Some exploit must be sought ... *for* it is shameful to desire long life when a man knows no relief from ill-fortune') is significant, for it shows that the decision has already been made and is presupposed as he rehearses his reasons. Extending life that is ruined beyond hope is shameful, cowardly; it follows that it will be *kalon* to curtail life, for Ajax's conception of the well-born man (*eugenês*) allows only these two ways – an honourable life or an honourable death (*ê kalôs zên ê kalôs tethnêkenai ton eugenê khrê* 479-80). The first way is *ex hypothesi* closed (474); therefore Ajax has no choice but to commit suicide, and in doing so he will show to his father (and to the world) that he is indeed *eugenês*.

- (iii) *Tecmessa's rhesis (485-526):* The 'tag' which the Chorus conventionally appends to Ajax's rhesis is a cue for Tecmessa. Her speech, too, is subtle and carefully organised, although not with the clearly articulated lines of argument which we found in Ajax's speech; there is, rather, an interweaving of themes, with sliding transitions and indirect connections of thought. Kamerbeek notes the contrasting manners of the two speeches, and adds in explanation that 'her motives are purely emotional'; but one should not think of the speech as an incoherent or uncontrolled outpouring of feeling; on the contrary, the themes on which she touches are shrewdly chosen to put pressure on Ajax through his heroic ideals.

The speech opens with a gnome on the harshness of ill-fortune, for which Tecmessa offers herself as an *exemplum*. This is subtle: the theme, 'others too ...', is a common consolatory *topos*; 'I, too ...' goes further, suggesting in

---

[30] Denniston, 1954: 273.

addition a bond of shared suffering and mutual sympathy. Moreover, since her own *anankaia tukhê* is her enslavement (by Ajax: hence the passing hint of praise of his prowess: 'by your hand most of all', *sêi malista kheiri*: 490), which means sharing Ajax's bed, she can show why she is well-disposed to him, and therefore an adviser to be taken seriously (490-1).[31] She can also show that she has two specific claims on Ajax: she appeals to him by Zeus *ephestios* (492), that is, as a member of his household, a dependant who can rightfully look to him for protection; and she appeals to him by their shared bed (493) – this latter point she will take up later in her speech: here, it is the theme of dependence that she develops. If you die, she says, you deprive me of your protection and abandon me to your enemies; she foresees slavery for herself – and for their child (499). Here (505ff.) she produces a brief vignette (marked off by ring-form: 'Someone will say ... so will someone say': *erei ... erei*) of the dishonour which her maltreatment after his death will bring to him; thus, in speaking of her fears for herself, she appeals, not just to pity, but to that sense of honour which we have seen over and again to be at the centre of Ajax's way of life, the core of his values. The dishonour will reflect not only on Ajax, but also on his family (505); this makes a sliding transition to the mention of his parents, and the introduction of another key element of heroic ethics, *aidôs* towards parents; but it also touches on the particular concern over his father which played so important a role in his speech. This appeal to the father is the pivot on which Tecmessa's speech turns; she now traces the themes over which she has ranged backwards (an elaborate ring-form), but in each case laying a slightly different emphasis. Her first mention of the child had appealed to Ajax's honour: the recapitulation is an appeal to pity, dwelling on the miserable future in store for him (510ff.: a scholiast on 506 observes that she does not appeal to Ajax to pity herself – a mark of the emotional control of her speech). The first reference to herself had emphasised the obligations imposed by dependence: in the recapitulation, although she does stress the complete-ness of her dependence on him (514-19), her main concern is with the obligations of gratitude. Here she takes up again the theme of their common bed: the *kharis* received imposes obligations on the recipient. (For the return of benefits in heroic ethics, see, for example, Teucer in 1266ff.; and note Ajax's concern with loyalty and the obligations of friendship in 378ff., 678ff.)

In this speech, therefore, in spite of the less clearly defined logical structure, Tecmessa is made to appeal to just those points which might sway an Ajax: to his obligations as *agathos* towards his dependants; to his sense of the *aiskhron*; to the *aidôs* owed to his parents; to the obligations imposed by the receipt of *kharis*.

(iv) *Eurysaces (527-595):* It appears at first that Ajax ignores Tecmessa utterly; he picks up the Chorus' tag (*ainoiês, epainou*) in such a way as to reject their appeal and change the subject. It turns out that this first impression is incorrect.

Ajax asks for his son to be brought to him (530); Tecmessa hedges

---

[31] Cf. E. *Tro.*665-6; on Tecmessa's status, see Winnington-Ingram 1980: 30 n.57; note also the scholion on 201.

cautiously;[32] but when Ajax's patience gives out (540) she is forced to summon the child. Her fears prove groundless; when Ajax speaks to his son it is, in his brusque way, with affection.[33] But out of what he says to Eurysaces emerges indirectly a reply to Tecmessa's arguments: there is no need to fear what Ajax's enemies will do after his death, since his brother Teucer will be able to protect them. Reinhardt is wrong, therefore, to say that 'the words of the wife die away without a syllable having reached her husband's ears';[34] he has heard, and now replies to her. If he is right (Winnington-Ingram claims that his confidence in Teucer is 'unrealistic':[35] even if that were true – and I shall argue for a more favourable estimate of Teucer's powers – the audience could not know that at this point), Tecmessa's appeal is groundless; and then the fact that her plea offered no other course of action that would resolve the difficulty expounded in Ajax's rhesis must be decisive against her. Ajax's death must be painful to all those closest to him; but it is forced on him by circumstances: he does indeed have no practicable and honourable alternative.

Ajax gives the Chorus final instructions to be passed on to Teucer about the care of the child and about the disposal of his weapons;[36] the last words of this section – 'They shall be buried with me' (577) – leave no doubt as to his intentions. He then hands back the child to Tecmessa, ordering her to shut up the tent and to refrain from public tears; the metaphor with which the speech ends is also very much to the point (582). The Chorus tags his speech. Tecmessa protests, and is firmly put in her place (586: a scholiast remarks approvingly that 'the *sôphrosunê* of women is best preserved if they do not

---

[32] 531 evades a clear instruction; 537 seems to hope that Ajax has forgotten about the child; 539 is again evasive, for Ajax did not ask where the child was and Tecmessa takes no further action to comply with his order, as the impatient 540 shows; only then does she summon the child. Staging: the child is brought on from an eisodos by an attendant; since this means a long entry there are some covering lines, the child being visible before he reaches the group on stage (cf. 544).

[33] 'Is it too much to suggest that he regards his son too primarily as an extension of himself?' (Winnington-Ingram 1980: 31, on 545-52). This is correct, and the comparison with S. *Tr.* is apt. But the significance of this should not be exaggerated; that the son should live up to the father's standards is a Homeric injunction (e.g. *Il.*6.209); and the attitude on which Winnington-Ingram remarks is deeply rooted in Greek culture (cf. Ar. *EN* 1134b10-11; perhaps also Pl. *Rep.* 589e1-90a2).

[34] Reinhardt 1979: 21; contrast the perceptive comments of the scholion on 570. Reinhardt also claims that the two speeches 'express ... incompatible philosophies of life, each justified from a different, totally separate standpoint' (p.22); I cannot accept this, since, as I have argued, the subtlety of Tecmessa's speech lies precisely in her appeal to those points of heroic ethics which would weigh most heavily with Ajax; Ajax here acknowledges but refutes her appeal to these points. Reinhardt's comments exemplify the danger – against which I warned in 4.44 – of reading citations of proverbial wisdom as expressions of a general viewpoint or 'philosophy of life', rather than as a response to a particular situation. (See also Easterling 1984.)

[35] Winnington-Ingram 1980: 31.

[36] Taplin (1978: 64) wavers over the introduction of the shield on stage: clearly it is not introduced; at what point would it arrive (unremarked, apparently)? What would be done with it (the child cannot *yet* carry it)? What would it be for? 574-6 obviously do not require its physical presence.

interfere in what their husbands are doing').[37] Her pleas now become more emotional (587-8), and are answered with a somewhat bitter irony (589-90); the rising emotional pitch is reflected in the shift to antilabe, but Tecmessa's wild appeals – she has now lost the emotional control of her rhesis – are firmly rejected. The eccyclema is withdrawn, bearing Ajax within the tent; Tecmessa collapses distraught.[38]

5.24 Act-dividing lyric (595-645)

The Chorus begins with an apostrophe of their (and Ajax's) home, Salamis: an emotive device designed here to introduce a contrast between the *eudaimonia* of Salamis and their own misery in Troy, which is thus set off and emphasised by the contrast. Their misery is, in the first instance, that of long absence on campaign; the textual difficulties of 600ff. cannot obscure the accumulation of emphasis which brings out the wearisome length of their absence (*palaios khronos, mênôn* – probably – *anêrithmos, aien, khronôi trukhomenos*; the *aien* of 604 echoes the end of the description of Salamis, pointing the contrast.) The stanza ends on a note of despair which intensifies the expression of misery.

But the general misery of their situation is itself only a preamble to their particular concern in this ode, the condition of Ajax, which crowns that misery; we may note the heightened emotional style in the apostrophe, with exclamations (610) and repetitions (620). The stanza has an 'a-b-a' structure; the initial statement of their trouble (*kai moi ... xunaulos*) is set against a contrast (*hon exepempsô ...*), and then there is a restatement (*nun d' au*). The element of contrast develops from the contrast of place introduced in the strophe; Salamis and Troy are still implicitly opposed as the *loci* of good and bad fortune, but to this is added a contrast (eased by the strophe's emphasis on the passage of time) between then and now: the man Salamis

---

[37] The scholiast's approval should remind us that Ajax's attitude to his wife is entirely Greek: Aristotle quotes 293 approvingly (*Pol.*1260a30), and see E.*Hcld.*476-7, *Tro.*654 (and more generally the evidence collected in 4.44). There is, even so, a hard edge to his words to her, and critics have rightly compared the Homeric model in *Il.*6: see Kirkwood 1965. The contrast should not be misrepresented, however. 'The pathos of the Homeric scene has darkened in the play into a desolate bitterness' (Kirkwood, p.57); of course: in Homer, Hector faces a glorious death in battle; in the play, Ajax is in a disastrously ruinous situation, and faces suicide as a desperate, but necessary, remedy: how could the scene not be more grim? One should not, I think, turn Ajax's brusqueness into 'brutal cruelty' (Stanford); when emotional pleading is met with an unloquacious firmness it is easy, but not necessarily fair, to represent the latter as cruel or callous. Ajax is stern, inflexible, grim (he has reason to be); we know this, and there is no reason for commentators to fuss over or be censorious about it. Could the scene have been written otherwise without introducing a wholly inappropriate sentimentality? (The scene is discussed also in Easterling 1984.)

[38] It is, in fact, rather uncertain what Tecmessa does here. The general opinion is that she enters the tent with Ajax at the end of the act (for dissent, see Gellie 1972: 281 n.9, Winnington-Ingram 1980: 32 n.65). The exit would be well-motivated (578ff.) but the unmotivated re-entry is a difficulty; it would be quite plausible to suppose that Tecmessa collapses, emotionally distraught, after her rebuff at 595, and so is on stage during the ode (this is no problem: Taplin 1977: 110-11), and already present to hear Ajax's speech when he reappears.

sent off (there, then) as a powerful warrior is (now, here) in the grip of an obsession which isolates him from his *philoi* so that he is beyond help, incurable. The 'now, here' side of this contrast is worked out in two parts: a hero such as Salamis sent forth would have been a joy to his friends and an object of respect and honour; Ajax is now a source of grief to his friends, while he has been betrayed and dishonoured by those who should have been his *philoi* (*aphila par' aphilois* 620).

The second strophe, in a particularly clearly realised image, pictures the grief of Ajax's mother who, on hearing of his 'madness', will lament him as one dead; the description is pathetic, with a strong emphasis on her age, and takes up a theme from the rhesis of Tecmessa. 'This is developed into a dirge as though for one dead, a vivid scene of mourning …'.[39] The mourning of the strophe is explained in the antistrophe: better dead than mad. This stanza reflects the 'a-b-a' structure of the first antistrophe. The first colon states the theme, in explanation of the strophe (*kreissôn gar* …); then a contrast is set up with Ajax's glorious past by means of the participle in the relative clause (*hos ... hêkôn*), before issuing back into an elaboration of the main theme (*ouketi* …). The stanza, and the ode, ends with a resumption of the motif of the bereaved parents, the father's grief being evoked as a complement to the mother's. But the closing words show how firmly, in this ode as in the whole play, attention is concentrated on Ajax himself, even when various subordinate foci are used to guide and enhance the attention we pay to Ajax: the ode began with the misery of the Chorus, and went on to the grief of the mother and father, but it ends by stating emphatically the point which underlies all these considerations, the unparalleled gravity of the disaster that has befallen Ajax.

5.3 Second and Third Acts (646-814)

5.31 Second Act: deception speech (646-692)

Ajax enters, holding a naked sword; the first part of his speech is delivered as a soliloquy, and he only turns to address Tecmessa and the Chorus briefly at 684. At 692 he leaves by an eisodos, while Tecmessa returns to the tent through the scene door.

The first step towards a misinterpretation of Ajax's soliloquy is to project its opening words onto too abstract or philosophical a plane, or to treat it as a discourse on time;[40] that would be to neglect both the rhetorical and the

---

[39] Burton 1980: 24-5. Although Burton brings out well the element of mourning in the ode, he is wrong to write as if the Chorus is predicting and in a sense wishing for Ajax's death: as Winnington-Ingram says (1980: 35), 635 means that his state is worse than death, so that his mother may as well lament as if for one dead, but they cannot agree with Ajax that he would be better off dead, since this is what they most fear. It remains true that Sophocles is using the ode to produce a funereal mood. (For Homeric use of the bereaved parents motif as a vehicle of emotive commentary, see Griffin 1980: index, s.v. 'parents, bereaved'.)

[40] 'This is something much more gravely philosophical than anything we have heard, or would have expected, from Ajax' (Kitto 1964: 188); the speech 'plunges directly into philosophical reflections on time' (Knox 1979: 136); similarly other commentators.

stylistic form of the words. Rhetorically, Sophocles is using a familiar kind of priamel;[41] as (for example) in 485ff., a speech is set in motion with a gnomic generalisation, which is then exemplified and applied to the speaker's specific concern. So to say that Ajax is preoccupied with the content of the opening generalisation is precisely to reverse the distribution of emphasis at which this device aims; as always, the speaker uses, not 'philosophy', but a conventional motif of folk-wisdom (drawing on tragedy's gnomic repertoire: 4.44) to gain indirect entry to the real topic of his discourse. Stylistically, the opening generalisation is less about time than about everything; the hyperbaton by which *hapanth'* ('everything') is displaced to the emphatic initial position has the effect of converting the logical and grammatical object of the sentence into its psychological subject, so that Ajax is saying, not so much that *time* brings everything to light, as that *everything* comes to light, in time; the difference of emphasis is important (and makes the remark more pertinent to his theme). The emphatic placing of *hapanth'* also makes it seem dominant within the object-clause; not 'time brings invisible things to light (all of them), and also hides visible things', but 'everything is brought to light in time, and it all gets hidden again'. So Ajax makes his way towards his main topic by means of a generalisation about the universality of change, and he uses an image of cyclic succession, a stock motif in Greek reflection, and one which will be developed later in this speech.

There is no exemption from change: the emphatically negative third line introduces the shift of focus towards the specific concern of Ajax's remarks. It is unhelpful to see any particular reference in *horkos* ('oath'):[42] that would simply be distracting; Ajax is giving a quite general example, as he does in *periskeleis phrenes* ('inflexible spirit') – these are things that one might expect to be unchanging. But the latter example does serve as a transition to the specific issue, the softening of his own *periskeleis phrenes* towards Tecmessa. Despite the outwardly stern inflexibility which he displayed in the last scene, Ajax has been moved to pity; and he remarks on the fact that his feelings are not exempt from the universal pattern of change with surprise and some indignation: he refers to his earlier inflexibility with a mocking irony, and to his weakening with contemptuous sarcasm (650-2). But the implications of that contempt show that he rejects the weakening he describes; his feelings have been stirred, but his will is unmoved.

All' eimi (654): 'the speaker breaks off his reflections, and announces his plan of action'.[43] But the connection of this proposed plan of action with what has gone before is unclear; and the proposal itself is couched in the ambiguous language that now begins to pervade the speech. It could be read (and is so taken by the audience *ad intra*) as an alternative to the plan of suicide: he will go to the shore, placate Athene by ritual purification, and dispose of his sword. But the words can also be understood in a sense consistent with the suicidal intent to which in fact (as the audience *ad extra* will discern: 5.32) he still adheres: it is by his own death that he will seek to

[41] Race 1982: 94-5.
[42] As, e.g., Knox 1979: 138.
[43] Denniston 1954: 8.

placate the goddess, and it is in his own body that he will bury the sword, of which the nether powers will take possession when it is placed in his own grave.[44] He goes on to explain why the sword is his foe (*ekhthiston*): since he received it from Hector, he has been dishonoured by the Greeks. It seems, then, that in his plan of action he seeks an end to the double hostility on which he has remarked before (cf. 397ff., 457ff.): an end to Athene's anger (656), and then also to the anger of his human enemies; the latter he will seek to end by disposing of the sword which, as he explains, seems to be bound up with the hostility of his allies. But what, in the 'change of mind' interpretation, appears to be two distinct acts is seen in the 'suicide' interpretation as a single act (his falling on his sword) described, with ironical obliquity, under two different aspects.

Toigar: after the digression which explains the point of his reference to the sword, Ajax resumes the thread of his thought with a particle that expresses connection 'with strong logical force'.[45] The connection is at first sight less than clear, and must remain obscure if it is taken to refer to the immediately preceding maxim; in fact, it ranges further back, taking up the consequences of the double 'reconciliation' of which he was speaking before the digression. If what he says about 'reconciliation' is ironical (if, that is, in speaking about reconciliation Ajax is speaking about his death), we should expect the continuation to be identifiably ironic also: and this is signalled, first by the shift into the plural (which tends to distance what is said from Ajax himself), and then by the noteworthy choice of words in 666-7. *Theois eikein* ('submit to the gods') in itself is not difficult, of course; nor, in itself, is the use of *sebein* ('revere') in a political context untoward; but when the two spheres are taken together, the reverse pairing would be natural, and the inversion of the expected order is, as the scholiast observed, striking. The pointed application of *eikein* not to men perhaps carries the implication that it was only the gods, and by no means his human enemies, who have brought about his submission (cf. 450-6); the pointed application of *sebein* to men (and of all men to the Atreidae) is so clearly inflated that the sense it appears to express is at once denied.[46]

Of course (he says mockingly) he must submit to the Atreidae: they are in authority, are they not? And even the most powerful natural phenomena yield to authority. We may observe how the examples which Ajax chooses to illustrate this point encourage us to understand 'submission' in the same ironical way that we understood 'reconciliation'; for in each case, the power that yields is extinguished: the simultaneous presence of winter and summer, night and day, storm and calm, sleep and waking, is impossible. So, too, Ajax

[44] Cf. Sicherl 1977: 79.

[45] Denniston 1954: 565.

[46] Fraenkel thought that the choice of words was rhetorical ornamentation without ironic significance (1977: 21, 25): this is perhaps true; but I – like the scholiast and most other commentators – have not been able to escape a sense that there is more to it. Certainly, the *context* is ironical, as the following line makes clear. It is important to observe, against Taplin 1979: 128, that it is the *juxtaposition* of the two words, and not the words *per se*, that is claimed to carry ironical significance.

will 'submit' by making way for his 'superiors' (the examples are of cyclic phenomena, but this should not be pressed, since this rhythm supplied the Greeks with their favourite image of impermanence, which is the point here). But there is another feature of these examples which is worth noting. In the previous scene Ajax opted for suicide as a way of restoring his honour and so reviving his fortunes; it was a healing operation (581-2). It is relevant, therefore, that the examples of submission by extinction all suggest in addition a movement from bad to good.[47] The section closes with a reminder of the point that introduced it (668ff., 677): if these submit, how can I not do so? The verb is, as in 666-7, plural, again drawing attention to the ironical brackets which enclose and qualify all that is said about 'submission'.

The transition to the next point is made uncertain by the controversial particles of 678; but Dawe's desperation is too extreme. Certainly, *egô de* breaking off into a parenthetic *gar* is not unusual; here, however, the syntax of the opening is not taken up. We could assume a simple anacoluthon; but perhaps the syntactical hiatus is a little more complex. We would be perfectly happy if we had: 'and I (since I know now that one's enemy must be looked on as a potential friend, one's friend as a potential foe – so faithless are most men) resolve henceforth to treat my enemies accordingly as future friends, my friends as future foes'. As it is, this repetitive pronouncement has been abbreviated by the conflation of the parenthesis and main clause: for their burden, the practical implications of the instability of friendship, is effectively the same. At any rate, the sequence of thought is clear. Ajax's ironical espousal of *to sôphronein*, of acquiescence in the conditions of human life, acts as a transition to the theme of the instability of human friendship, which he has found to be one of those conditions (cf. 348ff.). He has made the mistake of helping the Atreidae without the vital reservation, and has suffered the inevitable consequence – betrayal; it is a mistake which he will not make again. He ends his speech with a contemptuous dismissal of those who have betrayed his friendship.

At this point, he breaks off somewhat abruptly to address Tecmessa and the Chorus; and we should pause here to consider his intentions towards them in what he has already said: is the 'deception speech' a deception speech? Formally, the first part of the speech is a soliloquy; and this might suggest that we are not meant to understand it as designed for their ears and intended to deceive.[48] On the other hand, Ajax is aware of his auditors on stage (this is implied by the deictic in 652); and what he says is elaborately ambiguous, and does in fact conceal his intentions from them: so it is not clear that we could account for the way in which the speech is framed without assuming an intent to deceive. (Tecmessa concludes in 807-8 that Ajax did set out to deceive her; it is conceivable that we are meant to see that she is mistaken, but that is not the simplest hypothesis.)

---

[47] See (e.g.) Sicherl 1977: 87 ('The great images derived from nature have a light, as well as a dark side. Cold winter is followed by fruitful summer; the darkness of night by the light of day; the fetters of sleep ... by the freedom of waking; the blast of stormy winds by serene calm at sea.'); Moore 1977: 63; Winnington-Ingram 1980: 50-1.

[48] This point is emphasised by Knox 1979: 136-7.

If we do assume that Ajax intends to deceive, can we say why? If we ask this question about Sophocles' intentions, there is no mystery. He could have brought Ajax on to make a forthright statement of intent; in effect: 'I do feel pity for my wife and child, but must even so take my life; there is no choice, since I am hated by gods and men: I must yield, as all things yield in time, paying the price of my foolish trust in faithless men.' This would have been possible, but surely less effective: the rhetoric must have been less intriguing without its veil, the pathos less intense, the scorn less biting. Moreover, there could then have been no doubt in the mind of his dependants about Ajax's intentions; this would have robbed us of the particular emotional effect which, in the following ode, Sophocles extracts from the Chorus' misguided joy, and would have made impossible the sequence of events which ensues – a sequence which (as we shall see) is of great structural importance to the play. But Ajax is not Sophocles; why does *he* deceive? We must be cautious here: our task (as we said in 3.4) is not to furnish speculative motives, so much as to confirm the 'human intelligibility' of the deception. This is surely not impossible. On the one hand, it is credible that Ajax should wish to avoid the emotional outbursts that would have followed an open declaration of intent (cf. 579-80); on the other hand, the objection that deceit could not be reconciled with the forthright heroic *êthos* is perhaps disarmed by the very ambiguity of the speech: 'if he intends falsehood, and yet scruples to say anything verbally false, how can we say any longer that he is speaking out of character?'[49]

Ajax, then, intends to conceal his true intent from the audience *ad intra*; objections to this way of reading the speech founder on its closing lines, those addressed explicitly to Tecmessa and the Chorus; for these are certainly and deliberately misleading. Ajax carefully avoids explicit statement, using periphrases that suggest a more auspicious outcome:

ἐγὼ γὰρ εἶμ' ἐκεῖσ' ὅποι πορευτέον·
ὑμεῖς δ' ἃ φράζω δρᾶτε, καὶ τάχ' ἂν μ' ἴσως
πύθοισθε, κεἰ νῦν δυστυχῶ, σεσωμένον.

For I shall go where I must go: but you –
do as I tell you and you yet may hear
that I, though wretched now, am safe.   (690-2)

This is not 'plain speaking';[50] and to protest that the veil over his meaning is transparent is fruitless: it is nevertheless a veil, and if it is sufficiently opaque to succeed in deceiving, it is surely also opaque enough to be meant to deceive, as Tecmessa later supposes. For the audience *ad extra*, however, the very vagueness of his turns of phrase has an ominous ring, confirming the interpretation which they have put on his earlier words as a veiled statement of unchanged intent. Ajax will kill himself: and this is an act which (for the

[49] Moore 1977: 56; the contrary view is stated by (e.g.) Knox 1979: 135-6.
[50] As Knox calls it (1979: 137 – the paragraph can hardly be acquitted of special pleading).

reasons he gave in the previous act) he sees both as a necessity (*hopoi poreuteon*) and as a restoration of his fortunes (*sesômenon*).

5.32 Act-dividing lyric (693-718)

The audience of the deception speech *ad extra* should not be deceived. In the previous act, as we saw, Ajax expounded the necessity of suicide with an inescapable logic, and he has displayed sufficient rigidity of character to make us doubtful of any change of mind. The intervening ode, with its strongly funereal overtones, has reinforced the audience's expectations of death; and when he enters displaying (for the first time: n.7) a naked sword, this striking and ominous token should serve as a plain declaration of intent. The audience, therefore, should not be disposed to misconstrue Ajax's veiled language; they will find their way through its ambiguities with ease. But they will certainly perceive that they are ambiguities, and will understand that there is dissembling intent behind them; and this will raise the question: have Ajax's dependants been deceived?

As soon as the next ode begins, it becomes clear that they have: the Chorus respond to Ajax's supposed change of mind with an outburst of joy. It is a simple and single-minded song, that need not detain us long;[51] but one may feel that the loss of the musical setting of the words and of their choreographic accompaniment affects us most acutely here: for these would surely have expressed with great vividness the joyful mood of the Chorus, and made clearer the contrast with the funereal manner of the last, and still relatively recent, ode. Of course, this upsurge of joy rests on a misunderstanding; the incongruity of their emotions with the truth gives the ode its poignant effect.[52] The irony is particularly sharp when, echoing the first lines of Ajax's speech, they speak of the inescapable cycle of change that always defeats human expectation: an apt preparation for their disillusionment.

5.33 Third Act: Messenger (719-814)

A Messenger enters from an eisodos, and engages the Chorus in conversation. He soon introduces a note that jars with the closing words of their song: hostilities have not, as they optimistically suppose, ceased, at any rate on the Greek side. On the contrary, when Teucer arrived in the camp – and his long-awaited arrival (cf. 342-3, 562-4, 688-9) is the first thing that the Messenger reports – he was first reviled and then attacked by the other Greeks for his affinity with Ajax: so intense is their hatred. Teucer – naturally – defended himself, and swords were drawn before the elders soothed passions. The conflict is checked, but not resolved: even when calm is restored, Calchas' cordial gesture is isolated, and the Atreidae remain pointedly aloof (750-1).

The Messenger shows at first no sign of urgency. The relaxed pace of the

---

[51] See Burton 1980: 27-31 for a good account.

[52] For the pathos of illusion, see (e.g.) the scholia on S.*El.*1137, *Il.*22.443 T; cf. Griffin 1976: 165-6 (and Chapter 1 n.21 above).

opening of the scene quickens a little when he breaks off to enquire about Ajax – which is the real burden of his ostensible mission, the one that motivates his appearance on stage. The Chorus cannot understand the alarm with which he responds to their statement that Ajax is not in his tent; further explanation fails to penetrate their complacency (743-4), and the rising tension is, as it were, frozen while the Messenger delivers his rhesis. The burden of his report is given at once; by the time we have heard 755, the hopelessness of the situation should be evident even to the Chorus. But, as is the custom of tragic Messengers, he goes on to give a detailed elucidation. The first level of explanation is Athene's anger with the hero (756-7): of this we have been aware since the prologue, and Ajax, too, has attributed his ruin to her hostile action (401-3, 450-2, 656); now its origins are explained at greater length (758ff.), and in a way which confirms our interpretation of her anger in the prologue (5.1).[53] The explanation begins with a generalisation, of which Ajax is offered as *exemplum* (762); and two incidents from Ajax's career are mentioned, each affording clear evidence from his words that he falls under that generalisation: each shows how the intensity of his competitive spirit and heroic self-confidence has blinded him to the limits of human capacity, to the inescapable dependence even of the greatest men on the favour of the gods. The fact of the goddess's anger and its causes are summarised in 776-7; and the following lines come back to the critical point raised at the beginning of the speech.

When the rhesis has ended, the Chorus calls Tecmessa out of the tent;[54] she hears an abridged version of the Messenger's report, punctuating it with exclamations of distress: thus the pace of the recapitulation is quicker, its emotional tension greater. Indeed, Sophocles has kept Tecmessa off-stage during the rhesis, and so made the repetition of the Messenger's news necessary, for precisely this effect. He is working towards an unusual and spectacular climax to the scene, in which the stage is cleared in a flurry of urgent action: all those present (including the Chorus, in two parts) scatter

[53] Linforth attempted to discredit Calchas' words: a curiosity of interpretation that will not stand up to scrutiny; in effect he makes the following points (1954: 21-4): (i) The lively and circumstantial manner is suspicious: why? (ii) Calchas ignores the immediate occasion of Athene's anger, the murder-plot: this is a misreading of the prologue, as I argued in 5.1. (iii) The recommendation requires only insight into human motivation, not inspiration: if true (but Calchas tells us about divine motives and intentions as well) it would not mean that he was wrong in any point. (iv) The implication that Ajax can be saved is misleading: this is common enough in oracles and prophecies; for the ambiguity (Ajax will escape Athene's anger after this day because he will be dead: cf. 655-6) compare S.*Tr.* (cf.3.3). (v) The alleged impieties are too trivial to bear the weight put on them: an utterly un-Sophoclean scheme of values. (vi) If accepted, this makes Ajax's death 'the execution of a criminal', and therefore untragic: the truth is, as I showed in 5.1, more complex. It is worth asking how any audience could have been expected to follow the tortuous reasoning which Linforth's Sophocles demands of them; and why, if he is right, Sophocles would have thought the speech worth writing at all. By contrast, Winnington-Ingram's comments (1980: 12-13) seem entirely apt.

[54] When Tecmessa enters, one must assume (against the view of most commentators) that she is not accompanied by the child; 809 is no evidence for his presence – it is a distraught apostrophe (cf. 944); and if he is present, he would get in the way at the *exeunt* (he would have to be taken back into the tent by someone). No use is made of the child in this scene: contrast his first and last appearances, which are definitely functional.

in a desperate search for Ajax. To get to this climax, Sophocles must have something in reserve: after the rhesis has first frozen and then unfrozen the movement of the scene, there must be some further development in hand which can be thrown in to produce this sudden quickening of pace and tension; had Tecmessa been present from the beginning, her reaction to the news would have had to follow directly on the end of the rhesis, giving the scene a finale abrupt and therefore less effectively climactic.

5.4 Fourth Act (815-865)

5.41 The suicide of Ajax (815-865)

The scene changes from Ajax's tent to the lonely shore; Ajax enters – but how does the audience know that the scene has changed? what does Ajax do when he enters? above all: how does he make his exit? The actor who plays Ajax is needed in the later scenes; how, then, if he commits suicide on stage, does he get off again to perform his later duties? And how, when he has done so, is a substitute corpse brought on to replace him? This scene presents us with the play's most intractable problem of staging; and I will not pretend to have the solution to it. But one must regret the rash of question-begging which it has provoked. Many scholars, in considering this problem, have taken it as a *premise* of their reasoning that the scene involves 'an extraordinary venture in realism';[55] quite possibly it does: but we could say so with confidence only if we knew already how the scene was actually meant to be staged – the very point at issue. The consequences if we do make this assumption are sufficiently complex and laboured to give us pause: we are encouraged to set the eccyclema trundling backwards and forwards, or to make actors crawl about behind props. It would be worthwhile to reconsider the question, therefore.

To get an actor off a stage is in fact very easy: let him walk. If we were to conjecture that the actor playing Ajax made his exit in this rather simple way, what further inferences could be made? We might imagine the following inscenation (the suggestions are *exempli gratia* only):

(i)   After the *exeunt omnes* of 814 there is a pause; possibly stage-hands also effect some change of scenery (in our ignorance of contemporary arrangements in this respect, we are hardly in a position to take any firm decision on this point; the scenery, if there were any, would not have to be at all elaborate).

(ii) Ajax enters from the scene door; in his opening lines he explains what he has done immediately before his entry: he has fixed his sword in the

---

[55] Arnott 1962: 114; cf. 133. It must be conceded in favour (but not, I think, decisively so) of this view that the scholiast supposed that the suicide was enacted (to increase *ekplêxis*); and a note on 864 cites an anecdote which shows that in some (but not necessarily the original) performances this was so: cf. also Hesychius s.v. *suspaston*. Aristotle's reference to deaths *en tôi phanerôi* (*Poet.*1452a12) is also relevant.

ground, out of sight of the audience. (The repetition of the point about the sword – *hestêken, pepêge, epêxa* – might perhaps be taken to indicate that Sophocles is anxious to make very clear to the audience something that they have not witnessed.) If one felt that an entrance through the central door would be unduly confusing, the use of an eisodos would be possible; but this would make the fixing of the sword – presumably in the direction of his exit, which would have to be through the scene door – more obscure; an audience ought to be able to make sense of the central entry from what Ajax says, especially if there has been a change of scenery.

(iii) At the end of his speech Ajax makes an exit through the central door; the death itself, on this view, is not openly enacted.[56]

(iv)   This would leave us without a body on stage. Gardiner, who takes substantially the same line, suggests that at 891 Tecmessa's cries are heard within, and the eccyclema is extruded to display her and the corpse.[57] That is one possibility; but we have no evidence that the eccyclema was used except in 'the carefully prepared revelation or discovery of internal scenes',[58] and even if one were willing to concede the non-interior use here, the lack of preparation would remain a difficulty; moreover, Gardiner's suggestion that at the end of the play the Chorus and attendants leave by the eisodoi while the principals are withdrawn on the eccyclema materially damages the play's processional finale.[59] Joerden argues that at 913ff. the Chorus cannot see the corpse, so that it must still be within, and that in 920 Tecmessa is asking the Chorus or attendants to bring the corpse into view;[60] his reading of the latter line is clearly mistaken. It is possible that stage-hands simply bring on the corpse before the re-entry of the Chorus, and that Tecmessa discovers it near the central door. This would explain the absence of any signal to move the corpse into full view; and nothing can be inferred from the fact that the Chorus, in the orchestra, does not at once see the corpse near the scene: for there was a conventional separation of the two parts of the acting area, and characters entering from an eisodos often fail initially to notice characters at the scene (n.24).

I do not wish to claim that this *was* the intended manner of staging; for I do not see adequate grounds for making *any* confident assertions about the problem. But this suggestion seems no more open to objection than any other, and is considerably more economical than most. In the absence of further information about fifth-century stage technique, that we do not really

---

[56] I should emphasise, however, that I attach no weight to the alleged convention against the open enactment of violent death: cf. 4.43; my worries here are solely concerned with the practical problems involved in the open staging of *this* death.

[57] Gardiner 1979: 13.

[58] Taplin 1977: 443.

[59] See Taplin 1978: 42, Mills 1980/1:134 (on Mills' view of the substitution, see n.70 below).

[60] Joerden 1960: 67-72.

know the answer is all, I think, that we can honestly say.[61]

Ajax's speech begins with a studied placidity. Sophocles wishes to make the meaning of Ajax's entry perfectly clear, and to establish a contrast with the excited rush which ended the last act. So he supplies a preamble in which Ajax dwells on his preparations with a certain fascination with the means of his death. Note the alternating movement: the sword is the gift of a *xenos*, a friend: but of one who is also Ajax's bitter enemy; it is an enemy's gift, set in hostile soil, sharp and firmly fixed so as to be deadly: but it is also well-meaning – indeed, it is *therefore* well-meaning, as the instrument (or rather, as the agent: commentators have remarked on the personification) of the death he desires. The play of this paradox (which takes up themes from the deception speech: the unexpectedness of human affairs, the fluidity of human relationships) has a fascinating quality; it is also (as the scholion on 819 observes) pathetic.[62]

After this preamble, Ajax turns to the substance of his speech, which is cast into the form of a series of prayers. First, to Zeus; Ajax asks that Teucer will be the first to hear of his brother's death, so that he can secure the proper treatment of the corpse. This prayer takes up the recurrent theme of the threat to Ajax from his enemies, but it does so in a way that extends and very much sharpens the point. Hitherto we have been thinking of a threat to Ajax's life (but this is obviously no longer applicable), and of the danger facing his dependents once deprived of his protection; this aspect is still of importance, but it is no longer dominant: henceforth, it is the direct threat to Ajax after his death that is the main issue; and it is introduced here for the first time in a line full of charged Homeric resonance (830). The second prayer is to Hermes *pompaios* for a clean death. In the third prayer he calls in solemn phrases on the Erinyes, directing his curses against the Atreidae who have brought him to destruction (839ff.). This cursing section is capped by (as it were) the dispatch of the Erinyes to implement the curse (the language is vigorous: note the asyndeton of 844); but here he directs them against the whole army. This fact has outraged some critics;[63] but they are too squeamish. The play has offered a picture of mutual hostility between Ajax and the army as a whole; careful distinctions have not been made between the army, its leaders in general and the Atreidae in particular (cf. 95, 408-9, 440, 445, 458, 725-7, 1055); the general extension of the curse is therefore simply a continuation of this picture of general hostility. Winnington-Ingram argues that there is no evidence of hostility before the attack on the commanders; this is not quite the impression one gets from the parodos; but the argument from silence would in any case unwisely force precision on

[61] Our intuitions about what is or is not possible or proper on stage are more or less worthless in dealing with this problem. In the Chinese theatre, we are told, 'if an execution is to be enacted, a packet encased in red silk signifies the severed head; the man executed runs off stage, and an assistant displays the packet to the audience' (Brušák 1976: 63 – this paper is a useful antidote to theatrical parochialism).

[62] Macleod deleted 816 (Taplin 1978: 188): it could be defended, perhaps, in view of the deliberately slow pace of the opening of this speech; but note that one scholion (H²) bears witness to doubts about its authenticity. I do not understand Kamerbeek's note.

[63] E.g. Winnington-Ingram 1980: 45.

what Sophocles has left indeterminate. And even if Ajax has been drawn by the course of events deeper into a network of enmities, the enmities into which he has been drawn are not for that reason any less real.[64]

Finally, Ajax calls on the Sun as bearer of news to his parents,[65] and dwells on their grief, taking up the theme of Tecmessa's plea and the first stasimon: 'This, too, is full of pathos and humane feeling,' comments a scholiast (on 849: *kai tauta peripathê kai anthrôpina*). At this point he breaks off and utters his last words (854-8 are obviously unacceptable);[66] he takes his leave of the places emotionally most significant for him – his place of birth and the plains of Troy that nourished him (*ô trophês emoi*) poignantly in juxtaposition with his death. The last two lines (864-5) as it were act out verbally the moment of death, if (as I suspect) it is not physically enacted on stage.

5.42 Structure and unity

Many critics have claimed that *Ajax* falls into two parts around the death of the hero, that is, at the point we have now reached in our exegesis; it will be appropriate, therefore, before we proceed further, to examine the problem of structure and unity to which this partition allegedly gives rise. The claim, I shall argue, is in point of fact false, and betrays an excessively bookish and abstract point of view; for considered as a piece for the theatre, the play has evidently been constructed with some care just so as to avoid any sense of hiatus or discontinuity.

Consider first the Messenger's scene. We saw that Sophocles has made the Messenger give his report at length *before* Tecmessa is called on stage, so that he has to repeat it, in more urgent form and with excited interjections from the distraught Tecmessa; the effect of this shift from rhesis to agitated dialogue is a raising of the scene's emotional pitch; and this rising level of excitement is brought to a spectacular climax in Tecmessa's urgent instructions and in the flurry of excited action by which Sophocles clears the stage. The clearing of the stage is a relatively uncommon and certainly striking device, quite apart from its excited manner; and this ensures an unusually heavy structural break before the suicide-speech – a break which would be emphasised in performance by a perceptible pause, and which is certainly accentuated by the marked contrast of pace and tone between the two scenes: the excited climax of the Messenger-scene is set against the quiet, deliberative opening of Ajax's rhesis. Before the suicide-speech, therefore, there is the heaviest possible structural break; there is no comparable formal rupture after the speech, on which the re-entry of the Chorus follows (as

[64] Winnington-Ingram 1980: 45 n.103. Jebb comments: 'The punishment of the army is conceived as a further penalty on the chiefs. This would be thoroughly Homeric. Apollo avenges his priest on Agamemnon by plaguing the whole army, just as he might have punished a wicked shepherd by a murrain': the Homeric parallel is interesting, though too moralistically handled; suffice it to say that in this case, too, army and leadership are treated indiscriminately.

[65] I do not find anything 'extraordinary' in this poetical conceit, *pace* Winnington-Ingram 1980: 45 n.104.

[66] See Fraenkel ad loc. and West 1978b: 113-15.

Taplin observes) like a regular parodos on a prologue.[67]

If we had thereby succeeded simply in shifting a fault-line back some fifty lines, we would not have achieved very much. But it could hardly be claimed that the play is effectively complete before the suicide-speech; we are carried across the heavy formal break by the excited expectations, the sense of crisis, the forward momentum, that have been set up by the climax of the Messenger-scene. Similarly at the end of the suicide-speech, the expectations that were aroused by the beginning of the search for Ajax remain, and demand to be satisfied. So not only has Sophocles avoided the potentially disruptive coincidence of Ajax's death with the most marked formal juncture: he has also used the Messenger-scene so to form the audience's expectations that a forward pressure carries them through this whole sequence of events without allowing them to find any place where they can come to rest before the discovery of the body.

Meanwhile, he has been taking steps to ensure that we do not even then come to a resting-place: he has, so to speak, been loading our hands with further unfinished business; and he does this by drawing together themes that have recurred insistently throughout the first part of the play. The greatness of Ajax and the dependence on him of friends and family have been stressed from the prologue and the parodos on: so, too, has the unrelieved animosity that exists between Ajax and the rest of the army; taken together, these imply the insecurity of Ajax's dependants once deprived of his protection. This danger is most memorably expressed in Tecmessa's fruitless rhesis; and although Ajax does not believe the danger to be material (for he has complete confidence in Teucer's ability to provide protection) the theme does reappear in the deception speech (652-3). The Messenger's report of an attack on Teucer shows that the threat is not an illusory one; and the panic with which the scene ends vividly reinforces our sense of the dependants' peril. In the suicide-speech, the possibility of a threat to Ajax's corpse is raised for the first time; and in the latter part of the kommos following the discovery of the body, the possible reactions of Ajax's enemies will be mentioned repeatedly. Teucer's incisive action before his own lament over the body will also re-emphasise the threat. So, as I say, Sophocles is drawing together persistent themes, and he uses them to point the audience towards the crisis that is to break in the following scenes. If that is so, then clearly those scenes are not to be treated as an unnecessary afterthought, added just to keep the play going to a respectable length: in them are fought out conflicts that have been extensively anticipated; and without the resolution of those conflicts, the play would be obtrusively incomplete.

There is no structural dislocation, therefore; does this suffice to meet criticisms of the play's unity? To answer this question we must refer back to the criteria established in 3.2. In terms of continuity and completeness, the play is not open to objection: for I have been arguing precisely that the play does conserve the impression of continuity, and that the audience's

---

[67] Taplin 1978: 148: but even he makes what I regard as the error of treating the latter break as the stronger.

expectations are manipulated in such a way as to avoid a premature sense of closure or completeness, thus binding the earlier and later scenes of the play together as integral parts of a single dramatic whole. This line of argument goes some way towards a defence of the play's structure, but by no means the whole way; for it could still be argued that it was a mistake on Sophocles' part to make the later scenes so necessary and integral a part of the play. This could be argued, most obviously, if the unfinished business with which these scenes deal is intrinsically uninteresting, or if the way in which that business is handled is, or perhaps must be, artistically unsatisfactory. In short, there are outstanding problems with respect to the tragic *quality* of the scenes, and to their satisfaction of what I called in 3.2 the principle of *coherence*: do these scenes ruin the play as a coherent and aesthetically satisfying sequence of emotional experience? Many would claim that they do; we will return to the question once we have studied the scenes themselves a little more closely.

5.5 Second Parodos and Fifth Act (866-1222)

The first parodos of the play was introduced by anapaests; here, the prelude is partly sung (an astrophic lyric prelude, as in A. *ScT*, E. *Med* and *Ba.*); but this is not followed by a regular series of responding stanzas. After the first stanza Tecmessa enters (the only other case of a character entering during a parodos is in *IT*), and the continuation is in the form of a dialogue: iambic lines and couplets are punctuated by exclamations and brief lyric stanzas from the Chorus, summed up in a longer iambic speech by Tecmessa; and it is this whole complex which finds antistrophic correspondence. Although commentators speak of this as a kommos, the structural difference between this section and the kommos which opened the first act should not be overlooked. There the dialogue was formally distinct from the parodos, but here one cannot mark a formal break either at 879 (where there is no entry) or at 891 (where the entry falls within a metrical complex); so the kommos has been incorporated into the parodos. This results in a certain rapidity of movement.

The prelude expresses the Chorus' uneasiness in their fruitless search for Ajax. In the opening stanza of the strophe this is quickened into positive agitation or distress (879-90: note the dochmiac colouring); then Tecmessa's cries are heard as she enters and discovers the body. There is a brief dialogue in iambic lines, with the Chorus breaking into another brief stanza at the peak of emotion, when Tecmessa reveals that Ajax is dead. Iambic dialogue is resumed briefly; but when Tecmessa reveals that Ajax died by his own hand there is another emotional peak, again marked lyrically (909-14). Then Tecmessa makes a short connected iambic speech in which she covers the body with her cloak and looks for Teucer's arrival (Dawe's attribution of the last couplet to the Chorus is clearly wrong). The theme of friends and enemies begins to emerge in the last stanza of the strophe and in Tecmessa's speech; the opening stanza of the antistrophe dwells on the hostility between

Ajax and the Atreidae (925-36). This theme dominates the antistrophe: the two emotional peaks marked by lyric outbursts come when Tecmessa expresses fear for herself and for her child (944-5), and when she mentions the hated name of Odysseus (954-5). Tecmessa's concluding speech elaborates this, and takes up ideas we have heard in the parodos: of Ajax as the great man foolishly hated by those who depended on him, and who will miss him after his death.[68]

The next act begins with a short transitional scene. Teucer enters (attended) from an eisodos, uttering exclamations of grief; he has heard a rumour of Ajax's death. This is confirmed by the Chorus, and there follows a short (but effective) outburst of antilabe, in which the Chorus and Teucer work themselves into highly excited expressions of grief. But Teucer's thoughts quickly turn to practical matters, to the child and his safety, renewing the theme of hostile threat; he sends Tecmessa to fetch the child.

In the earlier part of the play Tecmessa was the main representative of Ajax's party; at this point Teucer takes over. Teucer, too much like Ajax in his way of thinking, would have been useless for the roles played by Tecmessa (as the scholion on 342 notes), just as she could not take the lead in the confrontations which fill the following scenes. So Tecmessa is abruptly faded out (she returns as a mute extra) after the discovery of the body, the last point at which emotional display is required – for Teucer's lament in the next part of this act is more measured: he takes over just at the point of the familiar shift from lyrics to iambic reprise. This change of roles is the main function of the transitional scene. But the scene also gives us our first opportunity to form an opinion about Teucer from observation. The impression is surely favourable: he assumes his responsibilities briskly (the style reflects his incisiveness: note the interruption in 985, and the position of *dêta* in 986 – cf. Jebb) and on his own initiative (he forestalls the Chorus' passing on of Ajax's instructions, as 990-1 remind us; see the scholion on 983). I emphasise this point, because Teucer has been roughly handled by many critics; Winnington-Ingram – whose animosity is carried to absurd lengths – writes that 'Teucer is an Ajax-substitute – and a poor one ... his inadequacy is pathetic'.[69] This judgment is, as we shall see, mistaken; and the point will have some bearing on our assessment of the later scenes of the play.

Tecmessa makes her exit by an eisodos, and Teucer turns his attention to the still shrouded corpse: the rumour when it reached him, he says, was painful, but the sight of his brother's body is far more so. Then he asks his attendants to remove the cloak, so that he can see the painful sight more

---

[68] Tecmessa's closing speech is damaged. It would end well at 968, and I do not find it in me to muster enthusiasm for the last five lines – in addition to their several problems, the extension of the consideration of the enemies seems weak and pointless after 966-7, which reads like an end to that theme and a transition to the speech's conclusion. There is a presumption in favour of numerical balance with the strophe (although in speeches of this length, the point should not be pressed too hard), so that deletion is not undesirable in itself; Dawe's lacuna after 965 (surely necessary) would supply at least one of the lines needed to restore precise balance if we removed 969-73.

[69] Winnington-Ingram 1980: 81.

fully. Taplin finds the action of covering and uncovering the corpse difficult:[70] but both gestures are full of pathos, and the act of uncovering the corpse marks off the more formal part of Teucer's lament and gives its opening a certain emphasis and dignity. (Tecmessa's covering of the corpse is a conventional gesture: Kamerbeek refers to E.*El.*1231, a better example than Jebb's S.*El.*1466, where the shroud is needed for the trick played on Aegisthus.)

Teucer's lament proper begins with a series of questions; this is a conventional form in the lament.[71] The questions emphasise Teucer's own loss, and carry a note of reproach; this, too, is a conventional motif: to reproach the deceased for his death is, after all, a way of formulating one's own sense of loss and of the dead man's importance.[72] In developing this theme, Sophocles – using a technique discussed in 3.2 – makes Teucer foreshadow events which fall outside the play's *praxis* as he speculates on his own fate. We are made to see Teucer as a man isolated, under threat from enemies at hand, and facing (as we know he will face) unjust rejection by his father for 'betraying' the brother to whom in fact he was and is passionately loyal. The image is calculated to excite the audience's sympathy: having seen Teucer as the brisk commander, we see also that he is a figure of pathos.

Teucer now breaks off from this line of thought with a new series of questions: again, a conventional form in the lament.[73] His attention is drawn to the sword by which Ajax died, which he draws from the body;[74] it prompts reflections on the curious and poignant features of the circumstances of Ajax's death: the false gift (*dôron adôron*: cf. 665) of each of the foes to the other, the strange interweaving of their two fates, the inescapable though elusive impression of a chilling logic and a guiding hand in events: Teucer resignedly concedes the subordinate and fragile position of man in the universe; and with these reflections he brings his lament to an end.[75]

The impending crisis now breaks: Menelaus enters (attended) from an eisodos. His opening words (1047) are abrupt and discourteous, his manner

---

[70] Taplin 1978: 189. Taplin suspects, and Mills (1980/1: 132) believes, that this action might be connected with the replacement of the 'dead' actor (see 5.41); but would Tecmessa have held her cloak up in outstretched arms long enough for one actor to crawl off and a dummy (or mute) to take his place?

[71] Alexiou 1974: 161-2.

[72] Alexiou 1974: 182-4.

[73] Alexiou 1974: 162.

[74] West (1978b: 116-17) corrects the punctuation in 1025-6 (period after *knôdontos*; the following words are exclamatory: in speaking of the *phoneus* Teucer is thinking of Hector, as the following words show). But I am not convinced by his arguments for the deletion of 1035. The dead taking vengeance on their living killers is a traditional motif: cf. A.*Ch.*886, which (as well as being a riddling reference to the false report of Orestes' death) is obviously meant to evoke the notion of the vengeance of the dead, thematic in both play and trilogy; also S.*El.*1417ff., *Tr.*1163.

[75] For parallels to the speech's concluding formula, see the commentaries. It is not as feeble and indecisive as it might appear: in Evenus fr.1, this kind of expression is quoted as a way of avoiding dispute with the foolish *polloi*, as opposed to the few intelligent men; and this is made explicit in S.*Ant.*496f., and is clearly implicit in *OC* 1665f. The meaning, then, is that the thing is so plain that anyone who cannot see it is a fool, and not worth arguing with. (The use in E.*Alc.*529 is different: avoidance of a dispute with a friend.)

imperious (1050). He speaks autocratically, and regards Ajax as an unruly subordinate, who was brought to Troy as an ally but proved unreliable; now, however, that a god has thwarted his treacherous designs he must be left unburied: if he could not be kept in order when alive, he will at least be under control when dead. Menelaus expands his complaints about Ajax's insubordination: he had never obeyed Menelaus, and this is a bad trait among subordinates, undermining discipline and threatening both individual and collective security. Menelaus is appealing in this to impeccable maxims: indeed, he echoes Athene's speech of institution in *Eumenides* (1.13); but that is typical of the stage-tyrant. His appeal to these maxims is an inadequate veil for his real motives, a weak man's envy and resentment of a greater (this recalls the parodos and Tecmessa's last speech). The tone of the speech, betraying weakness and arrogance, forbids sympathy; so, above all, does his blatantly and outrageously false arrogation of authority over Ajax – *andra dêmotên*, indeed, 'common man', as if Ajax were some recalcitrant Thersites!

It is to this last point that Teucer directs his reply, which is brief (Radermacher and Fraenkel have convinced me that 1105-6 are possibly, 1111-17 most probably, interpolated) and crushing. Bowra, to be sure, finds it 'intellectually inadequate'; and Winnington-Ingram imagines that Teucer is 'almost hysterical' in his rejection of 'the notion of discipline', 'the principle of supreme authority'.[76] But Teucer does not, and does not need to, reject or even to mention any general principles of this kind: he need only point out that Menelaus' appeal to them is fraudulent, resting as it does on a misrepresentation of his own and Ajax's status; and this is what he does.

The opposed speeches are followed by a passage of stichomythia, in which Teucer goads Menelaus to fury by his calm, apt and barbed retorts to the latter's taunts and threats. Menelaus eventually resorts to a fable – a rhetorical device of low character.[77] Teucer's reply distorts the form in mockery: Winnington-Ingram characteristically finds even in this evidence of Teucer's 'inadequacy': 'Teucer's attempt to use it is characteristically incompetent.'[78] This is absurd: the deliberately scornful tone of the distortion is shown quite clearly in the concluding words (*môn êinixamên*). And what tone is there more apt in a reply to this Menelaus than mocking contempt?

Menelaus' departure is followed by a brief recitative (1163-7); this serves to mark off the body of the act from the brief scene with which it closes, but without the heavy structural break that a full act-dividing lyric would have entailed. After the anapaests Tecmessa re-enters with the child, and a suppliant-tableau is posed round the corpse. This tableau is set up partly in readiness for the finale; Sophocles gathers together the elements which he requires for the funeral procession that is to constitute the play's final *exeunt*. But it is also highly emotive in itself: although silent and scarcely mentioned in what follows, it will remain as a constant and eloquent focus of pathos (as

---

[76] Bowra 1944: 51 (criticised by Long 1968: 155-6); Winnington-Ingram 1980: 61, 64.

[77] Fraenkel 1950: 773-4. (In 1141, Wecklein's conjecture should be adopted.)

[78] Winnington-Ingram 1980: 64 n.21.

the scholion on 1168 observes – without Christodoulou's curious emendations).

The dispute with Menelaus has shown Teucer as a firm defender of the corpse; but the crisis has not yet been resolved, and at the end of this scene he departs to hasten burial. There is a formal purpose to this exit: the act has been extended to allow the posing of the tableau, and the exit defines the end of the act sharply when it does come. But it also contributes to the presentation of Teucer as active and in control of the situation; he must be seen doing something at this point, and cannot be left on stage during the act-dividing song, passively awaiting developments.

The pathos of the supplication is enhanced in the act-dividing lyric that follows. The Chorus begin by speaking of their weariness and disgust with the war and its discomforts (developing themes used at the beginning of the first stasimon); the antistrophe turns this disgust into a curse of war's inventor, which reaches its climax in the alliterative and assonant exclamation of 1197, and comes to rest in a pregnant single-colon sentence.[79] In the second strophe the inventor of war is the point of departure for a movement of thought back to the theme of the first stanza, exploring further the discomforts of war (note the emotional repetitions and exclamations of 1205-6). The last stanza relates this to the contrast between 'then' and 'now': for all their discomfort, they did at least have Ajax as a protector; now he is dead, and they can only despair, longing helplessly for a sight of their home. Thus, as in the first stasimon, the starting-point of the ode, the miserable condition of the Chorus on campaign, is developed as a vehicle of lamentation over Ajax.

5.6 Final Act (1223-1420)

5.61 Conflict (1223-1315)

At the end of the lyrics Teucer enters in haste, and is soon followed by Agamemnon (attended). Agamemnon is exaggeratedly incensed by Teucer's retort to Menelaus, and his indignation is only intensified by recollection of the status of the man who made the retort, little better (he says) than a slave. It is Teucer's claim that Ajax was not a subordinate of the Atreidae that has outraged him; but for all his fury, he can offer no better defence against that claim than that Ajax was not unique in the Greek army – which is neither true nor to the point. His speech continues with specious but irrelevant maxims (irrelevant, that is, to the issue of the burial, which is what the conflict is supposed to be about), with extravagant insults, and with threats.

As in his confrontation with Menelaus, Teucer does not reply directly;[80] he begins with a preamble, couched in the form of a pathetic apostrophe to his dead brother, protesting at his opponent's behaviour. This technique allows

---

[79] For the rhythm of the clausula, see Dale 1968: 154.
[80] Cf. Stevens 1971: 135-6 (on *Andr.*319-23).

a speaker to seize, as it were, the high ground of moral superiority from which to launch his counter-attack: and having secured this advantageous position, Teucer rounds with great vigour on Agamemnon himself, to make the same point about disloyalty and ingratitude: Sophocles has made Agamemnon rely on the inconsequential falsehoods of his speech precisely so as to lay him open to this refutation. Moreover, the refutation draws on themes that have already acquired prominence in the play; Ajax's fall has been presented as the consequence of betrayal by small enemies who should have been friends, but who were jealous of one on whom they nevertheless depended. This presentation here finds its most eloquent and forceful expression: the more forceful, in that it is stated with detailed circumstantial backing in the face of a forthright denial of his debt by one of those friends, a man who is portrayed (as, indeed, we have been led to expect) as entirely odious and contemptible. Teucer next turns to Agamemnon's personal abuse, and turns the weapon back on its user, successfully impugning his origins with a catalogue of dubious forebears of great cumulative force; against this catalogue he sets a resonant defence of his own birth.

The function of personal invective in verbal conflict is to establish an ascendancy over the opponent: win points here, and one has by that alone put him into the position of an apparently beaten party, so that the whole of his case is bound to look shoddier; this section of Teucer's speech therefore delivers the final blow. Because Agamemnon has been deprived of any serious case, Teucer was able to make a show of demolishing his opponent's arguments; because in failing to make his case Agamemnon had imprudently tried to deny Ajax's outstanding worth, Teucer was able to adopt a tone of indignation and outrage at his opponent's disloyalty and ingratitude; and finally, Teucer can triumph in the exchange of abuse. He crushes Agamemnon's attack at every point, and emerges from the contest with complete ascendancy: argumentative, moral and personal.

In this speech, therefore, Teucer wins an overwhelming rhetorical victory (whether this is an entirely admirable thing to do is a question to which we shall return); this victory reflects the strength which, I have been arguing, is one characteristic of Sophocles' portrayal of Teucer. But I have said that Sophocles sets this figure of strength against a background of pathos that engages our sympathy for him in a desperate position. The end of the reply to Agamemnon brings out very well these two aspects. He proclaims his willingness to die in defence of his brother; this, with a gesture to the silent tableau around the body (1309), strikes the note of pathos which enlists our sympathies. But he goes on to close with a more positive and vigorous threat; and this strikes the note of strength, reaffirming the ascendancy he has won in the course of this devastating speech.

5.62 Resolution (1316-1420)

The Choral tag to Teucer's speech is the announcement of Odysseus' entry; Odysseus has heard the clamour of dispute, and come to investigate. He soon secures from Agamemnon an account of the trouble, and makes a noteworthy response. Although he does not wish to compromise his alliance with Agamemnon (1328-9), he delivers a short admonitory speech which, in effect, confirms the charges brought less eirenically by Teucer: Agamemnon is trampling on justice (1334-5); he is neglecting the outstanding worth of Ajax (1338-42); he is impiously breaking divine law (1343-4). Agamemnon grudgingly gives way – not, however, because he recognises the moral demands of the situation – and retires, leaving Teucer and Odysseus together: Ajax's brother and his former foe. Teucer responds to Odysseus' intervention with generous praise (1380ff.) and accepts the offer of friendship and assistance (1396-9), although quite properly respect for the dead man's feelings excludes Odysseus' participation in the most intimate parts of the funeral rite (1394-5). Odysseus accepts the reservation with a good grace (1400-1), and the exchange ends with the restoration of cordiality between the two firmly established.

We saw in our discussion of the prologue that although the traditional morality promoted competition and enmity, it also set limits to that enmity; when Odysseus intervenes in the confrontation between Teucer and Agamemnon, he is once again concerned only with the acceptable limits of enmity. He concedes that his relations with Ajax were hostile in the extreme (1336-8), but shows no sign of regret; on the contrary, he regards that enmity as something fine and honourable, *kalon*: 'I hated him,' he says, 'when hating was *kalon*' (1347). He does not deny to enmity its essential place in human life: but that place, he believes, is in honourable contest with a living foe, and not in the craven abuse of a corpse (1343-5), nor in the jealous denial of a great rival's worth (1348-52). This is, it should be needless to say, an entirely traditional outlook: Odysseus is supported by conventional, accepted wisdom (for respect for the dead see, for example, *Od.*22.412, Archilochus fr.134 W; for respect for an enemy, Pi.*P.*9.95, Theognis 1089-90); nothing here suggests a progressive or innovatory Odysseus. Rather, here as in the prologue, Odysseus has the highest regard for Ajax, and this esteem is founded entirely on a traditional scheme of values, centred on competitive *aretê* (1340, 1345, 1355, 1357, 1380: cf. 1190-20). Teucer responds favourably to him, with high praise: he is 'most excellent' Odysseus and a 'noble man' (*arist' Odusseu ... anêr kath' hêmas esthlos ôn* 1391, 1399); and he too must be applying a traditional set of values, for no one has yet been tempted to treat Teucer as a moral revolutionary. In fact, the *rapprochement* between Odysseus and Teucer is so warm, once purely partisan obstacles have been removed, just because they are both, in their own ways, admirable exponents of the same traditional set of values; they have the same ideals, admire the same kind of action and person, and so understand each other perfectly. Significantly, it is Agamemnon who finds Odysseus' attitude incomprehensible and alienating, despite their partisan association: for Agamemnon, with his brother, represents, not a different ethic, but contemptible failure in terms of the one, common ethic of the play. Everything they do or say, even in the judgment of their friend, confirms their moral failure; and the glaring contrast with Odysseus, who alone of Ajax's enemies belies his reputation, can only emphasise that failure. They are non-heroic, not in the sense of espousing an alternative code: for even their appeals to discipline and order are Homeric (recall the advice given to Achilles by Nestor in *Il*.1.277-81); they are non-heroic, quite simply as weak and dishonourable men. If there is any ethical polarity to be found in this play, it is to be found here: not in a contrast between old and new, but within the old, between the admirable and the contemptible.

Odysseus' intervention underlines the moral failure of the Atreidae, and ensures their defeat and withdrawal. Thus the crisis is resolved by a closing of ranks among those who are truly admirable in terms of the play's single ethic: a reconciliation that provides an appropriately calm conclusion to the scenes of conflict, a suitable lull before the funeral procession with which the play ends.[81]

5.63 *Quality and coherence*

In my excursus on structure and unity (5.42), I argued that the play satisfies the criteria of continuity and completeness, but pointed out that a defence was still required under the headings of quality and coherence: are the scenes in themselves good tragic material, and do they combine in such a way that the play as a whole is the vehicle of a coherent and aesthetically satisfying emotional experience? This would be denied by many critics, who find the latter part of the play uninteresting and undignified; and their view finds some support in ancient criticism; a scholion on 1123 comments: 'This kind of quibbling is inappropriate to tragedy; after the death of Ajax Sophocles wanted to prolong the play, but his artistic judgment failed and he dissipated the tragic emotion' (*epekteinai to drama thelêsas epsukhreusato kai eluse to tragikon pathos*).[82] This is echoed four lines later by another note: 'This sort of thing is more at home in comedy than in tragedy' (*to de toiouto kômôidias mallon ê tragôidias*). These criticisms are serious ones, coming from a Greek pen; for in Greek criticism (as we saw in Chapter 1) pathos, and the seriousness and dignity which distinguish tragedy from comedy, are cardinal principles in the aesthetics of tragedy. How far, then, are these charges justified?

To the first part of the charge, that concerning the interest of the material which the latter part of the play handles, a short answer is possible. The dispute over the burial of Ajax is not a matter of the disposal of some residual

---

[81] 'While they speak these words they form a funeral procession; and so Ajax's body has its final exit.' So a scholion on 1418, and it is clear that this direction is essentially correct: the only disputable point is whether the procession departs to the accompaniment of *these* words; for the case against their authenticity, see Dawe 1973: 173-5. The point is fortunately of little consequence for our purposes, since it is the visual impact of the procession, and the significance of that action, which are dramatically most important. That there are problems in these lines is clear: that excision is the best remedy is less so; but I will make only one comment on Dawe's argument. There will, I suppose, never be an end to those who think that plays do not fittingly end on platitudes (against this, see 3.2 and 4.21iii); but Dawe's objection to this play's platitude – that it 'is not in any degree applicable to this play, in which apprehension for the hero is expressed well in advance of the fatal hour' – is astounding, when one recalls 646ff., 714ff.

[82] Compare Ar.*Poet*.1451b37-52a1, and the scholia on S.*OC* 220, E.*Ph*.88. Note that it is the tragic quality of these scenes to which our scholiast objects, and not – as is often loosely supposed – to a violation of 'unity'.

rubbish, but most intimately touches on the personal fortunes (no less personal for being posthumous) of a character whose fortunes have been made for the audience a matter of intense concern: a focal character. The outcome of the debate *ought* to be of importance to us; and the debate itself should in that case not seem slack or irrelevant. I should perhaps stress that this line of argument does not depend on any consideration of Ajax's *post mortem* state of existence (on the 'peace of the departed spirit', as Jebb puts it); the point is simply that the withholding of burial is something degrading and repugnant, that one would not want to befall one's *philos*. Nor does my argument depend on Ajax's status as hero at Athens; it depends rather on the *dramatic* role which Ajax fills, as focus, that is, as a centre of intense and sympathetic emotional engagement.

The first part of the play, then, showed the collapse of Ajax's fortunes, and its aftermath; as the intention to commit suicide formed itself in Ajax's mind, it appeared to him as a way of restoration (581-2, 691-2); and the closing scenes work out the scheme of recovery which he then projected, so that they are an integral part of a single (that is, causally continuous and formally complete) action, the upturn of a falling line. The importance of this recovery to a sympathetically involved audience, and the severity of the threat, anticipated and here worked out, which almost plunges his fortunes into further ruin, ought to guarantee the interest and excitement of the closing scenes.

One might accept this line of argument in principle, however, and still feel that the execution of these scenes fails to excite the tension and interest that are present in the plot *in potentia*; the conflict which should have been the play's climax can be read as a degrading squabble between unimpressive figures, lacking both the emotive force and the poetic intensity of the play's earlier scenes. My reason for dissenting from this view lies partly in my favourable assessment of Teucer. As the character at the centre of the stage activity throughout these scenes, he obviously bears considerable responsibility for sustaining our interest in them. Many have denied that he is equal to this dramatic responsibility; Teucer has not excited the warmest admiration from the critics and commentators, who tend to deplore what they see as his vitriolic temper, his inability to rise above the low level of debate set by his opponents, and even his intellectual inadequacy in the face of their arguments. Yet this 'inadequate' figure is seen assuming his responsibilities as leader of Ajax's party promptly and efficiently after his brother's death; he crushes his opponents in debate; he is unwavering in his defence of his cause. Tycho Wilamowitz observed that the attack is made to come in two waves so as to display to the best advantage the unwavering staunchness of Teucer's loyalty to his brother;[83] this is true, but it should be added that his defence is not only staunch: it is also successful – as successful as any defence in these circumstances could be, and as successful as in the event it needs to be. What more could be required of him? This is surely not the picture of an inadequate man; only the most determinedly

[83] T. Wilamowitz 1917: 67-8.

unsympathetic observer could read it in that way. And Sophocles has, I have argued, taken steps to ensure that the audience is *not* unsympathetic, by showing Teucer as a figure of pathos as well as of strength.

Let us return to the debates. The verbal conflict in dramatic terms effectively is the defence of the body; and Teucer's ascendancy here is inevitably the chief factor in the impression that he gives of strength and capacity. But in one sense, it does not self-evidently advance my cause to point out Teucer's mastery in this kind of debate; for it is precisely to this kind of debate that so many critics have taken exception, from the censorious scholiast on. I take aesthetic commentary in the scholia seriously, because I think that on the whole their originators had a good grasp of the general principles of tragic aesthetics; but in this case, I believe that the important principle of tragic dignity has been misapplied, and misapplied for reasons that do not defy analysis. We are familiar from the Homeric scholia with that delicacy of taste that prompted athetesis on account of impropriety (*dia to aprepes*). When Achilles resorts to vigorous abuse in *Iliad* 1, modern critics do not complain that this is unheroic or degrading; but Plato singled out for disapproving comment the delightful passage in which Agamemnon is reviled as a drunken and shameless coward (*Il*.1.255-33: cf. Pl.*Rep*.289e-90a); and Zenodotus athetised it.[84] This parallel shows, I suggest, that coarse invective is not out of place in the heroic world, even though it may offend later Greek sensibilities; and I note that a scholion on 1285 finds the same parallel apt. That this commentator thought an apology necessary at all is perhaps an indication that he shared the distaste of his more censorious colleague; nevertheless, the defence which he offers is correct. Fifth-century tragedy is closer to the heroic than to the Hellenistic ethos; and one does not have to go far into the tragic corpus to see that the acceptability of personal invective as a weapon of debate is taken for granted: earlier in our own play, Ajax used some distinctly unflattering terms of Odysseus, and in a fragment of Aeschylus' play on the adjudication of Achilles' arms we find Ajax laying into Odysseus' shady ancestry (fr. 175). In short: there is nothing frigid or 'low' about these exchanges; they are entirely at home in the heroic world of epic, and of tragedy. Modern and ancient critics are of course welcome to their taste; but such squeamishness is anachronistic, and a treacherous guide to the interpretation of these scenes. We are meant to accept these speeches, and indeed to relish them: and certainly to admire Teucer's mastery in them.

There is a further point to be made here. The resort to invective raises the emotional pitch of the conflict, which becomes more angry, more bitter; and so it produces a more intense polarisation of the two sides. Since, as I have argued, the most appropriate role for the audience is that of a partisan of Ajax's and Teucer's faction, this polarisation should work to reinforce their prejudices: far from drawing back in distaste, we should be encouraged to take sides with more commitment. It is, therefore, with a firm prejudice against the Atreidae that we should approach the scenes of conflict; and what

---

[84] See the scholion on *Il*.1.222 A. The reason for the athetesis is not specified, but is not difficult to infer; Zenodotus athetised for impropriety at e.g. *Il*..3.423.

we find there should confirm that prejudice, for they are (as we have seen) moral failures, despicably unheroic.

I argued in Chapter 1 that the chief interest of poet and audience in tragedy was in its emotive force, and in the pleasure which accompanies the emotional response which that force can evoke; the most important question to ask of these scenes, therefore, concerns the nature of the emotional demands which they make on an audience – which means also, of their emotional reward. I shall approach this question by remarking on the unusual handling of focus in these scenes. For who occupies the focal position? There is still Ajax, of course; he may be dead, but he remains at the centre of everyone's attention, as he has been throughout the play, and it is his fortunes that are chiefly at stake; nevertheless, being dead he plays a somewhat passive role, and this prevents him from dominating the stage in the way he did before. There is also Tecmessa and the child, who join the corpse after Menelaus' rebuff to form a tableau; this remains a potent, if mute, centre of pathos through the following scene; but this group, too, is passive. It is Teucer, as the *active* representative of Ajax's faction, who must bear the greatest responsibility for providing the audience with a centre of dramatic interest; and I have argued that he is a strong and engaging figure, more capable of bearing this responsibility than is often allowed. But although I have argued that he is a strong character, I would not want to claim that he dominates the stage in anything like the way that Ajax did when he was alive; and although Sophocles has combined his strength with pathos, it is clear enough (one has only to compare the scenes of lamentation over a corpse in other tragedies) that he has not been trying to raise this pathos to the highest pitch. And it is tolerably obvious why Sophocles was compelled to write thus; for the appearance of a comparably dominant figure in the second part of the play would have detracted materially from our sense of Ajax's unique greatness. This point has often been made, of course, and it has been seen as one main root of Sophocles' failure in these scenes: he has, it is alleged, *compelled* himself to write a weak ending in order to protect the strong first half. We might formulate the arument thus: to avoid detracting from the first part of the play (which would have been a failure of coherence), Sophocles has had to work with a fragmented and underplayed focus in the latter part; but this means that the later scenes are lacking in tragic quality – and this in turn results in an anticlimax, and thus in a different (and perhaps more serious) fault in the play's coherence.

I suggest, however, that what Sophocles has done becomes more intelligible once we realise that his chief interest in these scenes is not with the sympathetic emotions at all, but with the antipathetic emotions – with the anger, contempt and hatred which the audience is invited to feel towards the Atreidae. In so far as Sophocles does exploit the sympathetic emotions here, it is instrumentally; the moderated pathos which he seeks to evoke has a subordinate and instrumental role, in that it reinforces our alignments in the conflict, and so indirectly increases our antipathy towards the characters who occupy the adversarial position; and the mute pathos of the suppliant-tableau stands, as it were, as a denunciation behind Agamemnon's tirade, again enchancing our outrage and hatred. If we look at the scenes in this way, it is clear that the fragmentation of focus, of the centre of *sympathy*, and the restrained treatment of pathos will not in any way diminish their emotive force: the scenes still possess, in the intense *antipathies* which they evoke, the emotional charge that can excite an audience, grip its attention, and afford the *oikeia hêdonê* of tragedy.

This being so, our defence of the play's 'unity' is complete. In fact, the attack on its unity in the strict sense was never compelling: the play's *praxis* does exhibit the causal continuity and closure that are the sufficient condition of unity. On this 'platform', Sophocles has – in accordance with the aesthetic principles set out in 3.2 – built a sequence of two contrasting emotional movements; and the charge that the latter movement is lacking in tragic quality is countered by our arguments for the tragic dignity of the scenes of invective, and for their possession of an unorthodox, but nevertheless real, emotive charge. Thus the quality of the scenes is established. We may perhaps still feel doubts about their aesthetic coherence with the earlier part of the play, a residual sense of anticlimax; the sense of disappointment is clearly felt by many, and I have myself sometimes (but by no means always) shared this feeling. But if we do feel thus, it is surely not because these later scenes are inherently weak: on the contrary, they are very good indeed; it must, therefore, be the exceptional excellence of the earlier scenes that is – as it were – at fault.

Teucer's overwhelming victory in the verbal contest is entirely satisfying to our sense of antipathy; and Odysseus' intervention, too, is both a confirmation of our contempt and anger, and a satisfaction of it: a confirmation, in that it underlines the moral failure of the Atreidae; and a satisfaction, in that it ensures the final defeat and withdrawal of the enemy. The play has shown us the humiliation of a great man by his divine antagonist; his anguish on discovering the nature of his downfall; his resolution to seek the restoration of his fortunes by suicide. It has traced the painful effects of this necessary decision on his dependants, and the danger which threatened to ruin his plan; it takes us, with partisan emotional engagement, through the conflict with the jealous and contemptible enemies who are the source of this threat to their defeat, to reconciliation with an unexpected protector – another great and good man – and to the burial of the hero. This sequence of events, and the pattern of emotional response which they demand of us, are the heart of this play: that is an elementary fact about the poetics of Greek tragedy; and whether we are in the last analysis entirely satisfied with *Ajax* or not, we certainly shall not be able to *understand* the play until we have grasped this simple truth.

Bibliography

(A) Editions

(i) Aeschylus is cited from the OCT of Page (Oxford 1972); Sophocles from Dawe (2 vols.: Leipzig 1975-9); Euripides from the new OCT by Diggle where available (II: Oxford 1981), and otherwise from Murray (I: Oxford 1902; III, ed.2: Oxford 1913).

(ii) Fragments of the tragedians are cited from the new *Tragicorum Graecorum Fragmenta* (Göttingen 1971-) where available, that is:
  I: Tragici minores, ed. B. Snell (1971)
  II: Adespota, ed. R. Kannicht and B. Snell (1981)
  III: Aeschylus, ed. S. Radt (1985)
  IV: Sophocles, ed. S. Radt (1977)
Euripides is cited from A. Nauck, *Tragicorum Graecorum Fragmenta* (ed.2: Leipzig 1889), and C. Austin, *Nova Fragmenta Euripidea* (Berlin 1968).

(iii) Other editions of fragments:
  Austin, C., *Comicorum Graecorum Fragmenta in papyris reperta* (Berlin 1972)
  Diels, H. & W. Kranz, *Die Fragmente der Vorsokratiker* (ed.6, 3 vols.: Berlin 1951-2)
  Kock, T., *Comicorum Atticorum Fragmenta* (3 vols.: Leipzig 1880-8)
  Lobel, E. & D. Page, *Poetarum Lesbiorum Fragmenta* (Oxford 1955)
  Snell, B. & H. Maehler, *Pindari Carmina, II* (ed.4: Leipzig 1975)
  West, M.L., *Iambi et Elegi Graeci* (2 vols.: Oxford 1971-2)

(iv) The scholia on Aeschylus are cited from the edition by O.L. Smith, where available (I: *Ag., Ch., Eu., Su.*: Leipzig 1976; II: *ScT*: Leipzig 1982); otherwise from O. Daenhardt (*Per.*: Leipzig 1894) and C.J. Herington (*PV*: Leiden 1972). For Sophocles I have cited P.N. Papageorgiou (Leipzig 1888), except for the scholia on *Ajax*, for which I have used the edition by G.A. Christodoulou (Athens 1977). Scholia on Euripides are taken from Schwartz (2 vols.: Berlin 1887-91).

Scholia on the *Iliad* are cited from the edition by H. Erbse (5 vols.: Berlin 1969-77), except for the solitary D-scholion, for which resort must still be had to Dindorf.

(B) Other books and articles

Abbreviations: *AJP*   *American Journal of Philology*
                     BICS   *Bulletin of the Institute of Classical Studies*

CJ   *Classical Journal*
CP   *Classical Philology*
CQ   *Classical Quarterly*
CR   *Classical Review*
G&R   *Greece and Rome*
GRBS   *Greek, Roman and Byzantine Studies*
HSCP   *Harvard Studies in Classical Philology*
JHS   *Journal of Hellenic Studies*
MH   *Museum Helveticum*
PCPS   *Proceedings of the Cambridge Philological Society*
YCS   *Yale Classical Studies*

Adkins, A.W.H., 1966, 'Aristotle and the best kind of tragedy': *CQ* 16:78-102

Alexiou, M., 1974, *The Ritual Lament in Greek Tradition* (Cambridge)

Arnott, Geoffrey, 1973, 'Euripides and the unexpected': *G&R* 20:49-64

Arnott, Peter, 1962, *Greek Scenic Conventions* (Oxford)

Atkins, J.W.H., 1934, *Literary Criticism in Antiquity, I: Greek* (Cambridge)

Bain, David, 1977, *Actors and Audience* (Oxford)

—, 1979, 'A misunderstood scene in Sophokles, Oidipous': *G&R* 26:132-45

—, 1981, *Masters, Servants and Orders in Greek Tragedy* (Manchester)

Barlow, Shirley, 1971, *The Imagery of Euripides* (London)

Barrett, W.S., 1964, (ed.) Euripides, *Hippolytus* (Oxford)

Beck, F.A.G., 1964, *Greek Education 430-350 b.c.* (London)

di Benedetto, V., 1969, (ed.) Euripides, *Orestes* (Florence)

Bond, G.W., 1963, (ed.) Euripides, *Hypsipyle* (Oxford)

—, 1974, 'Euripides' parody of Aeschylus': *Hermathena* 118:1-14

—, 1981, (ed.) Euripides, *Heracles* (Oxford)

Bowra, C.M., 1944, *Sophoclean Tragedy* (Oxford)

—, 1953, *Problems in Greek Poetry* (Oxford)

Bremer, J.M., 1976, 'Why messenger-speeches?': *Miscellanea Tragica in honorem J.C. Kamerbeek* (Amsterdam) 29-48

Brown, A.L., 1978, 'Wretched tales of poets: Euripides, *Heracles* 1340-6': *PCPS* 24:22-30

Brušák, K., 1976, 'Signs in the Chinese theatre': L. Matejka & I.R. Titunik (eds.) *Semiotics of Art: Prague School Contributions* (Cambridge, Mass.) 59-73

van Buitenen, J.A.B., 1968, (tr.) *Two Plays of Ancient India* (New York)

Burian, P., 1974, 'Pelasgus and politics in Aeschylus' Danaid trilogy': *Wiener Studien* 8:5-14

Burkert, W., 1955, *Zum altgriechischen Mitleidsbegriff* (diss. Erlangen)

Burton, R.W.B., 1980, *The Chorus in Sophocles' Tragedies* (Oxford)

Buxton, R.G.A., 1982, *Persuasion in Greek Tragedy* (Cambridge)

Bywater, Ingram, 1909, (ed.) Aristotle, *Poetics* (Oxford)

Calder, W.M., 1965, 'The entrance of Athene in *Ajax*': *CP* 60:114-6

Campbell, L., 1881, (ed.) Sophocles, *Plays and Fragments, II* (Oxford)

Chalk, H.O., 1962, '*Arete* and *Bia* in Euripides' *Heracles*': *JHS* 82:7-18

Coleman, R., 1972, 'The Chorus in Sophocles' *Antigone*': *PCPS* 18:4-27

Collard, C., 1972, 'The funeral oration in Euripides' *Suppliants*': *BICS* 19:39-53

—, 1975a, (ed.) Euripides, *Suppliants* (Groningen)

—, 1975b, 'Formal debates in Euripidean drama': *G&R* 22:58-71

—, 1980, 'On stichomythia': *Liverpool Classical Monthly* 5:77-85

Conacher, D., 1967, *Euripidean Drama* (Toronto)

—, 1981, 'Rhetoric and relevance in Euripidean drama': *AJP* 102:3-25

Coulson, M., 1981, (tr.) *Three Sanskrit Plays* (Harmondsworth)

Culler, Jonathan, 1975, *Structuralist Poetics* (London)

—, 1981, *The Pursuit of Signs* (London)

Dale, A.M., 1954, (ed.) Euripides, *Alcestis* (Oxford)

—, 1967, (ed.) Euripides, *Helen* (Oxford)

—, 1968, *The Lyric Metres of Greek Drama* (ed.2: Cambridge)

—, 1969, *Collected Papers* (Cambridge)

Dawe, R.D., 1963, 'Inconsistency of plot of character in Aeschylus': *PCPS* 9:21-62

—, 1966, 'The place of the hymn to Zeus in Aeschylus' *Agamemnon*': *Eranos* 64:1-21

—, 1967, 'Some reflections on Ate and Hamartia': *HSCP* 72:89-123

—, 1973, *Studies in the Text of Sophocles, I* (Leiden)

—, 1982, (ed.) Sophocles, *Oedipus Rex* (Cambridge)

Denniston, J.D., 1954, *The Greek Particles* (ed.2: Oxford)

Dingel, J., 1967, *Das Requisit in der griechischen Tragödie* (diss. Tübingen)

Dodds, E.R., 1951, *The Greeks and the Irrational* (Berkeley)

—, 1960, (ed.) Euripides, *Bacchae* (ed.2: Oxford)

—, 1973, *The Ancient Concept of Progress* (Oxford)

Dover, K.J., 1974, *Greek Popular Morality* (Oxford)

Drew-Bear, T., 1968, 'The trochaic tetrameter in Greek tragedy': *AJP* 89:385-405

Duchemin, J., 1968, *L'Agon dans la tragédie grecque* (ed.2: Paris)

Easterling, P.E., 1973, 'Presentation of character in Aeschylus': *G&R* 20:3-19

—, 1977, 'Character in Sophocles': *G&R* 24:121-9

—, 1982 (ed.) Sophocles, *Trachiniae* (Cambridge)

—, 1984, 'The tragic Homer': *BICS* 31:1-8

Finley, J.H., 1967, *Three Studies in Thucydides* (Cambridge, Mass.)

Fitton, F.W., 1961, 'The Suppliant Women and the Herakleidai of Euripides': *Hermes* 89:430-61

Forrest, W.G., 1960, 'Themistokles and Argos': *CQ* 10:221-41

Fraenkel, Eduard, 1950, (ed.) Aeschylus, *Agamemnon* (3 vols.: Oxford)

—, 1963, 'Sophokles Aias 68-70': *MH* 20:103-6

—, 1965, Review of W. Ritchie, *The Authenticity of the Rhesus of Euripides*: *Gnomon* 37:228-41

—, 1977, *Due Seminari Romani*, ed. L.E. Rossi *et al.* (Rome)

Fränkel, Hermann, 1960, *Wege und Formen frühgriechischen Denkens* (ed.2: Munich)

—, 1975, *Early Greek Poetry and Philosophy* (ET: Oxford)

Gardiner, C.P., 1979, 'The staging of the death of Ajax': *CJ* 75:10-14

Garton, C., 1957, 'Characterisation in Greek tragedy': *JHS* 77:247-54

—, 1972, 'The "Chameleon Trail" in the criticism of Greek tragedy': *Studies in Philology* 69:389-413

Garvie, A.F., 1969, *Aeschylus' Suppliants: Play and Trilogy* (Cambridge)

Gellie, G.H., 1972, *Sophocles: a reading* (Melbourne)

Gelzer, T., 1960, *Der epirrhematische Agon bei Aristophanes* (*Zetemata* 23: Munich)

Gerow, Edwin, 1977, *Indian Poetics* (= *A History of Indian Literature*, ed. J. Gond, V/3: Wiesbaden)

Gilmartin, K., 1970, 'Talthybius in the *Trojan Women*': *AJP* 91:213-222

Gould, John, 1973, 'Hiketeia': *JHS* 93:74-103

—, 1978, 'Dramatic character in Greek tragedy': *PCPS* 24:43-67

Greenwood, L.H.G., 1953, *Aspects of Euripidean Drama* (Cambridge)

Gregory, M. & S. Carroll, 1978, *Language and Situation* (London)

Griffin, Jasper, 1976, 'Homeric pathos and objectivity': *CQ* 26:161-85

—, 1980, *Homer on Life and Death* (Oxford)

Griffith, Mark, 1977, *The Authenticity of the Prometheus Bound* (Cambridge)

Grube, G.M.A., 1941, *The Drama of Euripides* (London)

Gulley, Norman, 1971, *Aristotle on the Purpose of Literature* (Cardiff)

Guthrie, W.K.C., 1969, *A History of Greek Philosophy, III: The Fifth-Century Enlightenment* (Cambridge)

Haigh, A.E., 1896, *The Tragic Drama of the Greeks* (Oxford)

Halliday, M.A.K., 1978, *Language as Social Semiotic* (London)

Halliwell, Stephen, 1986, *Aristotle's Poetics* (London)

Halloran, Michael R., 1985, *Stagecraft in Euripides* (London)

Hamilton, R., 1978, 'Announced entries in Greek tragedy': *HSCP* 82:63-82

Harding, D.W., 1962, 'Psychological processes in the reading of fiction': *British Journal of Aesthetics* 2:133-47

Havelock, E.A., 1963, *Preface to Plato* (Oxford)

Heath, M.F., 1985, 'Hesiod's didactic poetry': *CQ* 35:245-63

Hein, Piet, 1973, *Mist and Moonshine* (Oxford)

Hiriyanna, M., 1954, *Art Experience* (Mysore)

Hirsch, E.D., 1976, *The Aims of Interpretation* (Chicago)

Hourmouziades, N.C., 1965, *Production and Imagination in Euripides* (Athens)

Imhof, M., 1956, 'Tetrameterszenen in der Tragödie': *MH* 13:125-43

Janko, Richard, 1984, *Aristotle on Comedy* (London)

Jebb, R.C., 1896, (ed.) Sophocles, *Ajax* (Cambridge)

—, 1900, (ed.) Sophocles, *Antigone* (ed.3: Cambridge)

Jens, W., 1971, (ed.) *Die Bauformen der griechischen Tragödie* (*Beiheft zu Poetica* 6: Munich)

Joerden, K., 1960, *Hinterszenischer Raum und ausserszenischer Zeit* (diss. Tübingen)

de Joia, A. & A. Stenton, *Terms in Systemic Linguistics* (London)

Kamerbeek, J.C., 1953, (ed.) Sophocles, *Ajax* (Leiden)

Kannicht, R., 1969, (ed.) Euripides, *Helen* (Heidelberg)

Keith, A.B., 1928, *Sanskrit Drama* (Oxford)

Kells, J.H., 1973, (ed.) Sophocles, *Electra* (Cambridge)

Kirkwood, G.M., 1965, 'Homer and Sophocles' *Ajax*': M.J. Anderson (ed.) *Classical Drama and its Influence* (London) 51-70

Kitto, H.D.F., 1961, *Greek Tragedy* (ed.3: London)

—, 1964, *Form and Meaning in Drama* (ed.2: London)

—, 1966, *Poiesis: Structure and Thought* (Berkeley)

Knox, B.M.W., 1979, *Word and Action* (Baltimore)

Kopperschmidt, J., 1966, *Die Hikesie als dramatische Form* (diss. Tübingen)

Lanata, G., 1963, *Poetica Pre-Platonica* (Florence)

Lee, K.H., 1976, (ed.) Euripides, *Troades* (London)

Lefkowitz, M., 1985, 'The Pindar scholia': *AJP* 106:269-82

Lesky, Albin, 1972, *Die tragische Dichtung der Hellenen* (ed.3: Göttingen)

Linforth, I.M., 1954, 'Three scenes in Sophocles' *Ajax*': *University of California Publications in Classical Philology* 15:1-28

Lloyd-Jones, H., 1956, 'Zeus in Aeschylus': *JHS* 76:55-67

—, 1961, 'Some alleged interpolations in Aeschylus' *Choephori* and Euripides' *Electra*' *CQ* 11:171-84

—, 1971, *The Justice of Zeus* (Berkeley)

Long, A.A., 1964, 'Sophocles *Ajax* 68-70: a reply to Prof. Fraenkel': *MH* 21:228-31

—, 1968, *Language and Thought in Sophocles* (London)

Lucas, D.W., 1968, (ed.) Aristotle, *Poetics* (Oxford)

McLeish, K., 1980, *The Theatre of Aristophanes* (London)

Macleod, C., 1983, *Collected Essays* (Oxford)

Maas, Paul, 1962, *Greek Metre* (ET: Oxford)

Maehler, H., 1963, *Die Auffassung des Dichterberufs im frühen Griechentum* (*Hypomnemata* 3: Göttingen)

Marx, F., 1928, 'Der Tragiker Phrynichus': *Rheinisches Museum* 77:337-60

Mastronarde, D.J., 1979, *Contact and Discontinuity* (*University of California Publications Classical Studies* 21: Berkeley)

Meridor, R., 1978, 'Hecuba's revenge: some observations on Euripides' *Hecuba*': *AJP* 99:28-35

—, 1984, 'Plot and myth in Euripides': *Phoenix* 38:205-15

Michelini, A.N., 1982, *Tradition and Dramatic Form in the Persians of Aeschylus* (Leiden)

Mills, S.P., 1980/1: 'The death of Ajax': *CJ* 76:729-35

Moles, J., 1979, 'Notes on Aristotle, *Poetics* 13 & 14': *CQ* 29:77-94

—, 1984, '*Philanthrôpia* in the *Poetics*': *Phoenix* 38:325-35

Moore, J., 1977, 'The dissembling-speech of Ajax': *YCS* 25:47-66

Moorhouse, A.C., 1982, *The Syntax of Sophocles* (Leiden)

Navarre, O., 1900, *Essai sur la Rhétorique Grecque avant Aristote* (Paris)

Nickau, K., 1966, 'Epeisodion und Episode': *MH* 23:155-71

Norwood, G., 1930, ' "Episodes" in Old Comedy': *CP* 25:217-29

Owen, A.S., 1939, (ed.) Euripides, *Ion* (Oxford)

Padel, Ruth, 1974, 'The imagery of elsewhere: two choral odes in Euripides': *CQ* 24:227-41

Page, Denys, 1938, (ed.) Euripides, *Medea* (Oxford)

Parker, R.C.T., 1983, *Miasma* (Oxford)

Pathmanathan, R. Sri, 1965, 'Death in Greek tragedy': *G&R* 12:2-14

Pfeiffer, Rudolf, 1968, *History of Classical Scholarship from the beginnings to the end of the Hellenistic Age* (Oxford)

Pickard-Cambridge, A.W., 1946, *The Theatre of Dionysus* (Oxford)

—, 1962, Dithyramb, *Tragedy and Comedy* (ed.2: Oxford)

—, 1968, *The Dramatic Festivals of Athens* (ed.2: Oxford)

Race, W.H., 1982, *The Classical Priamel* (Leiden)

Radermacher, L., 1913, (ed.) Sophocles, *Ajax* (Berlin)

Reinhardt, Karl, 1979, *Sophocles* (ET: Oxford)

Richardson, N.J., 1980, 'Literary criticism in the exegetical scholia to the *Iliad*': *CQ* 30:265-87

de Romilly, J., 1975, *Magic and Rhetoric in Ancient Greece* (Cambridge, Mass.)

Russell, D.A., 1967, 'Rhetoric and criticism': *G&R* 14:130-44

—, 1981, *Criticism in Antiquity* (London)

Rutherford, W.G., 1905, *A Chapter in the History of Annotation* (London)

Schadewaldt, W., 1955, 'Furcht und Mitleid? zur Bedeutung der Aristotelische Tragödiensatzes': *Hermes* 83:129-71

Schmalzriedt, E., 1980, 'Sophokles und die Rhetorik': *Rhetorik* 1:89-110

Schmid, W. & O. Stählin, 1934, *Geschichte der griechischen Literatur I/2* (Munich)

Schroeder, O., 1914, *De laudibus Athenarum* (diss. Göttingen)

Shaw, M.H., 1982, 'The *êthos* of Theseus in "The Suppliant Women" ': *Hermes* 110:3-19

Sheppard, J.T., 1927, '*Electra*: a defence of Sophocles': *CR* 41:2-9

Sicherl, M., 1977, 'The tragic issue in Sophocles' *Ajax*': *YCS* 25:67-98

Sider, D., 1983, 'Atossa's second entrance': *AJP* 104:185-91

Sifakis, G.M., 1971, *Parabasis and Animal Choruses* (London)

Silk, M.S., 1974, *Interaction in Poetic Imagery* (Cambridge)

Sorabji, R., 1980, *Necessity, Cause and Blame* (London)

Srebrny, S., 1951, 'De Aeschyli Heraclidis': *Eos* 45:41-56

Stanford, W.B., 1963, (ed.) Sophocles, *Ajax* (London)

—, 1983, *Greek Tragedy and the Emotions* (London)

Steidle, W., 1968, *Studien zum antiken Drama* (Studia et Testimonia Antiqua 4: Munich)

Stevens, P.T., 1971, (ed.) Euripides, *Andromache* (Oxford)

—, 1978, 'Sophocles: *Electra*, doom or triumph?': *G&R* 25:111-20

Stinton, T.C.W., 1975, '*Hamartia* in Aristotle and Greek tragedy': *CQ* 25:221-54

—, 1976a, 'Si credere dignum est: some expressions of disbelief in Euripides and others': *PCPS* 22:60-89

—, 1976b, 'Notes on Greek tragedy, I': *JHS* 96:121-45

—, 1977, 'Notes on Greek tragedy, II': *JHS* 97:127-54

Strohm, H., 1957, *Euripides: Interpretationen zur dramatischen Form* (Zetemata 15: Munich)

Szlezák, T.A., 1981, 'Sophokles' Elektra und das Problem des ironischen Dramas': *MH* 38:1-21

Taplin, O., 1971, 'Significant actions in Sophocles' *Philoctetes*': *GRBS* 12:25-44

—, 1977, *The Stagecraft of Aeschylus* (Oxford)

—, 1978, *Greek Tragedy in Action* (London)

—, 1979, 'Yielding to forethought: Sophocles' *Ajax*': *Arktouros: Hellenic Studies presented to B.M.W. Knox* (Berlin & N.Y.) 122-9

—, 1983, 'Tragedy and trugedy': *CQ* 33:331-3

Thalmann, W.G., 1980, 'Xerxes' rags': *AJP* 101:260-82

Verdenius, W.J., 1970, 'Homer, the educator of the Greeks': *Mededeelingen der Koninklijke Nederlandse Akademie van Wetenschappen* 33.5

Vickers, Brian, 1973, *Towards Greek Tragedy* (London)

Walcot, Peter, 1976, *Greek Drama in its Theatrical and Social Context* (Cardiff)

Waldock, A.J.A., 1951, *Sophocles the Dramatist* (Cambridge)

Webster, T.B.L., 1967, *The Tragedies of Euripides* (London)

West, M.L., 1966, (ed.) Hesiod, *Theogony* (Oxford)

—, 1978a (ed.) Hesiod, *Works and Days* (Oxford)

—, 1978b 'Tragica, II': *BICS* 25:106-22

Wilamowitz-Moellendorff, T. von, 1917, *Die dramatische Technik des Sophokles* (Berlin)

Wilamowitz-Moellendorff, U. von, 1910, *Einleitung in die griechische Tragödie* (Berlin)

Wilson, J.R., 1967, 'An interpolation in the prologue of Euripides' *Troades*': *GRBS* 8:205-223

Wilson, Penelope, 1980, 'Pindar and his reputation in antiquity': *PCPS* 26:97-114

Winnington-Ingram, R.P., 1948, *Euripides and Dionysus* (Cambridge)

—, 1958, 'Hippolytus: a study in causation': *Fondation Hardt, Entretiens* 6:171-191

—, 1969, 'Euripides: *poietes sophos*': *Arethusa* 2:127-42

—, 1980, *Sophocles: an interpretation* (Cambridge)

—, 1983, *Studies in Aeschylus* Cambridge

Xanthakis-Karamanos, G., 1980, *Studies in Fourth-Century Tragedy* (Athens)

Index

act-dividing lyric, 20-2, 25-7, 90-1, 137-41, 152-3, 163, 184-5, 190, 197-8, 200-1

adversary, 16, 24, 75, 96-7, 148, 153; *see also* antipathy

Aeschines, 9-10, 35, 44-5, 49

Aeschylus, 13, 16, 33, 37, 41, 49, 61-2, 64, 152-3, 206
  Ag., 12, 16-26, 28, 30, 51, 70-1, 91-2, 95-7, 103, 112-13, 119-20, 123, 126-7, 135, 148, 152-3, 158, 160, 174
  Ch., 15, 24-8, 57, 71, 92, 112, 148, 152, 175, 199
  Eu., 17, 27-31, 56, 58, 65-6, 68-9, 71, 92, 112, 147, 153, 166, 200
  Per., 15, 37, 67-8, 82-3, 87, 96, 126, 144, 152-3, 161, 174, 176
  PV, 2, 12, 92, 109-10, 149, 161
  ScT, 66, 70, 82, 96, 121, 174, 176, 197
  Su., 2, 69-70, 76, 96, 129-30, 147, 149, 152-3, 174-6
  fragments, 51, 64-5, 69, 158, 161, 206

aetiology, 65, 68-9, 103

affective fallacy, 31

Agathon, 64, 161

agon, 58-9, 80-1, 91, 127, 130, 133-4, 138, 147, 199-202, 205-6, 208

aidôs, 58, 169, 182

Alcaeus, 176

allegory, 39-40, 90

analysis, 20, 102, 113-15, 117, 120, 137; *see also* conviction

anapaests, *see* metre

ancillary pleasure, *see* pleasure

anger, *see* antipathy

antipathy, 16, 23-4, 27, 58-9, 75, 87, 91, 93, 96, 98, 142, 148, 150, 164, 173, 206-8

Antiphanes, 150

apatê, see illusion

application, 44-6, 63, 72-3, 77-8, 88, 90

Archilochus, 150, 203

Areopagus, 29-30, 68-9

aretê, 74, 81, 83-4, 169, 182

Aristippus, 9

Aristophanes, 2, 45, 49-50
  Ach., 33-4, 41, 67, 116, 138
  Frogs, 13, 16, 33, 40-1, 44, 63-4, 72, 143
  Th., 63-4, 112, 116

Aristotle, 2, 4, 9-17, 28, 32-5, 38-9, 41-3, 45, 50, 59, 65, 67, 80-4, 86-7, 94-5, 99-102, 105-6, 108-9, 112, 114-19, 124-6, 131, 138, 141-3, 150, 152, 162, 173, 183-4, 192, 204

assistant, 97, 148

Astydamas, 105

atê, 18, 21, 23, 120-1

boêdromia, 147

burial, 73-6, 194, 196, 203-5, 208

Callinus, 176

Carcinus, 160

causality, 53, 98-102, 105, 108-10; *see also* continuity

Chaeremon, 159

character, 10, 42, 75, 81-8, 94, 96, 112, 114-23, 130-3, 154, 173-4, 189

Chinese theatre, 194

Chorus, 96, 127-8, 137-40, 151-3; *see also* act-dividing lyric, parodos

closure, *see* completeness

coherence, 35, 72, 102, 107-8, 112-13, 123, 163, 197, 204-8

comedy, 2-3, 7, 10, 17, 34-5, 41, 49, 63, 114, 126, 129, 138, 150, 204

competition, dramatic, 1, 45-6, 48, 64, 66-7

competitive ethic, 38, 82, 167-9, 173, 191, 203-4

completeness, 93, 99-103, 104, 108, 125, 163, 196-7, 208

consistency, 20, 35, 111-15, 117, 130-2, 137, 177

217